5

Senior Author

Rebecca Bowers Sipe, Ed.D.
Eastern Michigan University

Consulting Authors

Julie Coiro, Ph.D.
University of Rhode Island

Amy Humphreys, Ed.M., NBCT
Educational Consultant

Sara B. Kajder, Ph.D.
University of Pittsburgh

Mark Overmeyer, M.A.
Cherry Creek School District, Colorado

Senior Consultant

James Scott Miller, M.Ed.
National Writing Consultant

ZB Zaner-Bloser

Program Reviewers

Zaner-Bloser wishes to thank these educators who reviewed portions of this program and provided comments prior to publication.

Joe Anspaugh
Shelbyville Middle School
Shelbyville, IN

Michele Barto, Ed.D.
Fairleigh Dickinson University
Madison, NJ

Jackie Blosser
Lima City Schools
Lima, OH

Kim Bondy
South Arbor Academy
Ypsilanti, MI

Kelly Caravelli
Meadowbrook Middle School
Poway, CA

Cathy Cassy
St. Louis Public Schools
St. Louis, MO

Penny Clare
Educational Consultant
Lee, NH

Mary Dunton
Literacy Consultant
Sparks, NV

Emily Gleason
Beaverton School District
Beaverton, OR

Denise Gray, Ed.D.
Whiteriver Elementary School
Whiteriver, AZ

Laura Hall
Walton Charter Academy
Pontiac, MI

Donna Jett
Rockwood South Middle School
Fenton, MO

Christine Johnson, Ed.D.
Boonton Public Schools
Boonton, NJ

Dr. Roma Morris
Columbia School District
Columbia, MS

Rosanne Richards
Southern Nevada Regional Professional Development Program
North Las Vegas, NV

Sharlene E. Ricks
Alpine School District
American Fork, UT

Debbie Rutherford
Independent National Consultant
Omaha, NE

Melinda Springli
Lawton Public Schools
Lawton, OK

Kerry Stephenson
Pendleton County School District
Butler, KY

Photography: Cover © Richard Cummins/SuperStock; Interior models, George C. Anderson; Stopwatch image © Royalty-Free/Corbis; p. 3 © Daniel Dempster Photography/Alamy; p. 131 © David R. Frazier/ Photolibrary, Inc./Alamy; p. 249 © age fotostock/SuperStock; p. 363 © Bill Ross/Corbis; p. 367 © John Kershaw/Alamy; p. 369 © Myrleen Pearson/PhotoEdit; p. 455 © iStockphoto/Vjom

Art Credits: pp. 4, 32, 56, 132, 158, 180, 250, 274, 296, 364, 388, 412 Paul Montgomery; p. 17 Bill Ogden; pp. 82, 202, 318, 434 Chris Vallo

ISBN 978-0-7367-7280-8

Zaner-Bloser, Inc.
1-800-421-3018
www.zaner-bloser.com
Printed in the United States of America 13 14 15 19840 5 4 3

SUSTAINABLE FORESTRY INITIATIVE
Certified Chain of Custody
Promoting Sustainable Forestry
www.sfiprogram.org
SFI-00993

Hi, there! We're your *Strategies for Writers* Writing Partners!

We're here to guide you step-by-step through the stages of the writing process: Prewrite, Draft, Revise, Edit, and Publish.

In each unit, we'll focus on one mode of writing: **narrative, informative/explanatory, opinion,** or **descriptive**.

Have you ever wondered what makes a good fable? Or what the elements of a how-to essay are? How about some reasons for writing an editorial or an observation report? We'll answer those questions and more.

We'll focus on these six traits of effective writing: **Ideas, Organization, Voice, Word Choice, Sentence Fluency,** and **Conventions**. We'll explain how to apply the traits to each genre of writing, and we'll show you how the traits work together.

In each chapter, we'll first review a model writing sample. Then we'll use a rubric to score the model. Rubrics are a great way to know exactly what is expected as you plan and evaluate your writing. After that, it's your turn to write!

Narrative writing

Table of Contents

Play

LITERATURE CONNECTION

Narrative Test Writing

Informative/Explanatory writing

Table of Contents

Opinion writing

Table of Contents

Descriptive writing

Table of Contents

Appendices

Appendix A: Grammar Practice

Table of Contents

Appendix B: Rubrics

Narrative writing tells a story about real or imaginary events.

Hello, my name is Sasha. I want to learn all I can about narrative writing! When I go camping, I like to take notes about all the different things in nature that I see. Then I use my notes to write exciting adventure stories. Once I learn how to write my observations and descriptions in a way that is clear, my stories will be even better!

IN THIS UNIT

- Personal Narrative
- Fable
- Mystery
- LITERATURE CONNECTION ▶ Play
- Writing for a Test

Name: Sasha
Home: West Virginia
Favorite Activities: camping and swimming
Favorite Book: Tuck Everlasting by Natalie Babbitt

What's a Personal Narrative?

It's a true story that I write about something that happened in my life.

What's in a Personal Narrative?

Voice
My writing voice gives my story emotion. It's the mood I want to share with my audience. My tone might be unhappy, suspenseful, scary, or hilarious.

Character(s)
Characters are the people I include in my story. My story has a narrator, me, telling about a personal experience I had. I may also include other characters.

Plot
Plot is the action or sequence of events in a story. The plot has a beginning, a middle part, and an ending.

Setting
Setting is when and where my story takes place. It could be yesterday at home or last summer at the zoo. But no matter what the setting, using vivid words will bring my story to life!

Why write a Personal Narrative?

People have all kinds of reasons for writing a personal narrative. Here are some reasons I can think of for writing about something that happened to me.

Entertainment
A story is even better when it's shared. I like writing a story so that my readers get involved in the experience even though they weren't there when it happened. I like writing stories that my friends would enjoy reading.

Personal Reflection
Sometimes I feel mixed emotions about something that happens in my life. Writing about it can help me understand why I might feel happy and sad—or upset and amused—at the same time. If an experience leaves me confused or frustrated, writing about it can help me think it through and put it in perspective.

Linking Narrative Writing Traits to a Personal Narrative

In this chapter, you will write a story about an experience you want to share. This type of narrative writing is called a personal narrative. Sasha will guide you through the stages of the writing process: Prewrite, Draft, Revise, Edit, and Publish. In each stage, Sasha will show you important writing strategies that are linked to the Narrative Writing Traits below.

Narrative Writing Traits

	• a clear, focused topic, experience, or series of events • memorable details that bring the characters, plot, and setting to life
	• events told in the order they happened • an interesting beginning and a satisfying ending • transitions that signal the sequence of events
	• a voice and tone that are ideal for telling a story • dialogue that, when used, gives voice to the characters
	• precise words that describe the characters, plot, and setting
	• sentences that have flow and rhythm, making them enjoyable to read aloud
	• no or few errors in grammar, usage, mechanics, and spelling

Before you write, read Jackie Haley's personal narrative on the next three pages. Then use the personal narrative rubric on pages 10–11 to decide how well she did. (You might want to look back at What's in a Personal Narrative? on page 4, too!)

Personal MODEL Narrative

Don't Call Me Goldilocks

by Jackie Haley

narrator

beginning

Do you have a nickname? I do, and it's an absolutely horrible one. Everybody calls me Goldilocks! It wouldn't be so bad if I had blond, curly hair and fair skin. However, my hair is black, and my skin is dark. So how did I get this nickname? It all started on a family vacation at Yellowstone National Park.

setting

Yellowstone is spectacular. It has towering waterfalls, dramatic canyons, crystal-clear lakes, bubbling pools of boiling water and colorful mud, and incredible geysers that shoot steam and hot water high into the air. The wildlife is definitely not tame, and animals wander freely throughout the park. You can see lumbering bison, stately elk, soaring eagles, cutthroat trout, and graceful trumpeter swans. Naturally, Yellowstone also has bears.

vivid words

plot

On our first day at Yellowstone, my parents decided to plan all of our daily excursions. While they studied hiking and geological maps, I went outside for a walk. They told me to stay near the lodge; they also warned me about the bears. However, I wandered off, following a stream into a wooded area. It was cool, quiet, and dark underneath the trees. I was really enjoying my walk until I heard a loud snap!

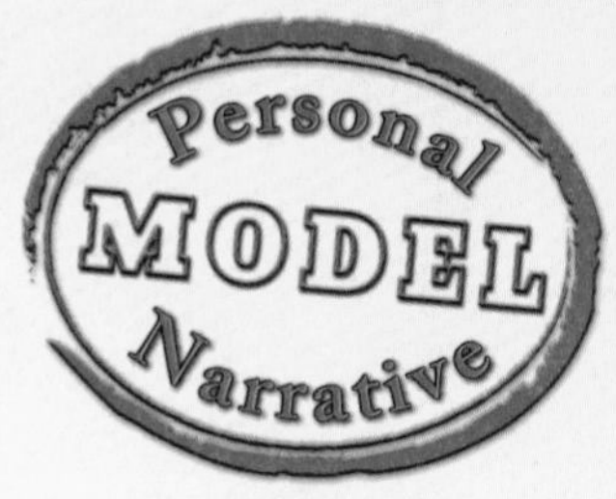

I jerked my head in the direction of the noise, but I didn't see a thing. Then the leaves rustled, and I saw something move. When I finally saw what it was, I froze on the spot. Three grizzly bears were looking right at me. The first bear was huge and looked ferocious. The second bear was not quite as large, and the third was a baby bear that would have looked cuddly—in a zoo!

I couldn't move a muscle, but my mind was racing. What did my parents say about bears? How was I supposed to get away from them? I tried to calm down. The bears didn't look too unhappy; that was good. I remembered that Mom said bears have a good sense of smell and bad eyesight. I hoped I didn't smell too good, and I really hoped they couldn't see me very well. She had also said that bears could run over 30 miles per hour. I took a deep breath and decided that I was in serious trouble.

middle part

I don't know how long I stood there, but it seemed like forever. I was starting to panic when I heard a low voice say, "Stay calm. I'm right behind you." I cannot tell you how happy I was to hear Dad's voice! He said not to look at the bears; he told me to back away quietly and carefully. As I moved backward very slowly, I knew the three bears were watching me closely.

character

After several long minutes, Dad said, "I think we're okay now, so turn around and follow me. Don't say a word until I do." When we reached the clearing, he grabbed me and hugged me. "What were you thinking?" he asked in a voice that shook a little. "You could have been killed!"

What could I say? I glanced back and breathed a long sigh of relief. The bears weren't anywhere in sight.

ending

As we hurried toward the lodge, Dad turned to me and said, "Guess we'll have to call you Goldilocks from now on. You could have gotten into a lot of trouble with those three bears today." I sighed; I knew what was coming. Dad went in and announced to everyone that he had saved me. He described the three bears and my predicament in great detail and with elaborate gestures. I got lots of hugs and lectures that afternoon, and, unfortunately, I also got a nickname.

voice

Personal Narrative Rubric

Use this 6-point rubric to plan and score a personal narrative.

	6	5	4
Ideas	The story shares the narrator's experience. Sensory details convey the experiences and events precisely.	The story shares the narrator's experience. Details help convey the experiences and events.	The story is mostly about the narrator's experience. Including more details would clarify and strengthen the story.
Organization	The events are arranged in a sequence that unfolds naturally. The story has a beginning that grabs the reader and an ending that satisfies.	The events are arranged logically. The story has a beginning, a middle, and an ending.	Most of the story's events are sequenced logically. A beginning, middle, and ending are present, but the beginning or ending is weak.
Voice	The writer maintains a narrative voice that connects with the reader.	The writer uses a narrative voice that connects with the reader most of the time.	The writer's voice connects with the reader at the beginning but fades as the story goes along.
Word Choice	The story uses precise, vivid words and descriptive language.	The story uses descriptive words to enhance the story.	The story uses descriptive words, but some are overused or imprecise.
Sentence Fluency	Varied sentence structures flow smoothly. Prepositional phrases connect important details.	The writing is smooth, easy to read, and many prepositional phrases connect details.	The writing uses some sentence structure variation. More prepositional phrases would help better connect details.
Conventions	All sentences are correct. The reader has no problem understanding the message.	The writer mostly uses conventional devices to enhance meaning.	Minor errors do not confuse meaning but require slight editing.

+Presentation White space helps organize the text on the page.

3	2	1	
The story can be inferred, but some details are unclear, missing, or irrelevant.	The story is unclear and needs to be developed. Very few details are included.	The writer's experience is not clear or focused. It is not a story yet.	Ideas
The time order of several details should be clarified or rearranged. There is no clear distinction between the beginning, middle, and ending.	Many details seem to be out of place or missing. The beginning does not connect to the ending.	The events are not in time order and do not tell a story.	Organization
The writer's voice fades in and out. The reader has to work to stay interested.	The writer's voice needs to connect with the reader more and match the story's action.	The writer's voice is absent and does not connect with the reader at all.	Voice
The story would be clearer with more descriptive words. Many words are vague or misleading.	The story contains too many general or overused words.	The story lacks energy due to vague or dull words and random word choice.	Word Choice
More sentence variety is needed. More prepositional phrases are needed. Many sentences are choppy.	Sentence structure variety is limited. The writing is choppy and difficult to read.	Sentences do not flow smoothly. Some may be incorrect or incomplete. Very few prepositional phrases are used.	Sentence Fluency
Several errors throughout the writing are distracting and impair readability and meaning.	Many errors throughout the story force the reader to reread. The meaning is difficult to follow.	The writer is not in control of the grammar, spelling, or usage.	Conventions

See Appendix B for 4-, 5-, and 6-point narrative rubrics.

Using the Personal Narrative Rubric to Study the Model

Did you notice that the model on pages 7–9 points out some key elements of a personal narrative? As she wrote "Don't Call Me Goldilocks," Jackie Haley used these elements to help her describe a personal experience. She also used the 6-point rubric on pages 10–11 to plan, draft, revise, and edit the writing. A rubric is a great tool to evaluate writing during the writing process.

Now let's use the same rubric to score the model. To do this, we'll focus on each trait separately, starting with Ideas. We'll use the top descriptor for each trait (column 6), along with examples from the model, to help us understand how the traits work together. How would you score Jackie on each trait?

- **The story shares the narrator's experience.**
- **Sensory details convey the experiences and events precisely.**

As Jackie begins her story, she includes so many memorable sensory details I can't help but feel excited to find out just how she got her nickname. She certainly makes it clear exactly how she feels!

> Do you have a nickname? I do, and it's an absolutely horrible one. Everybody calls me Goldilocks! It wouldn't be so bad if I had blond, curly hair and fair skin. However, my hair is black, and my skin is dark.

- **The events are arranged in a sequence that unfolds naturally.**
- **The story has a beginning that grabs the reader and an ending that satisfies.**

Jackie carefully organizes the events of her story in a natural way that's easy to follow. Her beginning caught my attention, the middle explained the whole story, and at the end I was relieved to learn that nothing had been hurt except Jackie's pride.

> I got lots of hugs and lectures that afternoon, and, unfortunately, I also got a nickname.

- **The writer maintains a narrative voice that connects with the reader.**

Jackie uses a friendly and energetic voice throughout her story. It's so easy to connect with her writing and stay interested until the end. I could almost "hear" her in my mind, wondering how to deal with the bears.

> I couldn't move a muscle, but my mind was racing. What did my parents say about bears? How was I supposed to get away from them? I tried to calm down. The bears didn't look too unhappy; that was good.

Using the Personal Narrative Rubric to Study the Model

- **The story uses precise, vivid words and descriptive language.**

Jackie uses vivid words like "crystal-clear lakes" and "bubbling pools of boiling water" to help me picture the scenery. I especially liked her descriptions of the animals.

Three grizzly bears were looking right at me. The first bear was huge and looked ferocious. The second bear was not quite as large, and the third was a baby bear that would have looked cuddly—in a zoo!

- **Varied sentence structures flow smoothly.**
- **Prepositional phrases connect important details.**

Jackie uses prepositional phrases like *on the spot* and *in a zoo* to add important details. Otherwise, all her sentences would be too vague. Notice how the prepositional phrases strengthen her story.

They told me to stay near the lodge; they also warned me about the bears. However, I wandered off, following a stream into a wooded area. It was cool, quiet, and dark underneath the trees. I was really enjoying my walk until I heard a loud snap!

- All sentences are correct.
- The reader has no problem understanding the message.

Jackie is careful to spell, punctuate, and capitalize correctly in her story. She has written some long sentences, but she is careful not to run any sentences together.

I jerked my head in the direction of the noise, but I didn't see a thing. Then the leaves rustled, and I saw something move.

+Presentation White space helps organize the text on the page.

My Turn!

Now it's my turn to write a personal narrative! I'll use the 6-point rubric on pages 10–11 and good writing strategies to help me. Read along to see how I do it.

Prewrite

Focus on **Ideas**

The Rubric Says The story shares the narrator's experience.

Writing Strategy Look at photographs to get ideas.

How do I decide what to write about for my personal narrative? My teacher says we should pick an experience that we remember really well. It can be a funny experience, or even a sad one. I've been on lots of thrilling river rafting trips, and I think I'd like to write about one of them, but which one?

I looked through our family photos, and I saw a whole bunch of pictures that reminded me of things my family has done together. I found a picture taken after my first rafting trip, which didn't go very smoothly. In the photo our whole family is dripping wet, but we're all smiling. Our adventure will make a great personal narrative!

Apply

Think about some interesting experiences you've had. Look through photographs to help jog your memory, and pick one event you'd like to write about.

Prewrite

Focus on **Organization**

The Rubric Says The events are arranged in a sequence that unfolds naturally.

Writing Strategy Use a Storyboard to organize ideas.

The rubric tells me that the events in my story need to be in a natural order. The action should have a definite beginning, middle, and ending. I think a Storyboard would help me organize my story. I'll draw pictures of what happened on our rafting trip.

Writer's Term

Storyboard

A **Storyboard** is a series of pictures. The pictures show the main events of a story in the order in which they happen.

Storyboard

Reflect

Look at the events. Are they arranged in a natural order?

Apply

Make your own Storyboard. Be sure to show events in the order they happened.

Draft

Focus on **Ideas**

The Rubric Says Sensory details convey the experiences and events precisely.

Writing Strategy Collect memorable details.

Writer's Term

Sensory Details

Sensory details tell what the writer saw, heard, tasted, felt, or smelled. These types of details help a writer share precisely what an experience was like for him or her.

I think I'm ready to draft my story now. I can use my Storyboard to help me remember details about my first rafting trip.

The rubric says I also need to include sensory details. Sensory details will help my readers feel the cold water and hear the waves. I want them to be as shocked as I was when the raft turned over. I want them to feel dripping wet!

As I write, I won't worry too much about mistakes. I'll do my best with grammar and spelling, but I can fix mistakes later.

Proofreading Marks

⊐	Indent	ℓ	Take out something
≡	Make uppercase	⊙	Add a period
/	Make lowercase	¶	New paragraph
∧	Add something	(sp)	Spelling error

sensory details

[DRAFT]

Famous Last Words

The day was supposed to be relaxing. That's what Dad said as the family left the house. I was nine years old, and this was my first rafting trip. Our plan was to raft down the calmer part of the New River. Mom and I would enjoy the ride and get some sun Dad was going to fish. He promised that we would go rafting on rougher rapids someday, but I needed to get some experience on calmer water. Then he said those words again: "We're going to have a relaxing day."

When we got to the New River, Dad rented a yellow raft and two paddles. Mom and Dad's task was to steer the raft; my task was simply to sit there and enjoy the ride. Each of us wore rafting clothes. We also wore helmets and life jackets.

We started down the river. We moved through some small waves that were as easy to handle as taking candy from a baby. Next, we came to a narrow channel where the water moved more swiftly. Finally, we came to a place where the river was as smooth as glass. Dad handed me the paddle and said, "You hold this awhile. I'm going to fish."

Reflect

Read the beginning of Sasha's draft. What sensory details stand out for you?

Apply

Use your Storyboard to write your first draft. Be sure to include sensory details.

Revise

Focus on **Organization**

The Rubric Says The story has a beginning that grabs the reader and an ending that satisfies.

Writing Strategy Connect the beginning of a story to the ending.

I looked back at the rubric after I finished my draft. It says that my beginning should grab the reader. I want my story to really pull readers in, but I'm not sure my beginning does that. It sounds a little dull. I'll add my thoughts to put the reader in my shoes.

Writer's Term

Beginning

The **beginning** of a story grabs the reader's attention. It makes the reader eager for the story to unfold.

[DRAFT]

attention-grabbing detail

Then he said those words again: "We're going to have a relaxing day." ^ Was he ever *wrong*!

Apply

Read your draft. Does your beginning grab your readers' interest? Add details that will make them want to read to the end of your story.

The rubric also says I need to end my story in a satisfying way. I want my readers to know that our river mishap ended just fine. Even though I fell in the water like I'd feared, I did not get hurt. I'd like my ending to be funny and to tie into the title and my beginning. Do you think this ending will work?

Writer's Term

Ending

The **ending** ties up loose ends and often reveals something a character learns from the experience.

By the time we got home that night, we were completely exhausted. Our clothes were still damp, our bruises were beginning to ache, and we didn't have a single fish. We were all smiling, though. Every time one of us mentioned our "relaxing day," we snorted with laughter. Mom called Dad's promise of a relaxing day his "famous last words." Perhaps he should have said, "This will be a day we'll never forget!"

connects to beginning

Reflect

Look at the ending. Did Sasha connect the beginning and ending of her story? In what ways?

Apply

Read your draft. Think of how to end your story in a way that your readers will like.

Revise

Focus on **Voice**

The Rubric Says The writer maintains a narrative voice that connects with the reader.

Writing Strategy Use the first-person point of view.

According to the rubric, my writing voice should connect with my readers. I will use first-person pronouns such as *I*, *we*, and *our* so that my readers know that I'm in the story. This will really help my readers connect with me as I tell my tale!

Writer's Term

First-Person Point of View

Point of view tells the reader who is telling the story. The point of view of a personal narrative is **first person** because the writer is telling his or her own story. Narrators use the words **I, me, my, mine, we, us, our,** and **ours** to tell their story in the first person.

first-person point of view

[DRAFT]

"We're going to have a relaxing day."

~~The day was supposed to be relaxing~~. That's what Dad said as we ~~the family~~ left our ~~the~~ house. I was nine years old, and this was my first rafting trip. Our ~~The~~ plan was to raft down the calmer part of the New River. Mom and I would enjoy the ride and get some sun Dad was going to fish.

Reflect

Look at the revisions. Did Sasha use the first-person point of view throughout her story? Find examples.

Apply

Look over your draft again. Make sure you have written in the first-person point of view.

Revise

Focus on **Word Choice**

The Rubric Says The story uses precise, vivid words and descriptive language.

Writing Strategy Replace clichés and overused words with precise, descriptive language.

My readers won't get a good sense of the story if I use clichés and overused words. Instead, I'll use a thesaurus. It will help me replace dull words with vivid ones and clichés with original language.

Writer's Term

Cliché

A **cliché** is a phrase that has been used over and over, such as **as smart as a fox** or **few and far between.**

Overused Words

Overused words include **said, beautiful, nice,** or **good.** They should be replaced with words that have more meaning, such as **whispered** or **mumbled.**

[DRAFT]

more precise words

We ~~moved~~ paddled through some ~~small~~ gentle waves that were ~~as~~ easy to handle ~~as taking candy from a baby~~.

took out a cliché

Apply

Replace dull words in your story with original, vivid descriptions.

Edit

Focus on **Conventions**

The Rubric Says All sentences are correct. The reader has no problem understanding the message.

Writing Strategy Use conjunctions to fix run-on sentences.

I'm finally ready to check my draft for spelling, punctuation, and capitalization. The rubric also reminds me to check my sentences. Look at how I fixed run-on sentences by adding a comma and a conjunction.

Writer's Term

Run-on Sentences

A **run-on sentence** happens when two sentences are joined only by a comma or by no punctuation at all.

[DRAFT]

created a compound sentence

Dad threw his line into the water ^[, and] he immediately caught a fish. It was a small-mouth bass. He cast his line again ^[, and] soon he had a muskie.

Reflect

What do you think? How have Sasha's edits helped her writing?

Apply

Conventions

Edit your draft for spelling, grammar, and punctuation.

For more practice fixing run-on sentences and using conjunctions, use the exercises on the next two pages.

Run-on Sentences

Know the Rule

When two sentences are joined together correctly, they become a **compound sentence**. When they are joined incorrectly, they become a **run-on**. Compound sentences can be formed by placing a **comma** and a **coordinating conjunction** (such as *and, or, but*) between two related sentences. Compound sentences can also be formed by placing a **semicolon** between two related sentences.

Examples:
Dad threw his line in the water, **and** he quickly caught a fish.
Dad threw his line in the water**;** he quickly caught a fish.

Practice the Rule

Correct each run-on sentence below by rewriting it as a compound sentence on a separate sheet of paper. Join the sentences with a comma and a coordinating conjunction or with a semicolon.

1. You should always swim with a friend it is dangerous to swim alone.
2. It is fun to swim in the sunshine the sun can burn your skin.
3. Sunscreen protects your skin you must apply it often.
4. There are often numbers on the side of a swimming pool they show the depth of the water.
5. You can swim in the shallow end you should never dive into shallow water.
6. The deep end of the pool can be dangerous only good swimmers should go there.
7. Many pools have lifeguards they are ready to help in emergencies.
8. Lifeguards must earn lifesaving certificates they must also have first-aid certificates.
9. Lifeguards must be alert they save many lives each year.
10. Most pools have rules swimmers must obey the rules.

Conjunctions

Know the Rule

Coordinating conjunctions (*and, but, or*) connect words or groups of words (including independent clauses) of equal importance. Coordinating conjunctions can be used to create compound sentences.

Examples:

Five-armed sea creatures are called starfish, **but** they are not fish.

You can call them starfish, **or** you can call them sea stars.

Practice the Rule

Number a sheet of paper 1–10. Write the coordinating conjunction that fits best in each sentence.

1. We could go to a movie, ____ I'd rather go to the aquarium.
2. Should we go to the seal show, ____ should we look at the fish tanks?
3. The fish tanks contain all kinds of sea life, ____ I find the shark tanks very interesting.
4. In this tank you can see an octopus, ____ in that tank you can see sea stars.
5. There are more than 1,000 kinds of sea stars, ____ they come in a variety of colors.
6. A sea star might lose an arm, ____ it can grow a new one.
7. Sea stars are interesting, ____ so are green moray eels.
8. Green moray eels look frightening, ____ they are not considered dangerous.
9. The average green moray eel is about six feet long, ____ the longest one ever found was ten feet long.
10. Next we could go to the octopus display, ____ we could go see the hammerhead sharks!

Publish

+Presentation

Publishing Strategy Submit the story to a magazine.

Presentation Strategy Use a limited number of clear fonts.

I've polished my personal narrative! Now I'll publish it. I think it's a story that other kids might like to read, so I'm submitting it to *Highlights for Children* magazine. To make my story easy to read, I will use just a couple of clear fonts. Then I'll mail a neat, double-spaced copy of my story to the magazine, along with a letter that asks the editor to publish my story. I'll include a return envelope for a reply. But first, I'll make sure that I've done everything on my final checklist.

My Final Checklist

Did I—

- ✔ remember to put my name on my paper?
- ✔ make a neat final copy?
- ✔ prepare an envelope?
- ✔ check for run-on sentences?
- ✔ edit and proofread carefully?

Apply

Use Sasha's checklist to check your own personal narrative. Be sure to use white space to help organize the text on the page.

Famous Last Words
by Sasha

"We're going to have a relaxing day." That's what Dad said as we left our house. I was nine years old, and this was my first rafting trip. I'd heard about people falling overboard and being swept away by swift currents. Our plan was to raft down the calmer part of the New River. Mom and I would enjoy the ride and get some sun; Dad was going to fish. He promised that we would go rafting on rougher rapids someday, but I needed to get some experience on calmer water. Then he said those words again: "We're going to have a relaxing day." Was he ever wrong!

When we got to the New River, Dad rented a yellow raft and two paddles. Mom and Dad's task was to steer the raft; my task was simply to sit there and enjoy the ride. Each of us wore a swimsuit, T-shirt, shorts, old sneakers, a windbreaker, sunglasses, and sunscreen. We also wore helmets and life jackets. We were well prepared and ready to go!

We headed down the stream. We paddled through some gentle waves that were easy to handle. Next, we encountered a narrow channel where the water flowed more swiftly. Finally, we came to a place where the river was bottle-green and perfectly still. Dad handed me the paddle and said, "You hold this awhile. I'm going to fish." Dad threw his line into the water, and he immediately caught a fish. It was a small-mouth bass. He cast his line again, and soon he had a muskie. Then he landed another and another! Fish were everywhere! Then it happened; Dad's hook got caught on something big. It was probably a rock, but we thought it might be a huge fish. "Watch out!" he yelled. "I'm going to need some room to get my line loose!"

Just then, we noticed that our boat was drifting into some waves that weren't so calm. Mom started to say something, but Dad completely lost his balance. He toppled over, and the raft rocked wildly back and forth! Dad's fishing rod flew up in the air, and the raft started to capsize. Water rushed over the sides of the raft, and we quickly began to bail it out with our hands. Suddenly, the raft flipped over! We tumbled into cold water, banging into rocks, the raft, and each other. Then we noticed that everything was floating away. We managed to snag the paddles and the fishing rod, but the lucky fish were long gone. We struggled to turn the raft right side up and finally crawled in. We were soaking wet and more than a little cranky!

By the time we got home that night, we were completely exhausted. Our clothes were still damp, our bruises were beginning to ache, and we didn't have a single fish. We were all smiling, though. Every time one of us mentioned our "relaxing day," we snorted with laughter. Mom called Dad's promise of a relaxing day his "famous last words." Perhaps he should have said, "This will be a day we'll never forget!"

Reflect

Use the rubric to score the story. Then use the rubric to check your own story.

What's a Fable?

It's a fictional story that teaches a lesson called a moral.

What's in a Fable?

Character(s)
Fables often have talking animal characters that think and act like people. At least one character has a good quality, such as kindness, or a bad one, such as laziness.

Plot
The plot is what happens in a fable. Each event causes an effect. These effects lead to the moral of the story.

Moral
A moral is a lesson that teaches people how to behave. Sometimes the moral is stated at the end of the fable. Sometimes you have to figure out the moral.

Dialogue
A fable is short, so well-written dialogue is important and used for several reasons. It reveals characters' traits, develops the plot, and moves the story along.

Why write a Fable?

Did you know that people have been creating fables for thousands of years? Many cultures around the world use fables to teach people how to behave. Here are two reasons for writing fables.

Entertainment
The stories are short, the plots are simple, and the endings are often funny. The characters and action are easy to picture in our minds. Once you know the story, you can retell your own version of the fable.

Instruction
Fables are simple stories, but they teach important lessons that are easy to remember. The moral tells us how we should act. If we think about it, we can see how the moral of an old fable applies to our lives today. I guess in some ways people haven't really changed that much!

Linking Narrative Writing Traits to a Fable

In this chapter, you will retell a story you know that has a moral. This type of narrative writing is called a fable. Sasha will guide you through the stages of the writing process: Prewrite, Draft, Revise, Edit, and Publish. In each stage, Sasha will show you important writing strategies that are linked to the Narrative Writing Traits below.

Narrative Writing Traits

 Ideas	• a clear, focused topic, experience, or series of events • memorable details that bring the characters, plot, and setting to life
 Organization	• events told in the order they happened • an interesting beginning and a satisfying ending • transitions that signal the sequence of events
 Voice	• a voice and tone that are ideal for telling a story • dialogue that, when used, gives voice to the characters
 Word Choice	• precise words that describe the characters, plot, and setting
 Sentence Fluency	• sentences that have flow and rhythm, making them enjoyable to read aloud
 Conventions	• no or few errors in grammar, usage, mechanics, and spelling

Before you write, read Rachel Randall's fable on the next page. Then use the fable rubric on pages 36–37 to decide how well she did. (You might want to look back at What's in a Fable? on page 32, too!)

THE FOX AND THE CROW

retold by Rachel Randall

character

One bitterly cold winter day, a skinny fox was walking through the woods. His red fur was scraggly, and his tongue was hanging out of his mouth. The fox was in a terrible mood because he hadn't had anything to eat for days. "Man, I'm hungry," he said to himself. "If I don't find something to eat soon, I'm toast!"

cause

character

Just then, a crow flew overhead and landed on a tree branch near the fox. In the crow's beak was an enormous piece of cheese. The fox's mouth watered as he gazed admiringly at the crow's cheese. Its delicious smell almost drove him crazy. I've got to get my paws on that cheese, thought the fox.

cause

Then a smile crept across the fox's lean and hungry face, and he sauntered slowly over to the tree. Looking up at the crow, the fox said in a friendly voice, "Hey, Crow! How's it going?"

dialogue

The crow glanced down at the fox with suspicion.

"I was just thinking about how sharp you look with those sleek feathers," the fox said smoothly. "Black is really your color, and I love the color of your eyes, too."

fox's trait revealed

The crow began to smile.

"I bet you're a terrific singer," continued the fox. "Any bird that looks as cool as you do has to have a great voice. I wonder if maybe you could just sing one song for me?"

cause

effect

The crow was so pleased at the fox's compliments that she opened her beak and let out her loudest caw. However, the moment she opened her mouth, the cheese fell to the ground with a plop. The fox strolled over to the huge piece of cheese and quickly snapped it up.

"Thanks a million, Crow," he said, smacking his lips. "Because you were so generous to give me your cheese, I'm going to give you a little piece of advice for the future—***Don't trust people who flatter you.***"

moral

Fable Rubric

Use this 6-point rubric to plan and score a fable.

	6	5	4
Ideas	The plot and characters all lead to the moral of the fable.	For the most part, the plot and characters lead to the moral.	The plot and characters lead to the moral, but there are a few unrelated details.
Organization	The plot events are in a natural sequence. Effective transitions show how one event leads to another.	Nearly all plot events are in logical order. Transitions are used.	Most of the plot events are in logical order. Transitions are used.
Voice	Well-written dialogue develops events and controls the pacing of the action.	Dialogue engages the reader most of the time and contributes to the development of the story.	Dialogue is present and sounds natural most of the time.
Word Choice	The writer uses sensory words, adjectives, and strong verbs to create memorable characters and scenes.	Sensory language, adjectives, and strong verbs develop characters and scenes.	Descriptive language is used but some words and phrases are confusing or vague.
Sentence Fluency	Sentences of various lengths and structures move the story along.	The story has a good variety of sentence lengths and structures.	There is variety in sentence beginnings, lengths, and structures most of the time.
Conventions	Negatives and the forms of *good* and *bad* are used correctly.	Negatives and the forms of *good* and *bad* are mostly correct, and the meaning is clear.	Double negatives and errors in the forms of *good* and *bad* distract the reader.

+Presentation Each paragraph is indented.

	3	2	1
Ideas	Disjointed or unrelated details add confusion and take away from the development of the moral.	The plot and characters do not lead clearly to the moral.	The plot and characters are not clear.
Organization	Some of the plot events are out of order. Transitions are predictable or overused.	The reader is confused by the lack of order. Transitions are few or poorly chosen.	Plot events are missing or confusing. Transitions are misleading or missing.
Voice	Dialogue contributes some to the story but does not always engage the reader.	Dialogue is present but sounds unbelievable, flat, or inconsistent and does not help move the story along.	There is little or no dialogue.
Word Choice	The writer underuses or overuses descriptive words and verbs. Many words are too general.	The writer uses some words and phrases incorrectly or repetitively.	Limited word choice throughout the story makes reading dull.
Sentence Fluency	Some repetitive sentence structures and lengths distract from the flow of the story.	Sentence beginnings, lengths, and structures are redundant and choppy.	There is little or no variation in sentence length or structure.
Conventions	Obvious, distracting errors with negatives and the forms of *good* and *bad* confuse the reader.	Serious errors with negatives and the forms of *good* and *bad* make the story hard to understand.	The writing contains many errors with negatives and the forms of *good* and *bad*. It is very hard to read.

See Appendix B for 4-, 5-, and 6-point narrative rubrics.

Using the Fable Rubric to Study the Model

Did you notice that the model on page 35 points out some key elements of a fable? As she wrote "The Fox and the Crow," Rachel Randall used these elements to help her retell a fable. She also used the 6-point rubric on pages 36–37 to plan, draft, revise, and edit the writing. A rubric is a great tool to evaluate writing during the writing process.

Now let's use the same rubric to score the model. To do this, we'll focus on each trait separately, starting with Ideas. We'll use the top descriptor for each trait (column 6), along with examples from the model, to help us understand how the traits work together. How would you score Rachel on each trait?

- **The plot and characters all lead to the moral of the fable.**

Every character and story event Rachel includes guides me to the moral. Fables are short, and there isn't any room for unimportant details. Her opening sets up the fable perfectly.

> One bitterly cold winter day, a skinny fox was walking through the woods. His red fur was scraggly, and his tongue was hanging out of his mouth. The fox was in a terrible mood because he hadn't had anything to eat for days.

- **The plot events are in a natural sequence.**
- **Effective transitions show how one event leads to another.**

Rachel tells the story events in order. She uses effective transitions like "just then" and "as he gazed" to move the story along and connect the events.

Just then, a crow flew overhead and landed on a tree branch near the fox. In the crow's beak was an enormous piece of cheese. The fox's mouth watered as he gazed admiringly at the crow's cheese.

- **Well-written dialogue develops events and controls the pacing of the action.**

Rachel's story is fun to read. She cleverly uses dialogue to reveal character traits and move the story from one event to the next.

Then a smile crept across the fox's lean and hungry face, and he sauntered slowly over to the tree. Looking up at the crow, the fox said in a friendly voice, "Hey, Crow! How's it going?"

Using the Fable Rubric to Study the Model

- **The writer uses sensory words, adjectives, and strong verbs to create memorable characters and scenes.**

I like Rachel's retelling because she chooses words that help me see, hear, taste, and smell what she's describing. I know exactly how the fox must feel at this moment.

Just then, a crow flew overhead and landed on a tree branch near the fox. In the crow's beak was an enormous piece of cheese. The fox's mouth watered as he gazed admiringly at the crow's cheese. Its delicious smell almost drove him crazy.

- **Sentences of various lengths and structures move the story along.**

Sentences of different lengths and types help readers stay interested in a story. Rachel's varied sentences—including the dialogue—build a sense of growing excitement for her readers.

The crow began to smile.

"I bet you're a terrific singer," continued the fox. "Any bird that looks as cool as you do has to have a great voice. I wonder if maybe you could just sing one song for me?"

- **Negatives and the forms of *good* and *bad* are used correctly.**

Rachel does a good job spelling, punctuating, and capitalizing correctly in her story. She's also very careful not to use any double negatives, especially in the moral. If she had written "Don't never trust people who flatter you," she would not have been correct.

"Thanks a million, Crow," he said, smacking his lips. "Because you were so generous to give me your cheese, I'm going to give you a little piece of advice for the future—***Don't trust people who flatter you.***"

+Presentation Each paragraph is indented.

My Turn!

Now it's my turn to write a fable! I'll use the rubric and good writing strategies to help me. Follow along to see how I do it.

Prewrite

Focus on **Ideas**

The Rubric Says The plot and characters all lead to the moral of the fable.

Writing Strategy Pick a fable with a plot and characters that are interesting.

I love to visit my grandparents' sheep farm. I help with the newborn lambs. I think I'll rewrite the fable "The Boy Who Cried Wolf" because the main character watches after lambs, too.

The original fable was set in ancient times. I'll include all the events in the original fable, but I'll update some of the details for my readers. I'll also use language that people use today. I'll start by taking some notes on the original fable.

The Boy Who Cried Wolf

- ✔ A boy got bored watching the sheep.
- ✔ He decided it would be funny to cry "Wolf!" and trick the villagers into running out to the pasture.
- ✔ His trick worked many times, and the boy laughed.
- ✔ Then a real wolf came.
- ✔ When the boy cried "Wolf!" this time, nobody came.
- ✔ Moral: Nobody will believe someone who lies all the time, even when he's telling the truth.

Apply

Pick a fable you'd like to retell. Jot down some notes about the events in the fable and list some details you can update.

Prewrite

Focus on **Organization**

The Rubric Says The plot events are in a natural sequence.

Writing Strategy Make a Cause-and-Effect Chain to organize the plot events.

I read in the rubric that all the events in a fable need to be told in a natural order. I'm going to use my notes to make a Cause-and-Effect Chain that will show how one thing leads to another. By the end of my chain, I'll have the whole plot organized.

Writer's Term

Cause-and-Effect Chain
A Cause-and-Effect Chain organizes events to show the reasons (causes) for the outcomes (effects). The final event leads to the moral of the story.

Cause-and-Effect Chain

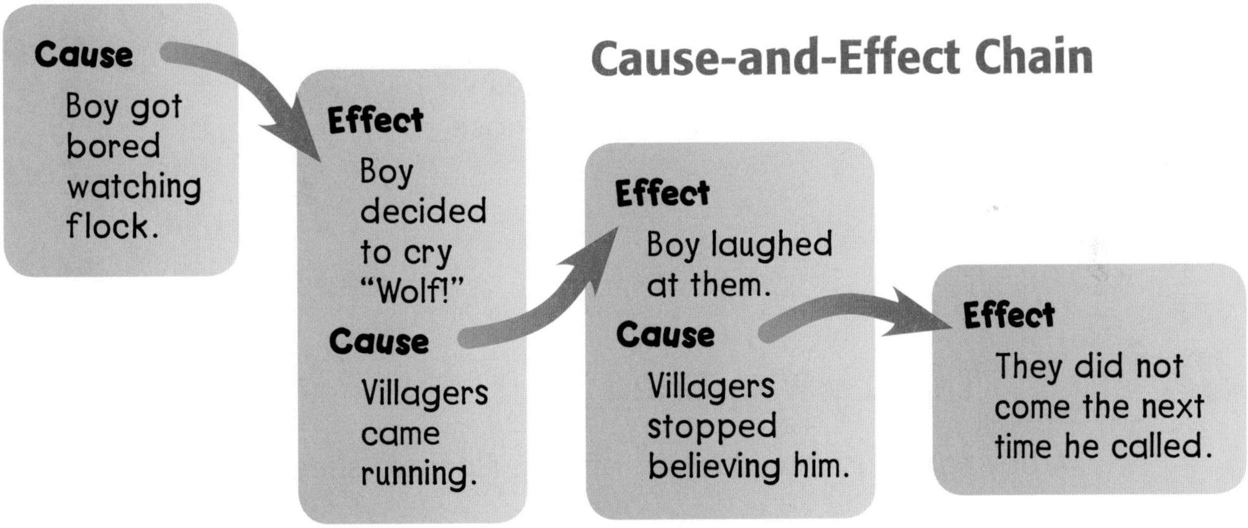

Cause
Boy got bored watching flock.

Effect
Boy decided to cry "Wolf!"

Cause
Villagers came running.

Effect
Boy laughed at them.

Cause
Villagers stopped believing him.

Effect
They did not come the next time he called.

Reflect

Are the events clear and in a natural order? Do they lead to the moral of the story?

Apply

Make a Cause-and-Effect Chain to organize your notes. Be sure to show clearly how one event causes another event.

Draft

Focus on **Organization**

The Rubric Says Effective transitions show how one event leads to another.

Writing Strategy Use carefully chosen transitions to show cause and effect.

Okay, I think I'm ready to start writing a draft. I can use my Cause-and-Effect Chain to help me keep the plot events the same as in the original fable, but I'll tell it my way.

The rubric says to use effective transitions to show cause and effect. I'll use *as soon as, because, but, however, if, since,* and *so* to help my readers connect the events and follow the story.

As I'm writing, I'll try not to make mistakes in grammar and spelling, but if I do, I can fix those mistakes later.

The Boy Who Cried Wolf

A boy named Michael looked after a flock of sheep for Mr. Baker, a local farmer. Because the sheep were in a pasture far from the barn, Mr. Baker gave Michael a cell phone. He told the boy to call him if he needed help.

Proofreading Marks

Indent	Take out something
Make uppercase	Add a period
Make lowercase	New paragraph
Add something	Spelling error

[DRAFT]

It didn't take long before Michael grew bored I thought I'd like this job, he grumbled to himself, but all sheep do is walk around and munch grass. One day when he was bored with his job, Michael had an idea. He pulled the cell phone out of his pocket and dialed Mr. Baker's number. As soon as the farmer answered, Michael told him wolves were attacking the sheep.

cause

effect

Soon the boy saw the farmer's truck speeding across the plain, a large tail of dust trailing after it. Mr. Baker stopped the truck at the top of the pasture and jumped out. All he saw was the flock of sheep munching peacefully on the green grass near the stream.

cause

Michael began laughing wildly. He thought Mr. Baker looked funny when he jumped out of the truck.

effect

Mr. Baker was not amused and he looked really angry. He spoke in an angry voice, telling Michael that it was wrong to play a trick on him.

Reflect

Read the beginning of Sasha's draft. Where does she use transitions to show cause and effect? How are the transitions helpful?

Apply

Use your Cause-and-Effect Chain to draft your fable. Connect the events with transitions to help your reader follow the story.

Revise

Focus on **Voice**

The Rubric Says Well-written dialogue develops events and controls the pacing of the action.

Writing Strategy Add dialogue to make the story and characters come alive.

After I finished my first draft, I remembered that the rubric says to use well-written dialogue to develop events and move the story along. Of course! I can use dialogue to show things that have already happened and reveal characters' feelings. That will liven up my fable!

Writer's Term

Dialogue

Dialogue is the conversation between characters in a story.

[DRAFT]

dialogue

"Do you realize that I drove up here as fast as I could?" he asked in an angry voice.

Mr. Baker was not amused ~~and he looked really angry. He spoke in an angry voice, telling Michael that it was wrong to play a trick on him.~~

Apply

Read your draft. Add dialogue to make characters and events seem more realistic and interesting.

Revise

Focus on **Word Choice**

The Rubric Says	The writer uses sensory words, adjectives, and strong verbs to create memorable characters and scenes.
Writing Strategy	Choose words and phrases to convey ideas precisely.

The rubric reminds me to use words that create strong, clear images for my readers. I think I can make the story even more memorable for my audience by using strong verbs and vivid descriptions.

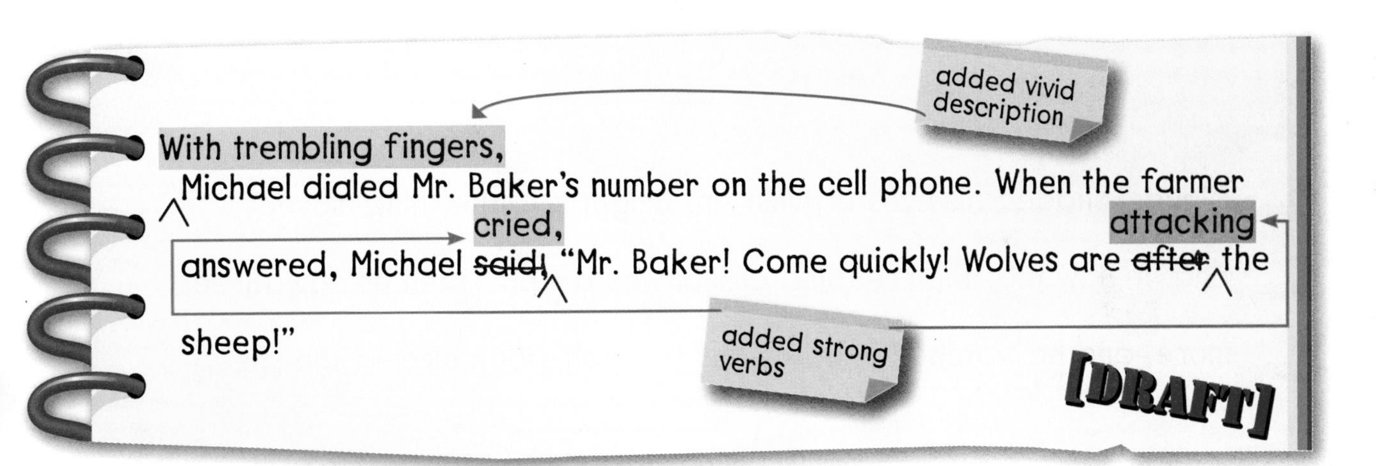

Reflect

Look at the changes. How do they help create a clearer image in the reader's mind?

Apply

Think of sensory words, adjectives, or strong verbs you can add to your fable.

Revise

Focus on **Sentence Fluency**

The Rubric Says Sentences of various lengths and structures move the story along.

Writing Strategy Separate sentences that are too long.

Now it's time to revise for sentence fluency. The rubric says I should vary my sentences to help my story flow. In some places, I used sentences that are too long. They may be confusing to my readers. I can divide long sentences into two sentences. See how I did this?

Michael shaded his eyes against the bright sun, the thing moved, and he saw that the creeping animal was a wolf. Then he saw three more, ~~and~~ he watched in horror as the wolf pack circled the sheep.

Shortened long sentences

[DRAFT]

Apply

Look over your draft again. Find sentences that are too long and separate them into shorter sentences.

Edit

Focus on **Conventions**

The Rubric Says Negatives and the forms of *good* and *bad* are used correctly.

Writing Strategy Check for double negatives and the forms of *good* and *bad*.

It's time to check my draft for correctness. Contractions sometimes create double negatives in my writing. I'll fix any I find. I'll also make sure I used forms of *good* and *bad* correctly.

Writer's Term

Double Negative

It is not correct to use two negatives together in the same sentence.

Incorrect: Tina **hasn't never** seen the ocean.

Correct: Tina **has never** seen the ocean.

[DRAFT]

This time, Mr. Baker was even angrier. He told Michael that if he ever played that trick again, he would lose his job. So Michael promised he wouldn't ~~never~~ trick Mr. Baker again.

corrected double negative

Reflect

Look at the editing change in the example. How did Sasha fix the double negative?

Apply Conventions

Edit your draft. Fix any double negatives and check your forms of *good* and *bad*.

For more practice, use the exercises on the next two pages.

Double Negatives

Know the Rule

Use only one **negative** in a sentence. Negatives include words such as *no, not, nothing, none, never, nobody, no one, nowhere, hardly, barely,* and *neither.* A sentence should not contain more than one negative. This error is called a **double negative**.

Incorrect: The man **didn't** say **nothing** when he heard the news.
Correct: The man **didn't** say anything when he heard the news.
Incorrect: Cody did **not** see **nobody** because it was so dark.
Correct: Cody saw **nobody** because it was so dark.

Practice the Rule

Number a separate sheet of paper 1–10. If the sentence contains a double negative, rewrite the sentence correctly. Write **Correct** on your paper if a sentence is correct.

1. Everyone has read fables, which usually feature talking animals.
2. Some readers have not never heard of Aesop.
3. Historians do not know nothing about his life.
4. Most experts believe that he was not a real person.
5. Aesop's fables are not hardly the only popular fables.
6. Another famous writer of fables was Jean de La Fontaine.
7. La Fontaine followed the pattern set by Aesop.
8. Many believe that La Fontaine's fables cannot be surpassed by no one.
9. Nobody can't forget his clever story "The Fox and the Crow."
10. Fable fans must not forget author Beatrix Potter neither.

The Forms of *Good* and *Bad*

Know the Rule

The words *good* and *bad* change form when they're used to compare. Use *better* and *worse* when you compare two people or things. Use *best* and *worst* when you compare three or more people or things.

Practice the Rule

Number a sheet of paper 1–10. Choose the word in ( ) that correctly completes each sentence. Write the word on your paper.

1. My friends and I all play sports, but Emma is the _______ (better/best) athlete of us all.
2. On the other hand, Jason is a _______ (better/best) baseball player than Emma.
3. Without a doubt, I'm the _______ (worse/worst) baseball player in the group.
4. I'm a _______ (better/best) soccer player than Mikayla, though.
5. Naturally, I'm _______ (worse/worst) at soccer than Emma.
6. Emma's team was the _______ (better/best) in the league last year.
7. Sadly, my team was the _______ (worse/worst) in the league.
8. Emma never bragged that my team was _______ (worse/worst) than hers.
9. She and our friends just cheered me on to become a _______ (better/best) player next year.
10. I have the _______ (better/best) friends a person could ask for.

Publish

+Presentation

Publishing Strategy Illustrate the fable and make it into a book for the classroom library.

Presentation Strategy Indent each paragraph.

My fable is finished! Do you think my classmates will recognize the original fable "The Boy Who Cried Wolf" in my version? I'm going to add illustrations to my fable and publish it as a book for the class library. I want my story to be easy to follow for the reader, so I'll make sure each paragraph is clearly indented. Before I put my book in a cover, I'll read through it to make sure I've done everything on my final checklist.

My Final Checklist

Did I —

✔ make sure I didn't use any double negatives?

✔ check my use of forms of *good* and *bad*?

✔ check my spelling, capitalization, and punctuation?

✔ indent every paragraph?

Apply

Use Sasha's checklist to check your own fable. Then add your illustrations and prepare a final copy to place in your class library.

The Boy Who Cried Wolf
retold by Sasha

A boy named Michael looked after a flock of sheep for Mr. Baker, a local farmer whose farm was located in the hills of West Virginia. Because the sheep were in a pasture far from the barn, Mr. Baker gave Michael a cell phone. He told the boy to call him if he needed help.

It didn't take long before Michael grew bored sitting under a tree watching the sheep all day long. I thought I'd like this job, he grumbled to himself, but all sheep do is walk around and munch grass. One day, when he was especially bored with his job, Michael had an idea. He pulled the cell phone out of his pocket and dialed Mr. Baker's number. As soon as the farmer answered, Michael cried, "Mr. Baker! Come quick! Wolves are attacking the sheep! Hurry, it's awful!"

Soon the boy saw the farmer's truck speeding across the plain, a large tail of dust trailing after it. Mr. Baker stopped the truck at the top of the pasture and jumped out. All he saw was the flock of sheep munching peacefully on the green grass near the stream.

Michael began laughing wildly. "You should have seen the look on your face when you jumped out of the truck!"

Mr. Baker was not amused. "Do you realize that I drove up here as fast as I could?" he asked in an angry voice. "And what do I find when I get here? You laughing and the sheep safe and sound!"

"OK," said Michael between giggles. "I'm sorry I made you come all the way up here, but I was just so bored out of my head, and you looked so funny!"

Mr. Baker was very angry, but he needed someone to watch his sheep because he had so many other chores to do. He warned Michael not to play the same trick again.

After a few more days, however, Michael grew even more bored than before. He looked at the cell phone lying on the ground next to him. He thought about how funny Mr. Baker looked when he found out Michael had played a trick on him. Then Michael picked up the cell phone and played the same trick again.

This time, Mr. Baker was even angrier. He told Michael that if he ever played that trick again, he would lose his job. So Michael promised he wouldn't trick Mr. Baker again.

A week later, Michael was sitting under a tree watching the sheep. Out of the corner of his eye, he saw something creeping toward a sheep on the edge of the flock. Michael shaded his eyes against the bright sun. The thing moved, and he saw that the creeping animal was a wolf. Then he saw three more. He watched in horror as the wolf pack circled the sheep. Some of the sheep started to run into the woods to hide.

With trembling fingers, Michael dialed Mr. Baker's number on the cell phone. When the farmer answered, Michael cried, "Mr. Baker! Come quick! Wolves are attacking the sheep!"

However, Michael heard only silence on the other end of the line. Finally, the farmer said, "I'm disappointed in you, Michael. You promised that you wouldn't do this again. I have no choice but to—"

"But Mr. B—"

"You heard me, Michael," said the farmer. "Today will be your last day working for me." Then Mr. Baker hung up.

Moral: No one will believe a liar, even when he is telling the truth.

Reflect

Use the rubric on pages 36–37 to score the story. Did Sasha use all the traits of a good fable? Then use the rubric to check your own story.

What's a Mystery?

It's a story that has suspense and secrets. Usually one of the characters is trying to solve a puzzle.

What's in a Mystery?

Character(s)
A mystery always has a main character who is like a detective and is trying to solve a puzzle. Other characters may help the detective or may get in the way.

Clues
A clue is something that guides characters or the reader to the solution of a mystery. The writer of a mystery leaves clues along the way.

Setting
The setting is where and when the story takes place. In a mystery, the setting helps create an atmosphere of suspense and excitement.

Plot
Plot is the action or sequence of events in a story. The events frame the central problem or puzzle. Usually the solution is revealed near the end.

Why write a Mystery?

I thought of a couple of fun reasons for writing a mystery.

Entertainment
Like adventure stories, mysteries can pull you into a world of suspense and excitement. Imagining the story really allows you to use your creativity.

Challenge
Any kind of puzzle makes us think. We keep trying different ways to tackle the puzzle until we finally find a solution. Inventing a mystery and then piecing it together with clues and characters can be fun!

Linking Narrative Writing Traits to a Mystery

In this chapter, you will write a story that revolves around a problem that has to be figured out. This type of narrative writing is called a mystery. Sasha will guide you through the stages of the writing process: Prewrite, Draft, Revise, Edit, and Publish. In each stage, Sasha will show you important writing strategies that are linked to the Narrative Writing Traits below.

Narrative Writing Traits

	• a clear, focused topic, experience, or series of events • memorable details that bring the characters, plot, and setting to life
	• events told in the order they happened • an interesting beginning and a satisfying ending • transitions that signal the sequence of events
	• a voice and tone that are ideal for telling a story • dialogue that, when used, gives voice to the characters
Word Choice	• precise words that describe the characters, plot, and setting
	• sentences that have flow and rhythm, making them enjoyable to read aloud
	• no or few errors in grammar, usage, mechanics, and spelling

Before you write, read Angela Massey's mystery on the next three pages. Then use the mystery rubric on pages 62–63 to decide how well she did. (You might want to look back at What's in a Mystery? on page 56, too!)

The Case of the Disappearing Soccer Shirt

by Angela Massey

characters

"Dad! Have you seen Jacob's soccer shirt?" called Shannon. "The red and yellow one with the long sleeves?"

Shannon was searching through her brother's room and getting desperate. She had looked on the bed, under the bed, in the closet, in the dresser, on the clothes pegs, and everywhere else she could think of.

beginning of plot

setting

"Gee, Rufus," she said to her big, shaggy red dog. "Jake told me he would leave his shirt right on the bed, so I could wear it to soccer tryouts." Shannon's older brother Jacob was a star player on the high school soccer team. Right now, he was away at soccer camp, but before he left, he had told Shannon she could wear his team shirt from last year to her tryouts.

another character

problem or puzzle

Rufus just looked at the empty bed, where the shirt was supposed to be. Then he looked up at Shannon and wagged his tail.

Shannon's dad came into the room holding the towel he had been using to dry some dishes. "Maybe Jake decided at the last minute to take the shirt to camp with him," he suggested.

solution?

"No," answered Shannon, "I'm sure he didn't. The last thing he said before he left was that his shirt would bring me good luck at my tryouts."

Her father shrugged and said, "Well, you'll just have to look around, I guess."

"I've already looked everywhere," moaned Shannon. "Haven't I, Rufus?"

Rufus just tilted his head to the side, as if he were thinking about what Shannon had just said. Whenever he did that, he made the whole family laugh.

"It's definitely a mystery," her dad said, "but you'll find a way to solve it. Maybe Rufus can help you. In fact, helping you might even cheer him up. I've noticed that he's been pretty unhappy since Jake went to soccer camp. All he does is hide behind the couch. I wonder why."

clue?

Shannon glanced down at her shaggy dog. "Rufus will be a huge help, I'm sure," she said with a smile. She used both hands to pull Rufus's long, tangled fur out of his eyes. "There," she said, "can you see better now? Are you ready to help me find Jake's shirt, old boy?"

"Why don't you ask Lizzie to help you, too?" Dad suggested. Lizzie was Shannon's younger sister.

"All right," answered Shannon, "but I'm not sure she'll be much help either."

another character

A few minutes later, Lizzie eagerly joined her sister in the search for the missing shirt. Lizzie looked in the basement, poked in and around the washer and dryer, and burrowed through all the closets. Meanwhile, Shannon scoured the car and garage. She also ransacked her room, Lizzie's room, and Jake's room—again! Rufus did not offer much assistance. Mostly, he lay in a lump on the living room rug or hid behind the couch.

setting

"I have to find that shirt really soon," Shannon reminded Lizzie. "Soccer tryouts start in three hours. If I don't find that shirt, I'll have to wear something else. I really want to wear Jake's shirt because I need all the good luck I can get at the tryouts. That shirt has got to be around here somewhere!"

suspense

Then Lizzie's eyes got big and round. "Maybe someone stole Jake's shirt!" she whispered. "I bet someone snuck in here and took it while we weren't looking!"

solution?

Shannon grinned and shook her head. "I don't think so, Lizzie, but I have to admit I don't have any better ideas right now. Anyway, Rufus would bark if a stranger came into our house." Then she spotted his tail sticking out from behind the couch. "But maybe not."

clue?

An hour later, Shannon had given up hope of locating the missing shirt. She was slouched on a kitchen chair, slowly helping her dad peel potatoes for their dinner.

Lizzie had gotten tired of searching, too, and was watching TV in the family room. She was lying on the couch, petting Rufus with her stockinged foot as she watched her favorite cartoons. "You really miss Jacob, don't you, boy?" Lizzie mumbled to the unhappy dog. "I bet that's why you didn't even notice when someone came in and stole his shirt."

clue?

Rufus got up slowly and sheepishly squeezed himself back behind the couch. After a while, Lizzie wondered how he was doing and peeped over the back of the couch. Then she let out a scream!

"Shannon! Dad! I found the thief!"

suspense

As Shannon and their dad rushed into the family room, Lizzie reached behind the couch, where Rufus was hiding. As the others watched in suspense, she pulled out the red and yellow shirt. Then Rufus crawled out from behind the couch and lay on the rug with his head on his front paws.

clue?

"Rufus had the shirt all along!" Shannon said with a sigh of relief. "Why would he take Jacob's shirt?"

"I think I know," said Dad. "Rufus really misses Jake, and dogs have a strong sense of smell. To Rufus, the shirt smells like Jake, so he pulled the shirt off the bed and carried it to his hideaway behind the couch. It probably made him feel as if Jake were nearby."

solution!

Shannon gave Rufus a warm hug, and the dog licked her face and wagged his tail. "Sorry, boy, but I need that shirt more than you do right now," she explained. "I'll give it back to you as soon as tryouts are over—I promise!"

Dad reached down and patted Rufus's head. "Why don't we take him with us to the tryouts? That way, he can keep a close watch over his favorite shirt!"

"It's everyone's favorite shirt today!" Shannon added.

end of plot

Mystery Rubric

Use this 6-point rubric to plan and score a mystery.

	6	5	4
Ideas	The story's setting, characters, and events are believable. Clever clues engage the reader.	Most of the details hold the reader's attention and develop story parts. Several clues are given.	The story is believable. Most clues support the story.
Organization	The plot events are well organized. The lead and transitions are strong; the conclusion is satisfying.	Most of the story is well organized. Transitions are helpful. The conclusion is clear.	The reader can follow the plot. Several transitions are used. The conclusion may leave the reader with questions.
Voice	A suspenseful tone and natural-sounding dialogue develop the plot and characters.	A suspenseful tone and the dialogue help develop the plot and characters.	Most of the tone and dialogue are helpful in developing the plot and/ or characters.
Word Choice	The writer uses sensory language and precise words to create a feeling of mystery and suspense.	The writer's sensory language and precise words create a feeling of mystery and suspense most of the time.	Most of the words create a feeling of mystery. Some too-general or weak words dull the story.
Sentence Fluency	The writer uses sentences of various lengths and structures. The story is enjoyable to read.	The writer should vary the length and structure of more sentences to add interest. Transitions are helpful.	Some sentence beginnings are repetitive, making reading dull in places.
Conventions	Dialogue and contractions are punctuated correctly.	Most of the dialogue and contractions are punctuated correctly, and the meaning is clear.	There are minor errors in punctuation of dialogue and contractions, but they do not make reading harder.

+Presentation Paragraphs are indented for each new speaker.

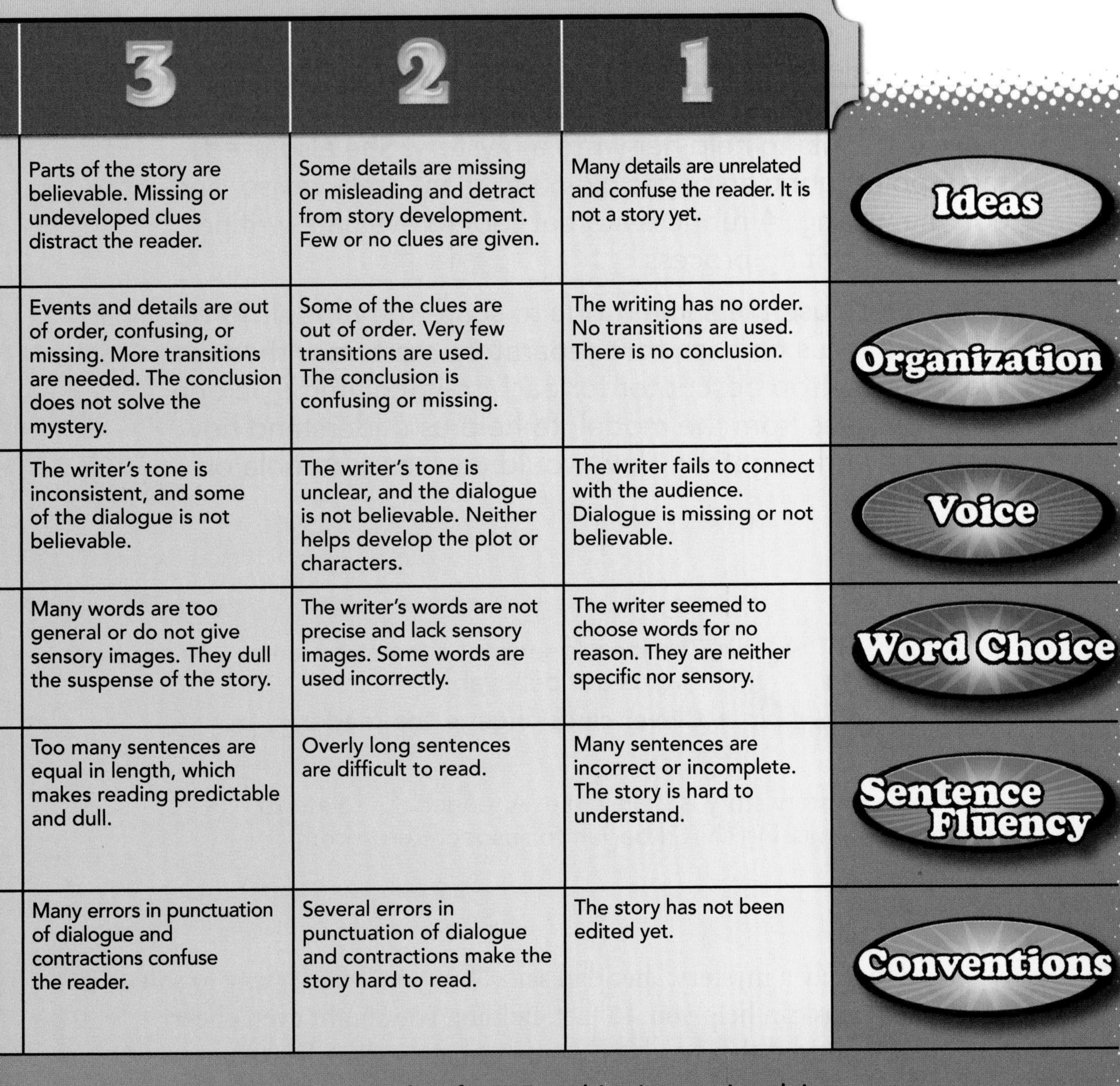

3	2	1	
Parts of the story are believable. Missing or undeveloped clues distract the reader.	Some details are missing or misleading and detract from story development. Few or no clues are given.	Many details are unrelated and confuse the reader. It is not a story yet.	Ideas
Events and details are out of order, confusing, or missing. More transitions are needed. The conclusion does not solve the mystery.	Some of the clues are out of order. Very few transitions are used. The conclusion is confusing or missing.	The writing has no order. No transitions are used. There is no conclusion.	Organization
The writer's tone is inconsistent, and some of the dialogue is not believable.	The writer's tone is unclear, and the dialogue is not believable. Neither helps develop the plot or characters.	The writer fails to connect with the audience. Dialogue is missing or not believable.	Voice
Many words are too general or do not give sensory images. They dull the suspense of the story.	The writer's words are not precise and lack sensory images. Some words are used incorrectly.	The writer seemed to choose words for no reason. They are neither specific nor sensory.	Word Choice
Too many sentences are equal in length, which makes reading predictable and dull.	Overly long sentences are difficult to read.	Many sentences are incorrect or incomplete. The story is hard to understand.	Sentence Fluency
Many errors in punctuation of dialogue and contractions confuse the reader.	Several errors in punctuation of dialogue and contractions make the story hard to read.	The story has not been edited yet.	Conventions

See Appendix B for 4-, 5-, and 6-point narrative rubrics.

Using the Mystery Rubric to Study the Model

Did you notice that the model on pages 59–61 points out some key elements of a mystery? As she wrote "The Case of the Disappearing Soccer Shirt," Angela Massey used these elements to help her write a mystery. She also used the 6-point rubric on pages 62–63 to plan, draft, revise, and edit the writing. A rubric is a great tool to evaluate writing during the writing process.

Now let's use the same rubric to score the model. To do this, we'll focus on each trait separately, starting with Ideas. We'll use the top descriptor for each trait (column 6), along with examples from the model, to help us understand how the traits work together. How would you score Angela on each trait?

- **The story's setting, characters, and events are believable.**
- **Clever clues engage the reader.**

Angela's mystery story is believable. A reader can relate to the problem, a missing shirt. I began to suspect Rufus from a clue in the story.

"It's definitely a mystery," her dad said, "but you'll find a way to solve it. Maybe Rufus can help you. In fact, helping you might even cheer him up. I've noticed that he's been pretty unhappy since Jake went to soccer camp. All he does is hide behind the couch. I wonder why."

- **The plot events are well organized.**
- **The lead and transitions are strong; the conclusion is satisfying.**

Angela's mystery story is tightly organized. She starts off with a strong introduction that tells me the problem right away. The solution to the mystery is satisfying. And along the way, Angela uses effective transitions to guide the reader.

Shannon gave Rufus a warm hug, and the dog licked her face and wagged his tail. "Sorry, boy, but I need that shirt more than you do right now," she explained.

- **A suspenseful tone and natural-sounding dialogue develop the plot and characters.**

Angela develops the story and characters with realistic dialogue. I could feel suspense build as I wondered if Shannon's luck would run out.

"I have to find that shirt really soon," Shannon reminded Lizzie. "Soccer tryouts start in three hours. If I don't find that shirt, I'll have to wear something else. I really want to wear Jake's shirt because I need all the good luck I can get at the tryouts."

Using the Mystery Rubric to Study the Model

- **The writer uses sensory language and precise words to create a feeling of mystery and suspense.**

I feel suspense in the story when Shannon and Lizzie react to possible solutions to the mystery. The writer uses visual words to help the reader "see" the action and feel what the characters are feeling.

"That shirt has got to be around here somewhere!"
Then Lizzie's eyes got big and round. "Maybe someone stole Jake's shirt!" she whispered.

- **The writer uses sentences of various lengths and structures.**
- **The story is enjoyable to read.**

Angela varies her sentences—short and long, simple and complex—to make the story flow smoothly. Her writing isn't boring. It's fun to read aloud!

Rufus got up slowly and sheepishly squeezed himself back behind the couch. After a while, Lizzie wondered how he was doing and peeped over the back of the couch. Then she let out a scream!

- **Dialogue and contractions are punctuated correctly.**

Angela follows the rules for writing dialogue. She uses quotation marks and other punctuation correctly.

> “Why don’t you ask Lizzie to help you, too?” Dad suggested. Lizzie was Shannon’s younger sister.
>
> “All right,” answered Shannon, “but I’m not sure she’ll be much help either.”

+Presentation Paragraphs are indented for each new speaker.

My Turn!

Now it’s my turn to write a mystery! I’ll use the rubric and good writing strategies to help me. Read on to see how I do it.

Prewrite

Focus on **Ideas**

The Rubric Says The story's setting, characters, and events are believable.

Writing Strategy Brainstorm some ideas about real people and events.

When our teacher asked us to write mysteries, several ideas popped into my head. Some came from things I like to do, but most came from the places I go and the people I know. Real-life mysteries are everywhere! Soon I had a whole list of possible topics.

Possible topics for mysteries:

- ✔ Friends: A word that has two meanings causes problems for friends who are trying to find something.
- ✔ Home: My brother is keeping a mysterious secret, and I want to know what it is.
- ✔ School: Something mysteriously appears at school and has all the kids talking.
- ✔ Camping: A strange sound late at night is making campers nervous.

After looking over my notes, I decided to write a mystery about school. Then I had a great idea! I would write about some mysterious posters showing up at school. What do they mean? Who put them there?

Apply

Think about places and people you know. Brainstorm some ideas for a mystery. Jot down some notes about these ideas.

Prewrite

Focus on **Organization**

The Rubric Says The plot events are well organized.

Writing Strategy Use a Story Map to organize the mystery.

I read in the rubric that organization is important in a mystery. I'll use a Story Map to organize the events in my mystery and decide where my clues will go.

Writer's Term

Story Map

A **Story Map** organizes the setting, characters, plot, problem, major events, and outcome of the story.

Story Map

Setting **Place:** elementary school hallways, cafeteria
Time: now

Main Characters Erin and Torrie, fifth-grade girls

Problem/Mystery to find out the meaning of mysterious posters and who put them up

Plot
Event 1: Erin and Torrie see the first poster and try to figure out what it means. **Clue**: Slippers
Event 2: They see the second poster and are still puzzled. **Clue**: Yellow road
Event 3: The girls see the third poster; Erin has an idea. **Clue**: Color of letters

Outcome Erin explains her idea to Torrie, and they find out Erin is right. The mystery is solved!

Reflect

Look at Sasha's Story Map. Is she ready to write a draft? How can you tell?

Apply

Make your own Story Map. Be sure to include the setting, characters, problem, clues, events, and outcome.

Draft

Focus on **Voice**

The Rubric Says A suspenseful tone and natural-sounding dialogue develop the plot and characters.

Writing Strategy Use dialogue to reveal the personalities of the characters.

Now I'll use my Story Map to begin drafting my mystery. The rubric reminds me to use natural-sounding dialogue to develop my story and its characters. Since my best friends are the main characters, it will be easy to write the way they speak. We all love going to the same school, having fun, and solving mysteries. I'll make sure my dialogue sounds like them, supports the suspense, and moves the story along.

As I draft my mystery, I'll try not to make mistakes. But, if I do, I'll be sure to fix them later on when I edit my writing.

Writer's Term

Dialogue

Dialogue is the conversation between characters in a story. It should sound natural and believable. Dialogue is like a window into what the characters are thinking and how they are feeling.

Proofreading Marks

⊐	Indent	ℓ	Take out something
≡	Make uppercase	⊙	Add a period
/	Make lowercase	¶	New paragraph
∧	Add something	(sp)	Spelling error

[DRAFT]

The Case of the Mysterious Posters

Those strange posters attracted a lot of attention at school. The first one appeared in the main hallway, just outside the cafeteria. My friend Torrie and I saw it when we were talking about our two favorite subjects—swim team and what the next Drama Club play might be. We were on our way to lunch.

dialogue

"Hey, Erin." Torrie said. "Look at this poster. What do you think it means?"

dialogue

I looked at it closely. It was in bright red letters on white paper. The poster said, "Don't forget your slippers." That's it—nothing more.

"Huh?" said Torrie. "Slippers at school? What's that supposed to mean? Maybe it's a new fashion trend."

I shruged my shoulders. "Beats me, I answered." Still, I couldnt stop thinking about the wierd poster for the rest of the day.

Reflect

Read the beginning of Sasha's draft. Do you think the dialogue sounds believable?

Apply

Use your Story Map to draft a mystery. Be sure to include natural-sounding dialogue.

Revise

Focus on **Ideas**

The Rubric Says Clever clues engage the reader.

Writing Strategy Check for meaning.

I read my draft to make sure that all the details, especially the clues, make sense to the reader. The part where Erin knew the answer but was still thinking about the posters was confusing! To make it clearer, I revised this part. My clues should also control the pace of the action. A slow-moving story is boring, but if too many clues appear at once, my reader won't be able to keep up! What do you think of my revision?

[DRAFT]

~~Then I knew the answer, but I decided not to tell Torrie until the next day.~~ Hmmm, I thought to myself. Maybe Torrie had something there. That night, I thought long and hard about the mysterious posters.

revised for meaning

Apply

Read your draft. Revise anything that doesn't make sense.

Revise

Focus on **Word Choice**

The Rubric Says The writer uses sensory language and precise words to create a feeling of mystery and suspense.

Writing Strategy Use a thesaurus to find words that add suspense.

The rubric says to use sensory language and precise words to create a feeling of mystery. I looked through my draft for words that were common or ordinary so I could replace them. In a thesaurus I found synonyms—words with similar meanings—that add suspense to my story.

Writer's Term

Thesaurus

A **thesaurus** is a resource in which you can find synonyms (words with a similar meaning) and antonyms (words with an opposite meaning).

[DRAFT]

The puzzle definitely got more ~~confusing~~ perplexing the next day. Torrie and I were leaving the cafeteria after lunch when she ~~spotted~~ spied another poster.

added suspenseful words

Reflect

Look at Sasha's revisions. Do the more precise words create more excitement and suspense for the reader? In what ways?

Apply

Read your draft. Use a thesaurus to replace ordinary words. You can use a print or an online version of a thesaurus.

Revise

Focus on **Sentence Fluency**

The Rubric Says The writer uses sentences of various lengths and structures.

Writing Strategy Revise sentences for a smooth flow.

The rubric says to use different kinds of sentences. I read my draft and found places where I had written the same kind and length of sentence several times in a row. I made some changes. Does my writing flow more smoothly now?

[DRAFT]

changed sentence structure

The second poster was completely different from the first one. It was written in yellow letters and ~~It~~ said, "Where does this road go?" A crowd of kids had gathered around it. From what they were saying, I could tell Torrie and I weren't the only ones who were puzzled. ~~They were all talking. Torrie and I were puzzled. They were puzzled, too.~~

combined three short, similar sentences

Apply

Read your draft aloud. Listen for similar sentences. Vary sentence length and structure in these places.

Edit

Focus on **Conventions**

The Rubric Says Dialogue and contractions are punctuated correctly.

Writing Strategy Check for errors in punctuating quotations and contractions.

I've finished drafting my mystery, and now I'll check my spelling, capitalization, and grammar, as I always do. The rubric reminds me to pay special attention to how I punctuate quotations and contractions.

Writer's Term

Direct Quotation

A **direct quotation** is the exact words of someone speaking.

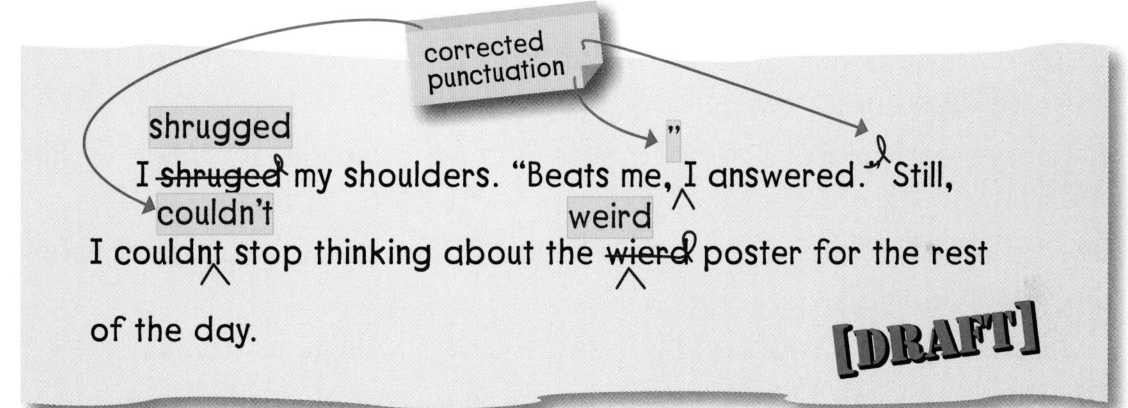

Reflect

Look at Sasha's edits. Is her spelling correct? Did she punctuate the direct quotation and contraction correctly?

Apply

Conventions

Edit your draft. Fix any errors in punctuating quotations and contractions.

For more practice in punctuating quotations and contractions correctly, use the exercises on the next two pages.

Quotations

Know the Rule

A **direct quotation** is a speaker's exact words. Use quotation marks at the beginning and the end of a quotation. Use a comma or end punctuation to separate the speaker's words from the rest of the sentence. Begin a quotation with a capital letter and add end punctuation before the last quotation mark.

Example:
Chloe said, "I think mysteries are both fun and interesting."

Practice the Rule

Read the sentences below. If the sentence contains an error in punctuating a quotation, rewrite the sentence correctly. If a sentence is correct, write **Correct**.

1. Many readers consider Edgar Allan Poe to be the inventor of the modern mystery story," said Professor Holman.
2. "Another early detective novel was *The Moonstone* by Wilkie Collins, she continued.
3. She added, "Collins was a good friend of Charles Dickens, another famous novelist."
4. I whispered to my mother, I've read a story by Wilkie Collins."
5. The professor said, "In 1887, the world's most famous literary detective appeared.
6. "Is there anyone who doesn't recognize Sherlock Holmes," the tall, thin detective with the pipe and famous hat? she asked.
7. "The Sherlock Holmes stories are told by his friend, Dr. Watson," Professor Holman continued.
8. She added, *The Hound of the Baskervilles* is my favorite Holmes tale.
9. Another English detective was Father Brown," said the professor.
10. Then she asked, "Does anyone have a favorite Agatha Christie character?"

Contractions

Know the Rule

A **contraction** is two words that have been shortened and combined. An apostrophe stands for letters that were dropped to make the contraction.

Example:
I am becomes **I'm,** and **does not** becomes **doesn't**. However, **will not** becomes **won't**.

Practice the Rule

Number a sheet of paper 1–10. Rewrite the underlined words as contractions.

1. I cannot go to a movie tonight.
2. I have not finished my homework yet.
3. My parents will not let me go out until it is all done.
4. They said I should not wait until the last minute to do my homework.
5. You did not do your homework either?
6. Let us do it together at my house.
7. If we help each other, we will finish faster.
8. After all, there are not many problems on the math worksheet.
9. Then we can ask my parents if they will take us out for ice cream.
10. I'm sure they would not mind taking us out for a treat, as long as our work is done.

Publish +Presentation

Publishing Strategy Read the mystery to the class on Authors' Day.

Presentation Strategy Indent paragraphs for each new speaker's dialogue.

I've finished writing my mystery! I can't wait for Authors' Day. I am a little nervous about reading my mystery to the class, but I'm pretty sure they'll like it! I also want people to be able to read my mystery for themselves. It's hard to follow dialogue when it's poorly presented, so I'll make sure I start a new paragraph for each new speaker. Here is the checklist I used to make sure my mystery was ready for the big day.

My Final Checklist

Did I—

- ✔ check my grammar, spelling, and capitalization?
- ✔ make sure I punctuated quotations and contractions correctly?
- ✔ indent a new paragraph for each new speaker's dialogue?

Apply

Make a checklist to check your own mystery. Then make a final copy to read to the class. You can add a couple of colorful illustrations to your mystery to help readers identify the clues, too.

The Case of the Mysterious Posters
by Sasha

Those strange posters attracted a lot of attention at school. The first one appeared in the main hallway, just outside the cafeteria. My friend Torrie and I saw it when we were talking about our two favorite subjects—swim team and what the next Drama Club play might be. We were on our way to lunch.

"Hey, Erin," Torrie said. "Look at this poster. What do you think it means?"

I looked at it closely. It was in big, bright red letters on white paper. The poster said, "Don't forget your slippers." That's it—nothing more.

"Huh?" said Torrie. "Slippers at school? What's that supposed to mean? Maybe it's a new fashion trend."

I shrugged my shoulders. "Beats me," I answered. Still, I couldn't stop thinking about the weird poster for the rest of the day.

The puzzle definitely got more perplexing the next day. Torrie and I were leaving the cafeteria after lunch when she spied another poster.

The second poster was completely different from the first one. It was written in yellow letters and said, "Where does this road go?" A crowd of kids had gathered around it. From what they were saying, I could tell Torrie and I weren't the only ones who were puzzled.

"I think we're in the middle of a really baffling mystery," Torrie said.

On the bus home that day, the posters were all Torrie and I talked about. We traded all sorts of theories about the posters. Who was putting them up? What did they mean? Why were they so mysterious and secretive? Would another poster appear tomorrow?

"We need to think about the mystery the way Charlie Chan or Sherlock Holmes would," Torrie said.

She was right. Those movie detectives from the 1930s could solve any mystery.

"We need to use our heads like the scarecrow in *The Wizard of Oz* does after he gets a brain," she added.

Hmmm, I thought to myself. Maybe Torrie had something there.

That night, I thought long and hard about the mysterious posters. Something about what Torrie said stuck in my mind, but I just couldn't come up with the right answer.

I finally drifted off to sleep, but I woke up with a start at about four in the morning. "That's it!" I cried. "That's the answer to the puzzle!"

I couldn't wait to get to school the next morning to tell Torrie what I'd figured out. I didn't see her until third period, when she came running up to me all excited.

"Guess what?" she practically yelled. "There's another poster!"

"What color are the letters?" I asked quickly.

She looked at me as if I were crazy, and then she answered, "They're bright green. Why?"

"Then I bet the poster says something like 'Welcome to the city!'" I said confidently.

Welcome to the city!

Torrie's eyes almost bugged out of her head. "You—you're exactly right! How did you know?"

"You told me yesterday," I explained.

"I did? But how?" she asked.

"Remember what you said about the scarecrow in *The Wizard of Oz*? And remember how the Drama Club is trying to keep the name of its next play secret as long as it can?"

"Yes, but so what?" Torrie asked.

"Auditions are next week, right? Think about it. The first poster was about slippers and written in red letters—ruby red letters. The second one asked about a road and was written in yellow letters. Does a yellow road ring a bell? The third one welcomed us to a city in emerald green letters. Do these three things remind you of any old movie?" I asked.

"Well, sure!" Torrie cried. "*The Wizard of Oz*! The class play is *The Wizard of Oz*!"

"Now you're using your brain, Scarecrow," I said.

Reflect

Use the rubric to score Sasha's story. Check your own mystery against the rubric, too!

What's a Play?

It's a story presented in a format so that actors can perform it, usually on a stage, or readers can imagine it in their minds.

What's in a Play?

Cast
The cast is the characters—the people or animals—in the play. Most plays have at least two characters, usually named in a cast list at the top of the play.

Dialogue
Dialogue is the conversation, or spoken lines, between characters. Spoken lines come after the name of the character that is speaking. Play dialogue is not enclosed in quotation marks.

Plot
Plot is the action or sequence of events in a story. Stage directions explain actions, lighting, and sound effects that help dramatize the events of the play.

Setting
The setting is where and when the events in a play take place. A short play is often divided into scenes to indicate changes in the setting.

Yosemite
National Park

Why write a Play?

People have many reasons for writing a play. Here are some reasons I can think of for writing a story in a form that can be acted out.

Entertainment
A good play entertains its audience by taking people out of their ordinary routines to enjoy the words and actions of a story happening right in front of them. Whether a play is performed on stage in a large theater or in a classroom, it can deliver the excitement, surprise, and fun of drama.

Information
I think it might be interesting to write a play about someone important I have learned about in class. I could really bring the topic to life that way.

Connections
Plays are a way for people to connect with each other. When you act in a play, you get to be a different character from your usual self to see how that feels. When you watch a play, you connect with certain characters and follow a story outside your familiar life. When I write a play, I will connect with my characters so that my audience can make the connection, too.

Linking Narrative Writing Traits to a Play

In this chapter, you will write a story in the form of a drama that can be acted out. This type of narrative writing is called a play. Sasha will guide you through the stages of the writing process: Prewrite, Draft, Revise, Edit, and Publish. In each stage, Sasha will show you important writing strategies that are linked to the Narrative Writing Traits below.

Narrative Writing Traits

	• a clear, focused topic, experience, or series of events • memorable details that bring the characters, plot, and setting to life
	• events told in the order they happened • an interesting beginning and a satisfying ending • transitions that signal the sequence of events
	• a voice and tone that are ideal for telling a story • dialogue that, when used, gives voice to the characters
	• precise words that describe the characters, plot, and setting
	• sentences that have flow and rhythm, making them enjoyable to read aloud
	• no or few errors in grammar, usage, mechanics, and spelling

Before you write, read Daniel Lee's play on the next three pages. Then use the play rubric on pages 88–89 to decide how well he did. (You might want to look back at What's in a Play? on page 82, too!)

North to Freedom

by Daniel Lee

cast list

CAST

Jess, plantation worker, age 9; **Tom,** plantation worker, age 13
Reba, Mother of Jess and Tom; **Harriet Tubman,** leader

SETTING: 1858, Maryland, a state that allowed slavery

setting

SCENE **1:** *Plantation cabin in Maryland, Saturday night, all gathered around a small table*

Jess: In the fields today, people sang, "Go Down, Moses."

Reba: That's the signal that Harriet Tubman has come again!

Tom: How do you know that, Ma?

Reba: Moses led his people out of slavery from Egypt. Harriet Tubman leads our people north, out of slavery to freedom!

Jess: Slavery is terrible! We work all day and never get paid.

dialogue

Tom: Slavery is wrong. I'll fight the slave owners!

Reba: Hush, Tom! Your father did that, and he was killed.

Tom: (*pounds fist on table*) Well, I would rather die than live in slavery!

stage directions

Reba: Then you must go to the North, where you can be free!

Jess: It's dangerous to go! Slave hunters, wild beasts, fever…

Reba: Harriet knows how to keep you safe. If you stay, you both will be sold and sent far down south. That's even worse.

Jess: I will go with Harriet only if you and Tom come, too!

Tom: This is our chance to stay together and to be free!

Reba: Well, then, I will go with you! We must pack quickly. Harriet waits at the secret meeting spot. She will leave tonight!

scene

SCENE 2: *Same night, forest, swamp, field*

Harriet: We will walk all night to get as far away from the plantation as possible. If we reach a safe place, we can rest by day and then go on when darkness comes.

Jess: Where are we going?

Harriet: We'll go north to Pennsylvania, where slavery is not allowed, about 100 miles from here.

stage directions

Tom: How long until we get there?

Harriet: Many, many days of walking mostly, so let us begin.
(*rumbling then booming thunder, heavy rain*)

Jess: The rain is so hard and cold. My clothes are soaked!

Harriet: Be glad for this rain. It washes away our scent, so the hounds of the slave hunters can't track us down.

Reba: (*whispers fearfully*) Oh, no! The rain has stopped! The sun is rising!
(*hounds barking, becoming louder*)

Harriet: See that tall marsh grass? Lie down and be very still.
(*a gun is fired*)

Jess: Slave hunters! They get money for shooting us!

plot

Reba: (*whispers urgently*) Hush! Please!
(*hounds barking very loudly, then fading away*)

Harriet: All right, now we can move again. We will crawl through this swamp; keep your heads down. (*all slog through swamp*)

Jess: We've been crawling so long. I'm tired and hungry.

Reba: Hush, Jess! I packed corn cakes. We'll eat them later.

Harriet: Soon we'll reach a cornfield. You can eat there.

SCENE **3:** *Morning, all hide among tall stalks in cornfield* (*an owl hoots*)

Tom: That's strange, to hear an owl in daytime.

Harriet: That's not an owl; it's a signal to us from folks ready to help! Up ahead is a safe house where we can rest. Then a kind man will hide us in his hay wagon and take us farther north.

Jess: Will we be in Pennsylvania then?

Harriet: No, this is just the first day of a long journey to the North, and then, to be safe, much farther on to Canada.

Tom: You were already free and safe. Why did you return?

Harriet: For nine years I have returned to Maryland to lead others north to freedom. I know the way quite well by now.

Reba: We are sure that you will lead us to freedom, too!

Play Rubric

Use this 6-point rubric to plan and score a play.

	6	5	4
Ideas	Plot, setting, and characters are well developed through details. Stage directions add details.	Plot, setting, and characters are developed. Most stage directions add details.	Plot and setting are developed. One character lacks details. Some directions are not clear.
Organization	The events are in a sequence that unfolds naturally. Scene changes divide the play into a strong beginning, middle, and ending.	The events are in order. Scenes divide the events into beginning, middle, and ending.	The events are in order. The final scene may leave unanswered questions or end abruptly.
Voice	Each character has a distinct voice. The dialogue is natural and realistic.	Each character has a distinct voice. Most of the dialogue is natural and realistic.	One character needs to sound more natural and realistic.
Word Choice	All words are used correctly and explained or defined, if necessary.	Most words are used correctly and explained or defined.	One or two words need definitions or have unclear definitions.
Sentence Fluency	Different types of sentences help the dialogue flow smoothly. It is easy to read aloud.	Most sentences are varied and make the dialogue flow.	More sentence variety in a couple of places would help make the dialogue flow.
Conventions	Sentences are punctuated correctly. Commas are used correctly.	Minor sentence errors are present but do not interfere with meaning. Commas are used correctly.	A few sentence errors cause confusion. One or two commas may have been used incorrectly.

+Presentation The script is formatted correctly.

	3	2	1
Ideas	Plot and setting are developed. Characters lack details. Some directions are missing.	Plot and setting are not developed. Characters lack details. Stage directions are not complete.	Plot and setting are not developed. Details may not be related. Stage directions are not provided.
Organization	Most events are in order. Some scene changes are not clear.	Many events are out of order. Scene changes are not clear. The play is hard to follow.	The writing is not organized. Play elements are not used.
Voice	The dialogue sounds awkward in some places. The voice may not fit the character(s).	The characters all sound the same. The dialogue is not natural or realistic.	The voice is weak or absent. Speaking parts are not present.
Word Choice	The meaning of many words is not clear. Definitions or explanations are lacking.	Some words may be confusing or overused. Definitions are not provided.	Many words are used incorrectly.
Sentence Fluency	Many sentences are the same type, which makes the dialogue somewhat choppy.	The play does not flow easily. Some sentences are incomplete.	The writing does not flow. It is very difficult to read.
Conventions	Many errors are repeated and cause confusion. Some commas are used incorrectly.	Serious errors interfere with meaning. Commas are missing or used incorrectly.	The writing has not been edited.

See Appendix B for 4-, 5-, and 6-point descriptive rubrics.

Using the Play Rubric to Study the Model

Did you notice that the model on pages 85–87 points out some key elements of a play? As he wrote "North to Freedom," Daniel Lee used these elements to help him write a play. He also used the 6-point rubric on pages 88–89 to plan, draft, revise, and edit the writing. A rubric is a great tool to evaluate writing during the writing process.

Now let's use the same rubric to score the model. To do this, we'll focus on each trait separately, starting with Ideas. We'll use the top descriptor for each trait (column 6), along with examples from the model, to help us understand how the traits work together. How would you score Daniel on each trait?

- **Plot, setting, and characters are well developed through details.**
- **Stage directions add details.**

From reading Daniel's play, I know that the play is set right before the Civil War. The details in the play show me what Tom, Reba, and Jess experience in their journey to the North. Details in the spoken lines reveal each character in the story. Stage directions add details about their feelings.

Tom: (*pounds fist on table*) Well, I would rather die than live in slavery!
Reba: Then you must go to the North, where you can be free!
Jess: It's dangerous to go! Slave hunters, wild beasts, fever…

- **The events are in a sequence that unfolds naturally.**
- **Scene changes divide the play into a strong beginning, middle, and ending.**

Daniel presents all the events in time order. He uses scene changes to tell when and where the action takes place, and there's a clear beginning, middle, and ending. The dialogue also helps me follow the timeline of the story.

Harriet: We'll go north to Pennsylvania, where slavery is not allowed, about 100 miles from here.
Tom: How long until we get there?
Harriet: Many, many days of walking mostly, so let us begin.

- **Each character has a distinct voice.**
- **The dialogue is natural and realistic.**

I notice that Daniel gives personalities to the characters through their dialogue. In Scene 2, Harriet Tubman talks like a leader, giving clear directions and explaining what to do. The sounds offstage are just as important, and they really add excitement!

Harriet: See that tall marsh grass? Lie down and be very still.
(*a gun is fired*)
Jess: Slave hunters! They get money for shooting us!
Reba: (*whispers urgently*) Hush! Please!

Using the Play Rubric to Study the Model

- **All words are used correctly and explained or defined, if necessary.**

The spoken lines in Daniel's play contain words like *North*, *slave hunters*, and *wild beasts*. They add realism to the play. Daniel uses the words correctly and adds clues to their meaning, such as saying that the North offers freedom.

Reba: Then you must go to the North, where you can be free!
Jess: It's dangerous to go! Slave hunters, wild beasts, fever…
Reba: Harriet knows how to keep you safe. If you stay, you both will be sold and sent far down south. That's even worse.

- **Different types of sentences help the dialogue flow smoothly. It is easy to read aloud.**

I think Daniel's spoken lines are easy to read aloud. He uses questions, exclamations, and statements to move the story along and make the dialogue flow.

Jess: The rain is so hard and cold. My clothes are soaked!
Harriet: Be glad for this rain. It washes away our scent, so the hounds of the slave hunters can't track us down.
Reba: (*whispers fearfully*) Oh, no! The rain has stopped! The sun is rising!

- Sentences are punctuated correctly.
- Commas are used correctly.

It's pretty obvious that Daniel edited his play carefully before he published it. Words are spelled correctly, even names and places. He also used end punctuation to animate the speaker's words and commas to show pauses.

Harriet: No, this is just the first day of a long journey to the North, and then, to be safe, much farther on to Canada.
Tom: You were already free and safe. Why did you return?
Harriet: For nine years I have returned to Maryland to lead others north to freedom. I know the way quite well by now.
Reba: We are sure that you will lead us to freedom too!

+Presentation The script is formatted correctly.

My Turn!

Now it's my turn to write a play! I'll use the rubric and good writing strategies to help me. Read along to see how I do it.

Prewrite

Focus on **Ideas**

The Rubric Says Plot, setting, and characters are well developed through details.

Writing Strategy Look through sources such as textbooks, reference books, and websites for topic ideas.

I want to write a play about someone who inspires me. My teacher says a good place to start is to think about real people we've read about in class.

I'll begin by looking through my literature book for ideas.

In the biography section, I remember reading a story about John Muir, who planned the first national parks. Since I love being outdoors and going camping with my family on our summer vacations, I would like to learn more about this amazing man. I want to share interesting details about his goal to save the most beautiful spaces in our country for future generations.

Now that I've chosen my topic, I'll meet with my writing partners to discuss my ideas. I'm sure putting our heads together will help all of us write our plays. To find information to use in my play, I'll search my school's library and reliable websites. The details I learn will help me shape the plot, characters, and setting.

Apply

Which leaders, inventors, or educators do you admire? List some different ideas. Then read more and talk with others to decide on your topic.

Prewrite

Focus on **Organization**

The Rubric Says The events are in a sequence that unfolds naturally. Scene changes divide the play into a strong beginning, middle, and ending.

Writing Strategy Create a Story Map to organize the play.

The rubric reminds me to organize the play carefully. I want to focus on the Yosemite hike John Muir and his daughters made in 1896. I'll put the events in order and make sure my plan includes information about the setting, characters, and plot.

Story Map

Setting **Place:** Sierra Nevada Mountains, Yosemite National Park
Time: Summer, 1896

Main Characters John Muir (mountain man, scientist, nature writer, conservation leader) and his daughters Wanda (age 15) and Helen (age 10)

Goal Girls want to know more about their father's life. All three want to reach a special mountain lookout.

Plot
Scene 1 Hike begins and John tells about his early life.
Scene 2 Stop to study wildlife and John tells about his life choices.
Scene 3 Stop for spectacular view and discuss the importance of national parks in protecting wildlife.

Outcome Girls learn more about their father. They enjoy the wilderness together.

Reflect

Look at Sasha's Story Map. How has she arranged the events?

Apply

Create a Story Map for your play. Be sure to put events in a natural order.

Draft

Focus on **Word Choice**

The Rubric Says All words are used correctly and explained or defined, if necessary.

Writing Strategy Check word use and define words that readers might not understand.

I think I'm ready to draft my play now. I can use my Story Map to remind me of information to use in my story. The rubric says that I should use words correctly and explain or define them if my readers might not understand them. I will try to explain words like *immigrate, wilderness,* and *botanist* in the dialogue.

As I write, I won't worry too much about punctuation, grammar, and spelling. I can fix those later. I'll use a computer to write my play so that I can use different kinds of type for dialogue and stage directions.

[DRAFT]

Hike with John Muir

CAST

Wanda Muir, age 15; **Helen Muir,** age 10

John Muir, scientist, writer, inventor, protector of nature

SETTING: Sierra Nevada Mountains, California, 1896

SCENE 1: *Mountain trail in Yosemite National Park*

Wanda: Thank you for taking us hiking with you, Father.

John: Of course, I want you both to know these great mountains!

Proofreading Marks

⊐ Indent	ℓ Take out something
≡ Make uppercase	⊙ Add a period
/ Make lowercase	¶ New paragraph
∧ Add something	(sp) Spelling error

[DRAFT]

unfamiliar word

Helen: Did you come here when you were my age?

John: Our family was still in Scotland until I was eleven. Then we left our home and immigrated to America. We settled in Wisconsin. I loved to explore the woods around our farm, but there were no mountains like these.

explanations

Wanda: Mother says you were an inventor, even as a boy.

John: I did like to invent things, like a giant thermometer and other gadgets to make farm work easier.

Wanda: Were you always interested in nature?

John: Yes, so in college, I decided to be a botanist. I filled journals with notes and drawings of everything I noticed about trees, flowers, and grass. As you know, I still keep journals wherever I go. (*holds up his pocket journal*)

Helen: Look at the beautiful blue butterflies on those bushes!

John: Let's stop and look more closely!

Wanda: Then let's have the fruit and bread I packed.

Reflect

What do you think about Sasha's choice of words for her play? How well did she explain unfamiliar words?

Apply

Follow your Story Map to write a draft. Try to include explanations for words from the time period in the dialogue.

Revise

Focus on **Ideas**

The Rubric Says Stage directions add details.

Writing Strategy Use clear stage directions to add details to the plot and characters.

I finished my draft and began to look at the rubric again. The Ideas rubric says that the stage directions add details. I see a place where a stage direction would clarify the dialogue. I'll be sure to put the stage directions in parentheses to set them off from the dialogue. Since I'm using a computer to write my play, I'll also use italics to make the stage directions stand out. Italics are letters that look like *this*. I don't want an actor to read aloud the stage directions!

[DRAFT]

Wanda: But you saved the wildlife. You wrote papers to get the government to protect Yosemite by making this a national park.
John: That helped somewhat, but not enough.
John: (*standing together at the lookout*) We're here! Look down there at the Yosemite Valley!

stage directions

Apply

Read your draft. Where can you add details that will explain the ideas you want to share?

Revise

Focus on **Organization**

The Rubric Says	Scene changes divide the play into a strong beginning, middle, and ending.
Writing Strategy	Use the scene changes to highlight a strong beginning, middle, and ending.

According to the rubric, the scenes help organize the action of the play. I have already organized my play into three scenes. However, I need to be sure that the beginning is nice and strong and leads to a memorable conclusion.

[DRAFT]

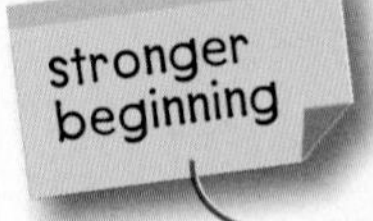

This is a steep trail! Where are we headed,

Wanda: ~~Thank you for taking us hiking with you~~, Father~~.~~?

A few miles up ahead we'll reach a splendid lookout.

John: ~~Of course, I want you both to know these great mountains.~~

I love to climb! hike

Helen: Did you ~~come~~ here when you were my age?

Reflect

How do the revisions make the beginning stronger?

Apply

Look over your draft. Is the beginning attention-grabbing? Is the ending satisfying?

Revise

Focus on Sentence Fluency

The Rubric Says Different types of sentences help the dialogue flow smoothly.

Writing Strategy Choose punctuation for effect.

The rubric reminds me to use different kinds of sentences to make the dialogue flow smoothly. The dialogue should have a good mix of questions, statements, and exclamations. The punctuation I use will help the reader know how to read the sentences. I'll read the dialogue aloud to see if I have enough variety.

Writer's Term

Dialogue

Dialogue is the conversation between characters. In a play, it takes on a very important role because it is the main way that the audience knows what is happening.

revised to include exclamations

[DRAFT]

Wanda: Aren't we in Yosemite right now?

John: Yes! The mountains here were the most magnificent I had ever seen. I stayed close to these mountains for many years. There was always more to study!

Apply

Read your play dialogue aloud with a partner. Revise your punctuation to include exclamations and questions where they're needed.

Edit

Focus on **Conventions**

The Rubric Says Sentences are punctuated correctly. Commas are used correctly.

Writing Strategy Use exclamation points, question marks, periods, and commas correctly.

I'm finally ready to check my draft for spelling, grammar, and capitalization. The rubric reminds me that I need to use appropriate punctuation for different sentences. The girls ask lots of questions. Their father makes many statements. Each type of sentence should be punctuated correctly.

corrected spelling

corrected punctuation

[DRAFT]

Helen: What about the giant ~~Seguoid~~ sequoia trees we saw yesterday?

John: Those spectacular ancient trees could be cut down for lumber soon.

Reflect

Look at Sasha's editing. Why did she make the changes she did? How have her edits made her play stronger?

Apply

Conventions

Edit your draft carefully. Mistakes can affect meaning and distract the reader.

For more practice identifying types of sentences and using commas, use the exercises on the next two pages.

Types of Sentences

Know the Rule

Remember to use punctuation to animate a speaker's words. Helen's first sentence, an **exclamatory sentence,** expresses strong feelings. It ends with an exclamation point. Her second sentence, an **interrogative sentence,** asks a question. It ends with a question mark.

Example:
Helen: I like to climb! Did you hike here when you were my age?

John's second sentence, an **imperative sentence,** gives a command.

Example:
John: We're here! Look down there at the Yosemite Valley!

Sentences that state information without too much emotion are called **declarative sentences,** and these end with a period.

Practice the Rule

Write the numbered sentences below on a separate sheet of paper, adding correct punctuation. Write **E** after each exclamatory sentence, **Im** after each imperative, **In** after each interrogative, and **D** after each declarative sentence.

1. Stop at the flat rock up ahead
2. Yes, that looks like a good place to rest
3. I will never, ever go back to that swamp again
4. Did you think we would ever get out of the swamp
5. It looks like your arm is bleeding
6. Get the first aid kit
7. Does your arm hurt
8. No, it's just a small cut
9. Hold still while I bandage your arm
10. Did you ever think of becoming a doctor

Commas

Know the Rule

Commas tell a reader where to pause. Use a comma to

- separate an introductory word from the rest of the sentence.

  Example:
  Yes, many immigrants came to the United States in the twentieth century.

- separate independent clauses in a compound sentence.

  Example:
  Some immigrants came to find a better life, but other immigrants came to be with their families.

- separate a noun of direct address from the rest of the sentence. A noun of direct address names a person who is being spoken to.

  Example:
  Maria, I'm so happy to see you!

Practice the Rule

Number a separate sheet of paper 1–10. Write each sentence correctly by putting the commas in the right places.

1. How many more days Mother until the ship lands in America?
2. I don't know but the sailors might.
3. Mother can Samuel and I go up on deck and watch the sailors working?
4. Yes but do not bother them with questions.
5. Come on Samuel let's go!
6. Hello son what can I do for you?
7. Sir can you tell us when we will land in America?
8. We should get there in six days but a storm could slow us down.
9. Help I almost slipped on the wet deck!
10. Be careful Samuel or you'll arrive in America with a broken leg!

Publish

+Presentation

Publishing Strategy Prepare a script for performance.

Presentation Strategy Use the computer to format the play.

I'll prepare a final copy of my play about John Muir for some friends in my class to act out. As I mentioned, I'll type my play on a computer so that I can use **dark print** to label the cast, setting, and scenes. I can use *italics* for the scene descriptions and stage directions. Also, I can add extra space between the speakers' lines to make reading the play easier. Then I'll print out three copies, one for each character, so we can rehearse together. A poster of Yosemite National Park would make a good background. Before we start rehearsing, I'll read through my draft to make sure I've done everything on my final checklist.

My Final Checklist

Did I—

- ✔ check my spelling, grammar, and capitalization?
- ✔ make sure I used commas and end punctuation correctly?
- ✔ use proper play format?
- ✔ add extra space between speakers' lines?

Apply

Use this checklist to publish your play. Make copies of the play for others to read and act out. Think about simple props or costumes to stage your play.

Hike with John Muir
by Sasha

CAST

Wanda Muir, age 15
Helen Muir, age 10
John Muir, scientist, writer, inventor, protector of wildlife

SETTING: Sierra Nevada Mountains, California, 1896

SCENE 1: *Mountain trail in Yosemite National Park*

Wanda: This is a steep trail! Where are we headed, Father?

John: A few miles up ahead we'll reach a splendid lookout.

Helen: I love to climb! Did you hike here when you were my age?

John: Our family was still in Scotland until I was eleven. Then we immigrated to America. We settled in Wisconsin. I loved to explore the woods around our farm, but there were no mountains like these.

Wanda: Mother says you were an inventor, even as a boy.

John: I did like to invent things, like a giant thermometer and other gadgets to make farm work easier.

Wanda: Were you always interested in nature?

John: Yes, so in college, I decided to be a botanist, a plant scientist. I filled journals with notes and drawings of everything I noticed about trees, flowers, and grass. As you know, I still keep journals wherever I go. (*holds up his pocket journal*)

Helen: Look at the beautiful blue butterflies on those bushes!

John: Let's stop and look more closely!

Wanda: Then let's have the fruit and bread I packed.

SCENE **2:** *Large flat rock for picnic*

Helen: Did you come to California after college, Father?

John: No, first I hiked mountains in Canada and then I moved to Indiana. I worked there as a factory engineer, until one fateful day.

Wanda: What happened, Father?

John: I was blinded in an accident at work.

Helen: But you are not blind, Father.

John: Luckily, I was cured after a month indoors in total darkness. I realized then how much I wanted to be outdoors in the light. I quit the factory job and began to hike and travel. I headed west to California and then Yosemite.

Wanda: Aren't we in Yosemite right now?

John: Yes! The mountains here were the most magnificent I had ever seen. I stayed close to these mountains for many years. There was always more to study! I loved living in this wilderness.

SCENE **3:** *Back on mountain trail, near lookout*

Wanda: Finally you left the mountains, met Mother, and married.

Helen: You managed the fruit ranch and helped to raise us.

John: And meanwhile Yosemite's wildlife was in grave danger.

Wanda: But you saved the wildlife. You wrote papers to get the government to protect Yosemite by making this a national park.

John: That helped somewhat, but not enough.

John: (*standing together at the lookout*) We're here! Look down there at the Yosemite Valley!

Wanda: What lovely meadows and amazing waterfalls!

John: Yes, but sadly the valley is not yet part of the national park land. Lumber companies, hunters, and sheep ranchers will destroy the wilderness if the United States government doesn't protect the land.

Helen: What about the giant sequoia trees we saw yesterday?

John: Those spectacular ancient trees could be cut down for lumber soon.

Wanda: Your writing will convince people to save the wilderness!

John: That's my hope, so I will keep writing about the glories of the wilderness. I'm so glad you hiked with me today.

Helen and Wanda: Thank you, Father! We will never forget what we saw today!

Reflect

Did Sasha use all the traits well? Be sure to use the rubric to score your own play.

Narrative test writing

Read the Writing Prompt

The first thing you'll read in a writing test is the writing prompt. Look for three helpful parts in the writing prompt.

Setup This part of the writing prompt gives you the background information you need to get ready for writing.

Task This part of the writing prompt tells you exactly what you're supposed to write: a personal narrative about an exciting event that you watched or took part in.

Scoring Guide This part tells how your writing will be scored. You should include everything on the list to do well on the test.

You've used rubrics for each narrative you've written using this book. When you take a writing test, you don't always have all the information that a rubric gives you. But the scoring guide looks a lot like a rubric. The scoring guide lists everything you need to think about to write a good paper. Many scoring guides will include the six important traits of writing that are in the rubrics we've looked at:

Word Choice

Conventions

Exciting events happen in everyone's life. Some exciting events are grand and important. Others are quiet events with family or a few friends.

Write a personal narrative about an exciting event you observed or experienced.

Be sure your personal narrative

- focuses on a memorable event and uses description to develop the events.
- includes events that unfold naturally and uses transitions to link events.
- uses first-person point of view to entertain and connect with the reader.
- uses concrete words and phrases and descriptive language to convey experiences and events precisely.
- flows smoothly with interesting sentences that vary in length and structure.
- has correct grammar, spelling, capitalization, and punctuation.

Writing Traits in the Scoring Guide

Take a look: Does the chart remind you of the rubrics you've used? Not all prompts include all of the writing traits, but this one does. Use them to do your best writing. Remember to work neatly and put your name on each page!

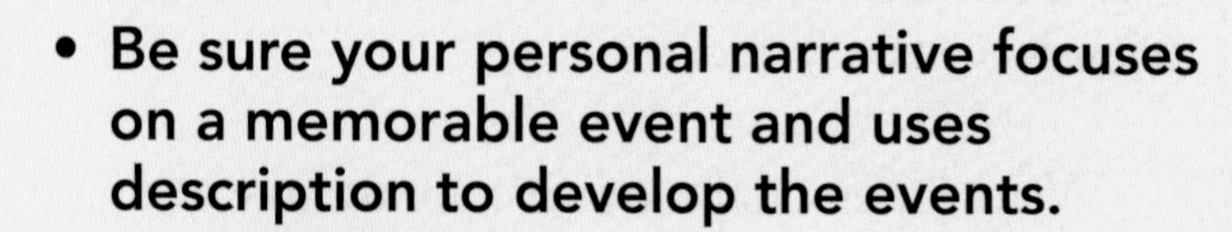

- Be sure your personal narrative focuses on a memorable event and uses description to develop the events.

- Be sure the events in your personal narrative unfold naturally and use transitions to link events.

- Be sure your personal narrative uses first-person point of view to entertain and connect with the reader.

- Be sure your personal narrative uses concrete words and phrases and descriptive language to convey experiences and events precisely.

- Be sure your personal narrative flows smoothly with interesting sentences that vary in length and structure.

- Be sure your personal narrative has correct grammar, spelling, capitalization, and punctuation.

Let's look at the personal narrative by Ramiro Gonzales on the next page. Did he follow the scoring guide?

When the Sun Hid Behind the Moon

by Ramiro Gonzales

It was July 20. I was eleven years old, so I didn't really understand what the fuss was about. My parents and aunt and uncle kept talking about "the eclipse." They had maps of Maine spread all over the kitchen table and had circled a big area in pencil. Dad was getting all excited.

"This is fantastic!" he said. "The kids will never forget an experience like this!"

We pitched camp not far from Pleasant Pond, the place Aunt Dotty thought would have the best view of the eclipse. What I really remember is that they set up our tents on this huge pile of sawdust. I guess they thought it would be soft, like a bed. We ended up with sawdust in everything: our sleeping bags, our clothes, even our hair.

The next morning, we headed over to Pleasant Pond. It was a nice day, pretty sunny, not too windy, and we spent most of the day swimming. I was glad I had brought a book along, because by lunchtime I was getting bored.

Finally the grownups showed us how to watch the eclipse. They said not to look at it directly. We had to get special boxes made from cardboard and keep special plastic lenses over our eyes the whole time that we looked at the sun.

Suddenly it seemed to be getting dark and cold. I thought that the sound of the lake lapping on the stony beach was loud, but it was just that the chirping and whistling of the birds had stopped. As I looked through my sunglasses, I could see a black shape moving over the sun. It was almost as if some invisible creature had nibbled it away, like a kid eating a cookie. Mom explained that we were looking at the moon. As the moon passed directly in front of the sun, it blocked the sunlight from getting to the earth.

The eclipse happened fast. In less than a minute, the black disk of the moon slipped from left to right across the glowing sun. For a few seconds, all we could see was a circle of light, like a halo, around the darkness. Then the moon continued on its way, uncovering the sun and bringing brightness and warmth back to Pleasant Pond.

Using the Scoring Guide to Study the Model

Let's use the scoring guide to check Ramiro's writing test, "When the Sun Hid Behind the Moon." We'll look for examples from his writing to show how well he did on each part of the scoring guide.

- **The personal narrative focuses on a memorable event and uses description to develop the events.**

Ramiro writes about the time he and his family observed a solar eclipse. He focuses on just one event, and he uses descriptive details that grab the reader's attention.

They had maps of Maine spread all over the kitchen table and had circled a big area in pencil. Dad was getting all excited.

"This is fantastic!" he said. "The kids will never forget an experience like this!"

- **The personal narrative's events unfold naturally, and transitions are used to link events.**

Ramiro remembers to put the details in order. He also uses effective transitions, so the reader has no trouble following the story.

The next morning, we headed over to Pleasant Pond.

I was glad I had brought a book along, because by lunchtime I was getting bored.

- **The personal narrative uses first-person point of view to entertain and connect with the reader.**

Ramiro uses first-person point of view to tell his story. He maintains an exciting tone throughout the story that really holds the reader's attention.

Suddenly it seemed to be getting dark and cold. I thought that the sound of the lake lapping on the stony beach was loud, but it was just that the chirping and whistling of the birds had stopped.

- **The personal narrative uses concrete words and phrases and descriptive language to convey experiences and events precisely.**

Ramiro uses precise, vivid words to describe the eclipse. For example, he adds "like a halo" to give a clear, concrete picture of what he saw. The reader can imagine exactly what the eclipse looked like.

For a few seconds, all we could see was a circle of light, like a halo, around the darkness. Then the moon continued on its way, uncovering the sun and bringing brightness and warmth back to Pleasant Pond.

Using the Scoring Guide to Study the Model

- **The personal narrative flows smoothly with interesting sentences that vary in length and structure.**

The scoring guide reminds you that sentences in your personal narrative should flow naturally. To get a natural flow, Ramiro uses different lengths and kinds of sentences. He also uses words like *and, but, so*, and *because* to join ideas.

Suddenly it seemed to be getting dark and cold. I thought that the sound of the lake lapping on the stony beach was loud, but it was just that the chirping and whistling of the birds had stopped.

- **The personal narrative has correct grammar, spelling, capitalization, and punctuation.**

Before turning in his story, Ramiro checked his writing for errors in grammar, spelling, capitalization, and punctuation. He added a title and his name to the page.

Planning My Time

My teacher usually tells us how much time we have to complete the test before giving us the writing prompt. Since I know how much time I have to write, I can plan how much time to spend on each part of the writing process. I also plan for time to study the writing prompt. Here's how I divided my writing time into four steps.

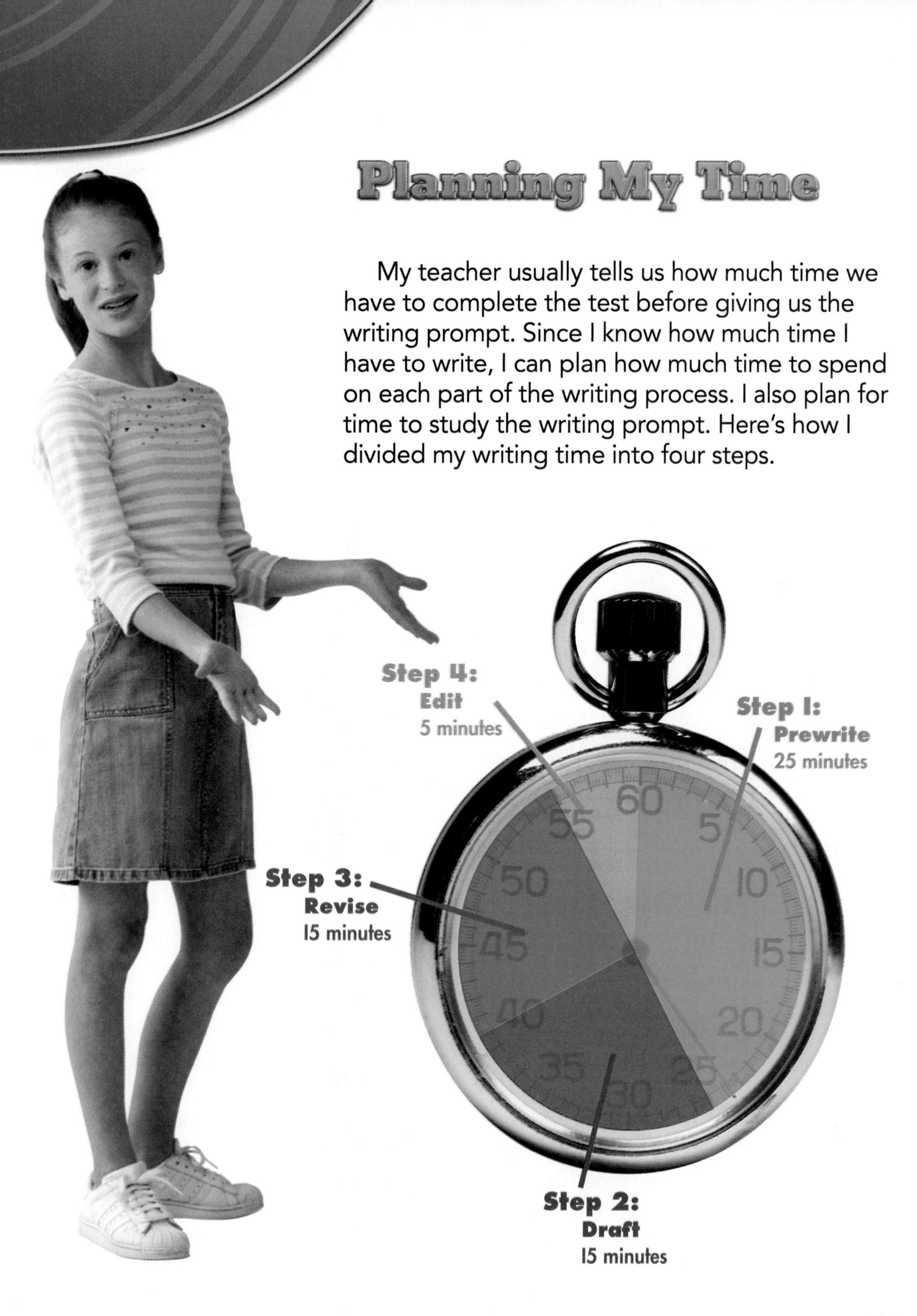

Prewrite

Focus on **Ideas**

Writing Strategy Study the writing prompt to find out what to do.

When my teacher gives us the writing prompt, I study it to make sure I know exactly what I'm supposed to do. Most writing prompts have three parts. You should find each part and label it: the setup, the task, and the scoring guide. See how I did this below? Then you can circle key parts in the writing prompt that tell you what kind of writing to do. I circled *Write a personal narrative* because it tells what kind of writing I'll be doing. Also I circled *an event in nature* because that is what I'll be writing about.

My Writing Test Prompt

Setup — Events in nature—from strong, stormy winds to quiet, rosy sunsets—can be powerful, inspiring, and sometimes scary.

Task — Write a personal narrative about an event in nature that surprised or amazed you.

Scoring Guide — Be sure your personal narrative

- focuses on a memorable event and uses description to develop the events.
- includes events that unfold naturally and uses transitions to link events.
- uses first-person point of view to entertain and connect with the reader.
- uses concrete words and phrases and descriptive language to convey experiences and events precisely.
- flows smoothly with interesting sentences that vary in length and structure.
- has correct grammar, spelling, capitalization, and punctuation.

Now that I've read the writing prompt, I'll think about how the scoring guide relates to the six writing traits I've studied in the rubrics. Not all rubrics will have all six traits, but I need to remember them all to write a good narrative.

Ideas

- **Be sure your personal narrative focuses on a memorable event and uses description to develop the events.**

I'll start by making a list of topics I might write about and choose the one I think readers will find the most memorable.

Organization

- **Be sure the events in your personal narrative unfold naturally and use transitions to link events.**

I'll use an organizer to arrange my details. I want to list them in the order I remember them happening.

Voice

- **Be sure your personal narrative uses first-person point of view to entertain and connect with the reader.**

I'll tell my story in my own voice. This means I will use first-person pronouns, like *I*, *me*, and *mine*.

- **Be sure your personal narrative uses concrete words and phrases and descriptive language to convey experiences and events precisely.**

I'll use vivid and precise words to describe the event so my reader can picture it.

- **Be sure your personal narrative flows smoothly with interesting sentences that vary in length and structure.**

I'll try to write interesting sentences that don't all begin the same way or run the same length.

- **Be sure your personal narrative has correct grammar, spelling, capitalization, and punctuation.**

I won't worry about making mistakes right now, but I'll make sure I proofread carefully later.

Prewrite

Focus on **Ideas**

Writing Strategy Respond to the task.

I know that writers collect ideas before they write. My task is to write a personal story about an event in nature that surprised or amazed me. To get started, I listed four ideas.

It's easy to choose the one I remember most vividly—the flood! I think my reader will understand why. I can think of lots of exciting details I'll be able to include.

Task—Write a personal narrative about an event in nature that surprised or amazed you.

Events I Could Write About
• the time it rained while the sun shined brightly
• the time the river near our house flooded
• the time it snowed on the first day of school
• the time the wind blew our garden shed across the yard

Apply

Think about how you'll respond to the task in the writing prompt before you write. To collect ideas, jot down some notes or make a short list.

Prewrite

Writing Strategy List details about the event.

Time is short! Now that I've chosen an event to write about, I need to start organizing my ideas. One good organizer for personal narratives is a Sequence Chain. It will help me remember what happened before, during, and after the flood. It will also help me retell the events in a natural order—the order in which they happened.

Before winter had brought more snow than usual

spring came early and was very warm; trees budded

During rain fell for many days on end, filling the river

the river became a muddy flood and carried tree branches downstream

the river overflowed its banks and kept rising, toward our house

After the rain finally stopped, and the river rose a little more and then began to fall

Reflect

How does Sasha organize her ideas? Does it work? Why?

Apply

When you write for a test, you don't have much time to revise. That means prewriting (planning what to write) is more important than ever!

Prewrite

Focus on **Organization**

Writing Strategy Make sure details are in the order in which they happened.

When you are writing for a test, there is very little time to revise. That means that I have to work quickly but accurately. I'll number the details to make sure they're in the right order. Then as I write, I'll use time-order transitions to connect them.

Before 1. winter had brought more snow than usual

2. spring came early and was very warm; trees budded

During 3. rain fell for many days on end, filling the river

4. the river became a muddy flood and carried tree branches downstream

5. the river overflowed its banks and kept rising, toward our house

After 6. the rain finally stopped, and the river rose a little more and then began to fall

Ideas

- **Be sure your personal narrative focuses on a memorable event and uses description to develop the events.**

I'll write only about the event I chose from my list, and I've listed several interesting details about what I experienced.

Organization

- **Be sure the events unfold naturally and use transitions to link events.**

My Sequence Chain will help me write my story. I'll use transitions to connect the details for my reader.

Voice

- **Be sure your personal narrative uses first-person point of view to entertain and connect with the reader.**

I'll imagine I'm speaking with my reader. That will make it easier to use first-person words like *I*, *me*, and *my* to describe my experience.

Word Choice

- **Be sure your writing uses concrete words and phrases and descriptive language to convey experiences and events precisely.**

I'll choose vivid, concrete words to retell the event. This way, my readers will be able to picture exactly what I describe.

Sentence Fluency

- **Be sure your personal narrative flows smoothly with interesting sentences that vary in length and structure.**

I don't want to write boring sentences. I'll write different kinds of sentences to make my writing flow.

Conventions

- **Be sure your personal narrative has correct grammar, spelling, capitalization, and punctuation.**

I'll check grammar and mechanics when I edit my draft.

Reflect

Is Sasha ready to respond to the prompt? Why do you think so?

Apply

Use the traits to write your draft. Be sure to keep your purpose (share a memorable event) and audience (your classmates) in mind as you write.

Draft

Focus on **Ideas**

Writing Strategy Use interesting details in descriptions.

The scoring guide reminds me to use description to develop the events. I think my details are exciting and surprising, and they create descriptions that develop the story well. I want my readers to remember my story. I have a feeling they will!

[DRAFT]

Almost Underwater
by Sasha

I had never seen the Greenbrier river that full. Normally it's a beautiful river, green as its name, and clear and clean. You can see the fish swimming. They swim on the sandy bottom. They dart in and out of water plants and around boulders. We get a lot of visiters who come here to paddle canoes or just walk the trails along the banks. We thought our house would end up underwater.

I live in Pocahontas County in West Virginia, and the Greenbrier stretches from one end of the county to the other. Then came the March thaw and the weather turned so warm that the trees budded up and the early flowers came into bloom. Winters are cold and we usually get alot of

Proofreading Marks

⊐	Indent	ℓ	Take out something
≡	Make uppercase	⊙	Add a period
/	Make lowercase	¶	New paragraph
∧	Add something	(sp)	Spelling error

snow. Still, people agreed that it had been a long time since they had seen drifts piled that high.

Soon it began to rain, This time, though, everyone got tired of gray clouds and the constant drumming of drops on the roof.

Water ran into the streets and part of our yard looked like a lake. Our house is about a hundred yards above the bank. We watched as the Greenbrier river turned from green water into a flood.

Each day the level of the river raised. Grandpa said we didn't have to worry. Until the Greenbrier reached the big Beech tree at the bottom of the yard.

Finally the rain stopped and the sun came out. We kept watching, though, and the waters kept heading toward the beech tree.

Then the Greenbrier stopped rising. We watched the waters go back as fast as they had come up.

Reflect

Read Sasha's draft. What do you think of her use of details?

Apply

Use interesting details to hold your reader's attention all the way through the story.

Revise

Focus on **Organization**

Writing Strategy Make sure the narrative's events are in a natural order.

Now that my draft is complete, I'll check it against the scoring guide to make sure I've included all the points I'll be graded on.

I'll reread my draft to make sure I told my story in the order in which it happened. I've included the details from my Sequence Chain, but I see I got one out of order. I'll fix that now.

Then came the March thaw and the weather turned so warm that the trees budded up and the early flowers came into bloom. Winters are cold and we usually get alot of snow. Still, people agreed that it had been a long time since they had seen drifts piled that high.

put details in natural order

Apply

Check your graphic organizer to be sure that all important details are in your draft and in the right order.

Revise

Focus on **Voice**

Writing Strategy Connect with the reader.

The scoring guide reminds me that I need to connect with the reader. I can do that by using first-person point of view and sharing my personal thoughts and reactions. I'll add my thoughts to the part where I describe the rain. I'll also revise to use first-person point of view.

I like rain and the beautiful smells it brings off the earth.

voice connects with the reader

Soon it began to rain. This time, though, ~~everyone~~ I got tired of the dark gray clouds and the constant drumming of drops on the roof.

Reflect

Look at Sasha's changes. How do they improve her story?

Apply

Use first-person point of view to tell your story and connect with the reader.

Revise

Focus on **Word Choice**

Writing Strategy Choose words and phrases to convey ideas precisely.

The scoring guide reminds me to use concrete words and phrases to describe the action in my story. I think my description of the overflowing river could be improved. I'll use stronger verbs and add some description. I want my reader to get a clear picture of what it looked like.

[DRAFT]

Water ~~ran into~~ poured down the streets and part of our yard looked like a lake. Our house ~~is~~ sits on a little rise about a hundred yards above the bank. We watched as the Greenbrier river turned from sparkling green water into a muddy flood.

used stronger verbs

added descriptive language

Edit

Focus on Conventions

Writing Strategy Check for errors in grammar, spelling, capitalization, and punctuation.

The scoring guide says to use correct grammar, spelling, capitalization, and punctuation. That's a lot to do, but I planned how to use my time. I'll read the draft carefully one more time.

FINAL DRAFT

Almost Underwater
by Sasha

I had never seen the Greenbrier river that full. Normally it's a beautiful river, green as its name, and clear and clean. You can see the fish swimming. They swim on the sandy bottom. They dart in and out of water plants and around boulders. We get a lot of visiters who come here to paddle canoes or just walk the trails along the banks. We thought our house would end up underwater.

[Edits marked: "river" → "River"; "swimming. They swim on" → "swimming on"; "bottom. They dart" → "bottom, darting"; "visiters" → "visitors"; "We thought" → "That year, though, we thought"]

¶ I live in Pocahontas County in West Virginia, and the Greenbrier stretches from one end of the county to the other. Winters are cold, and we usually get alot of snow. Still, people agreed that it had been a long time since they had seen drifts piled that high. Then came the March thaw, and the weather turned so warm that the trees budded up and the early flowers came into bloom.

[Edit marked: "alot" → "a lot"]

Apply

Always leave time at the end—about five minutes—to check your writing and make a neat final copy when you write for a test.

FINAL DRAFT

Soon it began to rain. I like rain and the beautiful smells it brings off the earth. This time, though, I got tired of the dark gray clouds and the constant drumming of drops on the roof.

Water poured down the streets, and part of our yard looked like a lake. Our house sits on a little rise about a hundred yards above the bank. We watched as the Greenbrier river turned from sparkling green water into a muddy flood. The current carried tree branches and anything else it could pick up downstream. My family was starting to get worried.

Each day the level of the river ~~raised~~ rose. Pretty soon the black birch and the aspen trees that lined the bank were surrounded by water. Grandpa said we didn't have to worry until the Greenbrier reached the big beech tree at the bottom of the yard.

Finally the rain stopped, and the sun came out. We kept watching, though, and the waters kept heading toward the beech tree.

Then the Greenbrier stopped rising. We watched the waters go back as fast as they had come up.

Reflect

How did the scoring guide help Sasha edit her draft? Can you suggest other improvements?

Hey, we did it! We used the writing prompt and scoring guide to write an interesting personal narrative! Remember these important tips when you write for a test.

TEST TIPS

1. **Study the writing prompt before you begin to write.** Look for the three parts that most writing prompts have: the setup, the task, and the scoring guide. Use the helpful information they give you.
2. **Make sure you understand the task before you start to write.**
   - Find and label the setup, task, and scoring guide.
   - Circle key words in the task. These tell you what kind of writing you need to do. They might also tell you who your audience is.
   - Read the scoring guide. It tells you how your paper will be graded.
3. **Plan your time, and then keep an eye on the clock.** Make sure you know how much time you have to write. Then decide how much time you'll spend on each part of the writing process. Try to stick to your plan. You want to have time to revise and edit your draft.
4. **Use the scoring guide to check your draft.** Like the rubrics you've used on other papers, the scoring guide reminds you of what is important. Reread your draft, and make sure that it does what the scoring guide says it should do.
5. **Leave time to edit your draft.** Look for the errors you make most often and correct them. Also, make sure your draft is neatly written. After all, the people scoring your test must be able to read it!

Informative/ Explanatory writing gives information.

Hi, my name is Mya. I'm learning all about informative/explanatory writing, and I think it's great! I am interested in informative/explanatory writing because my goal is to be a sports reporter for our school newspaper next year!

IN THIS UNIT

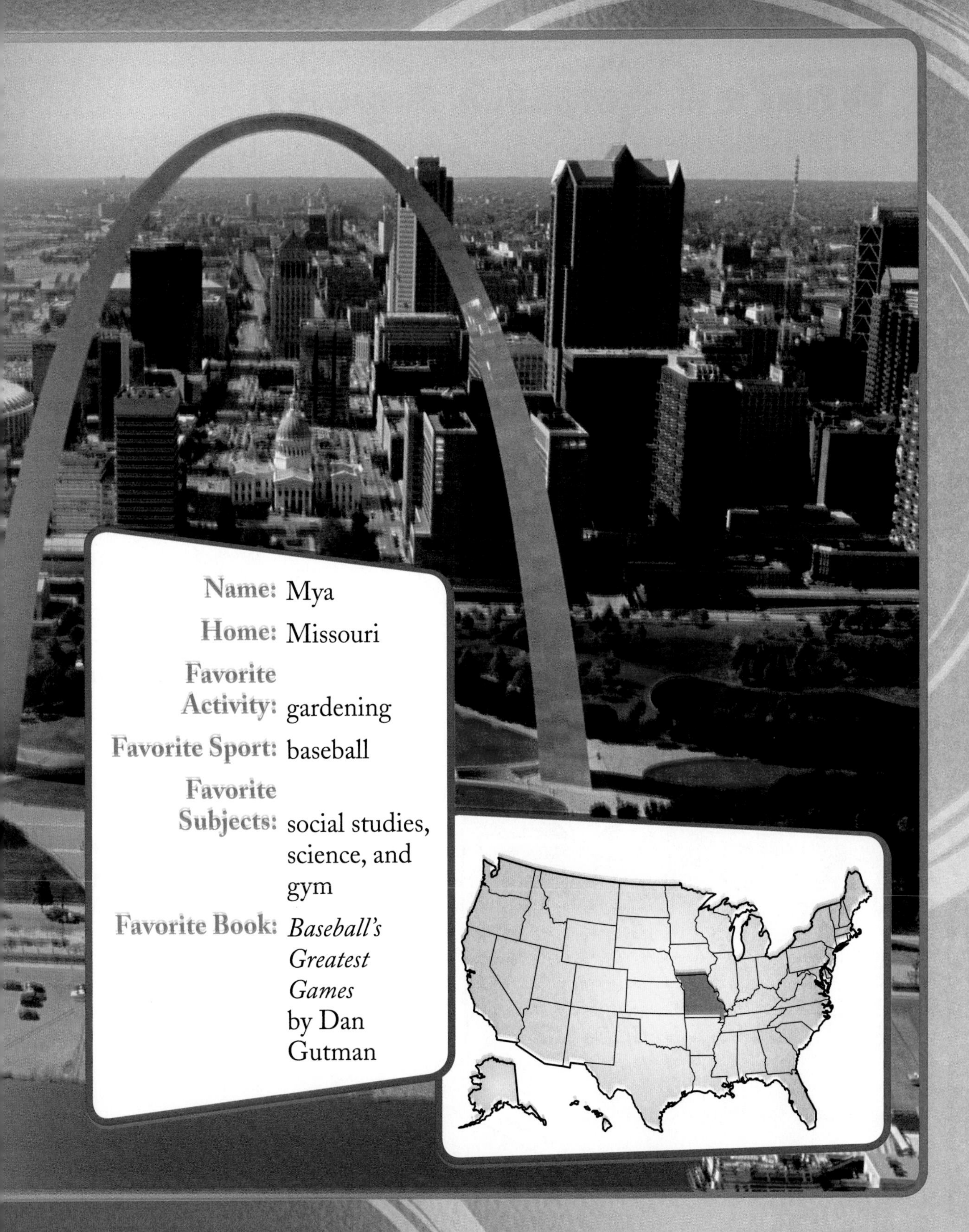
Name: Mya
Home: Missouri
Favorite Activity: gardening
Favorite Sport: baseball
Favorite Subjects: social studies, science, and gym
Favorite Book: *Baseball's Greatest Games* by Dan Gutman

What's a Research Report?

A research report is writing that gives information about a topic. The information comes from research the author has done.

What's in a Research Report?

Topic
That's the subject I'm going to write about.

Sources
A source is where research information can be found. The library is a great place to find sources.

Introduction
The introduction is the first paragraph. It will tell my readers my topic and get them interested in it.

Body
The body of my research report is the longest part. It's where I present most of the information about my topic.

Conclusion
The conclusion is my last paragraph. I'll restate the topic and summarize the main points.

Why write a Research Report?

There are many reasons to write a research report. Here are some reasons I thought of.

Information
Writing a research report is a good way to share information about a topic. People in many careers write them.

- In business, research reports help people make decisions about where to put up a building, what product to make, or how much money to charge for a product.
- In medicine, research reports help doctors decide the best treatment for their patients.
- In science, research reports inform scientists about work by other scientists. Sharing information helps scientists make new discoveries.

Understanding
Writing a research report is a great way to learn more about a subject. Researching something interesting is fun, and when my report is finished, I'll be a real expert on the topic!

Linking Informative/Explanatory Writing Traits to a Research Report

In this chapter, you will write a report that gives information about a topic you have researched. This type of informative/explanatory writing is called a research report. Mya will guide you through the states of the writing process: Prewrite, Draft, Revise, Edit, and Publish. In each stage, Mya will show you important writing strategies that are linked to the Informative/Explanatory Writing Traits below.

Informative/Explanatory Writing Traits

Ideas	• a topic that is clear and focused • facts, definitions, or details that develop the topic
Organization	• a strong introduction, body, and conclusion • well-organized paragraphs that contain transition words to connect ideas
Voice	• a voice that is appropriate for the purpose and audience
Word Choice	• language that is specific and appropriate for the audience
Sentence Fluency	• sentences that vary in length and structure to make the writing clear and easy to read
 Conventions	• no or few errors in grammar, usage, mechanics, and spelling

Before you write, read Matthew Hobbs's research report on the next page. Then use the research report rubric on pages 136–137 to decide how well he did. (You might want to look back at What's in a Research Report? on page 132, too!)

Chief Joseph

by Matthew Hobbs

introduction

Chief Joseph, a Nez Percé, was one of the greatest Native American leaders. There are not many Nez Percé left now. They once lived in the area known today as Idaho, Oregon, and Washington. Chief Joseph devoted his life to helping his people.

topic

Chief Joseph's leadership of the Nez Percé was tested beginning in 1860. That year, gold was discovered in their territory. The U.S. government wanted this land and tried to force the Nez Percé to move to a reservation in Idaho. Chief Joseph tried to preserve his people's right to the land where they had lived for hundreds of years. Finally, he did attempt to move his people to the reservation. However, U.S. troops attacked them along the way, and the Nez Percé War began.

body

Chief Joseph was a brave and intelligent leader. Under his leadership, the Nez Percé fought and won many battles against the U.S. troops. In time, Chief Joseph and other Nez Percé leaders knew they could not win the war. They decided to lead their people into Canada for safety. However, as they crossed Montana, U.S. troops pursued them. After a five-day battle, the Nez Percé surrendered. The survivors were sent to the Indian Territory of Oklahoma. There, many suffered and died.

Chief Joseph continued to fight for his people. He traveled to Washington, D.C. He convinced the lawmakers to send his people back to Idaho. Most of the remaining Nez Percé people still live there today.

conclusion

Chief Joseph fought for freedom and equality. When he spoke in Washington, he said, "Treat all men alike. Give them all the same law. Give them all an even chance to live and grow." These are still American ideals today.

sources

Sources

"Chief Joseph." The West Film Project and WETA. 2001, accessed October 21, 2012, http://www.pbs.org/weta/thewest/people/a_c/chiefjoseph.htm.

Nerburn, Kent. *Chief Joseph and the Flight of the Nez Percé.* New York: HarperCollins, 2005.

Research Report Rubric

Use this 6-point rubric to plan and score a research report.

	6	5	4
Ideas	The report is focused on one topic, uses two or more cited sources, and has no unnecessary information.	The report is focused on one topic, uses two or more cited sources, and has little unnecessary information.	The report has a focus, but not all of the information is related directly to the topic. Only one source is cited.
Organization	The report is well organized into paragraphs. The introduction and conclusion enhance the report. Appropriate and effective transitions link ideas.	The report is organized into paragraphs. The introduction is clear. The conclusion summarizes most of the points. Transitions link ideas.	The report is organized into paragraphs. The introduction and conclusion are clear. Transitions are limited.
Voice	The writer's voice is strong and knowledgeable. It connects with the audience.	The writer's voice is strong and knowledgeable in most places. It holds the reader's attention.	The writer's voice is appropriate for the topic, purpose, and audience.
Word Choice	Precise language informs readers about the topic.	The words are well chosen to give the information. A few unnecessary words are used.	Some vague or unnecessary words are used, but the reader is not confused.
Sentence Fluency	A variety of sentence lengths and structures makes the report easy to read and enjoyable.	Most sentences vary in length and structure. The report is easy to read and understand.	The writing is generally easy to read, although it may have a few choppy or run-on sentences.
Conventions	Proper nouns and proper adjectives are capitalized. The writing is easy to read and understand.	Most proper nouns and proper adjectives are used and capitalized correctly. The writing is easy to understand.	Some proper nouns and proper adjectives are capitalized incorrectly, distracting the reader.

+Presentation Electronic resources, such as photographs, sound clips, or video clips, enhance the presentation.

3	2	1	
The report is somewhat vague or confusing. Details are not expanded to develop the topic. Only one source is cited.	Information and details do not support the topic. The focus is inconsistent. Sources are cited improperly.	The report does not have a clear focus or direction. Information does not appear connected. No sources are cited.	Ideas
Information is not clearly organized into paragraphs. The introduction and conclusion are weak. Transitions are weak and limited.	It is hard to tell where paragraphs begin and end. The introduction and/or conclusion is missing or misleading. Transitions are missing.	The information is not organized as a report. It is difficult or impossible to read. Introduction and conclusion are missing.	Organization
The writer's voice is ordinary and/or inconsistent. It may not connect with the audience.	The writer's voice is inconsistent or too formal or informal. It only rarely connects with the audience.	The voice is weak or inappropriate and does not connect with the audience.	Voice
Several vague and/or unnecessary words distract the reader.	Too many words take up space but do not contribute to the meaning.	The writing is very wordy and confusing, or too brief and vague, making it difficult to read.	Word Choice
Sentence beginnings are repetitive, making the writing choppy and distracting.	Too many sentences of the same length make reading choppy and predictable.	Most sentences are the same length; some are incomplete or very awkward to read.	Sentence Fluency
There are some serious errors in capitalization of proper nouns and proper adjectives.	Many proper nouns and proper adjectives are not capitalized, making some sentences confusing to read.	Few or no proper nouns or proper adjectives are capitalized, causing confusion for the reader.	Conventions

See Appendix B for 4-, 5-, and 6-point informative/explanatory rubrics.

Using the Research Report Rubric to Study the Model

Did you notice that the model on page 135 points out some key elements of a research report? As he wrote "Chief Joseph," Matthew Hobbs used these elements to help him describe a person he found interesting. He also used the 6-point rubric on pages 136–137 to plan, draft, revise, and edit the writing. A rubric is a great tool for evaluating writing during the writing process.

Now let's use the same rubric to score the model. To do this, we'll focus on each trait separately, starting with Ideas. We'll use the top descriptor for each trait (column 6), along with examples from the model, to help us understand how the traits work together. How would you score Matthew on each trait?

- **The report is focused on one topic, uses two or more cited sources, and has no unnecessary information.**

I see that the topic of Matthew's report is Chief Joseph, and all the information is about Chief Joseph. Matthew does not include information about any other Native American leaders. I also see that Matthew cites two sources at the end of the report, so I know he got his information from reliable sources like the book below.

Nerburn, Kent. *Chief Joseph and the Flight of the Nez Percé.* New York: HarperCollins, 2005.

- **The report is well organized into paragraphs.**
- **The introduction and conclusion enhance the report.**
- **Appropriate and effective transitions link ideas.**

Each paragraph of Matthew's report tells something new about Chief Joseph. The introduction gets my attention by telling who Chief Joseph was and what he did with his life. Transitions such as *When he spoke* tell me how ideas are related. Do you see how the conclusion below gives a summary of Chief Joseph's accomplishments?

Chief Joseph fought for freedom and equality. When he spoke in Washington, he said, "Treat all men alike. Give them all the same law. Give them all an even chance to live and grow." These are still American ideals today.

- **The writer's voice is strong and knowledgeable. It connects with the audience.**

I can tell that Matthew knows what he is talking about in sentences like *Chief Joseph's leadership of the Nez Percé was tested beginning in 1860. That year, gold was discovered in their territory.* Then Matthew really helps me connect to the reason Chief Joseph is so interesting.

Chief Joseph was a brave and intelligent leader. Under his leadership, the Nez Percé fought and won many battles against the U.S. troops.

Using the Research Report Rubric to Study the Model

- **Precise language informs readers about the topic.**

All the words in Matthew's report are precise and useful. He does not repeat words or use words that are too general. For example, he uses the precise words *traveled* and *convinced* instead of general words such as *went* and *talked to.*

Chief Joseph continued to fight for his people. He traveled to Washington, D.C. He convinced the lawmakers to send his people back to Idaho. Most of the remaining Nez Percé people still live there today.

- **A variety of sentence lengths and structures makes the report easy to read and enjoyable.**

I was able to read through Matthew's report with no problem because the sentences flowed together well. He uses sentences of different kinds and lengths to make his paragraphs easy to read.

They decided to lead their people into Canada for safety. However, as they crossed Montana, U.S. troops pursued them. After a five-day battle, the Nez Percé surrendered.

- **Proper nouns and proper adjectives are capitalized. The writing is easy to read and understand.**

I didn't find any spelling, punctuation, or capitalization errors in Matthew's report. He must have proofread it really well! He was especially careful to capitalize words correctly.

Chief Joseph, a Nez Percé, was one of the greatest Native American leaders. There are not many Nez Percé left now. They once lived in the area known today as Idaho, Oregon, and Washington.

+Presentation Electronic resources, such as photographs, sound clips, or video clips, enhance the presentation.

My Turn!

Now it's my turn to write a research report! I'll use the rubric and good writing strategies to help me. Read along to see how I do it!

Prewrite

Focus on **Ideas**

The Rubric Says The report is focused on one topic, uses two or more cited sources, and has no unnecessary information.

Writing Strategy Pick a topic. Take notes from the Internet and at least one other source. Cite sources.

When my teacher told us to write a research report, I knew I wanted to write about Cesar Chavez. We have a street named after him in our town, so I wanted to find out who he was and why he was so famous.

When I researched Cesar Chavez on the Internet, my teacher said to use only credible sources. I chose to use the United Farm Workers website. I took notes from this website and from an interesting library book about Cesar Chavez. My teacher reminded me to avoid plagiarism by paraphrasing or summarizing information in my own words and to cite my sources on my notes.

Writer's Term

Citing Sources

When you **cite a source,** you tell readers where you found certain information.

To cite a book:
Author's last name, author's first name. Book title. City of publication: publisher, year of publication.

Example: Collins, David R. Farmworker's Friend: The Story of Cesar Chavez. Minneapolis: Carolrhoda Books, 1996.

To cite a website:
Author (if given), "Title of article." Sponsor of website.
Date of article. access date, website address.

Example: "The Story of Cesar Chavez." United Farm Workers. 2006, accessed October 23, 2012, http://www.ufw.org/_page.php?menu=research&inc=history/07.html.

My teacher also showed me how to put information on note cards. Each fact or group of closely related facts gets its own note card. I added headings to my note cards, too, so it would be easier to group them by topic later on. Here are three of my note cards.

Chavez Family ← heading

Mother – taught him about nonviolence and helping others
Father – taught him to stand up for his beliefs and for other people ← note

Farmworker's Friend: The Story of Cesar Chavez, p. 3 ← source

Basic Information on Chavez

Born: March 31, 1927 in Yuma, Arizona
Died: April 23, 1993 in San Luis, Arizona

"The Story of Cesar Chavez," p. 2

Chavez's Early Life

Did not like school because he spoke only Spanish – dropped out in 8th grade to work

"The Story of Cesar Chavez," p. 2

Reflect

Look at Mya's note cards. Does she have enough information to write a good research report? How do you think she decided which sources were credible?

Apply

Think about a topic that would make a good research report. Look it up in two credible sources—one on the Internet. Make note cards for the information you find, and cite your sources!

Prewrite

Focus on **Organization**

The Rubric Says The report is well organized into paragraphs.

Writing Strategy Use a Support Pattern to organize the notes.

I know from the rubric that organization is important. So I read through my cards and looked for information that I could group together. Then I decided to make a Support Pattern, which is kind of like an outline, to help me organize the information on my note cards. Each main point and its supporting facts will become a paragraph in the body of my report.

Writer's Term

Support Pattern

A **Support Pattern** is a chart that shows how main points are supported by facts.

Support Pattern

Topic: Cesar Chavez

Main Point: Cesar's best teachers were his parents.

Supporting facts

- Mother taught him violence is not a good way to settle problems.
- Mother taught him it is good to help other people.
- Father taught him to stand up for his beliefs.

Main Point: Cesar Chavez never forgot the lessons he learned as a child.

Supporting facts

- Family lost their farm and became migrant workers.
- Mexican Americans were often treated unfairly.
- The life of migrant farm workers is very hard.

Main Point: As Cesar got older, his beliefs became stronger.

Supporting facts

- He decided he should help migrant farm workers.
- Farm workers should have better pay, safer working conditions, and healthier living conditions.
- Nonviolent methods can bring about change.

Main Point: Cesar put his beliefs into action.

Supporting facts

- He registered voters and told Mexican Americans about their rights.
- He formed the National Farm Workers Association, and it became the U.F.W.
- U.F.W. and supporters held boycotts, marched in picket lines, and held strikes without violence.
- Cesar led marches, fasted, worked long hours, and helped improve the lives of the farm workers.

Reflect

Look over Mya's Support Pattern. How will it help her write a good research report?

Apply

Look at your note cards and make your own Support Pattern. Include at least two supporting facts for each main point.

Draft

Focus on **Ideas**

The Rubric Says The report is focused on one topic, uses two or more cited sources, and has no unnecessary information.

Writing Strategy Make sure all the information relates to the topic.

I did my research about Cesar Chavez using credible sources. Then I put my notes in a Support Pattern to help me see them clearly. Now I'm ready to draft my report.

The rubric reminds me to stay focused on my topic and not include unnecessary information. I'll write a body paragraph for each section in my Support Pattern. First I'll make sure each paragraph has a main point about Cesar Chavez's life and work. Then I'll write at least two details or facts to support it. I'll be careful to leave out information that is not about the main idea.

Proofreading Marks

- Indent
- Make uppercase
- Make lowercase
- Add something
- Take out something
- Add a period
- New paragraph
- sp Spelling error

[DRAFT]

Cesar Chavez

main point

Cesar's best teachers were his parents. He was born in Yuma, Arizona, in 1927. He did not like his early school years, partly because Mexican American children were often treated unfairly. Cesar's mother taught him that violence was not the way to settle problems. She encouraged him to help other people. Cesar's father taught him to stand up for his beliefs.

supporting detail

main point

Cesar never forgot the lessons he learned as a child. When he was still a boy, his family was cheated out of their farm. They had to become migrant farm workers in California. A migrant worker moves from place to place to pick crops. There Cesar discovered much more injustice. His family worked in the feilds for long hours. They got very little pay. They worked from Brawley to Oxnard. They often lived in one-room shacks. The shacks had no running water. His mother's name was Juana, and his father's name was Librado.

supporting detail

Reflect

Read the beginning of Mya's draft. Does each paragraph have a main point that is supported with enough well-researched information?

Apply

Use your Support Pattern to draft the body of your report. Make sure each paragraph has a main point and at least two details or facts to support it.

Revise

Focus on Organization

The Rubric Says The introduction and conclusion enhance the report. Appropriate and effective transitions link ideas.

Writing Strategy Write a strong introduction and conclusion. Connect ideas with transitions.

As I read back over what I've written, I realize that Cesar Chavez changed many lives. That's what I'll stress in my introduction and conclusion.

[DRAFT]

Cesar Chavez was a very determined man. He organized a union with more than 50,000 members, focused attention on migrant workers, and helped change laws. In these ways, he improved the lives of many farm workers. He was also a self-taught man. He learned many of his most important lessons during his childhood.

transition words

introduction

Cesar Chavez died in 1993, but his dream did not. He inspired many people, and they are continuing his work today. Cesar chavez saw a problem and decided he could do something about it. His life proves that one person can make a huge and lasting difference.

conclusion

Apply

Read your draft. Do you grab your reader's attention in your introduction and summarize your main points in your conclusion?

Revise

Focus on Voice

The Rubric Says The writer's voice is strong and knowledgeable. It connects with the audience.

Writing Strategy Use third-person point of view and sentences that contain facts.

When I read my research report to a classmate, she said my voice should be more knowledgeable. I went back and found places where I used first person to give facts. Do you think these sentences sound stronger in the third person?

[DRAFT]

~~I found out that~~ He told Mexican Americans about their rights in the U.S.A. ~~One source told me that~~ In 1962 Cesar founded the National Farm Workers Association.

changed to third person

changed to third person

Reflect

How do Mya's revisions make her voice sound more knowledgeable?

Apply

Read your draft. Make sure that your sentences contain facts. Change first person to third person.

Revise

Focus on **Word Choice**

The Rubric Says Precise language informs readers about the topic.

Writing Strategy Take out words that are unnecessary.

The rubric says to use only precise language about my topic. So I think I should take out any unnecessary words I might have used. They might distract the reader from the message of my report or repeat ideas. I see some places where I can get rid of words that don't help convey my message.

[DRAFT]

Union members also marched on picket lines and held strikes. Cesar led marches, held press conferences, and fasted (~~which means he~~ stopped eating). He worked long hours to help the workers get better pay and ~~also to get better~~ working conditions.

took out unnecessary words

Apply

Look over your draft again. Remove words that are not necessary or that repeat information.

Edit

Focus on Conventions

The Rubric Says Proper nouns and proper adjectives are capitalized. The writing is easy to read and understand.

Writing Strategy Check the capitalization.

I'll read through my draft now to check spelling and punctuation. The rubric reminds me to pay special attention to capitalization. Look at the revisions I've made below. Now my writing will be accurate and easy to read and understand.

Writer's Term

Capitalization

Capitalize:

- the first letter in proper nouns
- the first letter in proper adjectives
- initials in proper nouns
- abbreviations of words that are capitalized when written out

capitalized proper nouns

[DRAFT]

In 1962 Cesar founded the National Farm Workers association.

This union became the united farm workers, or the u.f.w.

capitalized abbreviations of proper nouns

Reflect

How do Mya's edits strengthen her writing? How can a word-processing program help you check for capitalization?

Apply

Conventions

Edit your draft for spelling and punctuation. Check for any mistakes with capitalization.

For more practice with capitalization, use the exercises on the next two pages.

Capitalization

Know the Rule

Proper nouns name a particular person, place, or thing. Proper nouns can include initials, and they can be written as abbreviations. The first letter in all of these forms of proper nouns should be capitalized.

1. All the important words in proper nouns are capitalized.
   Examples:
   Missouri **R**iver, **S**acajawea, **N**ational **F**arm **W**orkers **A**ssociation
2. The names of months and days of the week are proper nouns.
   Examples: **F**ebruary, **S**aturday
3. Capitalize the initials in proper nouns.
   Examples: **B**en **N.** **C**ampbell, **W. C. W**yeth
4. Capitalize abbreviations of words that are capitalized when written out.
   Examples: **U.S.** (**U**nited **S**tates), Elm **St.** (Elm **Str**eet)

Practice the Rule

Number a separate sheet of paper 1–10. Write each sentence with the correct capitalization. Also write the number of the rule you applied.

1. The story of Sacajawea has become a legend in america.
2. sacajawea means "bird woman" in the Shoshoni language.
3. Sacajawea was born in the 1780s in the area that is now lemhi county, Idaho.
4. She grew up in the area of the United States that became montana.
5. Sacajawea's husband was a French-Canadian fur trader named toussaint Charbonneau.
6. In may 1804, Lewis and Clark hired Charbonneau as an interpreter.
7. Lewis and Clark let charbonneau bring Sacajawea with him.
8. The u.s. silver dollar has a picture of Sacajawea on it.
9. Lewis and Clark bid farewell to Sacajawea in august 1806.
10. Sacajawea has also appeared on two u.s. stamps.

More Capitalization

Know the Rule

Here are some more rules for capitalization.

1. **Proper adjectives** are descriptive words formed from proper nouns.
   Examples: Native American, Alaskan
2. A **title of respect** is used before a person's name. Titles of respect are also capitalized.
   Examples: **Mr.** Lewis, **Chief** Joseph
3. The first, last, and all important words in **book titles** are capitalized.
   Examples: *Diary of a Wimpy Kid*

Practice the Rule

Read this paragraph about a journalist who was interested in migrant workers. Rewrite the paragraph on your paper, correcting all ten errors in proper nouns and proper adjectives.

Edward r. Murrow was a journalist who was interested in american migrant agricultural workers. In november of 1960, he presented a television documentary called *Harvest of shame.* This program showed how many workers lived and worked in very poor conditions for low wages. It was first broadcast soon after thanksgiving to remind viewers that a lot of the food they ate for the holiday was picked by these workers. mr. Murrow hoped to encourage people in Congress to pass laws to protect the rights of migrant workers. *Harvest of Shame* was the last program that he presented. After that he became the head of an agency in the united states government under president John F. kennedy.

Publish

+Presentation

Publishing Strategy Include the written report in a multimedia presentation to the class.

Presentation Strategy Enhance the presentation with electronic resources, as appropriate.

I've finished my research report! I'm ready to publish it now. Many of my classmates have never heard of Cesar Chavez. A multimedia presentation will allow them to see and hear him. I can include pictures, charts, and graphs as part of a slide show. I can also include recordings or short video clips of his speeches. Before I create my presentation, I'll check over my report one more time to make sure I've done everything right. Here's my final checklist.

My Final Checklist

Did I—

✔ use capitalization properly?

✔ include electronic "extras" to make my presentation more engaging?

✔ put my name on my report?

Apply

Use this checklist to check your report. Then make a final copy of your report and practice reading it.

Cesar Chavez

by Mya

Cesar Chavez was a very determined man. He organized a union with more than 50,000 members, focused attention on migrant workers, and helped change laws. In these ways, he improved the lives of many farm workers. He was also a self-taught man. He learned many of his most important lessons during his childhood.

CESAR CHAVEZ

Cesar's best teachers were his parents. He was born in Yuma, Arizona, in 1927. He did not like his early school years, partly because Mexican American children were often treated unfairly. Cesar's mother taught him that violence was not the way to settle problems. She encouraged him to help other people. Cesar's father taught him to stand up for his beliefs.

CESAR CHAVEZ

Cesar never forgot the lessons he learned as a child. When he was still a boy, his family was cheated out of their farm. They had to become migrant farm workers in California. A migrant worker moves from place to place to pick crops. There Cesar discovered much more injustice. His family worked in the fields for long hours and for very little pay. They often lived in one-room shacks that had no running water.

CESAR CHAVEZ

As Cesar got older, his beliefs became stronger. He believed that the farm workers should receive fair pay for their work. He believed that their working conditions should be safer. He knew that their living conditions should be healthier.

CESAR CHAVEZ

Cesar put his beliefs into action. He began by working to register Mexican American voters. He told Mexican Americans about their rights in the U.S.A. In 1962 Cesar founded the National Farm Workers Association. This union became the United Farm Workers, or the U.F.W. It used nonviolent ways to bring attention to the farm workers' problems. U.F.W. members led boycotts, urging people not to buy products from companies that were unfair to migrant workers. Union members also marched on picket lines and held strikes. Cesar led marches, held press conferences, and fasted (stopped eating). He worked long hours to help the workers get better pay and working conditions.

CESAR CHAVEZ

Cesar Chavez died in 1993, but his dream did not. He inspired many people, and they are continuing his work today. Cesar Chavez saw a problem and decided he could do something about it. His life proves that one person can make a huge and lasting difference.

Sources

Collins, David R. Farmworker's Friend: The Story of Cesar Chavez. Minneapolis: Carolrhoda Books, 1996.

"The Story of Cesar Chavez." United Farm Workers. 2006, accessed October 23, 2012, http://www.ufw.org/_page.php?menu=research&inc=history/07.html.

Reflect

Use the rubric to check Mya's report. Do you see all the traits of a good research report? Check your own research report against the rubric, too.

What's a Compare-and-Contrast Essay?

It's an essay that tells how two or more things are the same (compare) or different (contrast).

What's in a Compare-and-Contrast Essay?

Introduction
The introduction is my first paragraph. I'll tell the reader what things I am comparing and contrasting. I might compare two of my favorite fruits—apples and bananas.

Body
The body is at least two paragraphs. I'll write the similarities and differences in separate paragraphs.

Conclusion
My conclusion is my last paragraph. I'll summarize the most important similarities and differences I found.

Why write a Compare-and-Contrast Essay?

There are many reasons to write a compare-and-contrast essay. Here are a few.

Understanding
Writing an essay to compare and contrast something I don't know well with something I do know well can help me understand the one I didn't know.

Information
- In business, compare-and-contrast essays can help people make decisions about what products to make, how to make them, or where to build a factory.
- In science, compare-and-contrast essays can help people understand important similarities and differences between animals, oceans, medicines, or spacecraft.

Linking Informative/Explanatory Writing Traits to a Compare-and-Contrast Essay

In this chapter, you will write an essay that tells how two or more things are the same or how they are different. This type of informative/explanatory writing is called a compare-and-contrast essay. Mya will guide you through the stages of the writing process: Prewrite, Draft, Revise, Edit, and Publish. In each stage, Mya will show you important writing strategies that are linked to the Informative/Explanatory Writing Traits below.

Informative/Explanatory Writing Traits

Ideas	• a topic that is clear and focused • facts, definitions, or details that develop the topic
Organization	• a strong introduction, body, and conclusion • well-organized paragraphs that contain transition words to connect ideas
Voice	• a voice that is appropriate for the purpose and audience
Word Choice	• language that is specific and appropriate for the audience
Sentence Fluency	• sentences that vary in length and structure to make the writing clear and easy to read
Conventions	• no or few errors in grammar, usage, mechanics, and spelling

Before you write, read Karen Parkhill's compare-and-contrast essay on the next page. Then use the compare-and-contrast essay rubric on pages 162–163 to decide how well she did. (You might want to look back at What's in a Compare-and-Contrast Essay? on page 158, too!)

Television Goes to the Movies

introduction

by Karen Parkhill

compares and contrasts two things

"Danger, Will Robinson! Danger!" Do you recognize that line? It's from the movie *Lost in Space*—and from a TV show!

Some television shows are turned into movies. Sometimes the TV show and the movie are a lot alike, but sometimes they're very different.

One good example is *Lost in Space.* The 1998 movie was based on the 1960s TV show. The film and the TV show have much in common. The main similarity is the storyline: The Robinson family is lost in space. The main characters are also the same. John and Maureen Robinson head the Robinson family. Their children are named Judy, Penny, and Will. Will has a talking robot as his sidekick. The cast includes the pilot, Major Don West, and the evil Dr. Smith. The good guys on TV are still the good guys in the movie. The bad guys are still the bad guys.

similarities

body

differences

How are the film and the TV show different? First of all, movies are longer, usually about two hours. A TV episode lasts only 30 to 60 minutes, but a series can go on for years. The movie *Lost in Space* is less than two hours long. The television series *Lost in Space* lasted three years.

The biggest difference between the show and the movie is in the special effects. Computer-made special effects did not exist in 1964. For the TV show, tiny model spaceships were built to make the sets seem bigger. Ocean waves were created in a huge water tank. Actors in costumes played aliens and monsters. Today, if you watch a TV episode of *Lost in Space,* you might laugh at the effects. Still, you have to admit that they were very creative. For the movie *Lost in Space,* computer experts created special graphics, animation, and sound effects. The two-hour television pilot cost around $600,000 to make. The two-hour movie cost almost $90,000,000.

Lost in Space is just one of many TV shows that have been made into movies. The movie and TV show are much alike, but they're different enough to make each one interesting in its own way.

conclusion

Compare-and-Contrast Essay Rubric

Use this 6-point rubric to plan and score a compare-and-contrast essay.

	6	5	4
Ideas	The topic is appropriate for comparison. Facts and details develop the similarities and differences.	The topic is appropriate for comparison. The similarities and differences are mostly supported.	The two forms of the topic may not pair up well for comparison. Not all similarities or differences are supported.
Organization	Similarities and differences are grouped logically in paragraphs.	Most similarities and differences are presented clearly and logically.	Some of the similarities and differences are easy to follow.
Voice	The writer uses an unbiased, balanced tone.	The writer uses an unbiased tone most of the time.	The writer's tone is biased in a few places.
Word Choice	Precise language informs readers about the topic. The essay contains no jargon.	Word choice is precise in most cases. The essay contains very little jargon.	The essay uses some specific language and contains some jargon.
Sentence Fluency	Smooth, flowing sentences begin in varied ways with effective transition words.	Most sentences flow smoothly. Some begin with transition words.	Some sentences begin the same way, but only a few begin with transition words.
Conventions	Titles are capitalized correctly. Comparative and superlative adjectives are used correctly. The writing is clear.	There are a few minor errors in capitalization of titles and in the use of comparative and superlative adjectives. The errors do not confuse the reader.	There are some minor errors in capitalization of titles and in the use of comparative and superlative adjectives. The errors may distract readers in a few places.

+Presentation Handwriting is neat, or a limited number of clear fonts are used.

3	2	1	
The two forms of the topic do not compare and contrast well. Some similarities and differences are poorly supported.	There is a clear topic, but it may not be useful for comparison. The similarities and differences are not well supported.	The topic is too big or too small for effective comparison. The similarities and differences are not developed.	Ideas
Similarities and differences are present, but the organization is sometimes illogical.	Similarities and differences are present but not organized logically.	Comparisons are missing or unrecognizable.	Organization
Some of the essay has a biased tone.	Much of the essay has a biased tone.	The writing lacks tone or is completely biased.	Voice
The essay relies on vague, repetitive language and jargon.	The essay contains a lot of vague language and jargon.	Words are misused, unclear, or vague. Support is confusing or missing.	Word Choice
Many sentences begin the same way. A few begin with transition words that mislead the reader.	The flow is interrupted because almost all sentences begin the same way. There are no transition words.	Sentences do not flow or may be incomplete. There are no transition words.	Sentence Fluency
There are some errors in capitalization of titles and in the use of comparative and superlative adjectives. They make reading confusing in places.	There are some errors in capitalization of titles and in the use of comparative and superlative adjectives. Errors make the essay confusing to read.	Frequent, major errors in capitalization of titles and in the use of comparative and superlative adjectives make the essay hard to understand.	Conventions

See Appendix B for 4-, 5-, and 6-point informative/explanatory rubrics.

Using the Compare-and-Contrast Essay Rubric to Study the Model

Did you notice that the model on page 161 points out some key elements of a compare-and-contrast essay? As she wrote "Television Goes to the Movies," Karen Parkhill used these elements to help her compare and contrast two things. She also used the 6-point rubric on pages 162–163 to plan, draft, revise, and edit the writing. A rubric is a great tool for evaluating writing during the writing process.

Now let's use the same rubric to score the model. To do this, we'll focus on each trait separately, starting with Ideas. We'll use the top descriptor for each trait (column 6), along with examples from the model, to help us understand how the traits work together. How would you score Karen on each trait?

- **The topic is appropriate for comparison.**
- **Facts and details develop the similarities and differences.**

It makes sense to compare two versions of the same story. The movie and the TV show are both the same and different. I like the way Karen supports the similarities and differences with facts and details.

The film and the TV show have much in common. The main similarity is the storyline: The Robinson family is lost in space. The main characters are also the same.

How are the film and the TV show different? First of all, movies are longer, usually about two hours. A TV episode lasts only 30 to 60 minutes, but a series can go on for years.

- **Similarities and differences are grouped logically in paragraphs.**

Our teacher told us that compare-and-contrast essays have to present similarities and differences in a clear way for the reader to follow. Karen knows that, too. In each paragraph, she focuses on one aspect of her topic. Look how this paragraph contrasts the special effects in the TV and movie versions of *Lost in Space*.

> The biggest difference between the show and the movie is in the special effects. . . . For the TV show, tiny model spaceships were built to make the sets seem bigger. . . . For the movie *Lost in Space,* computer experts created special graphics, animation, and sound effects.

- **The writer uses an unbiased, balanced tone.**

Karen has made sure to keep opinion out of her essay. She gives facts and explanations, like this: *First of all, movies are longer, usually about two hours.* And as you can see in the paragraph below, she talks about each form with the same tone and gives the same amount of information.

> How are the film and the TV show different? First of all, movies are longer, usually about two hours. A TV episode lasts only 30 to 60 minutes, but a series can go on for years. The movie *Lost in Space* is less than two hours long. The television series *Lost in Space* lasted three years.

Using the Compare-and-Contrast Essay Rubric to Study the Model

- **Precise language informs readers about the topic.**
- **The essay contains no jargon.**

Jargon is all the technical words that people working together in any field use; for example, doctors use medical jargon. Karen is careful not to use jargon that would confuse readers. However, she does use precise language specific to her topic: *episode* and *series*. These words make her explanation clear, especially since she explains the words.

A TV episode lasts only 30 to 60 minutes, but a series can go on for years. . . . The television series *Lost in Space* lasted three years.

- **Smooth, flowing sentences begin in varied ways with effective transition words.**

I noticed that Karen begins some of her sentences with words that tell me right away how the next sentence connects with what I've already read. In the example below, she gets the reader ready for how TV shows and movies are the same or different. Then she signals that she will give an example.

Some television shows are turned into movies. Sometimes the TV show and the movie are a lot alike, but sometimes they're very different. One good example is *Lost in Space.*

- **Titles are capitalized correctly.**
- **Comparative and superlative adjectives are used correctly.**
- **The writing is clear.**

Karen uses correct spelling, punctuation, and capitalization—it's clear that she edited her essay! She even remembered to italicize *Lost in Space* and to capitalize the important words in the title. And she knew that the titles of movies and TV series are treated the same way. Finally she used a superlative adjective (*biggest*) correctly.

The movie *Lost in Space* is less than two hours long. The television series *Lost in Space* lasted three years.

The biggest difference between the show and the movie is in the special effects.

+Presentation Handwriting is neat, or a limited number of clear fonts are used.

My Turn!

Now I'm going to write my own compare-and-contrast essay. I'll use the rubric and good writing strategies to help me as I write! Come along to see how I do it!

Prewrite

Focus on **Ideas**

The Rubric Says The topic is appropriate for comparison.

Writing Strategy Choose a topic. Take notes on two forms of the topic.

When my teacher asked us to write a compare-and-contrast essay, I thought about the St. Louis Cardinals baseball game I went to last month. My friend Eli had watched the same game on television. I thought about how seeing the game in the ballpark was different from seeing it on TV. I decided to interview Eli. Here are some of the questions I asked and the notes I took.

Writer's Term

Interview

An **interview** is a way to gather information by asking someone prepared questions and recording his or her thoughts or opinions.

Questions for Eli

Q: What's the best thing about watching a ball game on TV?
A: announcers give history, tell stories
stats are always on screen
close-up shots and instant replays
always have a good view

Q: Have you been to a game at the ballpark?
A: Yes

Q: Is there anything you miss about the ballpark when you watch at home?
A: Yes, the crowd
fun to be with
other fans

Apply

Think about an interesting topic that has two forms. How are these two forms similar and different? Prepare some questions, and then ask another person to answer them.

Prewrite

Focus on **Organization**

The Rubric Says Simlarities and differences are grouped logically in paragraphs.

Writing Strategy Use an Attribute Chart to organize the notes.

I know that organization is important. I looked at the notes I wrote and thought about the game I saw in person. I decided to make an Attribute Chart to organize the notes and ideas. This organization will help me write strong paragraphs later.

Writer's Term

Attribute Chart

An attribute is a quality of something. An **Attribute Chart** can help organize information about how two things are alike and different.

Attribute Chart

Game on TV	Attributes	Game at the Ballpark
walk to couch	**Getting There**	by car or bus; find parking
close-ups, replays, stats on screen	**What You See**	whole field, stats on scoreboard
crowd; announcers	**What You Hear**	crowd; announcers
no crowds or interruptions	**Surroundings**	people; waiting in lines; fun to share experience
comfortable	**How You Feel**	could be hot, cold, wet; hard seats

Reflect

Look at Mya's notes in the Attribute Chart. How will they help her write a good compare-and-contrast essay?

Apply

Look at your interview notes. Then make your own Attribute Chart. Use it to organize your notes and ideas about the two forms of your topic.

Draft

Focus on Organization

The Rubric Says Similarities and differences are grouped logically in paragraphs.

Writing Strategy Introduce the topics in the introduction, and compare them in the body.

Now I'm ready to use my Attribute Chart to draft my essay. I know from the rubric that I need to present similarities and differences in logically organized paragraphs. In my introduction, I want to tell readers what my topics are. Next I could group all the similarities together and all the differences together. Or I could talk about one aspect of watching the game and show how it is both alike and different in the ballpark and on TV. My conclusion might tell readers to make up their own minds about how they prefer to watch a game.

I think I will group the similarities together and then talk about the differences.

As I draft, I'll do my best with spelling and grammar, but I know I can correct mistakes later. Here's part of my draft.

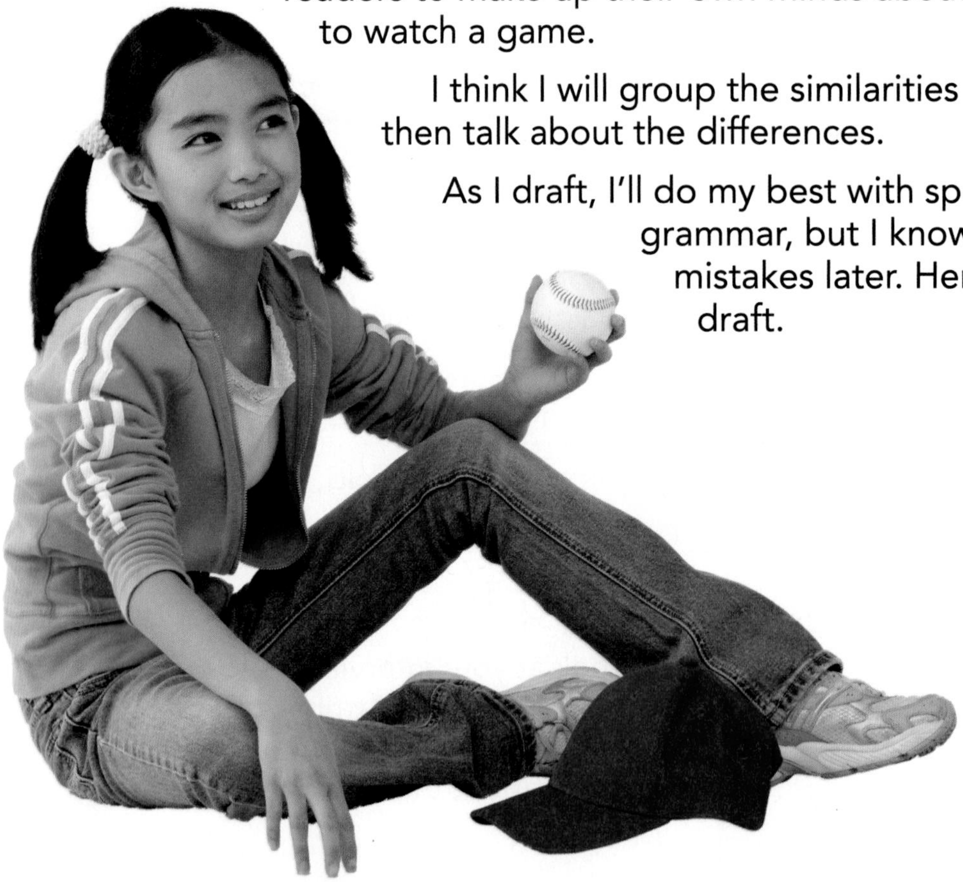

Proofreading Marks

Indent	Take out something
Make uppercase	Add a period
Make lowercase	New paragraph
Add something	Spelling error

[DRAFT]

Live or Televised?

Baseball is america's favorite pastime. Its also mine. I love books like Baseball's greatest Games by Dan Gutman. My favorite television show is Baseball Today. I even know a poem about baseball, Casey at the Bat. I follow the big leagues. The St. Louis cardinals are my favorite team. I watch all the cardinal games, sometimes on television and sometimes at the ballpark.

Is watching a game on television the same as watching it from the stands? Either way, you're going to see lots of action. You're also going to get lots of information about the players. At the ballpark, you can look at the scoreboard and see who is at bat and his jersey number. You can also get the count of balls, strikes, and outs. The scoreboard on a television screen is similar. It shows the score and the batting count right on your screen.

similarities presented together

Reflect

Read Mya's draft. How well does her introduction get her readers prepared to read the essay?

Apply

Use your Attribute Chart to draft your compare-and-contrast essay. Give your readers logical and clear information on both forms of the topic.

Revise

Focus on **Voice**

The Rubric Says The writer uses an unbiased, balanced tone.

Writing Strategy Use language that is fair to both forms of the topic.

I know that bias is a preference. Biased writing does not present both sides of an issue fairly and equally. I don't want my essay to be biased. That is, I want to give readers information without giving my opinion. Then readers can make up their own minds.

When I read my draft, I noticed that I included some biased writing. Do you think my revisions sound fair to both ways of watching baseball?

[DRAFT]

Television lets you watch the game from home~~, which is more comfortable~~. . . . At the ballpark, ~~it's a big advantage to~~ you can see the whole field at once. ~~This makes watching more fun~~.

deleted biased voice

deleted biased voice

Apply

Read your draft again. Take out any biased language. Make sure you are fair to both forms so readers can make up their own minds.

Revise

Focus on **Word Choice**

The Rubric Says Precise language informs readers about the topic. The essay contains no jargon.

Writing Strategy Replace jargon with more common words.

The rubric tells me to avoid jargon. Baseball fans know lots of jargon, like who the "ump" is, but using jargon in my essay can confuse readers. I replaced the jargon with more familiar terms. Precise language is important, too. The verb *follow* is perfect for the sentence below.

Writer's Term

Jargon

Jargon is technical language used by people who work or play together to name or describe their jobs or games.

[DRAFT]

television show is Baseball Today. I even know a poem about baseball, Casey at the Bat. ~~I follow the big leagues~~ I follow major league baseball. The St. Louis cardinals are my favorite team.

replaced jargon with common words

Reflect

Look at Mya's revision. How did replacing jargon with more familiar words strengthen her writing?

Apply

Read your draft again. Replace jargon with more common words.

Revise

Focus on **Sentence Fluency**

The Rubric Says Smooth, flowing sentences begin in varied ways with effective transition words.

Writing Strategy Start sentences with transition words.

Now I want to check my sentences for flow. My teacher says there are two kinds of flow: the sound of the sentences and the ideas. I know that transition words, like *however, on the other hand*, and *for example*, can show how ideas are related. If I put these words at the beginning of a sentence, they tell the reader right away how the ideas are connected. Plus, these words help my sentences flow smoothly. Check out my change to this paragraph. Does it connect the ideas and improve the sentence flow?

There's always an announcer at the ballpark. The announcer repeats information from the scoreboard and identifies the players. ~~T~~ However, television announcers talk a lot, too. They give statistics and news about teams and players. They also tell stories about famous players of the past.

[DRAFT]

Apply

Read your draft out loud. Listen for places to add transition words that connect ideas and smooth out sentences.

Edit

Focus on **Conventions**

The Rubric Says Titles are capitalized correctly. Comparative and superlative adjectives are used correctly. The writing is clear.

Writing Strategy Make sure all titles are capitalized and punctuated correctly and all adjectives are used correctly.

Now I'll proofread my essay. I'll check spelling, capitalization, grammar, and punctuation. The rubric reminds me to check titles and adjectives, too. I found some titles in the first paragraph that need to be fixed.

Writer's Term

Titles

Titles are the names of books, movies, poems, songs, stories, and television series and episodes.

It's

Baseball is america's favorite pastime. ~~Its~~ also mine. I love books like Baseball's greatest Games by Dan Gutman. My favorite television show is Baseball Today. I even know a poem about baseball, " Casey at the Bat. "

title of book

title of TV show

title of poem

[DRAFT]

Reflect

Look at Mya's editing. Would you have made the same edits?

Apply

Conventions

Edit your draft for spelling, punctuation, grammar, and capitalization. Check that all titles and adjectives are correct.

For more practice with titles and comparative adjectives, use the exercises on the next two pages.

Titles

Know the Rule

Titles are the names of books, movies, poems, songs, stories, and television series and episodes.

- For all titles, capitalize the first word, last word, and all other words except articles, short prepositions, and conjunctions.

  Example:
  Buzz Bissinger wrote Three Nights in August.

- Underline or italicize the titles of books, movies, and television series.

  Example:
  The St. Louis Cardinals in the 1940s is a book by Mel R. Freese.

- Use quotation marks around titles of songs, stories, poems, and television episodes.

  Example:
  America's favorite baseball song, "Take Me Out to the Ball Game," was written in 1909.

Practice the Rule

If a title is capitalized or punctuated incorrectly, rewrite it correctly. If a title is capitalized and punctuated correctly, write **Correct**.

1. When you were younger, you may have watched sesame street.
2. Did you know that Sesame Street has won more Emmy awards than any other children's program?
3. Young children love to sing Elmo's Song.
4. Older children are more likely to watch a show such as Nick News.
5. Some people enjoy National Geographic Special and other programs that take you around the world.
6. To find some science experiments, look for a book called Exploratopia by Pat Murphy.
7. A good song to sing while doing an experiment would be "check it out"!
8. Maybe I'll write a poem about an experiment and call it Ode to Science.

Comparative and Superlative Adjectives

Know the Rule

The **comparative form** of an **adjective** compares two people, places, or things. To create the comparative form of short adjectives, add *-er* followed by the word *than* (*fast**er** than, old**er** than*). Use the word *more* before long adjectives to create the comparative form (*more expensive, more thoughtful*).

The **superlative form** compares three or more people, places, or things. Add *-est* to short adjectives to create the superlative form (*rich**est**, steep**est***). Use the word *most* before long adjectives to create the superlative form (*most beautiful, most frightening*).

Practice the Rule

Number a separate sheet of paper 1–10. Choose the correct form of the adjective in parentheses for each sentence.

1. Many popular children's books become even (more/most) popular after they are made into movies.
2. The story in a movie is (shorter/shortest) than the story in a book because a lot of details are left out.
3. The movie *Polar Express* is much (longer/longest) than I thought it would be.
4. One of the (hotter/hottest) series of books and movies of all time is the Harry Potter series.
5. Of my three favorite movies, *The Wizard of Oz* is the (older/oldest).
6. I have seen all four Shrek movies, and the second one is (better/best).
7. Movies are (more/most) fun to watch with friends than alone.
8. I wonder which movie will be the (more/most) successful one this year.
9. The price of a movie ticket is (higher/highest) than it used to be.
10. The afternoon movies have the (cheaper/cheapest) tickets.

Publish

+Presentation

Publishing Strategy	Put the essay in a class time capsule.
Presentation Strategy	Use neat handwriting or a limited number of clear fonts.

Three cheers for me! I've finished my compare-and-contrast essay about watching baseball! The students in my class are making a time capsule. It will be opened 25 years from now to see how things have changed during that time. I thought my essay about live and televised baseball games would remind me of how we had fun.

Sloppy handwriting or hard-to-read fonts make reading an essay difficult. I want to be courteous to my readers, so before I place my essay in the time capsule, I will make a very neat copy. Then I will use this checklist to make sure the essay is ready.

My Final Checklist

Did I—

- ✔ proofread for errors in spelling and grammar?
- ✔ check to see that I wrote titles correctly?
- ✔ use adjectives correctly?
- ✔ use comparative and superlative forms correctly?
- ✔ use neat handwriting or word processing?

Apply

Use this checklist to check your compare-and-contrast essay. Then make a final copy.

Live or Televised?

by Mya

Baseball is America's favorite pastime. It's also mine. I love books like Baseball's Greatest Games by Dan Gutman. My favorite television show is Baseball Today. I even know a poem about baseball, "Casey at the Bat." I follow major league baseball. The St. Louis Cardinals are my favorite team. I watch all the Cardinal games, sometimes on television and sometimes at the ballpark.

Is watching a game on television the same as watching it from the stands? Either way, you're going to see lots of action. You're also going to get a lot of information about the players. At the ballpark, you can look at the scoreboard and see who is at bat. You can also get the count of balls, strikes, and outs. A television scoreboard is similar. It shows the score and the batting count right on your screen.

There's always an announcer at the ballpark. The announcer repeats information from the scoreboard and identifies the players. However, television announcers talk a lot, too. They give statistics and news about teams and players. They also tell stories about famous players of the past.

Even though you can catch all the action from your couch or from the stands, there are big differences. Television lets you watch the game from home. You don't have to catch a bus or ride in a car to the game. You don't have to find a parking space. You don't even have to buy a ticket. If you're watching a game on television, you can see instant replays. Most ballparks can't show replays. At the ballpark, you can see the whole field at once. On the other hand, television cameras follow the ball and take close-up shots of players.

Another thing that's different is the crowd. When you watch a game on television, you might be watching alone. No one will interrupt you to pass a bag of peanuts. When you're in the stands, you're with hundreds of other fans who share your excitement. You all clap and cheer together for your team.

You know, it really doesn't matter where or how you watch baseball. From the stands or from your couch, it's great entertainment!

Reflect

Use the rubric to check Mya's compare-and-contrast essay. Then use it to check your own essay.

What's a How-To Essay?

It's an essay that tells how to make or do something.

What's in a How-To Essay?

Point of View
Because I'm telling how to do something, I'll use the second-person point of view, which means I'll use the word *you*.

Materials
These are all the things I need to make or do what I'm writing about. If I'm gardening, I'll need gloves, a hat to protect myself from the sun, and gardening tools.

Introduction
The beginning of my essay will make it clear that I'm going to tell my readers how to do something.

Procedure
That's the order of steps I have to follow to do the project I'm writing about.

Conclusion
The end of my essay tells readers what they can expect after following the steps.

Why write a How-To Essay?

Some people who know how to do something very well will write how-to essays. They may publish these essays in books or magazines, or on the Internet. There are many reasons to write a how-to essay. Here are a few examples.

Information

- A person who fixes bicycles may write a how-to essay about adjusting the brakes or replacing a chain.
- Students may write how-to essays to tell their friends and classmates how to play a game or make a musical instrument.

Logical Thinking

To write a how-to essay, I have to think my project through from beginning to end. I have to imagine an audience that does not know how to do it. Writing a how-to essay is good exercise for the brain.

Linking Informative/Explanatory Writing Traits to a How-To Essay

In this chapter, you will write an essay that tells the steps for making or doing something. This type of informative/explanatory writing is called a how-to essay. Mya will guide you through the stages of the writing process: Prewrite, Draft, Revise, Edit, and Publish. In each stage, Mya will show you important writing strategies that are linked to the Informative/Explanatory Writing Traits below.

Informative/Explanatory Writing Traits

Ideas	• a topic that is clear and focused • facts, definitions, or details that develop the topic
Organization	• a strong introduction, body, and conclusion • well-organized paragraphs that contain transition words to connect ideas
Voice	• a voice that is appropriate for the purpose and audience
Word Choice	• language that is specific and appropriate for the audience
 Sentence Fluency	• sentences that vary in length and structure to make the writing clear and easy to read
 Conventions	• no or few errors in grammar, usage, mechanics, and spelling

Before you write, read Beyong Sun's how-to essay on the next page. Then use the how-to essay rubric on pages 184–185 to decide how well he did. (You might want to look back at What's in a How-To Essay? on page 180, too!)

A Home for Your Goldfish

introduction

by Beyong Sun

It's not just people who need homes. Pets need them, too. If the pets in question are goldfish, special care must be taken in choosing and preparing their new home. A goldfish's home is called an aquarium, and many factors must be looked at when choosing the aquarium that's right for your fish—and for you.

second-person point of view

The aquarium container, or tank, is available in many different sizes and shapes, depending on your needs. Goldfish need plenty of space, so when selecting your tank, make sure you get one that's large enough. That way, your fish will be more likely to stay healthy. A 20-gallon tank will usually be large enough for two goldfish.

materials

Once you have selected the tank, you will need to prepare it for your fish. The bottom should be covered in gravel; use about one pound for every gallon of water. Because gravel is available in many colors, you can choose the one you like best. Also, it is very important to include a filter to keep the water fresh.

To make your aquarium look nicer, you might want to consider adding rocks, plants, and small decorations. Pet stores have all kinds of stones in different colors: green, red, white, even striped. Some rocks look like towers. Others have holes the fish could swim through. Plants are important because goldfish like to nibble on them. They also like to hide behind the leaves.

Are you ready to set up your aquarium? First you need to put in the gravel and rocks. Begin by washing the tank, the gravel, and the rocks. As they are drying, set up the tank in a safe spot so no one will be likely to tip it over. After you spread the gravel around the bottom of the tank, arrange the rocks and other decorations.

procedure

You are now ready to put water in the aquarium. Start by filling the tank halfway with water and adding the plants. When everything is in place, you can continue adding water until the tank is full. Then attach the filter to the side of the tank, and turn it on. Be careful to allow the water to cycle for a while before adding the fish.

Finally your pets' new home is ready. Place your fish gently in the aquarium. As they get used to their surroundings, be prepared for the hours of entertainment you will receive from watching them swim around in the beautiful home that you have created for them!

conclusion

How-To Essay Rubric

Use this 6-point rubric to plan and score a how-to essay.

	6	5	4
Ideas	The topic is developed with concrete details. All the steps are explained clearly.	The topic is developed with details. Most of the steps are explained clearly.	A few details are missing but not enough to lose the reader. Some steps need more explanation.
Organization	Related information is grouped in easy-to-follow paragraphs. Appropriate transitions move the reader from one idea to the next.	The steps are organized in paragraphs. Some transitions are used.	Some steps are not clearly organized in paragraphs. Some transition words are missing or out of sequence.
Voice	The writer uses second-person point of view and a friendly tone to connect with the reader.	The writer uses second-person point of view. The tone connects with the reader most of the time.	The writer uses second-person point of view and a friendly tone most of the time.
Word Choice	Precise language, such as specific nouns and lively verbs, explains the topic.	The essay contains some specific nouns and lively verbs.	Verbs and nouns are present but may be used inappropriately.
Sentence Fluency	The sentences are a pleasing mix of statements, questions, and exclamations.	Most sentences are a mix of statements, questions, and exclamations.	Sentence types are repetitive in a few places.
Conventions	Dependent clauses and irregular verbs are used correctly. The essay is easy to read and understand.	There are a few errors in the use of dependent clauses and irregular verbs, but they do not interfere with meaning.	Minor errors in the use of dependent clauses and irregular verbs may distract the reader.

+Presentation Paragraphs are indented.

3	2	1	
Some details are missing. Some steps are not explained.	Key details are missing. The directions are not presented in steps.	Information is unclear or missing. The directions do not tell how to do something.	Ideas
Some steps are not organized in paragraphs. Transition words are out of sequence.	Steps and pattern seem confusing or missing. Transition words are used improperly or not at all.	The process is not organized. Transition words are missing. There is no structure.	Organization
The writer uses second-person point of view or a friendly tone inconsistently.	The writer does not use second-person point of view or a friendly tone.	Voice is lacking. The writing is flat and lifeless.	Voice
Many of the words are repetitive, misleading, or vague.	The writing lacks lively verbs, and the nouns are too general.	The words are not specific. Many are inaccurate.	Word Choice
Most sentences are the same type. The writing does not flow well.	Repetitive sentence types cause choppy, awkward sentences.	The sentences lack variety. They are all the same type.	Sentence Fluency
Some errors in the use of dependent clauses and irregular verbs confuse the reader.	The writer does not appear to be in control of dependent clauses and irregular verbs.	Many errors in the use of dependent clauses and irregular verbs distract the reader.	Conventions

See Appendix B for 4-, 5-, and 6-point informative/explanatory rubrics.

How-To Essay Using the Rubric to Study the Model

Did you notice that the model on page 183 points out some key elements of a how-to essay? As he wrote "A Home for Your Goldfish," Beyong Sun used these elements to help him explain how to set up an aquarium. He also used the 6-point rubric on pages 184–185 to plan, draft, revise, and edit the writing. A rubric is a great tool for evaluating writing during the writing process.

Now let's use the same rubric to score the model. To do this, we'll focus on each trait separately, starting with Ideas. We'll use the top descriptor for each trait (column 6), along with examples from the model, to help us understand how the traits work together. How would you score Beyong on each trait?

- **The topic is developed with concrete details.**
- **All the steps are explained clearly.**

Did you know that goldfish need a lot of space? I sure didn't! I'm glad Beyong told me that information, or I might have bought a tank that was too small. Beyong is very careful to add concrete details that he knows his readers need if they've never set up an aquarium before.

> The aquarium container, or tank, is available in many different sizes and shapes, depending on your needs. Goldfish need plenty of space, so when selecting your tank, make sure you get one that's large enough. That way, your fish will be more likely to stay healthy. A 20-gallon tank will usually be enough for two goldfish.

- Related information is grouped in easy-to-follow paragraphs.
- Appropriate transitions move the reader from one idea to the next.

I had no idea how to set up an aquarium until I read Beyong's essay. He tells me all the materials I need to gather. Then he gives me every step in order—he doesn't leave anything out. I especially like the way Beyong uses time-order transitions like *first, next,* and *then,* so that I know exactly what to do in the correct order.

First you need to put in the gravel and rocks. Begin by washing the tank, the gravel, and the rocks. As they are drying, set up the tank in a safe spot so no one will be likely to tip it over.

- The writer uses second-person point of view and a friendly tone to connect with the reader.

I think Beyong's instructions are easy to follow because he makes them sound like a conversation. He uses the word *you* to make the writing friendly and easy to understand.

You are now ready to put water in the aquarium. Start by filling the tank with water and adding the plants. When everything is in place, you can continue adding water until the tank is full.

How-To Essay Using the Rubric to Study the Model

- **Precise language, such as specific nouns and lively verbs, explains the topic.**

From Beyong's specific information, I know exactly what kinds of things to put in an aquarium—even the colors of the stones! He also uses precise, lively verbs like *nibble* and *hide* to explain how the fish will use all the materials I choose for them.

Pet stores have all kinds of stones in different colors: green, red, white, even striped. Some rocks look like towers. Others have holes the fish could swim through. Plants are important because goldfish like to nibble on them. They also like to hide behind the leaves.

- **The sentences are a pleasing mix of statements, questions, and exclamations.**

I like the way Beyong uses statements, questions, and exclamations in his essay. This variety makes it more fun to read. See how using a question livens up Beyong's writing. At the end of the essay, he uses an exclamation to add excitement.

Are you ready to set up your aquarium? First you need to put in the gravel and rocks.

- Dependent clauses and irregular verbs are used correctly.
- The essay is easy to read and understand.

Beyong's essay looks free of spelling, punctuation, or capitalization errors. He uses a comma when he begins a sentence with a dependent clause, and he spells irregular verbs correctly. Good proofreading!

Once you have selected the tank, you will need to prepare it for your fish. The bottom should be covered in gravel; use about one pound for every gallon of water. Because gravel is available in many colors, you can choose the one you like best.

+Presentation Paragraphs are indented.

My Turn!

Now it's my turn to write a how-to essay! I'll use the rubric and good writing strategies to help me. Read along to see how I do it!

Prewrite

Focus on **Ideas**

The Rubric Says The topic is developed with concrete details. All the steps are explained clearly.

Writing Strategy Make a list of everything needed for the project.

My teacher said that for my how-to essay I should choose a topic that most of my classmates aren't familiar with. That way, they can learn something new by reading my essay. I can teach my classmates how to grow great tomatoes like my grandma taught me. I'll have to remember that most of them have never gardened, so they'll need exact instructions and a complete list of materials. I'll list all the materials they'll need before I write my draft.

Materials

packet of tomato seeds
bag of seed starter soil
small growing tray
water
plastic wrap
pots

Apply

Think about all the things you know how to do or make. Choose one, and make a list of all the materials your reader will need.

Prewrite

Focus on **Organization**

The Rubric Says Related information is grouped in easy-to-follow paragraphs.

Writing Strategy Use a Sequence Chain to organize the items in the list.

I have put my list of materials in the order that they're needed. However, it's harder to put the steps for growing tomatoes in order. I'll use a Sequence Chain to organize the steps. Later this will help me write easy-to-follow paragraphs.

Writer's Term

Sequence Chain

A **Sequence Chain** shows steps or events in the order they happen.

Sequence Chain

Topic: Growing Tomatoes

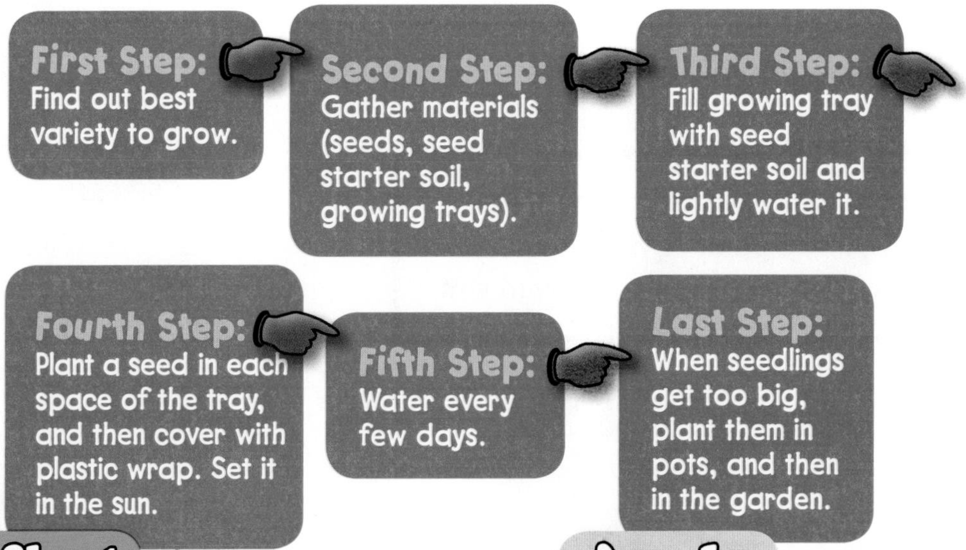

First Step: Find out best variety to grow.

Second Step: Gather materials (seeds, seed starter soil, growing trays).

Third Step: Fill growing tray with seed starter soil and lightly water it.

Fourth Step: Plant a seed in each space of the tray, and then cover with plastic wrap. Set it in the sun.

Fifth Step: Water every few days.

Last Step: When seedlings get too big, plant them in pots, and then in the garden.

Reflect

How will the list of materials and the Sequence Chain help Mya to write a good how-to essay?

Apply

Look at your list of materials. Create your own Sequence Chain with steps and materials. Be sure not to leave out any steps your reader might need.

Draft

Focus on **Voice**

The Rubric Says The writer uses second-person point of view and a friendly tone to connect with the reader.

Writing Strategy Use second-person point of view.

I've got my Sequence Chain done, and I'm ready to write now. The rubric reminds me that I need to use second-person point of view to create a friendly tone. That means I'll use the word *you* to talk to my audience. I can also use contractions, such as *it's*, to help make my language sound more casual.

I know I'll make a few mistakes in grammar and spelling as I write my draft. I can correct those mistakes later when I proofread. I will especially watch out for words that need capital letters, such as names of tomato varieties.

Here's the beginning of my draft.

Writer's Term

Second-Person Point of View

Second-person point of view addresses the reader directly by using the word **you**.

Proofreading Marks

] Indent	Take out something
≡ Make uppercase	⊙ Add a period
/ Make lowercase	¶ New paragraph
∧ Add something	(sp) Spelling error

[DRAFT]

The Best Tomatoes Ever

friendly tone

second-person point of view

It's very easy to grow your own tomatoes. Read on and you will see how.

First, you need to decide which variety of tomato to grow. Some varieties are Celebrity and Beefmaster. When you're ready to get started, go to your local garden center. Buy a packet of the seed variety you want, a bag of soil, and a starter tray.

Fill the spaces in the tray with the soil. Carefully pour water over the soil to make it damp.

Plant a seed in each space in the tray. Next, lay a piece of plastic wrap over the tray.

Reflect

Read the draft. How does second-person point of view help create a friendly tone?

Apply

Use your Sequence Chain to draft your how-to essay. Be sure to use the second-person point of view as you write.

Revise

Focus on **Ideas**

The Rubric Says All the steps are explained clearly.

Writing Strategy Add information that was left out.

I asked my friend to read my draft to see if she could follow my instructions. When she got to my materials list, she said she didn't know what kind of soil to buy or what a starter tray was. She made me see that I've left out some information that readers who have never gardened will need. Is my materials list clearer now?

Some varieties are Celebrity and Beefmaster. When you're ready to get started, go to your local garden center. Buy a packet of the seed variety you want, a bag of ^seed starter^ soil, and a ~~starter~~ ^small^ tray ^with six spaces in it^.

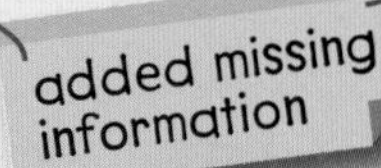

Apply

Read your draft. Did you include all of the information your reader needs?

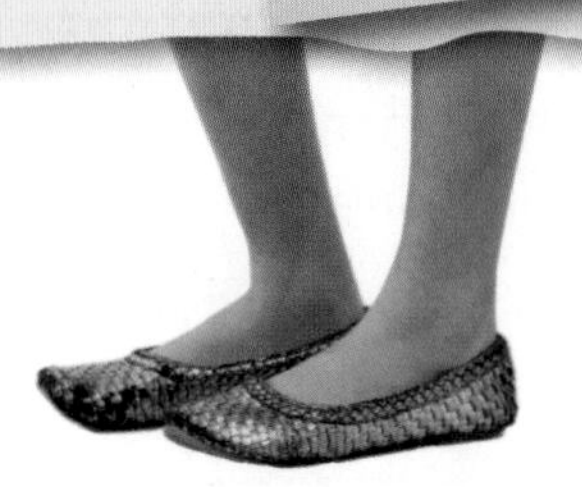

Revise

Focus on **Word Choice**

The Rubric Says Precise language, such as specific nouns and lively verbs, explains the topic.

Writing Strategy Choose words and phrases for effect.

The rubric says I should include specific nouns and lively verbs. I know that choosing my words and phrases carefully can make a big difference. It can help make my writing sound better and keep my readers interested. Do you think the changes to this paragraph make it more specific and lively?

[DRAFT]

When you are sure the weather will stay warm, ~~make~~ dig a hole for each plant about three feet apart in the garden. Remove the plants from their pots, set them in the holes, and press the dirt firmly around the ~~plants~~ roots. Finally, water the plants.

precise language

Reflect

Look at Mya's revisions. How does the new precise language improve her writing?

Apply

Read your draft. Check for places where you can make your nouns specific and your verbs more lively.

Revise

Focus on **Sentence Fluency**

The Rubric Says The sentences are a pleasing mix of statements, questions, and exclamations.

Writing Strategy Use different types of sentences.

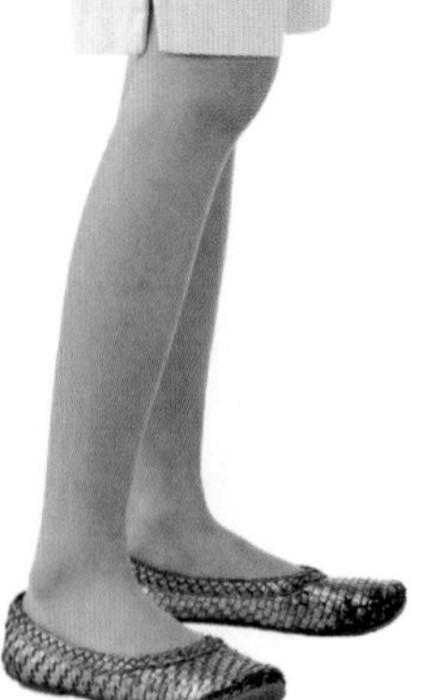

The rubric says that my sentences should be a mix of statements, questions, and exclamations. I know this variety will help make my essay sound more pleasing—and it will be more fun to read! Do you think the revisions below add variety to my sentences?

[DRAFT]

After about ten days, you should see tiny dots of green. This means the seeds have sprouted! Who knows? Maybe you've got a tomato there worthy of *Home Grown Magazine*!

use variety of sentences

Apply

Read your draft out loud. Listen for where you need to add some sentence variety.

Edit

Focus on **Conventions**

The Rubric Says Dependent clauses and irregular verbs are used correctly. The essay is easy to read and understand.

Writing Strategy Make sure dependent clauses and verbs are correct.

I'm going to check my draft now for spelling, punctuation, and capitalization. The rubric reminds me I should check my use of dependent clauses and irregular verbs.

Writer's Term

Dependent Clause

A **dependent clause** is a group of words that has a subject and a predicate but cannot stand on its own.

[DRAFT]

Once they are in the garden. Your tomato plants should grow really fast. As they grew, you will begin to see thick leaves and little yellow flowers.

corrected dependent clause error

fixed irregular verb

Reflect

Do the different types of sentences make the writing flow in a pleasing way? Are the dependent clauses and irregular verbs all correct?

Apply

Conventions

Edit your draft for spelling, punctuation, and capitalization. Use dependent clauses and irregular verbs correctly.

For more practice using dependent clauses and irregular verbs correctly, use the exercises on the next two pages.

Dependent Clauses

Know the Rule

An **independent clause** is a sentence that makes sense by itself. A **dependent clause** has a subject and a verb, but it does not make sense by itself. It needs—or is dependent on—an independent clause. A dependent clause often begins with a word such as *although, because, if, as,* or *when*. These words are called subordinating conjuctions.

Example:
When the tomato turns a deep red, it is ripe.

Example:
Do not pick a tomato **before it is ripe**.

Practice the Rule

Number a separate sheet of paper 1–10. Rewrite each sentence below. Underline each dependent clause. Circle the word that begins each dependent clause.

1. If you want to make a mold jar garden, I can tell you how.
2. All you need is a jar with a lid, a piece of bread, and some water, although you can use a slice of apple instead of bread.
3. If you use an apple, try to use a bruised one.
4. When you've got a piece of bread, wipe it on a dirty floor.
5. After you've gotten the bread dirty, you need to sprinkle it with water.
6. Don't get the bread too wet because it will fall apart.
7. Put the wet bread in the jar and screw on the lid, if you have one.
8. Although a lid works best, you can also use tight plastic wrap.
9. When you have the jar tightly closed, you need to place it in a warm, dark place for a week.
10. If you get the jar out after one week, you'll be amazed to find a mold garden!

Irregular Verbs

Know the Rule

Regular verbs form the past tense by adding *-ed*. However, **irregular verbs** change their spelling in the past tense.

Examples:

I like to **grow** all kinds of vegetables in my garden.

When I was little, my grandpa told me that he **grew** a 10-inch tomato plant one summer!

I've **grown** some big tomatoes, but none were that big.

Last year I **had** only tomatoes in my garden, but this year I **have** some peppers, too.

Practice the Rule

Number a sheet of paper 1–10. Write the correct form of the verb in parentheses for each sentence.

1. Last May my dad and I _____ (bought/buy) flower seeds for our garden.
2. My dad _____ (take/took) me with him to the garden store.
3. By the end of the week, he _____ (takes/had taken) me there three times to buy more seeds.
4. First, we _____ (dug/dig) rows for marigolds, daisies, and sunflowers.
5. Finally, my dad said we _____ (dig/had dug) enough rows.
6. Next, we _____ (take/took) the seeds out of the packets and dropped them in the rows.
7. It turned out that we did not _____ (buy/bought) enough seeds for all the rows!
8. After several days, the seeds _____ (grew/grown) into little green shoots.
9. Over the summer I watched one sunflower _____ (grow/had grown) to over eight feet tall!
10. When Grandpa _____ (saw/see) the sunflower, he was amazed.

Publish +Presentation

Publishing Strategy Read the essay to the class.

Presentation Strategy Indent the beginning of each paragraph.

My how-to essay on growing tomatoes is done! I'm ready to publish it now. I could make it into an instruction pamphlet or submit it to a newspaper, but my teacher also wants us to read our essays aloud in class. Before I read my essay aloud, I need to make sure it looks neat and I have done everything I need to do. I'll check to make sure I've indented all my paragraphs. Indenting organizes the information visually. Here's my final checklist.

My Final Checklist

Did I—

- ✔ check to see that all dependent clauses are part of a sentence?
- ✔ use irregular verbs correctly?
- ✔ indent every paragraph?
- ✔ use neat handwriting or word processing?
- ✔ put my name on my paper?

Apply

Use this checklist to check your own how-to essay. Then make a final copy to read aloud to your classmates.

The Best Tomatoes Ever

by Mya

It's very easy to grow your own tomatoes. Read on and you will see how.

First, you need to decide which variety of tomato to grow. Some varieties are Celebrity and Beefmaster. When you're ready to get started, go to your local garden center. Buy a packet of the seed variety you want, a bag of seed starter soil, and a small tray with six spaces in it.

When you get everything home, fill the spaces in the tray with soil. Then carefully pour water over the soil to make it damp.

Plant a seed in each space in the tray. Next, lay a piece of plastic wrap over the tray to keep the soil from drying out. Finally set the tray on a windowsill where it will get a lot of sun and stay warm. Then wait.

Every couple of days, take the plastic wrap off the tray and spray the soil lightly with water. Then put the plastic back on. After about ten days, you should see tiny dots of green. This means the seeds have sprouted! Who knows? Maybe you've got a tomato there worthy of *Home Grown Magazine*!

Eventually the seedlings will probably get too big for the tray. If it is too early in the growing season to plant them in the garden outside, you can put each one in its own pot.

When you are sure the weather will stay warm, dig a hole for each plant about three feet apart in the garden. Remove the plants from their pots, set them in the holes, and press the dirt firmly around the roots. Finally, water the plants.

Once they are in the garden, your tomato plants should grow really fast. As they grow, you will begin to see thick leaves and little yellow flowers. Soon little green tomatoes will appear. Before long, you should be able to pick big, red, ripe tomatoes!

Reflect

Use the rubric to check the essay. Does it include all the traits of a good how-to essay? Now check your own how-to essay against the rubric.

What's an Explanatory Essay?

An explanatory essay explains a concept or an idea. Often the information comes from research the author has done.

What's in an Explanatory Essay?

Introduction
The introduction is my first paragraph. It lets the reader know what my essay is about.

Thesis Statement
The thesis statement appears in the introduction. It tells the reader what to expect from my essay.

Body
In the body of the essay, I give support for my thesis statement.

Transitions
Transitions are words or phrases that guide the reader from one idea to the next.

Conclusion
The conclusion brings the essay to a close and summarizes my major points. A strong conclusion makes an impression on the reader.

Why write an Explanatory Essay?

There are many reasons to write an explanatory essay. Here are two reasons.

Explanation
Writing an explanatory essay could help me learn more information about a topic that interests me and explain what I've learned to others.

Exploration
I might want to explore a topic just to understand it better. Writing an explanatory essay would help me share my growing interest in a topic.

Linking Informative/Explanatory Writing Traits to an Explanatory Essay

In this chapter, you will write to explain a concept you have learned in social studies class. This type of informative/explanatory writing is called an explanatory essay. Mya will guide you through the stages of the writing process: Prewrite, Draft, Revise, Edit, and Publish. In each stage, Mya will show you important writing strategies that are linked to the Informative/Explanatory Writing Traits below.

Informative/Explanatory Writing Traits

	• a topic that is clear and focused • facts, definitions, or details that develop the topic
	• a strong introduction, body, and conclusion • well-organized paragraphs that contain transition words to connect ideas
	• a voice that is appropriate for the purpose and audience
	• language that is specific and appropriate for the audience
	• sentences that vary in length and structure to make the writing clear and easy to read
	• no or few errors in grammar, usage, mechanics, and spelling

Before you write, read Kemena Rivera's explanatory essay on the next page. Then use the explanatory essay rubric on pages 206–207 to decide how well she did. (You might want to look back at What's in an Explanatory Essay? on page 202, too!)

Our Government

introduction

by Kemena Rivera

Most people think that the United States is a democracy. We think this because voters elect our representatives. However, many people don't know that our democracy is not a pure democracy. It is a democratic republic. We should all be glad that we live in a democratic republic rather than a pure democracy. Let me explain why.

thesis statement

In a pure democracy, the majority (a number that equals more than half) rules. In a pure democracy the majority decides everything. What this means is that every time someone has an idea for a new law, everyone gets to vote on that new law. It sounds like a good idea until you take the time to think about it.

body

Suppose, for example, a majority of voters does not ride bicycles. The majority argues that bicycle riders are a nuisance and a danger on the road. Then someone proposes a new tax for people who ride bicycles. As a result, the majority could vote to create a law that would impose a tax on bicycle riders. In a pure democracy this could happen.

A democratic republic, on the other hand, protects the rights of all people within society. Using the same example, bicycle riders can form their own group and elect representatives to protect their interests.

transitions

The United States is a democratic republic. Our Constitution, a document that sets up the basis of our government, protects the rights of all citizens and prevents rule by the majority alone. Rather than making decisions by majority rule, we elect people to represent our interests and pass laws. A democratic republic limits the power of government over its people and protects the rights of all citizens. This is why we should be glad that we live in a democratic republic!

conclusion

Explanatory Essay Rubric

Use this 6-point rubric to score an explanatory essay.

	6	5	4
Ideas	A thesis statement clearly tells the reader what to expect. Concrete details and examples explain the topic clearly.	A thesis statement tells the reader what to expect. The essay would benefit from one or two more concrete details or examples.	A thesis statement tells the reader what to expect. More concrete details and examples are needed.
Organization	The essay has an introduction, body, and conclusion. Transitions link ideas and show how they are related.	The essay has an introduction, body, and conclusion. A few more transitions are needed.	The essay has an introduction, body, and conclusion. Transitions are needed in the body.
Voice	The writer's voice sounds knowledgeable and informative. The tone fits the purpose.	The voice sounds knowledgeable most of the time. The tone fits the purpose.	The voice sounds knowledgeable at first but then fades. The tone may not fit the purpose.
Word Choice	Domain-specific content vocabulary is used correctly and defined.	Domain-specific content words are used. One or two definitions are needed.	Domain-specific content words are used. One definition is incorrect.
Sentence Fluency	Sentence beginnings are varied for interest. Ideas flow smoothly and are easy to follow.	Most sentence beginnings are varied. Most of the ideas flow well.	A few sentence beginnings are varied. Most of the ideas flow well.
Conventions	Spelling, grammar, and punctuation are correct. Appositives and parentheses, if used, are correct.	There are a few minor errors, but they do not interfere with meaning.	There are a few errors that may cause confusion. Appositives or parentheses may be incorrect.

+Presentation Clear formatting guides readers through the essay.

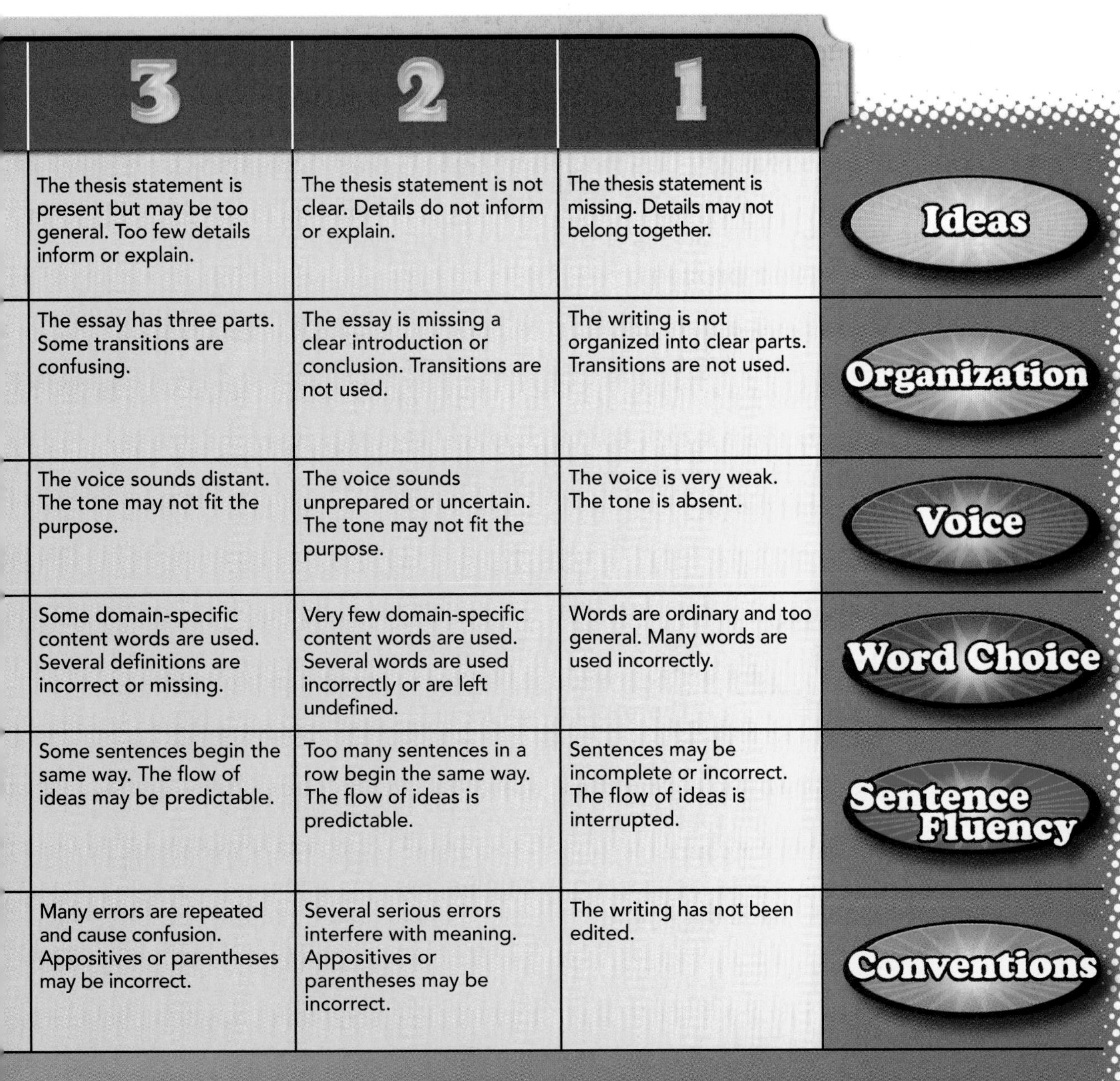

3	2	1	
The thesis statement is present but may be too general. Too few details inform or explain.	The thesis statement is not clear. Details do not inform or explain.	The thesis statement is missing. Details may not belong together.	Ideas
The essay has three parts. Some transitions are confusing.	The essay is missing a clear introduction or conclusion. Transitions are not used.	The writing is not organized into clear parts. Transitions are not used.	Organization
The voice sounds distant. The tone may not fit the purpose.	The voice sounds unprepared or uncertain. The tone may not fit the purpose.	The voice is very weak. The tone is absent.	Voice
Some domain-specific content words are used. Several definitions are incorrect or missing.	Very few domain-specific content words are used. Several words are used incorrectly or are left undefined.	Words are ordinary and too general. Many words are used incorrectly.	Word Choice
Some sentences begin the same way. The flow of ideas may be predictable.	Too many sentences in a row begin the same way. The flow of ideas is predictable.	Sentences may be incomplete or incorrect. The flow of ideas is interrupted.	Sentence Fluency
Many errors are repeated and cause confusion. Appositives or parentheses may be incorrect.	Several serious errors interfere with meaning. Appositives or parentheses may be incorrect.	The writing has not been edited.	Conventions

See Appendix B for 4-, 5-, and 6-point informative/explanatory rubrics.

Using the Explanatory Essay Rubric to Study the Model

Did you notice that the model on page 205 points out some key elements of an explanatory essay? As she wrote "Our Government," Kemena Rivera used these elements to help her explain some ideas she learned in social studies. She also used the 6-point rubric on pages 206–207 to plan, draft, revise, and edit the writing. A rubric is a great tool for evaluating writing during the writing process.

Now let's use the same rubric to score the model. To do this, we'll focus on each trait separately, starting with Ideas. We'll use the top descriptor for each trait (column 6), along with examples from the model, to help us understand how the traits work together. How would you score Kemena on each trait?

- **A thesis statement clearly tells the reader what to expect.**
- **Concrete details and examples explain the topic clearly.**

Kemena has written a clear thesis statement in her introductory paragraph. It tells me that her essay will explain the difference between a democratic republic and a pure democracy. As I read her essay, the concrete details and examples help me better understand her thesis statement.

We should all be glad that we live in a democratic republic rather than a pure democracy.

- **The essay has an introduction, body, and conclusion.**
- **Transitions link ideas and show how they are related.**

Kemena's essay has three easy-to-follow parts: an introduction that includes her thesis statement, a body or middle part that includes examples, and a conclusion that summarizes her findings. Kemena also makes the essay easy to follow by using transition words and phrases. In this passage, she uses *for example*, *Then*, and *As a result* to connect the ideas.

Suppose, for example, a majority of voters does not ride bicycles. The majority argues that bicycle riders are a nuisance and a danger on the road. Then someone proposes a new tax for people who ride bicycles. As a result, the majority could vote to create a law that would impose a tax on bicycle riders.

- **The writer's voice sounds knowledgeable and informative.**
- **The tone fits the purpose.**

Kemena's voice sounds like she is an expert on the topic. She clearly knows what she's talking about and wants me to understand it, too. Her tone is objective, which fits the purpose. She simply explains the facts without giving her opinion. She sounds a lot like my teachers when they explain things in class!

Most people think that the United States is a democracy. We think this because voters elect our representatives. However, many people don't know that our democracy is not a pure democracy. It is a democratic republic.

Explanatory Essay
Using the Rubric to Study the Model

- Domain-specific content vocabulary is used correctly and defined.

Kemena does a great job defining all domain-specific content vocabulary, like *pure democracy, democratic republic,* and *majority*. I'm glad she does because these words are new for me. Without the explanation, I wouldn't be able to understand the main points of her essay!

In a pure democracy, the majority (a number that equals more than half) rules.

- Sentence beginnings are varied for interest.
- Ideas flow smoothly and are easy to follow.

Reading Kemena's essay was a breeze! She kept her writing smooth and interesting by mixing up the way she started sentences. She begins some of her sentences with transition words, which help me follow her ideas easily.

Most people think that the United States is a democracy. We think this because voters elect our representatives. However, many people don't know that our democracy is not a pure democracy.

- **Spelling, grammar, and punctuation are correct.**
- **Appositives and parentheses, if used, are correct.**

I didn't find any spelling, punctuation, or capitalization errors in Kemena's essay. She even used appositives, words that explain nouns, and parentheses correctly.

The United States is a democratic republic. Our Constitution, a document that sets up the basis for our government, protects the rights of all citizens and prevents rule by the majority alone.

In a pure democracy, the majority (a number that equals more than half) rules.

+Presentation Clear formatting guides readers through the essay.

My Turn!

Now it's my turn to write an explanatory essay. I'll use the rubric and good writing strategies to guide me through. Read along to see how I do it.

Prewrite

Focus on **Ideas**

The Rubric Says A thesis statement clearly tells the reader what to expect. Concrete details and examples explain the topic clearly.

Writing Strategy Choose an interesting topic and take notes about it.

My teacher wants us to write a social studies essay on a topic we've studied. How do I decide what to write about? My teacher says we should ask ourselves what interests us or what we'd like to know more about. I decided to do some research to find out how our government really works.

I started my research with a reliable source: www.usa.gov. There I found information about the three branches of government: the executive, legislative, and judicial branches. Then I took notes. As I reread my notes, I realized that I've never really understood how these branches work together. I think figuring this out will be interesting for me and my readers.

Writer's Term

Credible Source

A **credible source** is any source that can provide you with accurate, trustworthy, and up-to-date information. Some examples of credible sources include encyclopedias, reliable websites, such as www.britannica.com, and notable magazines, such as *National Geographic Kids*.

Apply

Think about a topic in social studies that interests you. Choose a topic and do some research using credible sources. Don't forget to take notes, make a new words list, and keep track of your sources.

U.S. Government
Has three branches
- Executive enforces laws
- Judicial (courts) decides meaning of laws
- Legislative (Senate, House of Representatives) makes laws

Prewrite

Focus on **Organization**

The Rubric Says The essay has an introduction, body, and conclusion.

Writing Strategy Use a Support Pattern to organize information.

I know from the rubric that organization is important. I need a good way to put my notes in order. I looked for information on my topic that I could group together. Then I used a Support Pattern to help organize the information for my essay.

Writer's Term

Support Pattern

A **Support Pattern** is a chart that shows how main points are supported by facts.

Support Pattern

Topic: Branches of Government

Main Point: There are three branches of our government.

Supporting Facts

- The executive branch of government enforces the laws.
- The judicial branch, the courts, decides the meaning of laws.
- The legislative branch makes laws. It is composed of the Senate and the House of Representatives.

Reflect

Look at Mya's Support Pattern. Do the facts support her main point?

Apply

Make your own Support Pattern. State your main point. Then group the supporting facts.

Draft

Focus on **Word Choice**

The Rubric Says Domain-specific content vocabulary is used correctly and defined.

Writing Strategy Explain or define words that readers may not know.

From my research, I've learned a lot of new words that relate specifically to my topic. I listed them in my notes, along with their definitions. This way, I can refer to them easily as I write my draft.

I know from the rubric that I should define or explain words that are related to my topic but may be unfamiliar to my readers. My purpose is to inform my readers, so it's my job to make sure they fully understand the words I use.

While I'm writing my draft, I won't worry about making mistakes because I know that I will take time to edit my writing later. I just need to make sure that I can read my writing!

Proofreading Marks

Indent	Take out something
Make uppercase	Add a period
Make lowercase	New paragraph
Add something	Spelling error

[DRAFT]

Three Branches of Government

by Mya

Have you ever thought about what's really great about our government? The founding fathers, who planned how their new government would work, worried a lot about giving a lot of power to just a few people in the government. They decided to seperate the government into three branches or parts.

The executive branch of government includes the President, Vice President, and cabnet members. Cabnet members are important people who are part of the President's team, such as the Secretary of State. The President appoints Supreme Court Justices (the judges on the Supreme Court. The President has the power to veto bills before they become law.

domain-specific content words

Reflect

Read the beginning of Mya's draft. Are the domain-specific content vocabulary words defined clearly?

Apply

Use your Support Pattern to write your draft. Be sure to define or explain all domain-specific words.

Revise

Focus on **Ideas**

The Rubric Says A thesis statement clearly tells the reader what to expect. Concrete details and examples explain the topic clearly.

Writing Strategy Write a thesis statement that tells what the essay will be about. Use details to support the thesis.

I looked back at the rubric after I finished my draft. I don't think I've told my reader what to expect from my essay. I'll add a thesis statement to my introduction that tells my main point.

Writer's Term

Thesis Statement

A **thesis statement** tells the main idea of the whole essay. All the details and examples should support the thesis statement.

[DRAFT]

added thesis statement

Have you ever thought about what's really great about our government? The founding fathers, who planned how their new government would work, worried a lot about giving a lot of power to just a few people in the government. They decided to seperate the government into three branches or parts. ^ The three branches of our government are the executive, judicial, and legislative, and here's how they work.

Reflect

How does Mya's thesis statement tell the reader what to expect?

Apply

Read your introduction. Did you write a thesis statement that tells your main idea?

Revise

Focus on Organization

The Rubric Says Transitions link ideas and show how they are related.

Writing Strategy Use transitions to connect ideas.

When I read my draft to a classmate, some parts confused her. I reread those parts and decided that transitions would link my ideas and show how they are related. I think my points are easier to follow now. What do you think?

[DRAFT]

The President appoints Supreme Court Justices (the judges on the Supreme Court. In addition, the President has the power to veto bills before they become law.

added transitions to connect ideas

Reflect

How do Mya's revisions strengthen her writing?

Apply

Read over your draft. Use transitions to link ideas and show how they are related.

Revise

Focus on Sentence Fluency

The Rubric Says Sentence beginnings are varied for interest. Ideas flow smoothly and are easy to follow.

Writing Strategy Begin sentences in a variety of ways.

The rubric says to vary my sentence beginnings. As I reread my conclusion, I noticed that all the sentences began the same way. When too many sentences in a row begin the same way, they can sound predictable and boring. I revised this part of my essay to improve the flow of ideas and to make an impression on my reader.

[DRAFT]

The founding fathers did not want any part of government to have too much power. ~~They separated the government into three branches.~~ By separating government into three branches, they balanced the power. Each branch has its own work to do ~~. Each branch~~ and depends on the other branches to get it done.

changed sentence beginning

connected ideas

Reflect

Look at Mya's revisions. How will the new sentences hold her reader's attention and help the flow of ideas?

Apply

Read your draft. Be sure to vary sentence beginnings for interest and flow.

Edit

Focus on **Conventions**

The Rubric Says Spelling, grammar, and punctuation are correct. Appositives and parentheses, if used, are correct.

Writing Strategy Punctuate appositives and parentheses correctly.

Now I'm ready to check my draft for errors. I found my spelling mistakes and corrected each of them. The rubric also reminds me to make sure I use appositives and parentheses correctly, so I'll check them over now.

Writer's Term

Appositives and Parentheses

An **appositive** is a noun or noun phrase that identifies or describes the noun it follows. Appositives are set off from the sentence in one of two ways:

- with commas before and after the appositive when it falls inside a sentence, or with one comma to separate it from the rest of the sentence when it falls at the end of a sentence
- by **parentheses**

[DRAFT]

appositive at the end of the sentence

The President appoints Supreme Court Justices (the judges on the Supreme Court.

The judicial branch of government ~~the courts~~ decides the meaning of laws and whether or not laws violate the Constitution.

appositive within the parentheses

Reflect

Look at Mya's edits. How do they make the writing clearer and easier to understand?

Apply

Conventions

Fix any appositives that are punctuated incorrectly in your essay. Check for other errors in spelling, capitalization, and punctuation.

For more practice with appositives and parentheses, use the exercises on the next two pages.

Appositives

Know the Rule

An **appositive** is a noun or noun phrase that renames or explains the noun it follows. Appositives add information to sentences.
Use commas to separate an appositive from the rest of the sentence when it falls inside a sentence.

Example:
Maria**, my best friend,** is having a hard time deciding on a social studies topic.

Use one comma to separate it from the rest of the sentence when it falls at the end of a sentence.

Example:
She might write about Ben Franklin**, one of the nation's founding fathers**.

Practice the Rule

Number a separate sheet of paper 1–10. Write each sentence correctly.

1. I think I will write about Thomas Jefferson the nation's third president.
2. Jefferson the third of ten children was born in Virginia.
3. His father Peter Jefferson was a planter and surveyor.
4. Jane Randolph Jefferson's mother came from Virginia.
5. Jefferson a gifted writer was not a very good speaker.
6. The Declaration of Independence the nation's announcement of war with England was almost entirely written by Jefferson.
7. In 1790 George Washington Jefferson's friend appointed Jefferson secretary of state.
8. Jefferson supported the Lewis and Clark expedition a vast exploration of the western part of the country.
9. After many years of public service, Jefferson retired to Monticello his home in Virginia.
10. I think that John Jay the first chief justice of the United States would make an interesting topic for my next essay.

Parentheses

Know the Rule

Parentheses are used to make writing clearer. Use them to set off an explanation or example that is useful but not necessary to the meaning of a sentence.

Example:

The three branches of government **(executive, judicial, and legislative)** have separate work to do.

Practice the Rule

Number a sheet of paper 1–8. Rewrite the sentences correctly. Use parentheses to set off the explanation or example in each sentence.

1. The Preamble of the Constitution the introduction explains what the Constitution does.
2. The first ten amendments to the Constitution the Bill of Rights protect the rights of all Americans.
3. Before it became law in 1788, nine states were needed to ratify approve the Constitution.
4. Today the Constitution the supreme law of the land protects the rights of Americans in 50 states.
5. The legislative branch of government the House of Representatives and the Senate writes and passes new laws.
6. Before becoming a law, a bill a proposal for a new law is sent to the president for approval.
7. If the president does not act within ten days not including Sundays the bill becomes a law.
8. Sometimes a bill has so many pages one recent bill was longer than the novel War and Peace that the president certainly would need lots of time to read it!

Publish

+Presentation

Publishing Strategy	Include the report in a multimedia presentation to the class.
Presentation Strategy	Use text features effectively.

I've finished my explanatory essay! I'm ready to publish it now. I've decided to present my essay to my classmates and use a slide show for my main points. I'll use a computer to create my slides. I'll also be sure that each slide shows the information from one paragraph, or each main point. I'll remember to create headings and include two or three bullet points on each slide. Using special text features like headings, bullets, illustrations, and white space will help my audience see and follow my ideas. But first I need to make sure I've done everything on my final checklist.

My Final Checklist

Did I—

✔ punctuate all appositives and parentheses correctly?

✔ create a slide for each of the main points?

✔ use bullets to list my details?

✔ use special text features to present my essay and slides?

Apply

Use Mya's checklist to prepare your final copy. If you create a slide show, be sure it guides your audience through your essay.

The Three Branches of Government

by Mya

Do you know that our government has three separate but equal branches? The founding fathers, who planned how their new government would work, worried about giving too much power to just a few people in the government. For this reason, they decided to separate the government into three branches, or parts. The three branches of our government are the executive, judicial, and legislative, and here's how they work.

The Executive Branch

The executive branch of the government includes the president, vice president, and cabinet members. Cabinet members are important people who are part of the president's team, such as the secretary of state. The president appoints Supreme Court justices, the judges on the Supreme Court. In addition, the president has the power to veto (refuse to approve and sign) bills before they become law.

The Judicial Branch

The judicial branch of the government (the courts) decides the meaning of laws and whether or not laws violate the Constitution. The Supreme Court is the highest court of the land. When other courts can't agree on the meaning of the law, the Supreme Court figures it out. Once Supreme Court justices are appointed, they are free from the president's or anyone else's control.

The Legislative Branch

The legislative branch of government is Congress, which includes the Senate and House of Representatives. The Senate and House of Representatives (Congress) write and pass our laws. For example, in order to become law the 2010 health care bill had to be passed by both the Senate and House of Representatives. The House of Representatives can impeach (accuse of a crime) the president and other high officials. The senate approves the president's appointments to the Supreme Court.

The founding fathers did not want any part of government to have too much power. By separating government into three branches, they balanced the power. Each branch has its own work to do and depends on the other branches to get it done.

The Three Branches of Government

- Executive
- Judicial
- Legislative

Slide 1

Executive Branch

- Includes the president, vice president, cabinet
- President appoints Supreme Court justices
- President can veto laws

Slide 2

Judicial Branch

Supreme Court

- Decides the meaning of laws
- Decides if laws are constitutional
- Highest court in the land

Slide 3

Legislative Branch

- Includes Senate and House of Representatives
- Congress writes and passes laws

Slide 4

Reflect

How did Mya do? Use the rubric to score Mya's explanatory essay. Then use the rubric to check your own essay.

Informative/ Explanatory test writing

Read the Writing Prompt

When it's time to take a writing test, you will get a writing prompt. Most writing prompts have three parts.

Setup This part of the writing prompt provides background information for the writing test.

Task This part of the writing prompt tells you exactly what you're supposed to write: an essay that explains how you use a skill.

Scoring Guide This section tells how your writing will be scored. To do well on the test, you should make sure your writing does everything the scoring guide lists.

You've used a rubric to help you write each informative/ explanatory piece in this book. When you are writing for a test, you won't always have all the information that a rubric gives you. But don't worry! You can use the scoring guide in the same way you used the rubrics. Like the rubric, the scoring guide lists everything you need to think about as you write for a test. Scoring guides will often include the six important traits of writing that you've already seen in rubrics:

Organization

Conventions

A skill is the knowledge of how to do something. Each person has many skills, and each person can teach these skills to others. You have agreed to explain to young children how you do or make something.

Write an essay that explains how you use a skill.

Be sure your how-to essay

- includes a clear topic and concrete supporting details that are related to the topic.
- explains the steps of the skill in order and is well organized, with an introduction, body, and conclusion.
- has a voice that connects directly with the audience.
- has precise language (specific nouns and verbs).
- has a variety of sentence types.
- has correct grammar, spelling, capitalization, and punctuation.

Writing Traits in the Scoring Guide

Take a look: Does the chart remind you of the rubrics you've used? Not all prompts include all of the writing traits, but this one does. Use them to do your best writing. Don't forget to work neatly and put your name on each page!

- **Be sure your essay includes a clear topic and concrete supporting details that are related to the topic.**

- **Be sure your essay explains the steps of the skill in order and is well organized, with an introduction, body, and conclusion.**

- **Be sure your writing voice connects directly with the audience.**

- **Be sure your essay has precise language (specific nouns and verbs).**

- **Be sure your essay has a variety of sentence types.**

- **Be sure your essay has correct grammar, spelling, capitalization, and punctuation.**

Take a look at Nathan Rubin's essay on the next page. Let's use it to check whether Nathan used the scoring guide to write a good essay.

Tell Me a Story!

by Nathan Rubin

Last summer I visited the storytelling tent at the Bristol County Fair. That's where I discovered that anyone can be a terrific storyteller.

First, find a story that's worth telling. It should be funny, spooky, or surprising in some way. Pick something your audience will remember.

It's important to tell the story in your own words. Don't try to repeat the story just the way you heard it. If you memorize a story, it won't sound fresh and interesting when you tell it.

To begin, picture the main characters. What details would make them stand out for your listeners? Think about how they move, and try to move that way when you pretend to be them in the story. For example, a very old person might hunch over a little and move with a slow shuffle.

Also, think about the characters' voices. Are they low and gravelly or high and squeaky? Change your voice to fit each character. Then think about sound effects that could help listeners imagine the setting. Is there a strong wind in the story? Could you make noise like traffic in the background? Can you make the sounds of animals in the story?

Next, picture the story events in the order they happen. Here's a tip to help you remember the story. Draw empty boxes in a line on a sheet of paper. Then draw stick figures in each box. You will show the story events in the order they take place. When you're finished, each box should show some details that you want to remember and include in your story.

Now try your story out on an audience. Choose your family or some good friends, so you won't feel nervous. Watch your audience to see how they react. Do they laugh? Do they seem surprised? Each time you tell the story, keep the parts that get the reaction you want. Then think about ways to make the other parts of your story more interesting.

When you're ready to tell your story to a real audience, relax. Take a deep breath and look around. Remember to make eye contact with members of the audience as you talk. Let your listeners know that you are having fun, and they will have a good time, too.

When you're done, take a bow, and make a quick exit. It's always a good idea to leave your audience begging for more.

Using the Scoring Guide to Study the Model

Now let's use the scoring guide to study Nathan's writing test, "Tell Me a Story!" We'll look for examples in his essay that show how well he did on each part of the scoring guide.

- **The essay includes a clear topic and concrete supporting details that are related to the topic.**

Nathan introduces his topic by telling readers how he got into story-telling. Then, in the body, he provides concrete supporting details about storytelling. Here you can see how Nathan introduces his topic, and then how he gives details about why it's good to tell a story in your own words.

Last summer I visited the storytelling tent at the Bristol County Fair. That's where I discovered that anyone can be a terrific storyteller.

It's important to tell the story in your own words. Don't try to repeat the story just the way you heard it. If you memorize a story, it won't sound fresh and interesting when you tell it.

- **The essay explains the steps of the skill in order and is well organized, with an introduction, body, and conclusion.**

After Nathan's introduction about how he got into storytelling, the body of his essay includes all the steps in how to tell a story. Throughout his essay, he uses words like *First, Next,* and *When* to explain the order of the steps. Nathan's last paragraph makes a good conclusion.

When you're done, take a bow, and make a quick exit. It's always a good idea to leave your audience begging for more.

- **The voice connects directly with the audience.**

Nathan uses second-person point of view. That means he uses the word *you* to address his readers. This helps him connect directly with readers and make his voice sound friendly.

To begin, picture the main characters. What details would make them stand out for your listeners? Think about how they move, and try to move that way when you pretend to be them in the story.

- **The essay has precise language (specific nouns and verbs).**

Precise language, especially nouns and verbs, really helps the reader picture what the writer is describing. Nathan wants to keep his readers interested, and he also wants them to understand his topic. To do that, he uses specific nouns and verbs to paint a vivid picture. Words like *hunch* and *shuffle* help you truly "see" what Nathan is explaining.

For example, a very old person might hunch over a little and move with a slow shuffle.

Using the Scoring Guide to Study the Model

- **The essay has a variety of sentence types.**

The rubric says to include a variety of sentences. This helps keep readers interested and makes the essay enjoyable to read. Do you think Nathan uses a good variety of sentences? Are they pleasing to read?

Now try your story out on an audience. Choose your family or some good friends, so you won't feel nervous. Watch your audience to see how they react. Do they laugh? Do they seem surprised?

- **The essay has correct grammar, spelling, capitalization, and punctuation.**

The scoring guide will usually remind you to check grammar, spelling, capitalization, and punctuation. I can tell that Nathan completed this step. His final draft reads well because it doesn't have mistakes.

Planning My Time

Whenever we write a test in class, our teacher gives us the writing prompt and tells us how much time we'll have to complete the test. This gives me the chance to plan how I'll use the time I have to write the best test I can. I divide up the time into the different parts of the writing process. I make sure to plan time to study the writing prompt, to plan and write the essay, and to revise and proofread my essay. Look at how I've divided up the time for this test.

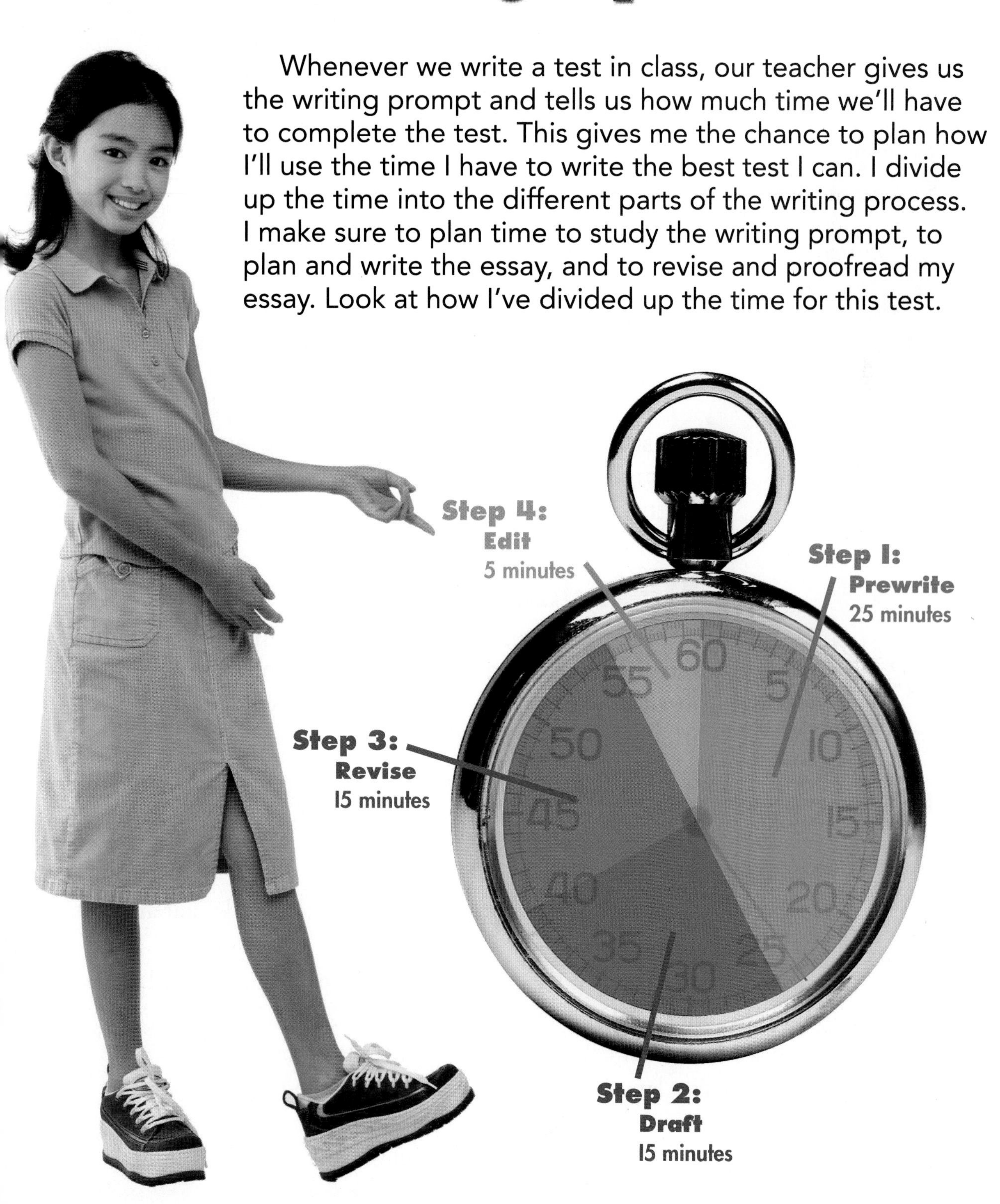

Prewrite

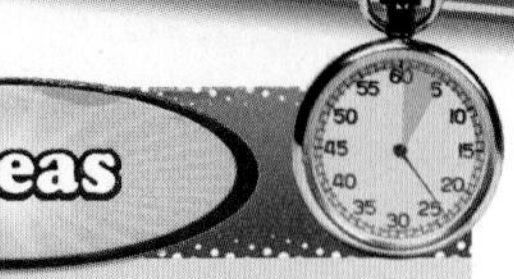

Writing Strategy Study the writing prompt to find out what to do.

The first thing I do when I get the writing prompt is study it. I want to make sure I know exactly what to do. Most writing prompts have three parts, but they usually won't be labeled. You'll need to find and label each part: the setup, the task, and the scoring guide. See how I did this below? Then I circled key words in the prompt that tell me what kind of writing to do. I circled *Write a how-to essay* because it tells what kind of essay I should write. Also, I circled *Explain the steps to complete the task in order* because it tells me how to structure my writing.

My Writing Test Prompt

Setup — Think of something you can do that you can teach others. Write a how-to essay that explains the steps to complete the task. You may write about how to make your favorite recipe, play your favorite sport, or do something else you know a lot about.

Task — Write a how-to essay that teaches others how to do something. Explain the steps to complete the task in order.

Scoring Guide — Be sure your how-to essay

- includes a clear topic and concrete supporting details that are related to the topic.
- explains the steps of the skill in order and is well organized, with an introduction, body, and conclusion.
- has a voice that connects directly with the audience.
- has precise language (specific nouns and verbs).
- has a variety of sentence types.
- has correct grammar, spelling, capitalization, and punctuation.

Now that I've taken time to study the prompt, I'll think about how the scoring guide relates to the six writing traits I've studied in the rubrics. This scoring guide has the six traits that a good essay needs. Not all scoring guides will have six traits, but if you think back to the rubrics you've used, you can remember what's important.

Ideas

- **Be sure your essay includes a clear topic and concrete supporting details that are related to the topic.**

I'll keep my topic clear and include lots of details.

Organization

- **Be sure your essay explains the steps of the skill in order and is well organized, with an introduction, body, and conclusion.**

I'll announce my topic in my introduction and then mention it again in my conclusion.

Voice

- **Be sure your writing voice connects directly with the audience.**

I'll use a friendly tone and address my readers directly.

Word Choice

- **Be sure your how-to essay has precise language (specific nouns and verbs).**

I'll use precise and vivid words to help readers better understand my topic.

Sentence Fluency

- **Be sure your essay has a variety of sentence types.**

To keep things interesting and flowing, I'll use a variety of sentences.

Conventions

- **Be sure your essay has correct grammar, spelling, capitalization, and punctuation.**

I'll proofread carefully and fix mistakes.

Prewrite

Focus on **Ideas**

Writing Strategy Respond to the task.

I've set aside time for gathering information. This will save me time when I write a draft. I'll start by seeing what information I can gather from the writing prompt. I'll look at the task section of the prompt because it tells me what to write. Then I'll think about it and make notes.

I know I have to explain how to do something. I don't have much time, so I'll quickly make a short list of things I know how to do. I can use one of my ideas to complete the writing prompt.

Task— Write a how-to essay that teaches others how to do something. Explain the steps to complete the task in order.

Things I Know How to Do

- Bake brownies
- Make macaroni and cheese
- Complete a homework assignment
- Give my dog a bath

Apply

Identify the parts of the task, and think about how you'll respond to the task. Then jot down a few notes to help you get started.

Prewrite

Focus on **Organization**

Writing Strategy Choose a graphic organizer.

I need to start organizing my ideas about the topic I've chosen—how to give a dog a bath! I think a Sequence Chain will help me get my ideas together. I'll start with my topic. Then in the circles, I can include the steps to complete the task in order.

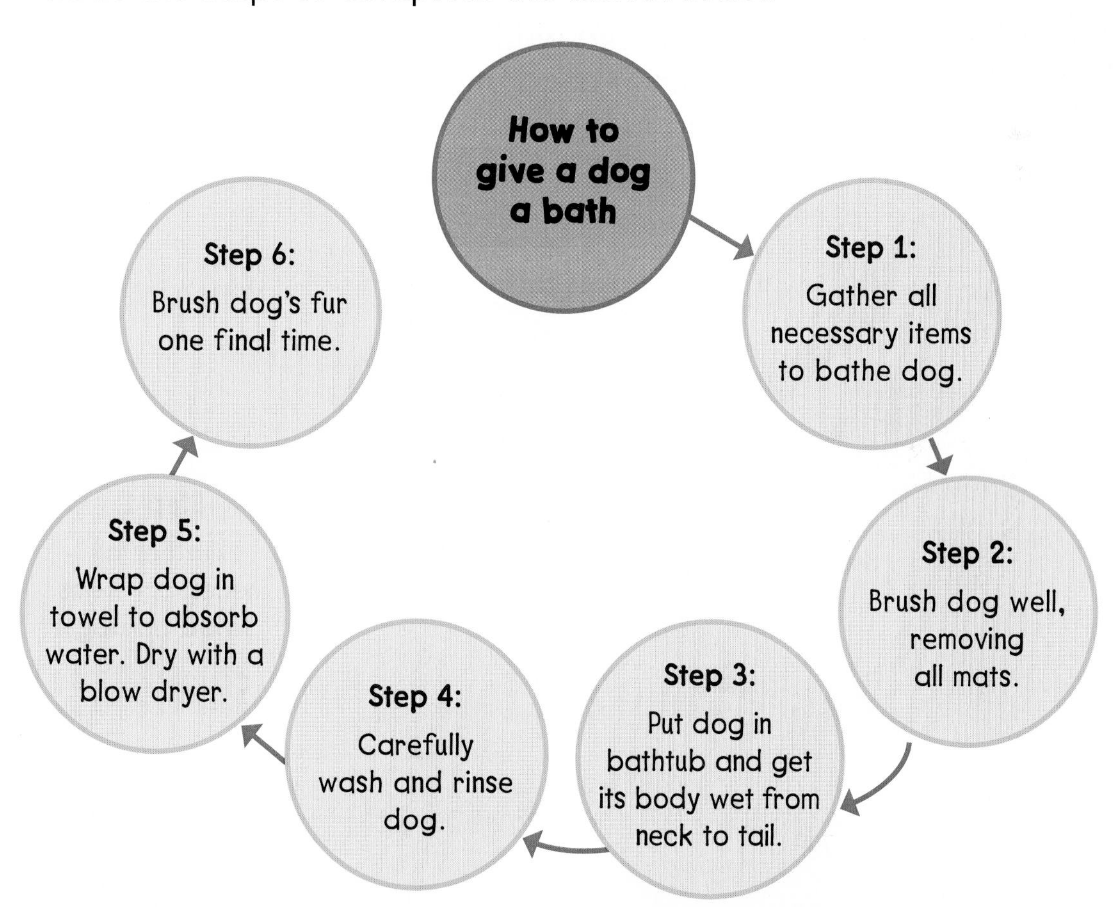

Reflect

Look at Mya's graphic organizer. Does it have all the information necessary for her to write a good essay?

Apply

Use the best graphic organizer for the assignment. Include the steps to complete the task in order and add details to explain each step.

Prewrite

Focus on **Organization**

Writing Strategy Check the graphic organizer against the scoring guide.

My writing plan reminds me that I won't have much time to revise my essay. That means that prewriting is even more important than usual. So, before I start writing my draft, I'll take a few minutes to check my Sequence Chain against the scoring guide in the writing prompt.

How to give a dog a bath

Step 1: Gather all necessary items to bathe dog.

Step 2: Brush dog well, removing all mats.

Step 3: Put dog in bathtub and get its body wet from neck to tail.

Step 4: Carefully wash and rinse dog.

Step 5: Wrap dog in towel to absorb water. Dry with a blow dryer.

Step 6: Brush dog's fur one final time.

Ideas

- **Be sure your essay includes a clear topic and concrete supporting details.**

How to give a dog a bath is my topic. The details I'll include are listed in my graphic organizer.

Organization

- **Be sure your essay explains the steps in order and is well organized, with an introduction, body, and conclusion.**

My Sequence Chain will help me write this part.

Voice

- **Be sure the writing voice connects directly with the audience.**

I can use first-person point of view and a friendly tone.

Word Choice

- **Be sure your essay includes precise language (specific nouns and verbs).**

I'll need to use precise words to create clear images in my readers' minds and hold their attention.

Sentence Fluency

- **Be sure your essay has a variety of sentence types.**

I'll use different types and lengths of sentences to make my how-to essay more interesting to read.

Conventions

- **Be sure your essay has correct grammar, spelling, capitalization, and punctuation.**

I will check grammar and mechanics when I edit my draft.

Reflect

How will Mya's Sequence Chain help her respond to the writing prompt?

Apply

Before you begin writing, take a look at your notes and your graphic organizer.

Draft

Focus on **Ideas**

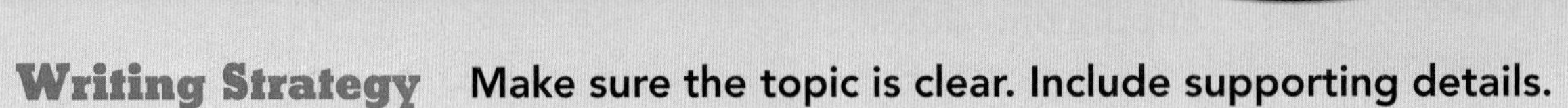

Writing Strategy Make sure the topic is clear. Include supporting details.

My Sequence Chain states my topic clearly, so I'll use that to tell my readers right away what I am writing about. The Sequence Chain reminds me of all the main ideas. As I write about them, I will be sure to support them with details. There's a lot to think about in a first draft! I think this one is a good start.

[DRAFT]

How to Give a Dog a Bath

Dog owners have to become good at giving their dogs a bath. It's not a very easy task to complete. A few key steps are important. If you follow these steps, bathing your dog will be simpler than ever before.

stated topic clearly

The first thing you must do to get ready to give your dog a bath is gather all the supplies I will need. Get shampoo, towls, a blow dryer, and a brush. You may also want to use conditioner if your dog has longer hair. Whatever you will need, make sure you have everything near the tub or area you will bathe your dog once you get started, you won't have time to go to grab whatever you forgot.

body paragraphs contain supporting ideas

Before you begin, brush you're dog. Be sure to get out all mats. Work slowly and carefully. Try to keep your dog still and comfortable.

Proofreading Marks

⊐	Indent	ℓ	Take out something
≡	Make uppercase	⊙	Add a period
/	Make lowercase	¶	New paragraph
∧	Add something	(sp)	Spelling error

The mats will only get worse when you get the hair wet, so work hard to get them out before you begin.

Then put your dog in the tub or area you are using to bathe. Get the dog's body wet from neck to tail. Then wash the dog's rear legs, tail, body, chest, and front legs. Use enough soap and rubbing to get a good lather. Next, wash the dog's head and face. Try to keep soap out of your dog's eyes.

After that, thoroly rinse all the soap out of your dog's hair. Rinse your dog until the water runs clear and you know all the soap is gone. Leaving soap on your dog will cause itching and skin irritation. If you think you got all the soap out, rinse a little longer to make sure.

Wrap your dog in a large towel. Dry your dog's hair with a blow dryer. Make sure the temperature isn't too hot for your dog. Then brush your dog's hair one last time making sure there are no mats.

That's it! You have successfully bathed your dog in just a few simple steps!

Reflect

Read the draft. Is the topic clear? How do the details support the topic?

Apply

To help readers understand your how-to essay, clearly state the topic early on and include plenty of supporting details.

Revise

Focus on **Organization**

Writing Strategy Explain the steps of your skill in order. Include an introduction, body, and conclusion.

Now my first draft is complete and ready for revision. The scoring guide says that the steps of my skill should be explained in order, and that my paper should have an introduction, body, and conclusion. Well, my paper has the three parts, but my steps need to be clearer.

For example, I looked at the paragraph about drying your dog and realized that I need to explain better that you wrap your dog in a large towel *after* you have rinsed out all the soap. I'll revise my writing to make it easier to understand.

[DRAFT]

added details

When you have finished rinsing your dog, to absorb the water After that,

~~W~~rap your dog in a large towel. ~~D~~ry your dog's hair with a blow dryer. Make sure the temperature isn't too hot for your dog. Then brush your dog's hair one last time, making sure there are no mats.

Apply

Read your draft. Add details that explain the steps of the skill in order.

Revise

Focus on **Voice**

Writing Strategy Use first-person point of view.

Now I need to consider how my writing voice sounds. The scoring guide tells me to connect directly with my audience. I know that using first person helps set a friendly tone, which then makes it easier for me to connect with my readers. Since I want my readers to feel I am speaking directly to them, I'll use first-person point of view in my introduction.

[DRAFT]

revised for first person

~~Dog owners have to~~ As a dog owner, I have become good at giving ~~their dogs~~ my dog a bath. It's not a very easy task to complete. I have discovered ~~A~~ a few key steps that are important. If you follow these steps, bathing your dog will be simpler than ever before.

Reflect

What do you think? Did Mya explain the steps of her skill in order? Did her use of first person in the introduction help you connect with her writing?

Apply

Look at your draft to find revisions you can make to use the first-person point of view.

Revise

Focus on **Word Choice**

Writing Strategy Use specific nouns and verbs.

The scoring guide tells me to check my essay to make sure I have used precise language. It is important that I use specific nouns and verbs so readers understand exactly how they should give their dogs a bath. Specific nouns and verbs will make sure the steps are easy to understand. I've used precise language in most of my paragraphs, but I found a few sentences where I could be more specific.

[DRAFT]

specific words

specific words

Then put your dog in the ^bath^ tub or area you are using to bathe. ^Using a large cup or hose,^ ~~G~~get the dog's body wet from neck to tail. Then ^carefully^ wash the dog's rear legs, tail, body, chest, and front legs. Use ~~enough~~ ^plenty of^ soap and rubbing ^action^ to get a good lather. Next, wash the dog's head and face. Try to keep soap out of your dog's eyes.

Apply

Use specific nouns and verbs.

Edit

Focus on **Conventions**

Writing Strategy Check the grammar, spelling, capitalization, and punctuation.

The scoring guide reminds me that I should use spelling and grammar correctly. It's a good thing I planned time to proofread! As I read my revised draft, I found many little mistakes. My final draft is much easier to read!

How to Give a Dog a Bath
by Mya

As a dog owner, I have become good at giving my dog a bath. It's not a very easy task to complete. How long does it take you to give your dog a bath? I have discovered a few key steps that are important. If you follow these steps, bathing your dog will be simpler than ever before!

The first thing you must do to get ready to give your dog a bath is gather all the supplies ~~I~~ ^you^ will need. Get shampoo, tow^e^ls, a blow dryer, and a brush. You may also want to use conditioner if your dog has longer hair. Whatever you will need, make sure to have everything near the tub or area you will bathe your dog ⊙ once you get started, you won't have time to grab whatever you forgot.

Before you begin, brush ~~you're~~ ^your^ dog. Be sure to get out all mats, and work slowly and carefully. Try to keep your

Apply

Always leave time to proofread your essay and to correct any errors in grammar, spelling, capitalization, and punctuation.

FINAL DRAFT

dog still and comfortable. The mats will only get worse when you get the hair wet, so work hard to get them out before you begin.

Then put your dog in the bathtub or area you are using to bathe. Using a large cup or hose, get the dog's body wet from neck to tail. Then carefully wash the dog's rear legs, tail, body, chest, and front legs. Use plenty of soap and rubbing action to get a good lather. Next, wash the dog's head and face. Try to keep soap out of your dog's eyes.

After that, ~~thorol~~ thoroughly rinse all the soap out of your dog's hair. Rinse your dog until the water runs clear and you know all the soap is gone. Leaving soap on your dog will cause itching and skin irritation. If you think you got all the soap out, rinse a little longer just to make sure.

When you have finished rinsing your dog, wrap your dog in a large towel to absorb the water. After that, dry your dog's hair with a blow dryer. Make sure the temperature isn't too hot for your dog. Then brush your dog's hair one last time, making sure there are no mats.

That's it! You have successfully bathed your dog in just a few simple steps!

Reflect

Could you find any mistakes Mya might have missed? Did she include everything in the scoring guide on her test? Remember to use the scoring guide when taking your own writing test.

Now we're all done, and that wasn't so hard after all! Using the setup, task, and scoring guide really helped me write my essay. Remember these important tips—they can help when you're writing for a test.

1. **Analyze the writing prompt before you begin to write.** Remember, the three important parts—setup, task, and scoring guide—may not be labeled. You will have to find and label them.
2. **Follow these steps to be sure you understand the task—before you start writing!**
   - Find and label the setup, task, and scoring guide.
   - Circle key words in the task. Key words tell you what kind of writing you need to do. They may also tell you who your audience is. Say the assignment in your own words to yourself.
   - Read the scoring guide so that you know how your essay will be graded.
3. **Plan your time, and keep an eye on the clock.** Decide how much time you can use for each part of the writing process. Plan your time accordingly. Stick to your plan as closely as you can so that you'll have time to revise and edit your draft.
4. **Check your draft against the scoring guide, at least twice.** Use the scoring guide. Like the rubrics you've used on other essays, the scoring guide tells you what's important. Read your draft to check that it does what the scoring guide says it should do.
5. **Plan, plan, plan!** You don't get much time to revise during a test, so planning is more important than ever.
6. **Don't forget the last step: editing!** Watch out especially for errors you often make, and correct them. Also write neatly so that the people scoring your test can read your essay!

Opinion writing convinces the reader to take action or to have or change an opinion.

Hi, my name is Miles, and I'm learning all about opinion writing. It is really exciting! I have lots of opinions to express about a variety of topics. Now I'll be able to do that better than ever before.

IN THIS UNIT

- Book Review: Response to Literature
- Letter to the Editor
- Opinion Essay
- SCIENCE CONNECTION ▶ Opinion Speech
- Writing for a Test

Name: Miles

Home: New Jersey

Favorite Activities: coin collecting, caring for my pets, and reading

Favorite Food: Thai food

Favorite Sport: basketball

Favorite Subjects: social studies and language arts

Favorite Author: Harriette Gillem Robinet

What's a Response to Literature?

It's when I write my thoughts about what I have read. I will write a book review, which will tell my opinion about a book.

What's in a Response to Literature?

Thesis Statement
My thesis statement tells my opinion of the book and gets the reader interested in learning more about the book.

Quotations and Examples
I'll use quotations and examples from the book to support my opinion and main points.

Story Elements
I want to tell enough about the book so my readers understand what it is about. I need to tell the theme, describe the setting and main characters, and explain the plot.

Why write a Response to Literature?

There are many reasons to write a book review as a way to respond to literature. Here are three I thought of.

Expressing an Opinion
Writers of most book reviews want to share their opinion about a book with readers. The writer might be eager to spread the word about a wonderful new book. Or he or she might hope to warn readers to avoid a book that's poorly written.

Information
Some people read book reviews to find out what new books are about and whether to read one of the reviewed books because the topic interests them.

Deeper Understanding
People who write reviews help themselves remember or understand a book more deeply.

Linking Opinion Writing Traits to a Response to Literature

In this chapter, you will share your opinion about a book you have read. This type of opinion writing is called a response to literature. Miles will guide you through the stages of the writing process: Prewrite, Draft, Revise, Edit, and Publish. In each stage, Miles will show you important writing strategies that are linked to the Opinion Writing Traits below.

Opinion Writing Traits

- a clear opinion in a thesis statement
- strong supporting reasons and facts
- counterclaims anticipated and addressed

- a logical organization: the introduction has an opinion, the body has a strong argument, and the conclusion ends with a summary or call to action
- effective transitions that link opinions and reasons

- a voice and tone that are appropriate for the purpose and audience

- language that is fair, balanced, and precise

- a variety of sentences that add interest to the writing and are easy to read

- no or few errors in grammar, usage, mechanics, and spelling

Before you write, read Sharla Baker's response to literature on the next page. Then use the response to literature rubric on pages 254–255 to decide how well she did. (You might want to look back at What's in a Response to Literature? on page 250, too!)

And Now Miguel

by Joseph Krumgold

reviewed by Sharla Baker

story element: theme

How does a young person prove that he or she is ready for adult responsibilities? This question is the theme of *And Now Miguel* by Joseph Krumgold. This Newbery Award-winning novel is about 12-year-old Miguel Chavez. Miguel himself tells the story. The reader sees everything through his eyes. It is a powerful tale that I strongly recommend.

story element: characters

thesis statement

Miguel and his family live on a sheep ranch in New Mexico. The boy's goal is to join the men of his family when they take the sheep to their summer pasture. The pasture is high in the mountains. Miguel wants to prove that he is ready to share this important responsibility. The story of how he proves it takes place over a year. The setting of majestic mountains adds much to the story.

story element: plot

story element: setting

I felt that the book's greatest strength is its characters. They are interesting and true to life. Miguel's family includes his older brother, Gabriel, whom he admires. A younger brother is named Pedro. A secret that Miguel tells Pedro causes serious problems during the story. Another interesting character is Uncle Eli, a wise, old teacher.

examples

The ways the characters reacted to the plot's events seemed realistic. I also liked how the book showed both good and bad events in their lives. Miguel describes "how the worst thing happened, and then how the best thing happened, and then how everything got mixed up."

quotation

On the other hand, the novel seemed a little long. I also found that the dialogue sometimes sounded phony. Overall, however, *And Now Miguel* is an exciting story of a boy becoming a man. All young people—boys and girls—should read it.

Response to Literature Rubric

Use this 6-point rubric to plan and score a response to literature.

	6	5	4
Ideas	A clearly worded thesis statement states the writer's opinion. The reasons are supported by quotations and examples.	A thesis statement gives the writer's opinion. The reasons are supported by quotations and examples.	The writer includes a thesis statement, but the opinion could be stated more clearly. Most reasons are supported by quotations and examples.
Organization	A strong introduction, body, and conclusion organize the information logically. A concluding paragraph restates the opinion clearly.	An introduction, a body, and a conclusion organize the information logically. A concluding paragraph restates the opinion.	The review has an introduction, a body, and a conclusion, but some information is not logically ordered. The opinion is restated at the end.
Voice	The writer uses a formal, knowledgeable voice that connects with the reader.	The voice is appropriate and connects with the reader most of the time.	The writer uses a formal tone most of the time but sometimes fails to connect with the reader.
Word Choice	The language is fair and balanced. No negative, biased words are used.	The writer uses language that is fair and balanced most of the time.	The writer's language is fair and balanced sometimes. Some negative words are used.
Sentence Fluency	A variety of sentences, including questions, makes the writing flow smoothly.	Most paragraphs have a variety of sentences, including questions.	In some sections, the writing flows poorly because it lacks sentence variety and questions.
Conventions	Spelling, punctuation, and capitalization are correct. Each pronoun refers to a clear antecedent.	There are a few minor errors with pronouns and antecedents, but they do not confuse the reader.	There are a few errors, and a few pronouns have unclear antecedents.
+Presentation	The review is neat and legible.		

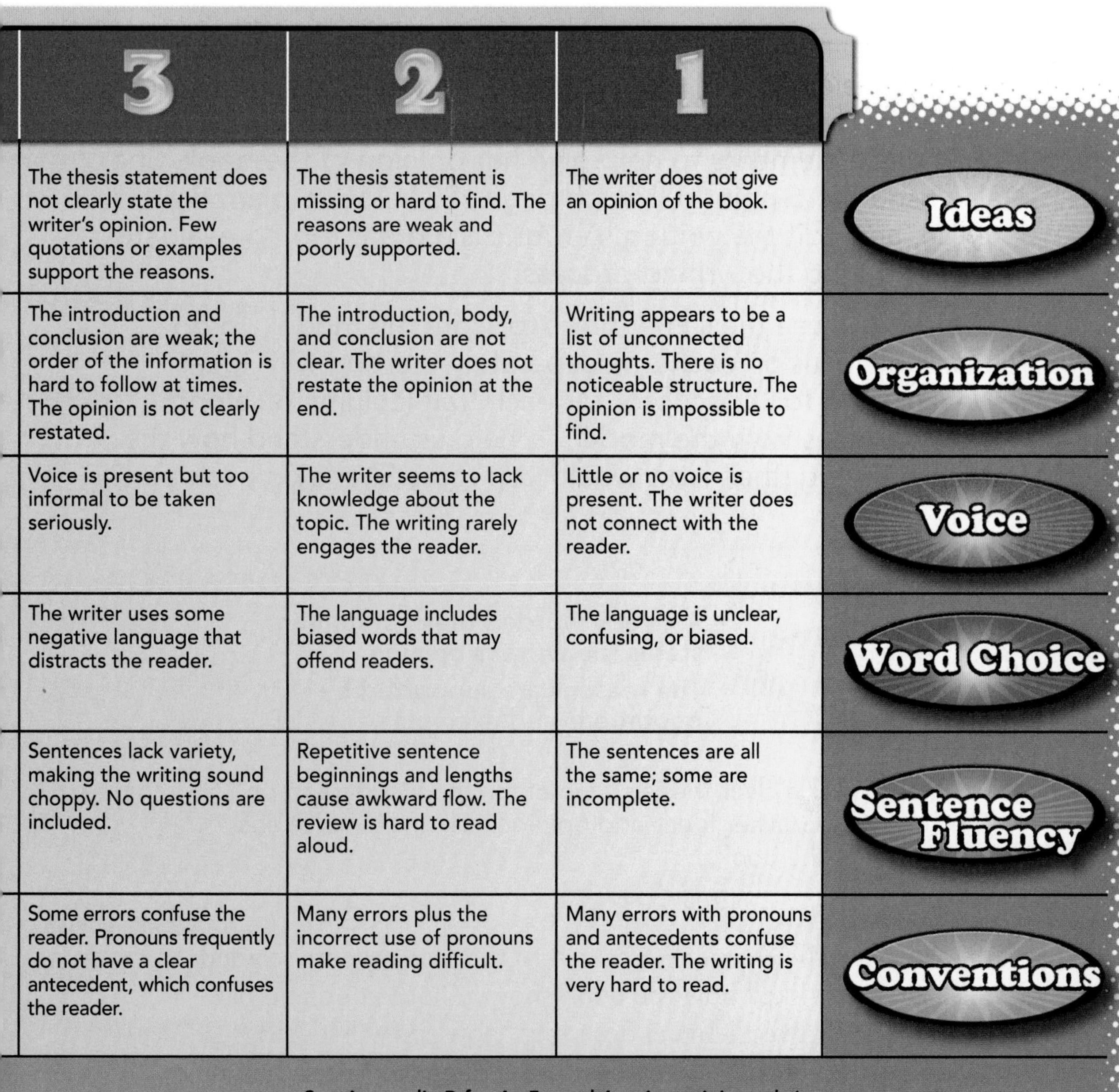

3	2	1	
The thesis statement does not clearly state the writer's opinion. Few quotations or examples support the reasons.	The thesis statement is missing or hard to find. The reasons are weak and poorly supported.	The writer does not give an opinion of the book.	Ideas
The introduction and conclusion are weak; the order of the information is hard to follow at times. The opinion is not clearly restated.	The introduction, body, and conclusion are not clear. The writer does not restate the opinion at the end.	Writing appears to be a list of unconnected thoughts. There is no noticeable structure. The opinion is impossible to find.	Organization
Voice is present but too informal to be taken seriously.	The writer seems to lack knowledge about the topic. The writing rarely engages the reader.	Little or no voice is present. The writer does not connect with the reader.	Voice
The writer uses some negative language that distracts the reader.	The language includes biased words that may offend readers.	The language is unclear, confusing, or biased.	Word Choice
Sentences lack variety, making the writing sound choppy. No questions are included.	Repetitive sentence beginnings and lengths cause awkward flow. The review is hard to read aloud.	The sentences are all the same; some are incomplete.	Sentence Fluency
Some errors confuse the reader. Pronouns frequently do not have a clear antecedent, which confuses the reader.	Many errors plus the incorrect use of pronouns make reading difficult.	Many errors with pronouns and antecedents confuse the reader. The writing is very hard to read.	Conventions

See Appendix B for 4-, 5-, and 6-point opinion rubrics.

Using the Response to Literature Rubric to Study the Model

Did you notice that the model on page 253 points out some key elements of a response to literature? As she wrote her response to literature of *And Now Miguel*, Sharla Baker used these elements to help give her opinion of the book. She also used the 6-point rubric on pages 254–255 to plan, draft, revise, and edit the writing. A rubric is a great tool to evaluate writing during the writing process.

Now let's use the same rubric to score the model. To do this, we'll focus on each trait separately, starting with Ideas. We'll use the top descriptor for each trait (column 6), along with examples from the model, to help us understand how the traits work together. How would you score Sharla on each trait?

- **A clearly worded thesis statement states the writer's opinion.**
- **The reasons are supported by quotations and examples.**

Sharla gives a clear thesis statement in the first paragraph. She then supports her ideas and opinions using examples and a quote from the book.

> The ways the characters reacted to the plot's events seemed realistic. I also liked how the book showed both good and bad events in their lives. Miguel describes "how the worst thing happened, and then how the best thing happened, and then how everything got mixed up."

- **A strong introduction, body, and conclusion organize the information logically.**
- **A concluding paragraph restates the opinion clearly.**

Sharla's introduction, body, and conclusion are strong and well organized. Each paragraph discusses one aspect of the book, giving her opinion of that aspect. Sharla's concluding paragraph adds some information and restates her opinion in clear, strong words. I know just what she thinks about *And Now Miguel*.

On the other hand, the novel seemed a little long. I also found that the dialogue sometimes sounded phony. Overall, however, *And Now Miguel* is an exciting story of a boy becoming a man. All young people—boys and girls—should read it.

- **The writer uses a formal, knowledgeable voice that connects with the reader.**

Sharla explains in a clear and knowledgeable way why she personally recommends the book to the reader.

Miguel himself tells the story. The reader sees everything through his eyes. It is a powerful tale that I strongly recommend.

Response to Literature
Using the Rubric to Study the Model

- **The language is fair and balanced.**
- **No negative, biased words are used.**

After describing many positive features of the book, Sharla notes two concerns. She treats the concerns fairly with her language. She does not offend her readers with negative words.

> On the other hand, the novel seemed a little long. I also found that the dialogue sometimes sounded phony. Overall, however, *And Now Miguel* is an exciting story of a boy becoming a man.

- **A variety of sentences, including questions, makes the writing flow smoothly.**

I know that using questions now and then keeps the pace lively and helps get readers interested in the ideas in the response to literature. Sharla sets the pace by starting off with an interesting question.

> How does a young person prove that he or she is ready for adult responsibilities? This question is the theme of *And Now Miguel* by Joseph Krumgold.

- **Spelling, punctuation, and capitalization are correct. Each pronoun refers to a clear antecedent.**

Sharla proofread her writing carefully. I couldn't find any errors in spelling, punctuation, or capitalization. She also made sure that all pronouns agree with their antecedents in number. In the first paragraph, for example, she is careful with a tricky antecedent. The pronouns *he or she* correctly match the antecedent *young person*.

How does a young person prove that he or she is ready for adult responsibilities?

+Presentation The review is neat and legible.

My Turn!

Now I'm going to write my own book review. Follow along to see how I use the rubric and good writing strategies.

Prewrite

Focus on **Ideas**

The Rubric Says A clearly worded thesis statement states the writer's opinion. The reasons are supported by quotations and examples.

Writing Strategy Take good notes during reading.

My teacher asked us to write a book review, but I couldn't think of a book that I had a strong opinion about. Then my teacher suggested *The Arrow Over the Door* by Joseph Bruchac. This book is based on real events during the American Revolution. After I read the book jacket, I really wanted to read the book. As I read, I took notes about ideas I might want to use in my review.

Notes on The Arrow Over the Door
by Joseph Bruchac

- ✔ Story takes place in 1777 during the Revolutionary War near Saratoga, (upstate) NY.
- ✔ Samuel Russell is young Quaker boy.
- ✔ Stands Straight is Abenaki Indian boy.
- ✔ Story is told from each boy's point of view.
- ✔ Theme: each boy learns about himself, his own strengths, and his people's beliefs.
- ✔ Story contains much interesting information about Quaker and Abenaki traditions and beliefs.

Apply

Pick a book about something that interests you. Take notes on the book's theme, characters, plot, and setting.

Prewrite

Focus on **Organization**

The Rubric Says A strong introduction, body, and conclusion organize the information logically.

Writing Strategy Use a Pros-and-Cons Chart to organize book notes.

After reviewing my notes, I decided to make a Pros-and-Cons Chart to help me remember the things I liked and disliked about the book. The rubric reminds me to organize my writing into an introduction, a body, and a conclusion. The chart will help me place the information in the right order.

Writer's Term

Pros-and-Cons Chart
A Pros-and-Cons Chart shows the positive points (pros) and negative points (cons) about a topic or issue.

Pros-and-Cons Chart

	Pros (what I liked)	**Cons** (what I disliked)
Plot	Two people tell a story, and the stories come together at the end.	Book ended too soon.
Theme	Each boy questions his own beliefs but comes to understand them better.	
Setting	The author uses the setting—upstate New York—to show the loneliness but also the friendliness of the wilderness.	
Characters	I learned how the two boys are similar and different.	
Other	I learned interesting details about Quakers and Abenakis; the author himself is Abenaki.	Author could have told more about some of the other characters.

Reflect

Look at the chart. Why do you think Miles listed so few cons?

Apply

Make a Pros-and-Cons Chart to organize your notes and ideas about your book.

Draft

Focus on **Ideas**

The Rubric Says A clearly worded thesis statement states the writer's opinion.

Writing Strategy State opinion in a thesis statement.

Now I'm ready to use my notes and Pros-and-Cons Chart to draft my book review. The rubric says to give my opinion clearly in my thesis statement. I'll make sure my thesis statement makes it clear why I think the book is a good one.

Then I will tell what I liked, such as the book's theme, which is the author's message. Also I will tell what I did not like, such as not enough details about some of the characters. I won't worry about grammar and spelling too much on this first draft. I can fix errors later. Here's the start of my draft.

Writer's Term

Thesis Statement

A **thesis statement** is the writer's opinion. In an essay or book review, the writer presents points to try to convince the reader that his or her thesis statement is correct.

Proofreading Marks

- Indent
- Make uppercase
- Make lowercase
- Add something
- Take out something
- Add a period
- New paragraph
- Spelling error

[DRAFT]

The Arrow Over the Door
by Joseph Bruchac

reviewed by Miles

Two boys, an American Quaker named Samuel Russell and an Abenaki Indian named Stands Straight, are the main characters in this novel by Joseph Bruchac. The boys are from very different backgrounds. When they meet, they learn about themselves and about other people's fears, hopes, and beliefs. I really liked this book because I could identify with how the boys tried to sort out their feelings and beliefs and better understand them.

thesis statement

The story is told from each boy's point of view. Readers get to know each character's thoughts We find out ways they are similar and ways they are different. The story takes place during the American Revolution. The setting is upstate New york.

Reflect

Read Miles's draft. Does his thesis statement clearly express his opinion? Did he include both pros and cons?

Apply

Use your Pros-and-Cons Chart to draft your book review. Include a strong thesis statement in the first paragraph to involve your readers.

Revise

Focus on **Organization**

The Rubric Says A concluding paragraph restates the opinion clearly.

Writing Strategy Restate the opinion in the conclusion.

Using the rubric, I looked at how I organized paragraphs for the beginning, middle, and conclusion. I thought I did a good job of organizing my information logically for the reader. Then I noticed that I had forgotten to restate my opinion at the end of my review!

I'll add another short paragraph. I'll remind readers that I really liked the book and that they probably will, too.

[DRAFT]

Other readers may agree with me that the book seems to end too soon. I wanted to know more about what happened to Samuel and Stands Straight as the Revolutionary War continued.

Overall, though, The Arrow Over the Door is an excellent novel. I recommend it for anyone who wants to read an exciting and interesting historical novel.

restated opinion

Apply

Make sure your conclusion paragraph restates your opinion of the book.

Revise

Focus on **Voice**

The Rubric Says	The writer uses a formal, knowledgeable voice that connects with the reader.
Writing Strategy	Use the right tone to connect with the reader.

From the rubric, I know that my voice should sound knowledgeable so that the reader trusts my opinion. I think I'll add what I learned about the author and his research. This will let my reader know I read beyond the book.

[DRAFT]

stronger voice

, who is an Abenaki. He has also researched the beliefs and actions of the Quakers during the Revolutionary War.
The two boys' beliefs are well described by the author.

Reflect

Look at the revisions. In what ways do they improve Miles's voice?

Apply

Find places in your review to share information about the author's life and work.

Revise

Focus on **Word Choice**

The Rubric Says The language is fair and balanced. No negative, biased words are used.

Writing Strategy Avoid biased or offensive language.

The rubric reminds me to use fair and balanced words in my review. I found one sentence toward the end where my words sound pretty negative. I don't want any of my readers to take offense to my book review. If that happens, they won't pay attention to my opinion.

I'll revise the sentence so my criticism sounds reasonable and complete.

[DRAFT]

Some readers may feel that the author focuses too closely on the two main characters. They were interesting, but I would have liked to know more about some of the other characters. ~~The worst thing about this book is the author forgot stuff.~~

used fair language

Apply

Look over your draft to find places where your statements could be more balanced and fair.

Edit

Focus on **Conventions**

The Rubric Says Spelling, punctuation, and capitalization are correct. Each pronoun refers to a clear antecedent.

Writing Strategy Make sure all pronouns are used correctly. Check to see that pronouns agree with their antecedents in number.

Now I need to check my spelling, capitalization, and punctuation. The rubric reminds me to check that every pronoun has a clear antecedent and that pronouns and antecedents agree in number. Here are a few of the corrections I made.

Writer's Term

Pronouns and Antecedents

A **pronoun** is a word that replaces a noun. An **antecedent** is the word or phrase that a pronoun replaces.

corrected pronoun-antecedent error

[DRAFT]

To both Samuel and Stands straight, the wilderness is a place where ~~he~~ they can look for answers to ~~his~~ their most puzzling questions.

Reflect

Look at Miles's edits. How do his changes improve the draft and strengthen his writing?

Apply

Conventions

Edit your draft for spelling, punctuation, and capitalization. Check that antecedents are clear and that all pronouns agree with their antecedents.

For more practice with pronouns and antecedents, use the exercises on the next two pages.

Pronoun Antecedents

Know the Rule

The **antecedent** of a pronoun is the word to which the pronoun refers.

Unclear: She checked the books and the reviews and is pleased with **them**. (Does *them* refer to *books* or *reviews*?)

Clear: She checked the **book reviews** and is pleased with **them**.

A **singular antecedent** requires a **singular pronoun**.

Example: Maggie thinks before **she** writes.

A **plural antecedent** requires a **plural pronoun**.

Example: Book reviewers choose **their** books carefully.

Practice the Rule

Number a sheet of paper 1–8. For each sentence, write the antecedent for the underlined pronoun.

1. Quakers are a small group of people, but they have had a strong influence on world history.
2. They consider George Fox to be the founder of their religion, the Society of Friends.
3. Early Quakers faced many challenges. Most English people were suspicious of them.
4. The Quakers refused to remove their hats when an important person passed.
5. Friends also used the familiar words *thee* and *thou* instead of the formal word *you*. Some people still use these words today.
6. Quakers have sometimes suffered for their beliefs in nonviolence.
7. From the start, women participated in the Society. They were considered equal to men.
8. If you meet a Quaker, you might ask her about what it means to be a Friend.

Personal and Possessive Pronouns

Know the Rule

Use the **personal pronouns** *I, me, we,* and *us* to speak or write about yourself.

Example: **We** picked out books to take with **us**.

Use the **personal pronouns** *you, he, him, she, her, it, they,* and *them* to refer to other people and things.

Example: **She** wants to read to **you** on the plane.

The **possessive pronouns** *my, your, his, her, its, our,* and *their* show ownership.

Example: Please bring **your** camera on **our** trip.

Practice the Rule

Find and list all personal pronouns in the following sentences.

1. My favorite books are mostly nonfiction, but one novel pulled me right in.
2. The novel he planned to review was suggested by his teacher.
3. Ann saw her teacher and asked him if she should choose another book.
4. They say that you can't judge a book by its cover, but sometimes you can.
5. We chose our books at the library, and most of them were fiction.

Now find and list all possessive pronouns in the following sentences.

6. I wrote my book review about *Jip: His Story* by Katherine Paterson.
7. My book and your book are both novels, but their themes are different.
8. Her book review changed my view about the future of our planet.
9. Would you want to read a book if its title was the name of your baby brother?
10. He decided to write his next book review about a biography.

Publish +Presentation

Publishing Strategy Submit the book review to a literary magazine.

Presentation Strategy Choose one or two clear fonts.

That's it! I've written my book review. I'm going to send my book review to our school district's literary magazine. This magazine publishes work by students like me. Now other kids can read my review and decide whether to read *The Arrow Over the Door.* I want my review to look professional to impress the magazine editors. I'll use just one or two clear fonts so that my writing will look clean and neat, not busy.

Before I send my review, I'll read it one more time, and I'll check that my work is neat. I'll use this checklist to make sure it's ready to be published.

My Final Checklist

Did I—

- ✔ check to make sure my pronouns are correct?
- ✔ check to make sure my antecedents are clear?
- ✔ name the book and the author?
- ✔ add my name as reviewer?
- ✔ use neat handwriting or word processing?

Apply

Use the checklist to prepare your final copy. Think about ways to publish your review.

The Arrow Over the Door
by Joseph Bruchac

reviewed by Miles

Two boys, an American Quaker named Samuel Russell and an Abenaki Indian named Stands Straight, are the main characters in this novel by Joseph Bruchac. The boys are from very different backgrounds. When they meet, they learn about themselves and about other people's fears, hopes, and beliefs. I really liked this book because I could identify with how the boys tried to sort out their feelings and beliefs and better understand them.

The story is told from each boy's point of view. Readers get to know each character's thoughts and feelings. We find out ways they are similar and ways they are different. The story takes place during the American Revolution. The setting is upstate New York.

A battle is coming. Samuel doubts that the Quakers' belief in nonviolence will be able to keep them from harm. Should he use a weapon to defend his people if danger approaches? The book focuses on his struggle to understand the beliefs of his Quaker people.

At the same time, Stands Straight questions the Abenakis' part in the war. Why have their leaders decided to fight for King George and against the Americans? They will be fighting people they do not know. How can he bring himself to make war against the young white boy? Samuel seems almost like his brother.

The two boys' beliefs are well described by the author, who is an Abenaki. He has also researched the beliefs and actions of the Quakers during the Revolutionary War. Bruchac's understanding of the two cultures is part of what makes this book special.

The language of the characters adds a lot to the story. For example, Samuel's parents know that he is worried. "What is troubling thy heart, Samuel?" his mother asks. Samuel is concerned about how his peace-loving family will react to the battle that will soon take place.

The author's use of setting is especially interesting. To both Samuel and Stands Straight, the wilderness is a place where they can look for answers to their most puzzling questions. In one scene, Samuel looks into a sparkling brook at his reflection. He feels unhappy and confused about his life and future. "He stared at it, wondering how another face might look," writes Bruchac. In another scene, Stands Straight prays to Elder Brother Sun. "I asked our Elder Brother if it is really war that he wants for us."

I have only a few criticisms of the novel. Some readers may feel that the author focuses too closely on the two main characters. They were interesting, but I would have liked to know more about some of the other characters. I was especially interested in the Quaker visitor, Robert Nisbet, and the Abenaki leader, Sees-the-Wind. Other readers may agree with me that the book seems to end too soon. I wanted to know more about what happened to Samuel and Stands Straight as the Revolutionary War continued.

Overall, though, *The Arrow Over the Door* is an excellent novel. I recommend it for anyone who wants to read an exciting and interesting historical novel.

Reflect

Use the rubric to score this review. What are some ways that it shows the traits of a good book review? Be sure to use the rubric to score your own review.

What's a Letter to the Editor?

That's a letter I write to a newspaper or magazine giving my opinion about a recent story or event.

What's in a Letter to the Editor?

Timely Topic
That's what I'm writing about. It should be a current topic or event. I might write about student council elections at my school or about something happening in my neighborhood.

My Opinion
That's how I feel about the topic. I'll try to convince readers that my opinion is correct.

Summary of the Argument
I'll sum up the reasons for my opinion at the end of my letter.

Supporting Reasons and Facts
I'll explain my reasons for my opinion and offer facts that support it.

The Six Parts of a Business Letter
That's the format—certain words and information I need to write and where I put them on the page. The six parts of a business letter are the heading, inside address, salutation, body, closing, and signature.

Why write a Letter to the Editor?

There are many reasons to write a letter to the editor. Here are a few.

Reaching Readers
People write letters to the editor to convince others to share their opinions. If a letter to the editor is published in a newspaper or magazine, many people will read it.

Expression
Citizens write letters to the editor of a local newspaper to express opinions about recent news items. The topic could be about schools, government, sports, or arts.

Linking Opinion Writing Traits to a Letter to the Editor

In this chapter, you will write a letter to convince the readers of a magazine or newspaper to agree with you about an important issue. This type of opinion writing is called a letter to the editor. Miles will guide you through the stages of the writing process: Prewrite, Draft, Revise, Edit, and Publish. In each stage, Miles will show you important letter-writing strategies that are linked to the Opinion Writing Traits below.

Opinion Writing Traits

- a clear opinion in a thesis statement
- strong supporting reasons and facts
- counterclaims anticipated and addressed

- a logical organization: the introduction has an opinion, the body has a strong argument, and the conclusion ends with a summary or call to action
- effective transitions that link opinions and reasons

- a voice and tone that are appropriate for the purpose and audience

- language that is fair, balanced, and precise

- a variety of sentences that add interest to the writing and are easy to read

- no or few errors in grammar, usage, mechanics, and spelling

Before you write, read Cody Allen's letter to the editor on the next page. Then use the letter to the editor rubric on pages 278–279 to decide how well he did. (You might want to look back at What's in a Letter to the Editor? on page 274, too!)

heading

114 Essex Street
Northville, OH 430—
October 16, 2012

Editor, *Northville Gazette*
1455 Washington Boulevard
Northville, OH 430—

salutation

Dear Editor:

timely topic

opinion

I am writing to address a serious problem. It is the lack of a town recycling program. Many cities and towns around the nation have recycling programs. Yet our town is one of the few without one. We are missing a great chance to save energy. We could also be lowering pollution and cutting down on the amount of trash going to our landfills. In addition, we could earn money for important community programs.

supporting reasons and facts

The most important reason to recycle is to save energy by reusing materials. Did you know that recycling a ton of paper saves 7,000 gallons of water? This water would have been used to produce new paper.

Did you know that recycling just one aluminum can saves energy? It is enough energy to run a computer for three hours! Did you know that recycling just one glass bottle can save energy? This energy can power a 100-watt light bulb for four hours!

When we conserve energy, power plants need to produce less energy. As a result, there is less pollution in our air. When we reuse materials, we send less trash to landfills. Finally, our town can sell the materials we recycle. In this way, we can earn money for programs we need and want.

summary of argument

Nearly 90 percent of all Americans recycle. However, our community does not. Who knows how many valuable resources we are throwing away every day? Now is the time to take this important step toward saving our environment and improving our community!

closing

Sincerely,

signature

Cody Allen

Cody Allen

Letter to the Editor Rubric

Use this 6-point rubric to plan and score a letter to the editor.

	6	5	4
Ideas	The writer's opinion is supported by valid reasons and facts. The argument includes a clear call to action.	Most of the writer's reasons and many facts are supported. The call to action is clear.	The writer shares at least three facts to support the viewpoint. There is a call to action.
Organization	Logically ordered reasons and smooth transitions move the reader along from beginning to end.	Reasons are presented in a logical order, and most transitions are smooth.	Most reasons are presented in a logical order. Some transitions are unclear.
Voice	The writer's sincere, knowledgeable voice convinces the reader.	The writer's voice is sincere and knowledgeable and connects with the reader.	The voice is usually appropriate and connects with the reader most of the time.
Word Choice	The writer uses specific language that supports the message.	The writer uses specific language. Nearly all the words support the message.	In a few places, the language is less specific or not connected to the message.
Sentence Fluency	A variety of sentences and transitions gives the writing rhythm and flow.	Variety in sentence length and structure is noticeable and appealing. It may need more effective transitions.	Some repetitive sentence beginnings and structures make parts awkward. Some transitions are weak.
Conventions	There are no sentence fragments. Initials and abbreviations are used correctly.	There are no sentence fragments. There are a few minor errors with initials and abbreviations.	There are a few sentence fragments and errors with initials and abbreviations.

+Presentation The letter is in proper business-letter format.

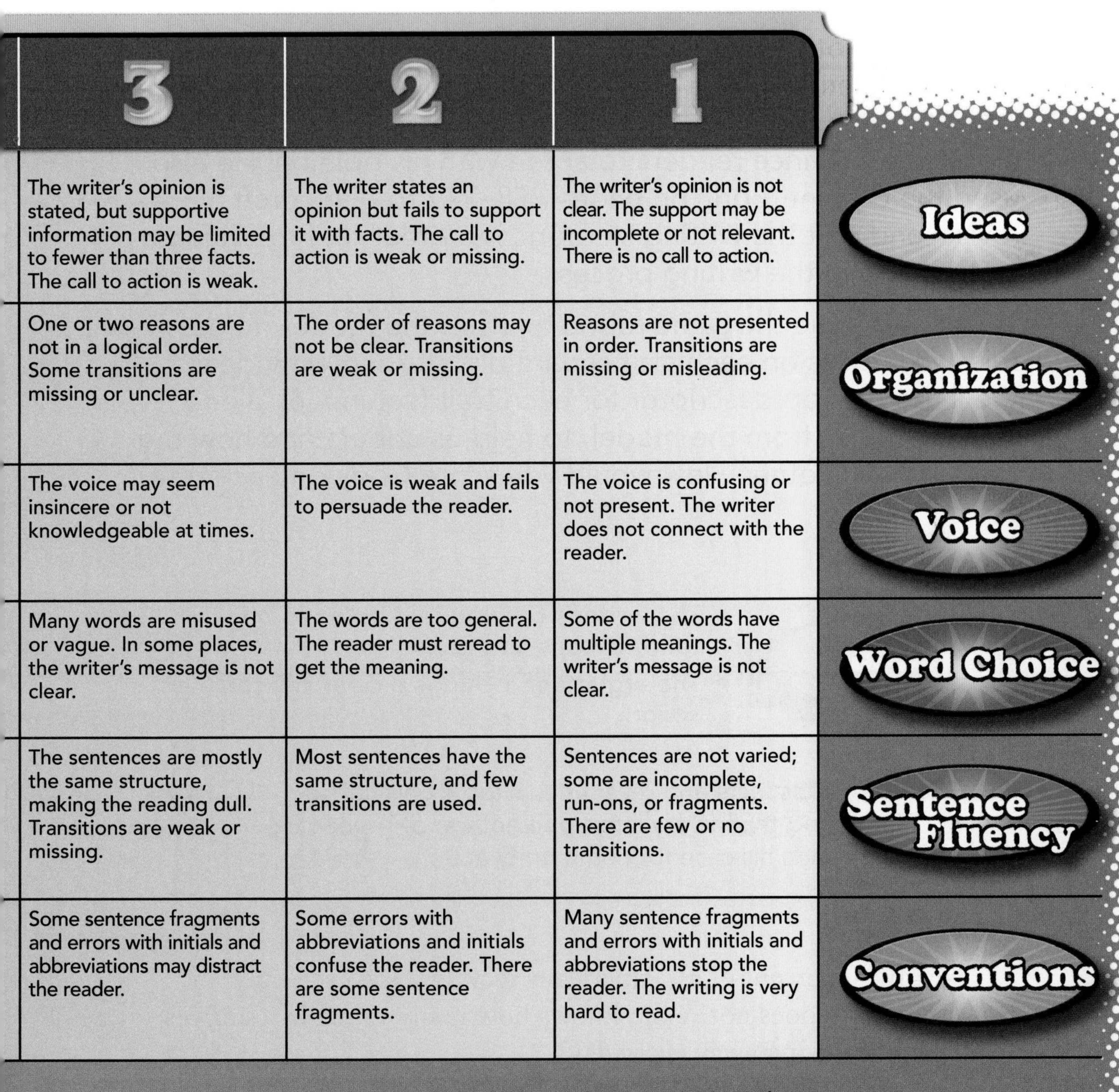

3	2	1	
The writer's opinion is stated, but supportive information may be limited to fewer than three facts. The call to action is weak.	The writer states an opinion but fails to support it with facts. The call to action is weak or missing.	The writer's opinion is not clear. The support may be incomplete or not relevant. There is no call to action.	Ideas
One or two reasons are not in a logical order. Some transitions are missing or unclear.	The order of reasons may not be clear. Transitions are weak or missing.	Reasons are not presented in order. Transitions are missing or misleading.	Organization
The voice may seem insincere or not knowledgeable at times.	The voice is weak and fails to persuade the reader.	The voice is confusing or not present. The writer does not connect with the reader.	Voice
Many words are misused or vague. In some places, the writer's message is not clear.	The words are too general. The reader must reread to get the meaning.	Some of the words have multiple meanings. The writer's message is not clear.	Word Choice
The sentences are mostly the same structure, making the reading dull. Transitions are weak or missing.	Most sentences have the same structure, and few transitions are used.	Sentences are not varied; some are incomplete, run-ons, or fragments. There are few or no transitions.	Sentence Fluency
Some sentence fragments and errors with initials and abbreviations may distract the reader.	Some errors with abbreviations and initials confuse the reader. There are some sentence fragments.	Many sentence fragments and errors with initials and abbreviations stop the reader. The writing is very hard to read.	Conventions

See Appendix B for 4-, 5-, and 6-point opinion rubrics.

Using the Letter to the Editor Rubric to Study the Model

Did you notice that the model on page 277 points out some key elements of a letter to the editor? As he wrote his letter to the editor, Cody Allen used these elements to help him try to convince readers to agree with his opinion. He also used the 6-point rubric on pages 278–279 to plan, draft, revise, and edit the writing. A rubric is a great tool to evaluate writing during the writing process.

Now let's use the same rubric to score the model. To do this, we'll focus on each trait separately, starting with Ideas. We'll use the top descriptor for each trait (column 6), along with examples from the model, to help us understand how the traits work together. How would you score Cody on each trait?

- **The writer's opinion is supported by valid reasons and facts.**
- **The argument includes a clear call to action.**

Cody includes facts and reasons to support his call for action. By noting that a very large percentage of Americans recycle, he builds his case for community action.

> Nearly 90 percent of all Americans recycle. However, our community does not. Who knows how many valuable resources we are throwing away every day?

- **Logically ordered reasons and smooth transitions move the reader along from beginning to end.**

Cody organizes his ideas by order of importance. He chose to put his most important reason first. Transition words such as *finally* and *in this way* guide the reader to the conclusion.

Finally, our town can sell the materials we recycle. In this way, we can earn money for programs we need and want.

- **The writer's sincere, knowledgeable voice convinces the reader.**

Cody uses the pronouns *we* and *our*, reminding readers that he is part of the community. This gives his voice a sincere, convincing tone that persuades the reader.

We are missing a great chance to save energy. We could also be lowering pollution and cutting down on the amount of trash going to our landfills. In addition, we could earn money for important community programs.

Letter to the Editor

Using the Rubric to Study the Model

- The writer uses specific language that supports the message.

Cody has chosen his words carefully to make his message clear and precise. He uses specific words such as *reusing* and *recycling* to make his meaning clear to the reader.

The most important reason to recycle is to save energy by reusing materials. Did you know that recycling a ton of paper saves 7,000 gallons of water?

- A variety of sentences and transitions gives the writing rhythm and flow.

Cody uses a lively rhythm of questions and exclamations to convey information. A variety of sentences keeps the reader interested and the writing flowing at a good pace.

Did you know that recycling just one aluminum can saves energy? It is enough energy to run a computer for three hours!

- **There are no sentence fragments.**
- **Initials and abbreviations are used correctly.**

I don't see any spelling, punctuation, or capitalization errors in Cody's letter. I don't see any sentence fragments, and abbreviations in the addresses are correctly punctuated.

When we conserve energy, power plants need to produce less energy. As a result, there is less pollution in our air.

+Presentation The letter is in proper business-letter format.

My Turn!

Now it's my turn to write a letter to the editor! I'll use the rubric and good writing strategies to help me. Follow along with me.

Prewrite

Focus on **Ideas**

The Rubric Says The writer's opinion is supported by valid reasons and facts.

Writing Strategy Read and listen to others to form an opinion about a topic.

Our local animal shelter doesn't have enough money or staff to care for animals properly. I decided to write a letter to the editor to persuade people to donate time and money to keep the shelter open!

Writer's Term

Opinion

An **opinion** is a belief, often strong, that cannot be proven to be true.

My letter needed solid information to be convincing. The librarian helped me find information on the Internet, and I went to the shelter and talked to the people there. Here are some of the notes I took on what I learned.

My Notes About the Local Animal Shelter

- The shelter finds homes for animals, helps people find lost pets, helps control rabies and other diseases, and investigates pet abuse and neglect.
- The shelter is understaffed. Cages get cleaned only once a week. Animals get little time outside their cages.
- The shelter needs volunteers to care for and play with the animals, clean cages and play areas, and raise money.

Apply

Choose an opinion about something timely and important that you'd like to convince others to share. Learn all you can about your topic and write notes about what you learn.

Prewrite

Focus on **Organization**

The Rubric Says Logically ordered reasons and smooth transitions move the reader along from beginning to end.

Writing Strategy Use an Outline to organize ideas.

I've got some great notes on the animal shelter. The rubric reminds me to put my reasons in a logical order. I am going to organize them from most important to least important. I decided to use an Outline to do that. I've got three main reasons. I'll put my most important one first.

Writer's Term

Outline

An **Outline** shows the main points or reasons and supporting details or facts in a piece of writing. Each main point or reason should have a Roman numeral. Each supporting detail or fact should have a capital letter.

Outline

I. The shelter provides important services.
   A. It finds homes for animals.
   B. It helps people find lost pets.
II. Staff is working hard, but there aren't enough people.
   A. There is only one staff person for every 40 animals.
   B. Cages get cleaned only once a week.
III. Community is not helping enough with money.
   A. Shelter needs more equipment and supplies.
   B. Our town spends more on holiday decorations.

Reflect

Look at Miles's Outline. How are the ideas organized?

Apply

Create an Outline using your notes. List your reasons from most important to least important.

Draft

Focus on **Organization**

The Rubric Says Logically ordered reasons and smooth transitions move the reader along from beginning to end.

Writing Strategy Organize ideas from most important to least important.

Now that I have my Outline, I'm ready to write a draft of my letter. I have to present my reasons in the best order to convince my reader. The fate of the animal shelter is at stake! I'll use transitions, such as *but* or *however*, to connect my ideas so the reader can follow them. I also need to make sure my letter is in the right format.

Here are two parts of my letter. I'll proofread my entire draft later for mistakes.

Writer's Term

Business Letters

A letter to the editor is one kind of business letter. It contains six parts:

- the **heading,** which gives your address and the date
- the **inside address,** which gives your reader's name and address
- the **salutation,** followed by a colon (Dear Editor:)
- the **body,** or your message
- the **closing,** followed by a comma (Sincerely,)
- your **signature,** with your typed name under it

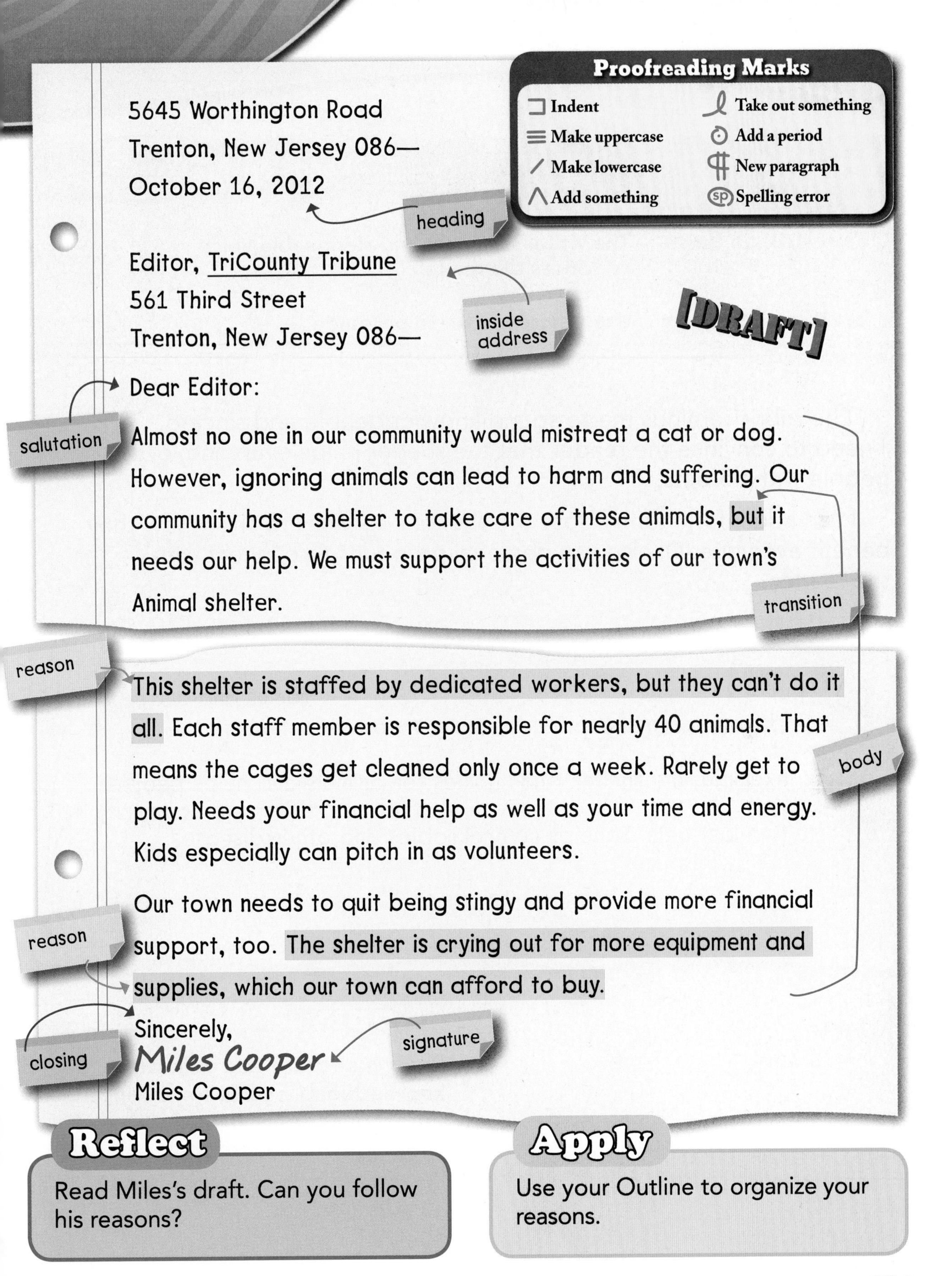

5645 Worthington Road
Trenton, New Jersey 086—
October 16, 2012

Editor, TriCounty Tribune
561 Third Street
Trenton, New Jersey 086—

Dear Editor:

Almost no one in our community would mistreat a cat or dog. However, ignoring animals can lead to harm and suffering. Our community has a shelter to take care of these animals, but it needs our help. We must support the activities of our town's Animal shelter.

This shelter is staffed by dedicated workers, but they can't do it all. Each staff member is responsible for nearly 40 animals. That means the cages get cleaned only once a week. Rarely get to play. Needs your financial help as well as your time and energy. Kids especially can pitch in as volunteers.

Our town needs to quit being stingy and provide more financial support, too. The shelter is crying out for more equipment and supplies, which our town can afford to buy.

Sincerely,
Miles Cooper
Miles Cooper

Reflect

Read Miles's draft. Can you follow his reasons?

Apply

Use your Outline to organize your reasons.

Revise

Focus on **Voice**

The Rubric Says The writer's sincere, knowledgeable voice convinces the reader.

Writing Strategy Use a sincere tone to persuade.

The rubric reminds me to sound knowledgeable and sincere. I need to convince the reader that the shelter helps everyone, even people with no pets.

I can add information about the shelter's services to show how they benefit everyone. I'll also use personal pronouns to connect with the reader.

[DRAFT]

The animal shelter provides many important services ^for us and our pets^. For example, the shelter finds homes for animals and helps people find lost pets. It helps control rabies and other diseases ^that can affect our community^.

added voice

Apply

Read your draft. Use a sincere, knowledgeable voice to convince the reader.

Revise

Focus on Word Choice

The Rubric Says	The writer uses specific language that supports the message.
Writing Strategy	Use words that are appropriate for the purpose.

As I reread my letter, I thought about my word choices. My purpose is to convince readers to help the shelter somehow. Making readers angry would harm my purpose, so I took out words that could hurt someone's feelings or have the wrong tone for a newspaper. Now there is a better chance that people will really want to help.

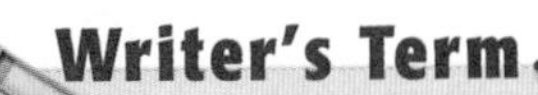

Purpose

Purpose is the specific reason a person has for writing.

used appropriate words

Our town needs to ~~quit being stingy and~~ provide more financial support, too. The shelter needs ~~is crying out for~~ more equipment and supplies, which our town can afford to buy.

Reflect

Look at the changes in the lines above. How do you think they make a difference to the reader?

Apply

Look at your draft again. Find places to add specific language that supports your message.

Revise

Focus on **Sentence Fluency**

The Rubric Says A variety of sentences and transitions gives the writing rhythm and flow.

Writing Strategy Use a variety of sentence lengths.

The rubric says I should use a variety of sentences and transitions to give my writing rhythm and flow. If I use nothing but long sentences, my writing will be dull. If I use nothing but short sentences, my writing will be choppy. If I use a variety of sentence lengths, my writing will flow and be enjoyable to read. I've found a paragraph with two long, dull sentences in a row. I'll break them up to create rhythm and flow. I'll also add an exclamation to grab readers' interest.

The shelter ~~is crying out for~~ needs more equipment and supplies~~,~~. ~~which our town can afford to buy~~ Our town can afford it. We now spend more on holiday decorations than we spend on the shelter~~,~~. ~~which is a situation that we must change~~ This must change!

added short sentences

Apply

Read your draft. Break up some long sentences to add variety.

Edit

Focus on Conventions

The Rubric Says There are no sentence fragments. Initials and abbreviations are used correctly.

Writing Strategy Check for complete sentences and use abbreviations and initials correctly.

I'm ready to check my draft now for spelling, punctuation, and capitalization. The rubric says I should also look for sentence fragments. Sometimes I am writing so fast that I don't write in complete sentences! I'll fix any fragments I find.

Writer's Term

Sentence Fragments

A complete sentence has a subject and a verb. A **sentence fragment** is missing either a subject or a verb. It does not state a complete thought.

corrected sentence fragments

[DRAFT]

Each staff member is responsible for nearly 40 animals. That means the cages get cleaned only once a week. The animals rarely get to play. Staff director J.D. Holmes says they need your financial help as well as your time and energy. Kids especially can pitch in as volunteers.

Reflect

Look at the edits. How do they improve this part of the letter?

Apply

Conventions

Edit your draft for spelling, punctuation, and capitalization. Correct any sentence fragments.

For practice fixing sentence fragments and abbreviations, use the exercises on the next two pages.

Sentence Fragments

Know the Rule

A **complete sentence** has both a subject and a verb and expresses a complete thought. If a group of words is punctuated like a sentence but lacks either a subject or a verb, it is a **sentence fragment**.

Examples:

Sentence Fragment: Shelters in many communities throughout the state. (a subject without a verb)

Sentence Fragment: Are working hard to come up with new ideas. (a verb without a subject)

Complete Sentence: Many **experts have** ideas for solving the problem of stray animals. (a complete sentence with both a subject and a verb)

Practice the Rule

Number a sheet of paper 1–10. Write **Correct** if the sentence is complete. If it is a sentence fragment, write **S** if the subject is missing. Write **V** if the verb is missing.

1. The Humane Society of the United States is the world's largest animal protection organization.
2. Has millions of supporters around the country.
3. Was founded in 1954.
4. The staff includes veterinarians, scientists, and lawyers.
5. The Society's focus on companion animals, such as dogs and cats.
6. Helps to train animal shelter workers.
7. Work with police and judges to prevent animal abuse.
8. Opposes cruel methods of hunting and trapping.
9. Humane Society International is a worldwide organization.
10. Also supports a youth education division.

Initials and Abbreviations

Know the Rule

An **abbreviation** is a shortened form of a word. **Titles of respect** such as *Doctor of Philosophy* (*Ph.D.*) are usually abbreviated. **Days of the week** and **months of the year** are often abbreviated. **Kinds of businesses** such as *Real Company* (*Co.*) and *Ace, Incorporated* (*Inc.*) are often abbreviated. Words in **addresses** such as *Street* (*St.*), *Avenue* (*Ave.*), and *Court* (*Ct.*) are usually abbreviated. Most abbreviations begin with a capital letter and end with a period. The two-letter postal abbreviations for states and *USA* are not punctuated.

An **initial** takes the place of a name. It is usually written as a capital letter followed by a period (*Maria E. Sanchez*).

Practice the Rule

Number a sheet of paper 1–10. Look at the lines below. Write the abbreviations for the words in dark print. Punctuate initials correctly.

1. **Monday**
2. **February**
3. MG Greenwald
4. 42 Bond **Street**
5. **Mister** Frank Jones
6. Frank Jones **Junior**
7. Zaner-Bloser, **Incorporated**
8. EE Cummings
9. Denver, **Colorado**
10. **United States of America**

Publish

+Presentation

Publishing Strategy Submit the letter to a newspaper or magazine.

Presentation Strategy Use proper business-letter format.

My letter to the editor is almost ready to send! It's going to my city newspaper's editor, so it has to have the proper format of a business letter. The parts of a business letter are the heading, inside address, salutation, body, closing, and signature. Before I send it in, however, I'm going to look it over one last time, using my final checklist.

My Final Checklist

Did I—

- ✔ correct sentence fragments?
- ✔ use abbreviations correctly?
- ✔ check my spelling, punctuation, and capitalization?
- ✔ double-check the addresses?
- ✔ include all the parts of a business letter?

Apply

Use this checklist to prepare your final copy. Then submit your letter to a newspaper or magazine.

5645 Worthington Road
Trenton, NJ 086—
October 16, 2012

Editor, *TriCounty Tribune*
561 Third Street
Trenton, NJ 086—

Dear Editor:

Almost no one in our community would mistreat a cat or dog. However, ignoring animals can lead to harm and suffering. Our community has a shelter to take care of these animals, but it needs our help. We must support the activities of our town's animal shelter. The shelter is a valuable but neglected resource in our community.

The animal shelter provides many important services for us and our pets. For example, the shelter finds homes for animals and helps people find lost pets. It helps control rabies and other diseases that can affect our community. In addition, it investigates pet abuse and neglect. All of these services require money, as well as people, to carry them out.

This shelter is staffed by dedicated workers, but they can't do it all. Each staff member is responsible for nearly 40 animals. That means the cages get cleaned only once a week. The animals rarely get to play. Staff Director J.D. Holmes says they need your financial help as well as your time and energy. Kids especially can pitch in as volunteers.

Our town needs to provide more financial support, too. The shelter needs more equipment and supplies. Our town can afford it. We now spend more on holiday decorations than we spend on the shelter. This must change!

Our community is good and caring. We must make sure this caring includes our pets. The best way to do this is to support our animal shelter. Students can help by feeding and playing with the animals, cleaning cages, and raising money. They can also tell people about the shelter. Call 555-8943 to see what you can do.

Sincerely,

Miles Cooper

Miles Cooper

Reflect

Use the rubric to score the letter. Did Miles use all the traits well? Then use the rubric to check your own letter.

What's an Opinion Essay?

It's an essay that states an opinion and gives reasons to support it.

What's in an Opinion Essay?

Introduction
That's my first paragraph. In it I'll state my opinion about something. I may run for student council president. I could write to convince other students to vote for me!

Claim
A claim is the writer's opinion. A good claim is supported by reasons and evidence. I'll develop my claim in the body of my essay.

Opposing Claim
An opposing claim is a point that might be made by someone who disagrees with me. It's important to mention opposing claims and explain why my opinion makes better sense.

Conclusion
That's my last paragraph. It's where I'll restate my opinion and sum up my argument.

MILES for PRESIDENT

VOTE FOR MILES

Why write an Opinion Essay?

There are many reasons to write an opinion essay. Here are a few I thought of.

Convincing
If I have a strong opinion about a subject, I want to try to convince others to agree with me. If enough of us agree, we might take action to try to change or improve a situation.

Explanation
I can use an opinion essay to explain why a topic is important to me or why I hold a certain opinion. This lets me share my thoughts with other people. It also might help me educate them on a topic they didn't know about before.

Understanding
Writing an essay is a good way to examine my own thoughts. As I lay out my argument and reasons, I understand better how I feel and why I feel that way. As I research details to support my reasons, I can also learn more about my topic.

Linking Opinion Writing Traits to an Opinion Essay

In this chapter, you will explain your opinion about a topic you care about. This type of opinion writing is called an opinion essay. Miles will guide you through the stages of the writing process: Prewrite, Draft, Revise, Edit, and Publish. In each stage, Miles will show you important writing strategies that are linked to the Opinion Writing Traits below.

Opinion Writing Traits

- a clear opinion in a thesis statement
- strong supporting reasons and facts
- counterclaims anticipated and addressed

- a logical organization: the introduction has an opinion, the body has a strong argument, and the conclusion ends with a summary or call to action
- effective transitions that link opinions and reasons

- a voice and tone that are appropriate for the purpose and audience

- language that is fair, balanced, and precise

- a variety of sentences that add interest to the writing and are easy to read

- no or few errors in grammar, usage, mechanics, and spelling

Before you write, read Carl Waggoner's opinion essay on the next page. Then use the opinion essay rubric on pages 300–301 to decide how well he did. (You might want to look back at What's in an Opinion Essay? on page 296, too!)

The Arts Belong in Every School

Opinion MODEL Essay

by Carl Waggoner

introduction

A good education is important. That's why children go to school. School is where they learn to read, write, and do math. It's also a place where many kids start thinking about what kind of work they want to do and how to live good lives. Learning about the arts helps kids develop skills they can use in any job, as well as skills they need for life. The arts should be a part of every student's education.

claim

The idea that only children who want to be performers and painters should take arts classes is like thinking that only students who plan to become doctors should take science! Children who take music and art classes in school learn skills they can use in all kinds of jobs. In music class, children learn about sounds and rhythms. They also learn about other cultures by listening to their music. In art class, children work with paint and clay and even computers. They look at colors, shapes, and lines, and they see how the little details can make a big difference. Many fields, such as law, teaching, and medicine, require good listening and looking skills. For example, doctors have to listen carefully and look closely to tell what is wrong with their patients.

opposing claim

Music and art also help children develop life skills. Children use their imaginations when they make art. A good imagination makes life more interesting. Who hasn't turned a long car ride or a rainy day into something fun by using imaginative games? A good imagination also helps us solve problems. An actor in a play has to imagine how his character feels. A musician on stage has to imagine how she wants the song to sound. The artist who designs a poster for a soccer team imagines what colors, pictures, and words will make people want to come to a game. A good imagination helps people do many things. Moms and dads use their imaginations to turn food they buy into delicious dinners. Teachers engage students' interest by creating games to learn grammar or math concepts. In business, salespeople come up with imaginative ad campaigns to promote products. A good imagination helps us see things from another person's point of view, and that helps all of us get along with each other.

conclusion

It's true. The arts are fun, interesting, and useful. The arts are an important part of every education, and they belong in every school.

Opinion Essay Rubric

Use this 6-point rubric to plan and score an opinion essay.

	6	5	4
Ideas	The writer presents a thoughtful, well-supported opinion. Opposing claims are addressed.	The writer expresses a clear opinion. Some examples need more explanation. At least one opposing claim is addressed.	The writer's opinion is clear and supported. More examples are needed. An opposing claim is presented but not addressed.
Organization	Reasons and their supporting details are well organized from beginning to end. The conclusion summarizes the opinion.	Most of the reasons and supporting details are well organized. The conclusion summarizes the opinion.	A few sections are not logically organized. The conclusion tries to summarize the argument, but it is not clear.
Voice	The writer uses a knowledgeable, convincing voice and speaks directly to the reader.	The writer uses an appropriate voice and connects with the reader most of the time.	The writer's knowledge and commitment are present in places. The voice connects with the reader sometimes.
Word Choice	Carefully chosen words with strong connotations convince the reader.	Vivid words with strong connotations support the message most of the time.	Some words are dull, have weak connotations, or do not support the message.
Sentence Fluency	The sentence structures are clear, complete, and varied. The essay is enjoyable to read.	The structure of most sentences adds to the flow of the writing.	The writing is easy to read in some places. Some sentences vary in length, sentence beginning, and structure.
Conventions	Adjectives and adverbs are used correctly. The essay is easy to read and understand.	There are a few minor errors with adjectives and adverbs, but they do not confuse the reader.	Several minor errors with adjectives and adverbs do not make the essay hard to read but may confuse the reader in places.

+Presentation Indent each new paragraph.

	3	2	1
Ideas	The writer's position may not be clear, or it may need more supporting examples. An opposing claim is presented but not clear.	The writer's opinion is not supported. No opposing claim is presented.	The writer does not express an opinion that the reader can identify.
Organization	The organization of the reasons and supporting details is often not logical. The conclusion may not summarize the argument.	The essay is poorly organized and hard to follow. There is no summary of the argument.	The writer has not attempted to organize the essay. There is no summary of the argument.
Voice	The voice is often not convincing. The reader has a hard time connecting with the writer.	The voice is weak. The writing lacks energy or passion and falls flat.	The voice does not match the writer's purpose or connect with the reader.
Word Choice	Ordinary or overused words weaken the writer's opinion.	Dull words with weak or poor connotations fail to connect with the reader.	Word choice is very limited, repetitive, and not convincing.
Sentence Fluency	Some weak and repetitive sentence structures interfere with the writer's message.	Many sentences are awkward and the same length. There are some run-ons and fragments.	Most of the sentences have the same structure or are incomplete.
Conventions	Some errors confuse the reader. Adjectives and/or adverbs may have been used incorrectly.	Many serious errors stop the reader. Adverbs, if used, are not correct.	Many serious, repeated errors with adjectives and adverbs make the essay hard to read and understand.

See Appendix B for 4-, 5-, and 6-point opinion rubrics.

Opinion Essay Using the Rubric to Study the Model

Did you notice that the model on page 299 points out some key elements of an opinion essay? As he wrote his opinion essay, Carl Waggoner used these elements to help him try to convince readers to agree with his opinion. He also used the 6-point rubric on pages 300–301 to plan, draft, revise, and edit the writing. A rubric is a great tool to evaluate writing during the writing process.

Now let's use the same rubric to score the model. To do this, we'll focus on each trait separately, starting with Ideas. We'll use the top descriptor for each trait (column 6), along with examples from the model, to help us understand how the traits work together. How would you score Carl on each trait?

- **The writer presents a thoughtful, well-supported opinion.**
- **Opposing claims are addressed.**

Carl states a strong opinion in the introduction. Then he addresses and answers a counterargument. He responds to the opposing viewpoint with a strong example that supports his opinion.

The arts should be a part of every student's education.

The idea that only children who want to be performers and painters should take arts classes is like thinking that only students who plan to become doctors should take science! Children who take music and art classes in school learn skills they can use in all kinds of jobs.

- Reasons and their supporting details are well organized from beginning to end.
- The conclusion summarizes the opinion.

Carl states his opinion that the arts belong in every school in the introduction. Then he presents his reasons and supporting details in clear, logical categories. He summarizes his argument in the conclusion.

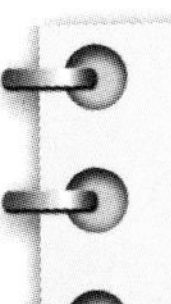

It's true. The arts are fun, interesting, and useful. The arts are an important part of every education, and they belong in every school.

- The writer uses a knowledgeable, convincing voice and speaks directly to the reader.

Carl speaks directly to the reader in his essay. He asks questions to engage the reader in the argument. He also uses the pronoun *us* to include the reader.

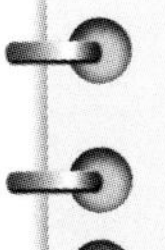

Who hasn't turned a long car ride or a rainy day into something fun by using imaginative games? A good imagination also helps us solve problems.

Opinion Essay
Using the Rubric to Study the Model

- **Carefully chosen words with strong connotations convince the reader.**

Carl makes effective word choices. In explaining how a good imagination helps people do things, he chooses *delicious dinners* to make his point. Chances are the reader will remember this example.

A good imagination helps people do many things. Moms and dads use their imaginations to turn food they buy into delicious dinners.

- **The sentence structures are clear, complete, and varied. The essay is enjoyable to read.**

Carl writes confidently. He uses a lot of straightforward, declarative sentences, and he uses the word *should* a lot, as in the sentence "The arts should be a part of every student's education." Rather than use a whole bunch of exclamation marks, Carl uses just one well-placed exclamation mark in one powerful sentence.

The idea that only children who want to be performers and painters should take arts classes is like thinking that only students who plan to become doctors should take science! Children who take music and art classes in school learn skills they can use in all kinds of jobs.

- **Adjectives and adverbs are used correctly. The essay is easy to read and understand.**

Carl did a great job proofreading his essay for mistakes. He also uses adjectives and adverbs correctly.

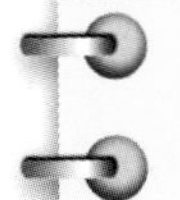

Many fields, such as law, teaching, and medicine, require good listening and looking skills. For example, doctors have to listen carefully and look closely to tell what is wrong with their patients.

+Presentation Indent each new paragraph.

My Turn!

Now it's my turn to write an opinion essay! Follow along to see how I use the rubric and good writing strategies to help me.

Prewrite

Focus on **Ideas**

The Rubric Says The writer presents a thoughtful, well-supported opinion.

Writing Strategy Decide what your opinion is. List reasons to support the opinion.

My teacher said that our essay topics should be something we feel really strongly about. I started thinking about the time a lot of plants and animals died because of a chemical spill near my favorite beach. I decided to write an essay to convince people to prevent pollution in the ocean.

First I have to think of reasons why ocean pollution is a problem. I'll start by making a list of all the reasons I can think of.

Reasons why ocean pollution is a problem

- ✔ Trash washes into the ocean. It is dangerous for ocean animals.
- ✔ Chemicals wash into the ocean. They are dangerous for plants and animals.
- ✔ Trash and chemicals affect people, too. They can harm people. They can hurt business for people who make a living from the ocean.

Apply

What issue do you feel strongly about? What would you like to change? Make a list of all the reasons you can think of to support your opinion.

Prewrite

Focus on **Organization**

The Rubric Says Reasons and their supporting details are well organized from beginning to end.

Writing Strategy Use a Network Tree to organize the reasons in a list.

My list gives three solid reasons why ocean pollution is a problem. My paragraphs will need details and examples to support my reasons. Otherwise I'll never convince my readers to prevent pollution. A Network Tree will help me organize my reasons and details.

Writer's Term

Network Tree

A **Network Tree** organizes information about a central idea. The central idea goes at the top. Main points for the central idea go on the next level. Details about each main point go on the bottom level.

Network Tree

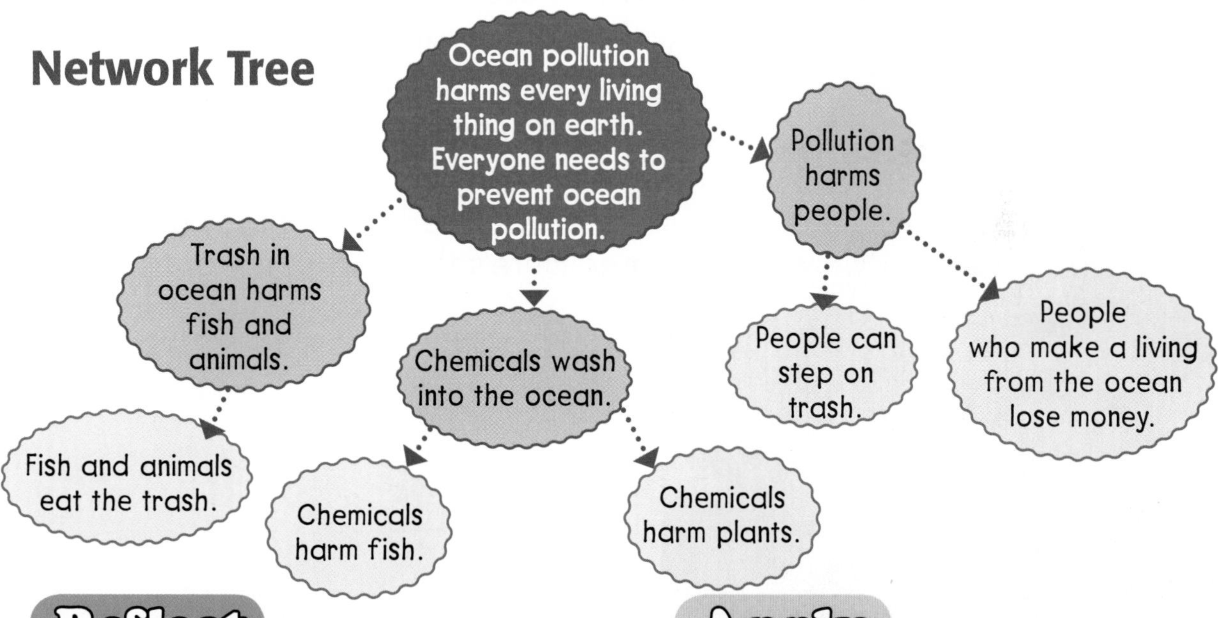

Reflect

Look closely at the Network Tree. What are the three main points and supporting details?

Apply

Use your notes to make a Network Tree. Be sure to include supporting details and examples for each reason you provide.

Draft

Focus on **Voice**

The Rubric Says The writer uses a knowledgeable, convincing voice and speaks directly to the reader.

Writing Strategy Connect with the reader.

I have a good idea now of the arguments I want to make in my essay. My Network Tree helped me see that I have three main points and support for each point. As I write, I'll add even more support.

The rubric also reminds me that my voice should reach out to the reader. Since pollution is a problem we all face, I'll share what I know and use pronouns like *us* and *we* to speak to the reader.

I'm sure I'll make a few mistakes in grammar and spelling as I write. Right now I'll concentrate on getting my ideas down clearly. I'll edit my draft later. Here's the start of my draft.

[DRAFT]

Cleaning Up Ocean Pollution Starts With You and Me

Proofreading Marks

Indent	Take out something
Make uppercase	Add a period
Make lowercase	New paragraph
Add something	Spelling error

Ocean pollution is a problem for every living thing on earth. It effects fish, animals, and plants that live in oceans, as well as people who depend on the oceans for many things. Ocean pollution is a problem everyone should care about, and everyone should work to help stop pollution.

speaks directly to the reader

Did you know that some of the trash that is dropped on the ground will end up in the oceans? A lot of this trash is very dangerous to fish and animals. Some of it looks like food to fish, seals, and turtles. If they eat the trash, they can get very sick and die.

Some chemicals that we use on land are also a big problem. When the chemicals get into the ocean, they make the fish sick. The chemicals also harm the plants in the water. The plants are food for some fish, and they help keep the water clean and full of oxygen. When the plants disappear, there isn't enough oxygen in the water for the fish.

Reflect

Read the beginning of Miles's draft. Where do you hear his voice coming through in his writing?

Apply

Use your Network Tree to draft your own opinion essay. Be sure to convey your knowledge and connect directly with readers.

Revise

Focus on **Ideas**

The Rubric Says Opposing claims are addressed.

Writing Strategy Answer any questions the reader might have.

Sometimes readers will question a writer's claim. If I can predict what my readers will ask and answer those questions in my writing, I will have a very strong argument.

Writer's Term

Opposing Claim

An **opposing claim** is an argument that could be used against the claim, or opinion, that is central to an opinion essay. By addressing opposing claims, writers make their own claims stronger.

[DRAFT]

Some chemicals that we use on land are also a big problem. When the chemicals get into the ocean, they make the fish sick. Many companies say that they keep chemicals far away from the ocean. In fact, chemicals wash into storm drains and rivers that flow to the ocean! The chemicals also harm the plants in the water.

added and answered opposing claim

Apply

Read your draft. Include an opposing claim and answer it with your reasons.

Revise

Focus on **Word Choice**

The Rubric Says Carefully chosen words with strong connotations convince the reader.

Writing Strategy Choose words and phrases for effect.

Now I am ready to choose the best words to get my ideas across. I looked for words that were vague and replaced them with specific words that have more meaning.

Writer's Term

Connotations

Connotations are extra meanings or emotions you think of when you read certain words. For example, the word *loud* simply describes a noise at high volume. *Screechy* means the same thing but also has painful connotations.

[DRAFT]

Most (replaces ~~A lot~~) of this trash is life-threatening (replaces ~~very dangerous~~) to fish and animals. Some of it looks like food to fish, seals, and turtles. If they eat the trash, they can become gravely ill (replaces ~~get very sick~~) and die.

used stronger words

Reflect

Look at Miles's revisions. How do his changes strengthen his examples?

Apply

Read your draft again. Replace vague or overused words with specific ones.

Revise

Focus on **Sentence Fluency**

The Rubric Says The sentence structures are clear, complete, and varied. The essay is enjoyable to read.

Writing Strategy Write a variety of strong sentences.

I'm going to check my sentences now. I want my readers to agree with me about taking action for clean beaches, but I won't convince them by using boring or weak sentences. To create some interest, I'm going to start my conclusion with a question. I'll also delete some unnecessary words to make my sentences stronger and more direct.

[DRAFT]

What can we do?
Cleaning up ocean pollution ~~is something that~~ starts with you and me. Each of us has to ~~do something that~~ helps.

made stronger sentences

Apply

Look over your draft again. Revise any sentences that are wordy or confusing.

Edit

Focus on **Conventions**

The Rubric Says Adjectives and adverbs are used correctly. The essay is easy to read and understand.

Writing Strategy Check that adjectives and adverbs are used correctly.

I always check my writing for spelling, punctuation, and capitalization. The rubric says I should make sure I use adjectives and adverbs correctly, too. Here's a part of my draft that I've edited.

Writer's Term

Adjectives and Adverbs
An **adjective** is used to describe nouns and pronouns. An **adverb** is used to describe verbs or adjectives.

adjective

walking and playing on the beach are barefoot. If they step on something ~~sharply~~ sharp, such as a piece of glass or metal, they can get hurt ~~bad~~ badly.

adverb

[DRAFT]

Reflect

What do you think of Miles's revised sentences? How do his edits improve the essay?

Apply

Conventions

Edit your draft for spelling, punctuation, and capitalization. Correct any errors with adjectives and adverbs.

For practice identifying and correcting adjectives and adverbs, use the exercises on the next two pages.

Adjectives and Adverbs

Know the Rule

Adjectives describe nouns or pronouns. Some adjectives tell what kind, such as *gray* or *furry*. Other adjectives tell how many, such as *two* or *many*. The adjectives *this, that, these,* and *those* tell which one. The articles *a, an,* and *the* are also adjectives.

Examples: Wednesday was a **windy** day. (what kind) A **dozen** socks fell off the clothesline. (how many) **Those** pots were knocked over, too. (which one)

Adverbs describe verbs or adjectives. They tell how, when, where, or to what extent (how much). Many adverbs end in *-ly*. Other common adverbs are *fast, very, often, again, sometimes, soon, only, however, too, later,* and *then.*

Examples: The wind whipped **violently** around the corner. (how) **Later** the door burst open and was **completely** knocked off its hinges. (when, to what extent) Even the jars placed **high** over the bookcase were broken. (where)

Practice the Rule

Make two columns on a sheet of paper. Label the left column **Adjectives** and the right column **Adverbs**. Write the adjectives in the left column and the adverbs in the right column. Do not include articles.

1. Coral reefs have a remarkable ability to survive violent forces such as hurricanes.
2. Coral is actually a small, soft-bodied animal called a polyp.
3. Coral polyps naturally form a hard, chalky shell for protection.
4. Corals feed on the small animals that drift unsuspectingly near their stinging tentacles.
5. Corals also get food from tiny algae that live in their stomach cells.
6. These algae give corals their brightly colored appearance.
7. Lately global warming has caused corals to lose their algae.
8. Coral reefs are also increasingly threatened by fishermen.

Predicate Nouns and Adjectives

Know the Rule

A **predicate noun** follows a linking verb and renames the subject.

Example:

An ant is an **insect.**

A **predicate adjective** follows a linking verb and describes the subject.

Example:

The worker ants are **strong**.

Practice the Rule

Number a sheet of paper 1–10. Write the predicate noun or predicate adjective that you find in each sentence. Label it **PN** or **PA**.

1. The students in our science group were truly cooperative.
2. Our teacher is also a scientist who studies insects.
3. Observation of live insects is difficult but rewarding.
4. Ants are more fascinating than I thought.
5. The largest ant is the queen.
6. Some ants are relatively slow.
7. All the ants seem busy.
8. The smallest ants look very tiny.
9. Building an ant farm is this month's project.
10. The ant farm has become fun for the whole class.

Publish +Presentation

Publishing Strategy Publish the opinion essay on the class website.

Presentation Strategy Indent all paragraphs.

I want to do more than just give this opinion essay to my teacher. If I put it on our class website, many people will see it. I'll make sure to indent each paragraph. Indenting helps to group together information that belongs together. Before I put my essay in a place where lots of people can read it, I will use my final checklist to check it one more time.

My Final Checklist

Did I—

- ✔ check my spelling, punctuation, and capitalization?
- ✔ use adjectives and adverbs correctly?
- ✔ include my title and name at the top of the first page?
- ✔ indent every paragraph?

Apply

Make a checklist to check your own opinion essay. Then make a neat final copy.

Cleaning Up Ocean Pollution Starts With You and Me

by Miles

Ocean pollution is a problem for every living thing on earth. It affects fish, animals, and plants that live in oceans, as well as people who depend on the oceans for many things. Ocean pollution is a problem each one of us should care about. We can work together to help stop pollution.

Did you know that some of the trash that is dropped on the ground will end up in the oceans? Most of this trash is life-threatening to fish and animals. Some of it looks like food to fish, seals, and turtles. If they eat the trash, they can become gravely ill and die.

Some chemicals that we use on land are also a big problem. Many companies say that they keep chemicals far away from the ocean. In fact, chemicals wash into storm drains and rivers that flow to the ocean! When the chemicals get into the ocean, they make the fish sick. The chemicals also harm the plants in the water. The plants are food for some fish, and they help keep the water clean and full of oxygen. When the plants disappear, there isn't enough oxygen in the water for the fish.

Ocean pollution affects people, too. Sometimes pollution comes back onto the land. It looks ugly, and it can be dangerous. Many people walking and playing on the beach are barefoot. If they step on something sharp, such as a piece of glass or metal, they can get badly hurt. Many people depend on the oceans for a living. Some people work in the fishing business. Others work at hotels, restaurants, and shops at the seashore. Polluted oceans cause many problems.

What can we do? Cleaning up ocean pollution starts with you and me. Each of us has to help. We can recycle trash in our neighborhoods or throw it away properly. We can use safer soaps and chemicals. Together, we can make the oceans clean and safe for every living thing.

Reflect

Use the rubric to score Miles's opinion essay. Which traits were strongest? Then use the rubric to check the traits in your essay.

What's an Opinion Speech?

That's a speech I write telling others my opinion on a topic and convincing them to share the same opinion.

What's in an Opinion Speech?

Call to Action
After hearing my speech, I want listeners to take action. I'll urge the audience to do something as a result of my argument.

Argument
This is my opinion that I'll support with evidence and specific facts about the subject.

Opposing Claim
An opposing claim gives the reasons why someone might disagree with my argument. I'll mention at least one opposing claim to explain why my argument makes more sense.

Convincing Tone
This is how I want my speech to sound. I'll use a sincere and convincing tone to convince my listeners to agree with me and take action.

Why write an Opinion Speech?

The main purpose for writing an opinion speech is to convince the audience to agree with a point of view and to take action.

Convincing
People write opinion speeches to share their opinions and convince others to agree with their arguments. The goal is to show the audience that the speech writer's opinion is important. He or she usually wants listeners to take some kind of action in response to the speech.

Awareness
Students, business owners, and citizens give opinion speeches to make others aware of their concerns and the research they have done on their topics.

Linking Opinion Writing Traits to an Opinion Speech

In this chapter, you will give a talk to convince your readers to agree with you about an important issue. This type of opinion writing is called an opinion speech. Miles will guide you through the stages of the writing process: Prewrite, Draft, Revise, Edit, and Publish. In each stage, Miles will show you important writing strategies that are linked to the Opinion Writing Traits below.

Opinion Writing Traits

	• a clear opinion in a thesis statement • strong supporting reasons and facts • counterclaims anticipated and addressed
	• a logical organization: the introduction has an opinion, the body has a strong argument, and the conclusion ends with a summary or call to action • effective transitions that link opinions and reasons
	• a voice and tone that are appropriate for the purpose and audience
	• language that is fair, balanced, and precise
	• a variety of sentences that add interest to the writing and are easy to read
	• no or few errors in grammar, usage, mechanics, and spelling

Before you write, read Megan Crosby's model speech on the next page. Then use the opinion speech rubric on pages 322–323 to decide how well she did. (You might want to look back at What's in an Opinion Speech? on page 318, too!)

Help Save the Animals!

by Megan Crosby

The endangered species list is made up of over 1,000 plants, birds, fish, mammals, and other species. Some species on the list may live in our neighborhoods or migrate through our communities each year. Did you know that there are many ways we can protect wildlife and plants that don't take much time, money, or special equipment?

argument

For example, you can plant a school garden to attract wildlife, butterflies, and birds. Students can help plant trees to provide shelter for birds and animals. Some people say that it takes too much time to care for gardens and trees. However, if each class does its share, it would take only a few minutes each week to maintain an inviting, natural space.

There are things you can do at home, too. If you own a cat that goes outdoors, put a bell on it to warn wildlife. Cats hunt birds, butterflies, mice, frogs, and other small animals. Each plays an important role in the ecosystem. They deserve our protection.

convincing tone

To protect the wildlife and plants in your community, there is a variety of things you can do. For example, you can help organize a clean-up day in your neighborhood. Every piece of paper, aluminum can, or soda bottle you pick up is one less that will end up in streams, ponds, and forests. Some will say, "Why should I spend a day picking up litter? It's just not worth it. Tomorrow there will be more." This simply isn't true! By setting a good example, you will help others think before littering.

opposing claim

We all need to play a bigger role in protecting the wildlife and plants in our communities. Start today to keep more species from being added to the endangered species list! Teach others about the many ways they can help preserve wildlife in your community.

call to action

Opinion Speech Rubric

Use this 6-point rubric to plan and score an opinion speech.

	6	5	4
Ideas	The writer expresses a clear opinion supported by strong facts. Opposing claims are addressed thoroughly.	The writer expresses a clear opinion. Most facts are strong. Opposing claims are addressed.	The writer expresses a clear opinion supported by facts. One opposing claim is addressed.
Organization	The reasons and facts are organized logically to suit the writer's purpose. The conclusion includes a clear call to action in response to the opinion.	The reasons and facts are organized logically. The conclusion includes a call to action that relates to the opinion.	Most reasons and facts are organized logically. The conclusion includes a call to action, but it is not clearly stated.
Voice	The writer's voice is convincing. The tone is ideal for the topic and audience.	The writer's voice is convincing. The tone is appropriate most of the time.	The writer's voice sounds convincing in the beginning. The tone may be too informal.
Word Choice	The language is fair and balanced. No negative or inflammatory words are used. The writer avoids repetition or overused words.	Most of the language is fair and balanced. Some words are overused.	The writer uses language that is fair. One or two words could be more positive.
Sentence Fluency	A variety of sentence structures gives the speech rhythm and flow.	Most of the sentence structures give the speech rhythm and flow.	Several sentences could be combined to improve rhythm and flow.
Conventions	Spelling, grammar, punctuation, and capitalization are correct. Pronouns are used correctly.	There are a few minor errors, but they do not interfere with meaning.	There are a few grammatical errors that may cause confusion.

+Presentation White space helps organize the text on the page.

3	2	1	
The writer expresses an opinion supported by facts. Some evidence may be unimportant or weak.	The writer expresses an opinion supported by facts. Some facts may be unrelated.	The writer's opinion is not clear or wavers between viewpoints.	Ideas
Several reasons or facts are out of order or do not support the writer's purpose. The call to action is weak or hard to understand.	The organization of facts and reasons is hard to follow. The call to action is missing.	The writing is not organized. Few or no reasons or facts are given, and there is no call to action.	Organization
The writer's voice tries to sound convincing. The tone may be too uninterested or uninformed.	The writer's voice is weak and not convincing. The tone may be too neutral.	The voice is absent. The writer does not try to connect with the audience.	Voice
The language is not balanced. It shows only the writer's opinion.	The writer uses some language that distracts or offends the audience.	The writing includes words that are used incorrectly.	Word Choice
Most sentences share the same structure. The rhythm is predictable.	Sentences are not varied. Several are very long and hard to follow.	Many sentences are incomplete and do not have a smooth rhythm.	Sentence Fluency
Many errors are repeated. Some pronouns are used incorrectly.	Several serious errors interfere with meaning. Most pronouns are not used correctly.	The writing has not been edited.	Conventions

See Appendix B for 4-, 5-, and 6-point opinion rubrics.

Using the Opinion Speech Rubric to Study the Model

Did you notice that the model on page 321 points out some key elements of an opinion speech? As she wrote "Help Save the Animals!" Megan Crosby used these elements to help her try to convince her listeners to agree with her opinion. She also used the 6-point rubric on pages 322–323 to plan, draft, revise, and edit the writing. A rubric is a great tool for evaluating writing during the writing process.

Now let's use the same rubric to score the model. To do this, we'll focus on each trait separately, starting with Ideas. We'll use the top descriptor for each trait (column 6), along with examples from the model, to help us understand how the traits work together. How would you score Megan on each trait?

- **The writer expresses a clear opinion supported by strong facts.**
- **Opposing claims are addressed thoroughly.**

Did you know all the things you could do to protect natural habitat? I didn't! Megan states her opinion clearly. Then she backs up her opinion with good reasons and specific facts. She anticipates her listeners' concerns and addresses opposing claims.

Students can help plant trees to provide shelter for birds and animals. Some people say that it takes too much time to care for gardens and trees. However, if each class does its share, it would take only a few minutes each week to maintain an inviting, natural space.

- **The reasons and facts are organized logically to suit the writer's purpose.**
- **The conclusion includes a clear call to action in response to the opinion.**

Megan organizes her speech into things we can do at school, at home, and in our community to protect the wildlife and plants. This perfectly suits her purpose of convincing listeners to help. She wraps up with a clear and exciting call to action.

Start today to keep more species from being added to the endangered species list! Teach others about the many ways they can help preserve wildlife in your community.

- **The writer's voice is convincing.**
- **The tone is ideal for the topic and audience.**

Megan's voice is convincing from beginning to end. She speaks directly to her audience and suggests things we can do to help in our communities.

To protect the wildlife and plants in your community, there is a variety of things you can do. For example, you can help organize a clean-up day in your neighborhood.

Using the Opinion Speech Rubric to Study the Model

- The language is fair and balanced. No negative or inflammatory words are used.
- The writer avoids repetition or overused words.

I noticed that Megan avoids negative or emotional language. For example, she did not say, "What's wrong with some people? Don't they know cats can kill a ton of baby animals?" It's obvious that she chose words that are reasonable and address the problem.

If you own a cat that goes outdoors, put a bell on it to warn wildlife. Cats hunt birds, butterflies, mice, frogs, and other small animals.

- A variety of sentence structures gives the speech rhythm and flow.

Megan varies her sentences. She uses questions and strong statements to get her points across. The variety also gives her speech rhythm and flow.

Some will say, "Why should I spend a day picking up litter? It's just not worth it. Tomorrow there will be more." This simply isn't true! By setting a good example, you will help others think before littering.

- **Spelling, grammar, punctuation, and capitalization are correct.**
- **Pronouns are used correctly.**

I didn't find any errors in the speech. All the pronouns in Megan's speech are correct. It is clear when she refers to herself and when she refers to others. When she uses *we*, she really engages the audience.

We all need to play a bigger role in protecting the wildlife and plants in our communities.

Presentation White space helps organize the text on the page.

My Turn!

Now it's my turn to write an opinion speech. I'll use the rubric and good writing strategies to help me. Read on to see how I do it.

Prewrite

Focus on **Ideas**

The Rubric Says The writer expresses a clear opinion supported by strong facts. Opposing claims are addressed thoroughly.

Writing Strategy Decide on a topic and take notes about it.

I need to write an opinion speech for a science assignment. I have decided to research the topic of healthy school lunches. I think it's an important topic. In order to convince my listeners to agree with me, I'll need to find strong supporting facts. I will also need to think about opposing claims, viewpoints that are the opposite of mine.

As I begin my research, I'll look for information on the Internet that I can use in my speech. I'll take notes on the key concepts and the facts I find. I'll also think about the opposing claims I'll want to address in my speech.

My Notes About Healthy School Lunches

- ✔ The number of overweight children may double in 20 years
- ✔ Good nutrition can prevent disease
- ✔ Healthy eating habits can last a lifetime

Apply

Research a topic and form an opinion you'd like to convince others to share. Learn all you can about your topic, including opposing claims, and write notes about what you learn.

Prewrite

Focus on **Organization**

The Rubric Says The reasons and facts are organized logically to suit the writer's purpose.

Writing Strategy Use a Concept Map to organize ideas.

The rubric reminds me to organize my ideas logically to support my purpose. I'll use a Concept Map to list my arguments and the facts I have gathered to support each argument. I'll be sure to use reliable sources, too.

Writer's Term

Concept Map

A **Concept Map** includes a space to list my opinion, my reasons, and my supporting facts. Finally, there is a space to write my call to action statement.

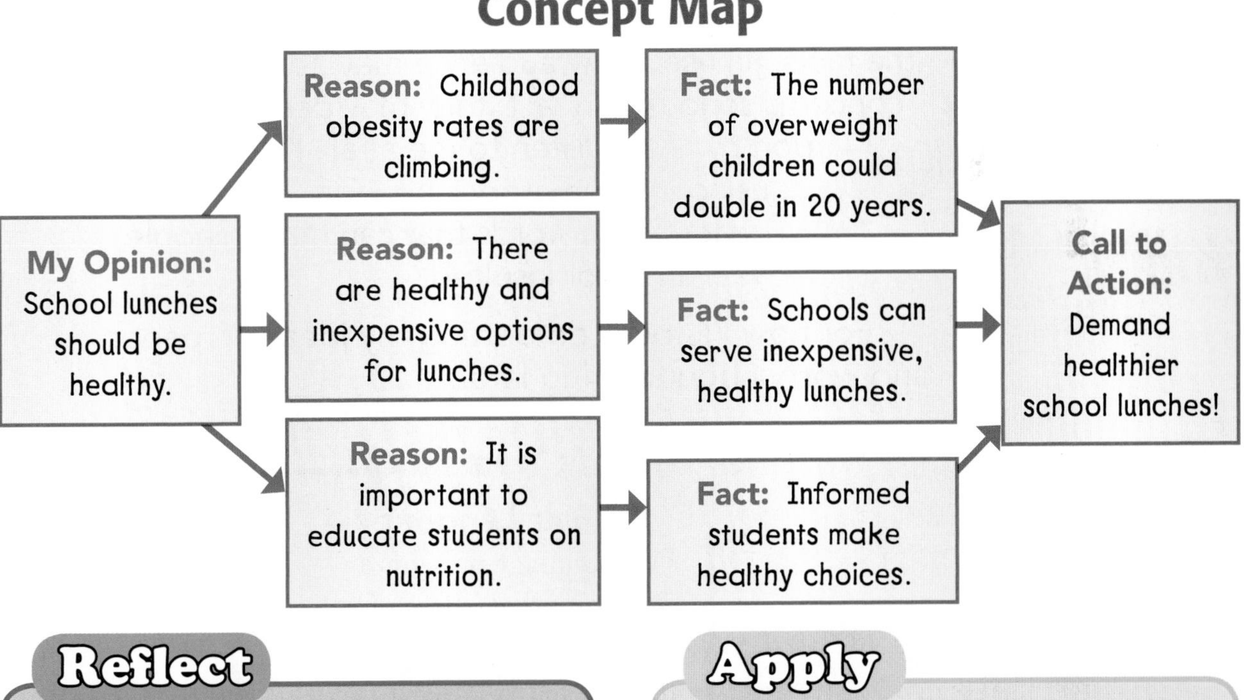

Reflect

How does the Concept Map organize Miles's notes?

Apply

Create a Concept Map. List your reasons and the facts you found. Then write a call to action statement.

Draft

Focus on **Word Choice**

The Rubric Says The language is fair and balanced. No negative or inflammatory words are used.

Writing Strategy Use words that make the argument sound strong and believable.

Now that my Concept Map is complete, I'm ready to begin my draft. I want to make my speech sound convincing so my audience will take action. Our health is important, and I want others to know how school lunches can affect us.

I need to make sure that I should use fair language. That means I should avoid words that sound negative. Negative language usually doesn't convince people of the facts. If I use it, my audience may not take my concerns seriously. In fact, they may decide that they don't want to listen to me at all. I'll also avoid using inflammatory language. *Inflammatory language* is words that can make people feel angry or insulted.

For now I'll focus on getting my ideas on paper and worry about editing later.

Writer's Term

Fair Language

Fair language presents a viewpoint that is free of negative wording. Opinions that are stated fairly are taken seriously by the audience. Negative words usually create a negative response.

Proofreading Marks

⊐ Indent	Take out something
≡ Make uppercase	⊙ Add a period
/ Make lowercase	¶ New paragraph
∧ Add something	(sp) Spelling error

[DRAFT]

Healthy School Lunches Aren't Optional

Did you know that your school lunch may be harmful to your health? Everyone agrees that meals that are high in fat and low in nutritional value do not belong in school. Yet, childhood obesity rates continue to climb. So it's important that we act now!

used fair language

Studies show that if children develop healthy eating habits early in life, them will continue good eating habits into adulthood. Most people agree that unhealthy foods can cause obesity, but some argue that healthy foods cost more. This just isn't true! Some schools even have gardens to help lower food costs.

Schools should also provide students with information on good nutrition. Students need to learn that a good diet can prevent many medical problems. They need to learn that a good diet can prevent diabetes, obesity, and heart disease. Some argue that there isn't enough time in the school day to teach nutrition, but many teachers already use the government's food pyramid to remind students about the healthy food groups.

strong and fair conclusion

Schools should play a bigger role in helping children make informed choices about food. Demand healthier school lunches today!

Reflect

Can you find other examples of fair language in Miles's draft? How does using fair language strengthen the writing?

Apply

Check your speech for fair language. Write a strong, but fair, conclusion so your audience will take action.

Revise

Focus on **Ideas**

The Rubric Says Opposing claims are addressed thoroughly.

Writing Strategy Include the other side of an argument.

The rubric tells me to address opposing claims in my speech. I found a place where I can add more details. This will help me strengthen my argument and show my audience that I have thought about opposing viewpoints. Here's how I did it.

Writer's Term

Opposing Claims

An **opposing claim** is the opposite of an argument. A writer should explain why an opposing claim is weak and why it should not be taken seriously by the audience.

[DRAFT]

addressed an opposing claim

Most people agree that unhealthy foods can cause obesity, but some argue that healthy foods cost more. This just isn't true! ^ Many school districts offer real cheap meals, such as bean chili and black beans and rice, as healthy meals.

Apply

Read your draft. Be sure to address opposing claims.

Revise

Focus on **Organization**

The Rubric Says The conclusion includes a clear call to action in response to the opinion.

Writing Strategy State what the audience can do.

The rubric says to include a call to action in the conclusion. The call to action is the reason I am writing my speech. I have to be clear about what I want the audience to do after hearing my speech. I need to make sure my conclusion is clear and specific. I've added some details to my conclusion. Do you think I've improved my call to action?

Writer's Term

Call to Action

A **call to action** urges the audience to take action right away. It asks the reader or listener to respond by doing something specific.

[DRAFT]

Schools should play a bigger role in helping children make informed choices about food. Demand healthier school lunches today! Ask your school to add wholesome grains, fruits, and vegetables to the menu. Your health depends on it!

added a clear call to action

Reflect

How did Miles strengthen his call to action?

Apply

Read your conclusion. Be sure your call to action is specific.

Revise

Focus on **Sentence Fluency**

The Rubric Says A variety of sentence structures gives the speech rhythm and flow.

Writing Strategy Combine sentences that repeat information.

The rubric reminds me that I should use a variety of sentence structures. I reread my draft aloud and found a place where two sentences in a row repeated some of the same information and words. So I combined them to improve the flow.

[DRAFT]

Schools should also provide students with information on good nutrition. Students need to learn that a good diet can prevent many medical problems, including diabetes, obesity, and heart disease. ~~Students need to learn that a good diet can prevent many medical problems. They need to learn that a good diet can prevent diabetes, obesity, and heart disease.~~

combined sentences

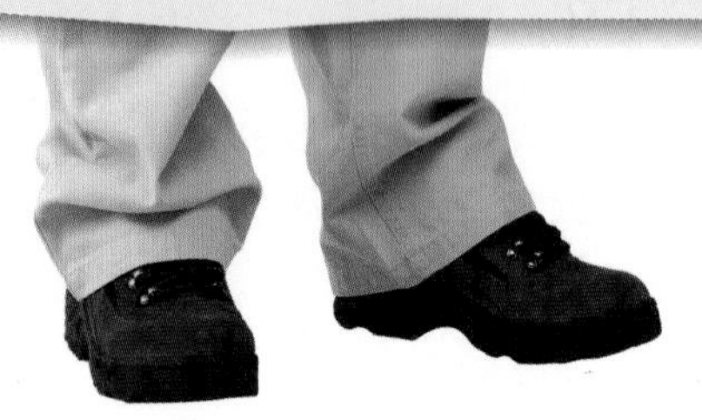

Apply

Read your draft. Look for places where you can combine sentences and improve the flow.

Edit

Focus on **Conventions**

The Rubric Says Pronouns are used correctly.

Writing Strategy Use the correct form of each pronoun.

The rubric says I should make sure pronouns are used correctly to make my message clear. When I wrote my draft, I focused on getting my ideas down on paper, so I may have made mistakes. I should check for accurate spelling, grammar, and punctuation, too. I'll fix any errors I find.

Writer's Term

Subject and Object Pronouns

Subject pronouns include **I, he, she, we,** and **they**. **Object pronouns** include **me, him, her, us,** and **them**. The pronouns **it** and **you** can be either subject or object pronouns.

[DRAFT]

Studies show that if children develop healthy eating habits early in life, ~~them~~ they will continue good eating habits into adulthood.

corrected pronoun

Reflect

Look at Miles's edit. How does his change make the message clear?

Apply

Conventions

Edit your draft for spelling, punctuation, and capitalization. Correct any pronouns that are used incorrectly to make sure your writing is clear.

For more practice using subject and object pronouns, use the exercises on the next two pages.

Conventions **Grammar, Usage & Mechanics**

Subject and Object Pronouns

Know the Rule

A pronoun can be the subject or the object in a sentence.
Subject pronouns include *I, he, she, we,* and *they.*

Example:
They started a Healthy School Lunch campaign.

Object pronouns are used after an action verb or a preposition. Object pronouns include *me, him, her, us,* and *them.* The pronouns *it* and *you* can be either subject or object pronouns.

Examples:
The principal wants to plan the campaign with **them.**
She'll meet **him** in the cafeteria.

Practice the Rule

Number a separate sheet of paper 1–10. Read the sentences below. Then write the correct pronoun for each sentence.

1. It's important that (we/us) all make healthy food choices as young children.
2. His mom is teaching (he/him) good eating habits.
3. Our lunch committee is working to improve the food (we/us) eat.
4. (I/she) am trying to learn more about making healthy food choices.
5. What kinds of snacks will (they/them) put in our vending machines?
6. Learning to read food labels will help (we/us) choose healthy snacks.
7. A healthy diet and exercise will help (it/you) from becoming overweight.
8. My mom placed a bowl of apples on the table for my sister and (I/me).
9. (They/Him) shared healthy school lunch ideas with each other.
10. The Healthy School Meals act will reward school districts with money if (they/you) offer vegetarian food choices.

Pronouns in Pairs

Know the Rule

When you use two pronouns or a noun and a pronoun together, be sure you use the correct form of each pronoun. Use the pronouns *I, we, he, she,* and *they* as **subjects** in sentences. Use the pronouns *me, us, him, her,* and *them* as **objects** in sentences. The pronouns *it* and *you* can be either subjects or objects. When you include yourself, put *I* or *me* last. Remember to use this rule when you speak, too.

Practice the Rule

Number a separate sheet of paper 1–10. Write the correct pronoun in each sentence. Then write **S** if the pronoun is a subject pronoun. Write **O** if the pronoun is an object pronoun.

1. Andi and (I/me) created a large poster to advertise "Herb Garden Day" at our school.
2. Principal Tate asked her and (I/me) to display it at the main entrance.
3. He and (we/us) hope that many parents will be able to attend.
4. It will help them and (we/us) learn how to grow herbs.
5. Andi and (I/me) will introduce Mr. Green from the garden center.
6. (He/Him) and we will distribute seed packets of herbs to the parents.
7. Mr. Green will show (they/them) and the students how to plant herbs.
8. Then he will ask for parent volunteers to help the teachers and (we/us).
9. Mr. Green and (they/them) will build a greenhouse for the school.
10. They will post pictures of the herbs and (we/us) on the school website.

Publish

+Presentation

Publishing Strategy Give the speech in person or as a podcast.

Presentation Strategy Use white space effectively.

My opinion speech is done! Now I'll present it to my class. My science teacher wants to record our speeches as a podcast for students and their families. I hope my speech encourages students to make healthy choices about their eating. When I give my speech, I want to be sure that I don't lose my place. Good margins and indented paragraphs will help me keep my place as I read. Before I consider my speech finished, I'll make a final checklist.

My Final Checklist

Did I—

✔ use pronouns correctly?

✔ check my spelling, grammar, punctuation, and capitalization?

✔ use white space to organize the text on the page?

Apply

Make a checklist to prepare your final copy. Then present your speech to your class.

Healthy School Lunches Aren't Optional

by Miles

Did you know that your school lunch may be harmful to your health? Everyone agrees that meals that are high in fat and low in nutritional value do not belong in school. Yet, childhood obesity rates continue to climb. One recent study found that the number of overweight children could double in the next 20 years. So it's important that we act now!

Studies show that if children develop healthy eating habits early in life, they will continue good eating habits into adulthood. Most people agree that unhealthy foods can cause obesity, but some argue that healthy foods cost more. This just isn't true! Many school districts offer budget-friendly meals, such as bean chili and black beans and rice, as healthy options. Some schools even have gardens to help lower food costs. The teachers and students at my cousin's school grow their own vegetables. This is a great idea! Children learn to grow, harvest, and enjoy healthy food.

Schools should also provide students with information on good nutrition. Students need to learn that a good diet can prevent many medical problems, including diabetes, obesity, and heart disease. Some argue that there isn't enough time in the school day to teach nutrition, but many teachers already use the government's food pyramid to remind students about the healthy food groups.

Schools should play a bigger role in helping children make informed choices about food. Demand healthier school lunches today! Ask your school to add wholesome grains, fruits, and vegetables to the menu. Your health depends on it!

Reflect

Use the rubric to check Miles's opinion speech. Did he use all the traits of a good opinion speech? Be sure to check your own speech against the rubric.

Opinion test writing

Read the Writing Prompt

When it's time to take a writing test, you will get a writing prompt. Most writing prompts have three parts.

Setup This part of the writing prompt gives you background information that helps you get ready for writing.

Task This part of the writing prompt tells you exactly what you're supposed to write: an opinion essay about one way to make your town a better place.

Scoring Guide This part tells how your writing will be scored. Make sure that your writing test includes everything on the list.

You've already used a rubric to help you write convincingly. When you are writing an opinion test essay, you won't always have all the information that a rubric gives you. That's okay! You can use the scoring guide in the same way you use a rubric. Like the rubric, the scoring guide lists everything you need to think about as you write your test essay. Scoring guides often include the six important traits of writing that you've already seen in rubrics:

Every town or city has good features: places to go, things to do, services for its citizens. But no town or city is perfect. There's always room for improvement! Town leaders listen to citizens who express their opinions clearly and thoughtfully.

Write an opinion essay about one way to make your town a better place.

Be sure that your opinion essay

- gives reasons that are supported by facts and details.
- introduces the topic clearly and concludes with a call to action.
- has a writing voice that speaks directly to the audience.
- includes specific words.
- has sentences that have varied beginnings, use transitions, and flow smoothly.
- has correct grammar, spelling, capitalization, and punctuation.

Writing Traits
in the Scoring Guide

This chart was made using the scoring guide from the writing prompt on page 341. Does the chart remind you of the rubrics you've used? Not all prompts include all of the writing traits, but this one does. Use them to do your best writing. Remember to work neatly and put your name on each page!

- **Be sure your opinion essay gives reasons that are supported by facts and details.**

- **Be sure your opinion essay introduces the topic clearly and concludes with a call to action.**

- **Be sure your opinion essay has a writing voice that speaks directly to the audience.**

- **Be sure your opinion essay includes specific words.**

- **Be sure your opinion essay has sentences that have varied beginnings, use transitions, and flow smoothly.**

- **Be sure your opinion essay has correct grammar, spelling, capitalization, and punctuation.**

Look at Hattie Beck's essay on the next page. Did she follow the scoring guide?

Mallville Needs a Playground

by Hattie Beck

There is a problem here in Mallville. The town's problem is not crime or pollution. It's not poverty or violence. But it's still a real problem. The problem is that Mallville doesn't have a good place for kids to play. It needs a playground very badly.

Mallville has grown rapidly over the past 20 years. As a result, this growth has caused open space to shrink. Fields where kids used to be able to run, play, and ride their bikes are gone. There used to be woods and vacant lots where kids could climb trees and learn about nature. Now there are houses and shopping malls instead. There are almost no places, other than backyards, for kids to play together outside. Because of this, kids spend more time watching television or playing video games. The only time some of them have a chance to get together to play outside is during team sports such as soccer or baseball.

Many people believe that it is important for children to play together for their health and well-being. Playing with their friends teaches kids to be independent and to get along with others. It gives them chances to use their imaginations. In addition, playing often on playground equipment such as swings, slides, and seesaws improves kids' balance and helps their muscles grow stronger. Finally, kids need another choice for entertainment besides playing video games and watching television. They need another choice for exercise besides team sports.

If Mallville had a playground, kids would have a place where they could go to get exercise and to have fun together. We all need to work together to convince the town leaders that having a playground for the town's kids is very important. Right now, having a playground is just a dream. If everyone works together, this dream could come true.

Using the Scoring Guide to Study the Model

Now let's use the scoring guide to study Hattie's writing test, "Mallville Needs a Playground." We'll look for examples in her essay to show how she did on each part of the scoring guide.

- **The essay gives reasons that are supported by facts and details.**

Hattie believes Mallville needs a playground. She develops her opinion by sharing facts she has learned about the benefits of play.

> Many people believe that it is important for children to play together for their health and well-being. Playing with their friends teaches kids to be independent and to get along with others.

- **The essay introduces the topic clearly and concludes with a call to action.**

Hattie's essay is well organized. She gives her opinion in the title and then repeats it clearly in the introduction. She develops her opinion in the body paragraphs. Notice how she includes a call to action in her conclusion.

> We all need to work together to convince the town leaders that having a playground for the town's kids is very important.

- **The writer speaks directly to the audience.**

Hattie's first sentence states that the problem is *here*. This tells us that she and her readers live in the same community. Once she makes this connection and gets their attention, she reveals the problem.

There is a problem here in Mallville. The town's problem is not crime or pollution. It's not poverty or violence. But it's still a real problem.

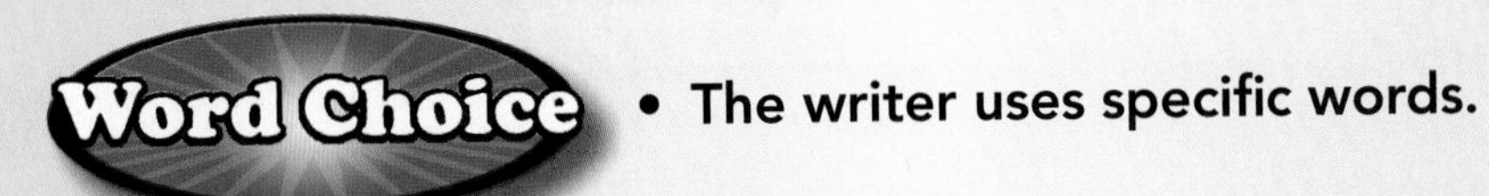

- **The writer uses specific words.**

Hattie convinces the reader with specific examples that include words such as *fields, woods,* and *trees.* She creates a powerful image by saying that natural spaces have been replaced by buildings and parking lots.

As a result, this growth has caused open space to shrink. Fields where kids used to be able to run, play, and ride their bikes are gone. There used to be woods and vacant lots where kids could climb trees and learn about nature. Now there are houses and shopping malls instead.

Using the Scoring Guide to Study the Model

- **The sentences in your opinion essay have varied beginnings, use transitions, and flow smoothly.**

Hattie uses a variety of sentences in her essay. Some begin with transitions like *As a result* or *Because of this*, which link important ideas and keep the essay flowing.

> There are almost no places, other than backyards, for kids to play together outside. Because of this, kids spend more time watching television or playing video games.

- **The opinion essay has correct grammar, spelling, capitalization, and punctuation.**

The scoring guide reminds you to check grammar, spelling, capitalization, and punctuation. Hattie must have remembered this step, because her final draft is free of errors and easy to read.

Planning My Time

To do the best job I can when writing for a test, I need time to plan and prewrite, to draft, to revise, and to edit. So I find out right away how much time I have to write, and then I divide up the time for each step of the process. I may not stick exactly to my plan, but I try to stay close! Here's how I've divided my time into four steps for this test:

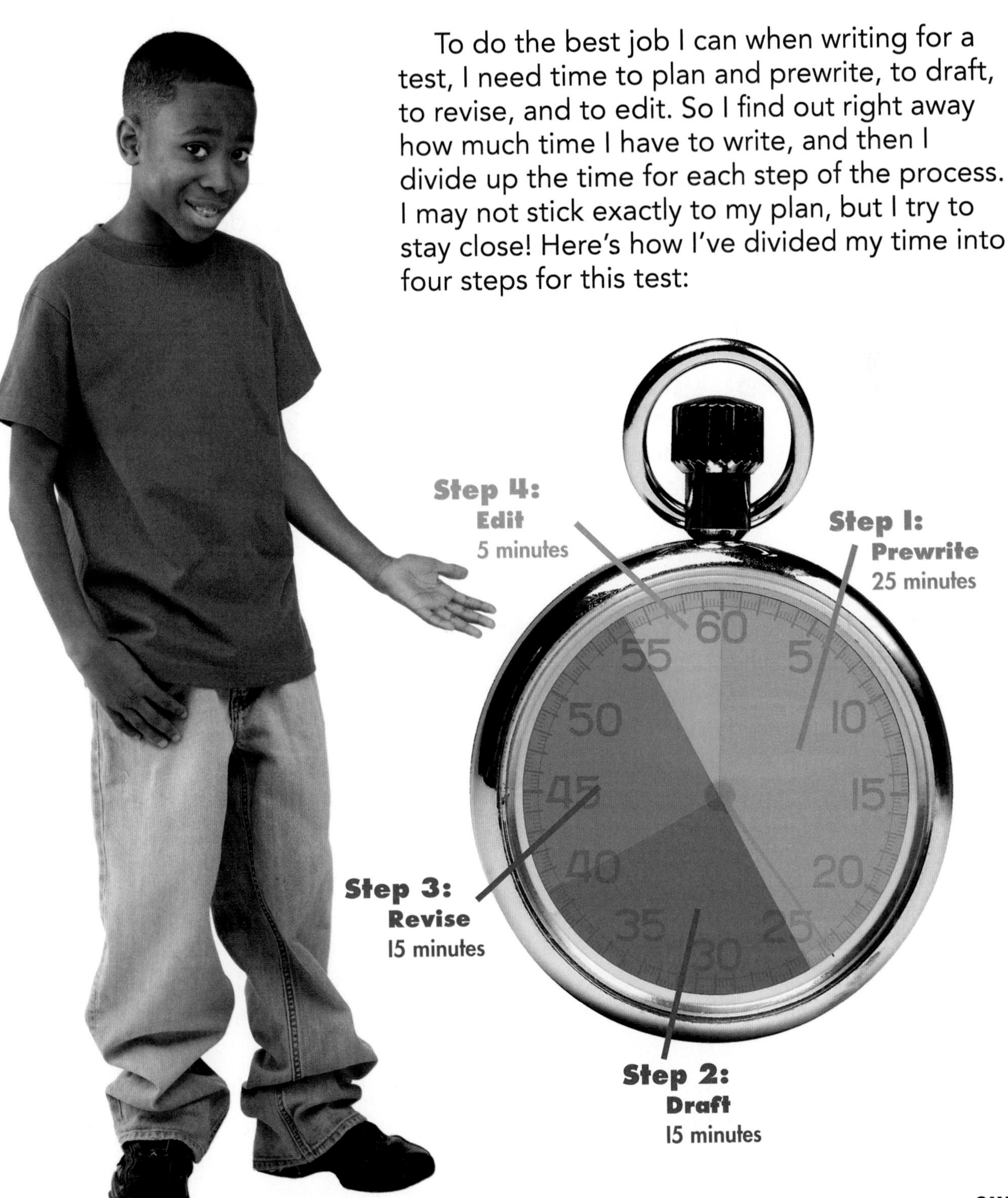

Prewrite

Focus on **Ideas**

Writing Strategy Study the writing prompt to find out what to do.

When my teacher hands out the writing prompt, I study it to make sure I know exactly what to do. Most writing prompts have three parts. You need to find and label each part: the setup, the task, and the scoring guide. Look at how I did this below. Then you should circle key words in the prompt that tell what kind of writing to do. I circled *Write an essay* because it tells what kind of writing I should do. Also, I circled *to convince your school's leaders to make a change* because it tells me what to write about.

My Writing Test Prompt

Setup — Your school's got a lot to offer students: great teachers, interesting courses, fun events. But what if you could do one thing to your school to make it even better? What would you change to improve your school?

Task — Write an essay to convince your school's leaders to make a change to your school.

Scoring Guide — Be sure that your opinion essay

- gives reasons that are supported by facts and details.
- introduces the topic clearly and concludes with a call to action.
- has a writing voice that speaks directly to the audience.
- includes specific words.
- has sentences that have varied beginnings, use transitions, and flow smoothly.
- has correct grammar, spelling, capitalization, and punctuation.

Now that I've had time to study and label the prompt, I'll think about how the scoring guide relates to the six writing traits I've studied in the rubrics. This scoring guide has the six traits that a good essay needs. If your scoring guide doesn't have all six traits, think back to the rubrics you've used. Try to remember what's important in a good essay.

Ideas

- **Be sure your opinion essay gives reasons that are supported by facts and details.**

I'll state my opinion and jot down notes for the strongest points. I'll also include supporting facts and details.

Organization

- **Be sure your opinion essay introduces the topic clearly and concludes with a call to action.**

I'll state my opinion clearly in the introduction and make sure I wrap up with a strong call to action.

Voice

- **Be sure your opinion essay has a writing voice that speaks directly to the audience.**

My writing voice should draw readers in and keep that connection all the way through.

Word Choice

- **Be sure your opinion essay includes specific words.**

I'll choose words for their power to convince.

- **Be sure your opinion essay has sentences that have varied beginnings, use transitions, and flow smoothly.**

I'll use a variety of sentence structures to support my opinion and link my ideas with transitions.

- **Be sure your opinion essay has correct grammar, spelling, capitalization, and punctuation.**

I'll try to leave time for proofreading, but I'll also do my best to use good grammar and spelling as I draft.

Prewrite

Focus on **Ideas**

Writing Strategy Respond to the task.

Prewriting is an important step when you write for a test, so I've set aside a big chunk of time for it. First I'll gather as much information as I can from the task part of the writing prompt. It tells me what kind of writing to do: an essay. I also know I'm trying to convince people, so it's an opinion essay. That means I need to present my opinion and supporting reasons.

I also know that I need to think about something I would change to make our school better. The first thing I'll do is brainstorm a short list of things I would change.

Task— Write an essay to convince your school's leaders to make a change to your school.

Changes We Could Make at Our School

- more fresh fruits and veggies in the cafeteria
- longer recess time to stretch and run off energy
- computer lab where all students could learn skills
- extra library hours in the evening so that study groups can meet

Apply

Identify the parts of the task and know what kind of writing to do before you start drafting. Then you can make notes to help you gather information.

Prewrite

Writing Strategy Choose a graphic organizer.

I've decided to write about adding a computer lab to our school. I already have some good information about this idea. I think a Support Pattern will help me get my ideas together. I'll list each of my main points, or reasons, and the information that supports each one.

Reasons to Add a Computer Lab to Our School

Reason: Students need to know how to use computer programs.

Supporting facts
- word processors help with writing
- spreadsheets help with math
- knowledge to make simple computer repairs

Reason: Students need to know how to use the Internet.

Supporting facts
- Internet permits students to do research
- Internet connects students to the world
- Internet can be hard to use

Reason: Students need to learn from teachers who have training and time.

Supporting facts
- in a lab, students learn together
- in a lab, students have time to learn
- in a lab, teachers have time to teach

Reflect

Look at Miles's reasons and supporting facts. How does the organizer help him plan his writing?

Apply

Organize information before you draft. Use a graphic organizer that fits the topic and kind of writing you've been assigned.

Prewrite

Focus on **Organization**

Writing Strategy Check the graphic organizer against the scoring guide.

Prewriting is important when you write a timed test because you won't have time to start over. To be sure that I'm ready to start drafting, I'll take a few minutes to check my Support Pattern against the scoring guide in the writing prompt.

Reasons to Add a Computer Lab to Our School

Reason: Students need to know how to use computer programs.

Supporting facts
- word processors help with writing
- spreadsheets help with math
- knowledge to make simple computer repairs

Reason: Students need to know how to use the Internet.

Supporting facts
- Internet permits students to do research
- Internet connects students to the world
- Internet can be hard to use

Reason: Students need to learn from teachers who have training and time.

Supporting facts
- in a lab, students learn together
- in a lab, students have time to learn
- in a lab, teachers have time to teach

Ideas

- **Be sure your opinion essay gives reasons that are supported by facts and details.**

I've listed strong facts and details for each main point. If I think of others, I'll make sure they support the reasons and add them to my draft.

Organization

- **Be sure your opinion essay introduces the topic clearly and concludes with a call to action.**

I'll make a clear statement of my opinion in my introduction, and I'll end with a call to action.

Voice

- **Be sure your opinion essay has a writing voice that speaks directly to the audience.**

I'll want to engage my readers right away in order to convince them to act on my suggestion.

Word Choice

- **Be sure your opinion essay includes specific words.**

I'll use specific words throughout the essay.

Sentence Fluency

- **Be sure your opinion essay has sentences that have varied beginnings, use transitions, and flow smoothly.**

I'll use a variety of sentences to connect and link ideas.

Conventions

- **Be sure your opinion essay has correct grammar, spelling, capitalization, and punctuation.**

I will leave time to proofread my draft.

Reflect

How does Miles use the scoring guide to plan his writing?

Apply

Before you begin writing, check the scoring guide.

Draft

Focus on **Ideas**

Writing Strategy Use facts to support the reasons.

The graphic organizer has three reasons. I'll write a paragraph for each and include the three facts I have listed. As I write, I'll keep in mind my opinion: Our school needs a computer lab. Here's my first draft.

[DRAFT]

A New Computer Lab
by Miles

reason

There are many reasons why we need a computer lab in School. Today computers are part of allmost everything we do in life. There are many skills we must learn to be able to use computers well. We need to know how to use computer programs. We should know how to do reports' on the computer, we need to know how to make charts and drawings on the computer. It would also be very useful to learn how computers work. And how to fix simple problems with our computers.

Students also must understand and be able to use the internet. The internet connects the classroom to the whole world.

Proofreading Marks

⊐ Indent	ℓ Take out something
≡ Make uppercase	⊙ Add a period
/ Make lowercase	¶ New paragraph
∧ Add something	(sp) Spelling error

It is becoming more and more important as a research tool. Students need to find information quickly. Students need to learn how to judge whether the information is factual and reliable. To learn these skills, students need a computer lab in school.

reason

There is often little time to learn computer skills during class. These skills are best learned in a computer lab. There, students can learn about computers from a specially trained teacher. Mr. Badelt would make a good computer lab teacher. This also gives us a chance to practice the skills as they are being learned.

As our education progresses, computer skills will become even more important. The best way to help students get ready for the future is to set up a computer lab and make computer classes part of the regular school day.

Reflect

Read the draft. Did Miles support his reasons?

Apply

Use the facts and reasons in your graphic organizer as you write your draft. Make sure to state and support your opinion.

Revise

Focus on Organization

Writing Strategy Make a clear opinion statement, and end with a call to action.

Now I'm ready to revise. The scoring guide says I should introduce my topic clearly. My first sentence gives my opinion, but I could say it better.

I also need to add a call to action in my conclusion. I'll tell my classmates what they can do to help get a computer lab for the school. Then my essay will end on a strong note, too!

Here are two parts of my draft. I'll proofread my entire draft later.

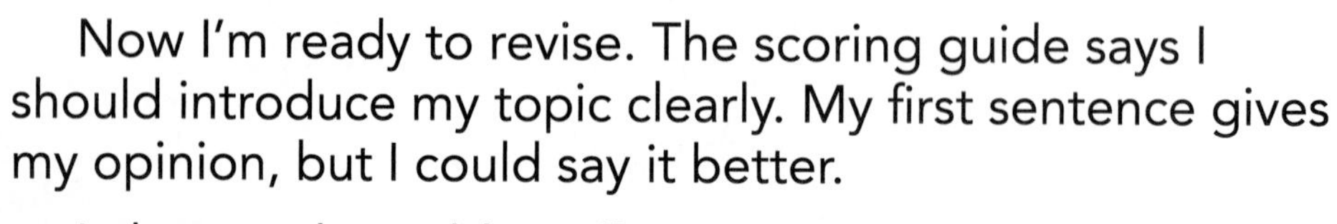

[DRAFT]

We really need a computer lab in our school! When you read ~~There are many reasons why we need a computer lab in~~ my reasons, I'm sure you'll agree. ~~School~~.

stronger introduction

Talk to your parents and the principal about why we need a computer lab. Let's make sure it happens soon!

classes part of the regular school day. ^

added call to action

Apply

Read your draft. Make sure you start with a clear statement about your opinion and end with a strong call to action.

Revise

Focus on Voice

Writing Strategy Use first person to speak directly to the audience.

The scoring guide reminds me to speak directly to my audience. I'm writing to the students in my school. I think my voice will be stronger if I use first-person words like *we* and *our* all the way through my essay.

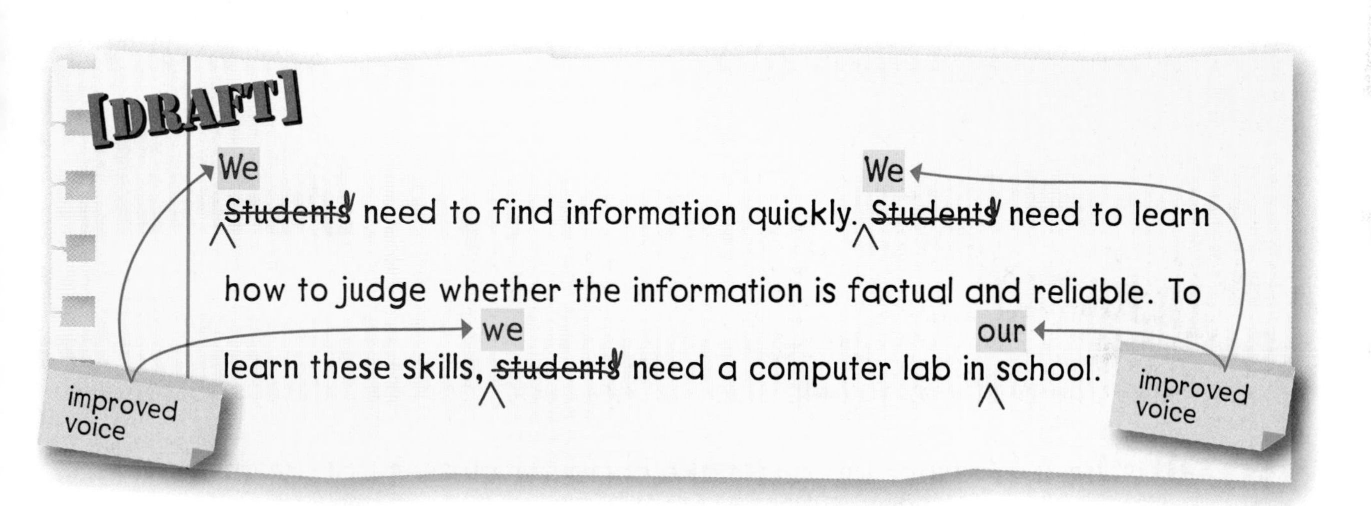

Reflect

Look at Miles's changes. How do they improve his voice?

Apply

Read your draft and use first-person voice all the way through.

Revise

Focus on **Word Choice**

Writing Strategy Replace weak or vague words.

The scoring guide reminds me to use specific words. Sometimes it's not just one word but the way I use a group of words that makes a difference. I improved this sentence by using a stronger verb and getting rid of ordinary words.

[DRAFT]

stronger words

prepare

The best way to ~~help~~ students ~~get ready~~ for the future is to set up a computer lab and make computer classes part of the regular school day.

Apply

Look for places in your essay where you can replace vague or ordinary words with specific ones.

Edit

Focus on **Conventions**

Writing Strategy Check the grammar, spelling, capitalization, and punctuation.

Now I'll use the time I set aside to edit and proofread. During this time I will focus on spelling, grammar, punctuation, and capitalization. You will have time to edit if you revise your draft first. I corrected the errors I found as neatly as I could.

A New Computer Lab

by Miles

We really need a computer lab in our school! When you read my reasons, I'm sure you'll agree. ~~There are many reasons why we need a computer lab in school.~~ Today computers are part of ~~allmost~~ almost everything we do in life. There are many skills we must learn to be able to use computers well. For example, we need to know how to use computer programs, including word processing, spreadsheets, and desktop publishing. We should know how to do reports on the computer. In addition, we need to know how to make charts and drawings on the computer. It would also be very useful to learn how computers work and how to fix simple problems with our computers.

Apply

Every time you write for a test, leave time at the end to proofread and fix any errors in grammar, spelling, capitalization, and punctuation.

Students also must understand and be able to use the internet. The internet connects the classroom to the whole world. It is becoming more and more important as a research tool. ~~Students~~ We need to find information quickly. ~~Students~~ We need to learn how to judge whether the information is factual and reliable. To learn these skills, ~~students~~ we need a computer lab in our school.

There is often little time to learn computer skills during class. These skills are best learned in a computer lab. There, students can learn about computers from a specially trained teacher. ~~Mr. Badelt would make a good computer lab teacher.~~ In a computer lab, all students can learn at the same time. This also gives us a chance to practice the skills as they are being learned.

As our education progresses, computer skills will become even more important. The best way to ~~help~~ prepare students ~~get ready~~ for the future is to set up a computer lab and make computer classes part of the regular school day. Talk to your parents and the principal about why we need a computer lab. Let's make sure it happens soon!

FINAL DRAFT

Reflect

Use the scoring guide to check Miles's writing. How did he use the traits to write his essay?

We're done! Using the setup, task, and scoring guide really does help you write for a test. Just remember these important tips.

TEST TIPS

1. **Study the writing prompt before you begin to write.** Remember, look for the three important parts—setup, task, and scoring guide. They may not be labeled, but you can find and label them yourself.
2. **Follow these steps to be sure you understand the task—before you start writing!**
   - Find and label the setup, task, and scoring guide.
   - Circle key words in the task. Look for words that tell you what kind of writing to do, what to write about, and sometimes even what kind of audience to write to.
   - Read the scoring guide so that you know how your paper will be graded.
3. **Plan your time, and then watch the clock.** Decide how much time you can use for each step of the writing process. Stick to your plan as closely as you can so that you'll have time to revise and edit your draft.
4. **Check your draft against the scoring guide at least twice.** Like the rubrics you've used for other writing assignments, the scoring guide tells you what's important. Make sure your draft does what the scoring guide says it should do.
5. **Plan!** You won't have much time to revise, so planning what you will write is very important.
6. **Don't skip the last step: editing!** Look for the errors you tend to make, and correct them. Write neatly so that the people scoring your test can read your essay easily!

Descriptive writing paints a picture for the reader.

Hi, my name is Joe. I'm learning all about descriptive writing, and I love it! My grandfather takes me on fishing trips, and I can't wait to write about my experiences. I'm going to describe the environment, write an observation report, create a poem, and even write a description of my great-grandfather.

IN THIS UNIT

- Descriptive Essay
- Observation Report
- Biographic Sketch
- MATH CONNECTION ▶ Poem
- Writing for a Test

Name: Joe
Home: Colorado
Favorite Activities: writing stories and spending time with my grandfather and great-grandfather
Favorite Sport: fishing

What's a Descriptive Essay?

It's an essay that gives a clear, detailed picture of a specific person, place, or thing.

What's in a Descriptive Essay?

Topic
This is what my essay is about. My topic could be anything I can describe with words.

Introduction
My first paragraph will introduce my reader to my topic. I'll begin with the most interesting information. That way my reader will want to find out more.

Body
That's the middle part of my essay. It's where I'll develop my topic and give a lot of specific details.

Details
These are words used to describe what I'm writing about. For example, if I'm writing about a fish I caught, I could give details about how big and what color the fish was.

Conclusion
That's my last paragraph. I will end with what I thought was most interesting about my topic. It's also how I started my essay. I will go back to that idea but say it differently this time.

Why write a Descriptive Essay?

There are many reasons to write a descriptive essay. Here are a few that come to mind.

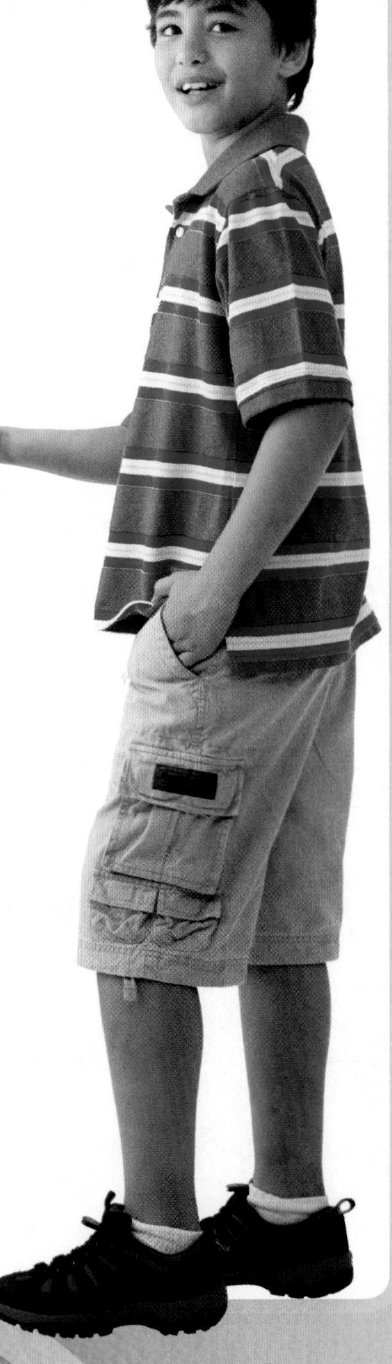

Entertainment
Writing about an interesting person, place, thing, or event can be fun. If I describe something that is special to me, maybe others will enjoy it, too.

Information
I can share important information about my topic with my readers. I might even teach them something they didn't know.

Personal Learning
A descriptive essay can also be my starting place for investigating a topic that interests me. I will learn interesting facts and details as I write my essay.

Linking Descriptive Writing Traits to a Descriptive Essay

In this chapter, you will write an essay to describe an interesting person. This type of descriptive writing is called a descriptive essay. Joe will guide you through the stages of the writing process: Prewrite, Draft, Revise, Edit, and Publish. In each stage, Joe will show you important writing strategies that are linked to the Descriptive Writing Traits below.

Descriptive Writing Traits

 Ideas	• a clear, focused, and complete topic • sensory details that are related to and develop the main ideas
 Organization	• well-constructed paragraphs that are organized into an introduction, a body, and a conclusion • paragraphs that each have a topic sentence and supporting details • transitions that connect ideas
 Voice	• a voice and tone that are appropriate for the purpose and audience
 Word Choice	• precise, descriptive language that creates a picture for the reader
 Sentence Fluency	• a variety of sentences that make the writing interesting and easy to read aloud
 Conventions	• no or few errors in grammar, usage, mechanics, and spelling

Before you write, read David Morrow's descriptive essay on the next three pages. Then use the descriptive essay rubric on pages 370–371 to decide how well he did. (You might want to look back at What's in a Descriptive Essay? on page 364, too!)

Descriptive MODEL Essay

Sarah the Sound Engineer

by David Morrow

topic

introduction

most interesting information

Every weekday morning, Sarah and Tex take a taxi to her job. Sarah is a sound engineer for a radio reading service. She happens to be blind. Tex is her guide dog. Radio reading service is for people who are blind or visually impaired. Each day, the service broadcasts articles from newspapers, chapters of books, and interviews. In this way, people who cannot see can receive the same information as sighted people.

body

At work, Sarah wears headphones and sits at a control desk. In front of her is a panel with small sliding knobs called faders. Faders control the sound that comes from the microphones and the CD and tape players. Sarah has memorized the positions and functions of all the knobs on her panel. Her hands move like lightning across the panel. She quickly adjusts the faders as she listens to the different sounds coming through her headphones. She makes sure that every sound is clear. Her supervisor says Sarah is one of the best sound engineers the reading service has ever had.

specific details

Sarah likes her job because she spends the day listening to interesting information and music. Tex likes Sarah's job because the floor underneath her desk is as cool as a cave.

When Sarah gets home from work each day, she takes off her sunglasses and lets her long auburn hair out of its barrette. It flows like a waterfall over her shoulders. Then she puts on her favorite outfit: jeans and a T-shirt. She has trouble finding jeans that are short enough. She is only 5 foot 1 inch tall, as short as a minute, her father says.

specific details

body

After changing clothes, Sarah turns on classical music, waters her plants, listens to phone messages, returns calls, and cooks dinner. In the evening, she often visits with friends or her sister Meg, who lives in the same town. Sarah and Meg go out to eat at least once a week, usually at their favorite Mexican restaurant.

specific details

Sometimes Sarah just stays home and reads. She uses a computer and a scanner. The scanner transmits words from printed pages to the computer, and then the computer reads the words aloud, just like a person. Sarah also has a small computer called Braille'n Speak. It has buttons for the braille alphabet, the raised dots that blind people touch to read. Sarah uses this machine to type in braille or to turn braille dots into printed words. It can read for her, too. Like Tex, both of these machines help Sarah "see."

While Sarah reads, Tex usually sleeps. He's a large black Labrador retriever, and he has been trained to help her. Tex seems as smart as most people. Absolutely nothing escapes his attention. When he is working, he always wears a harness that Sarah holds in her left hand. He watches traffic, pauses at steps, and understands Sarah's commands.

specific details

You can see Sarah and Tex all around town. They get on buses, cross busy streets, ride elevators, and sometimes buy lunch at a vendor's stand. They go to restaurants, ice cream shops, concerts, and friends' homes. It's hard to talk about Sarah without talking about Tex. They are a team.

Sarah's life is a lot like most people's lives, but she is different in one way. She never travels alone. She always has the help of a friend named Tex.

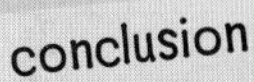

Descriptive Essay Rubric

Use this 6-point rubric to plan and score a descriptive essay.

	6	5	4
Ideas	Vivid sensory details support and develop a clear topic.	Most details support and develop the topic.	The writer uses some sensory details, but more are needed.
Organization	The introduction presents the topic, the body develops it, and the conclusion wraps it up in a satisfying way.	The introduction presents the topic, the body contains details, and the conclusion wraps it up.	The essay has an introduction, but it is not clear in places. The body mostly relates to the topic, and the conclusion may be weak.
Voice	The voice conveys the writer's purpose and engages the reader.	The writer's purpose comes through and engages the reader most of the time.	The writer's voice connects with the reader and is acceptable for the topic, purpose, and audience.
Word Choice	Descriptive and figurative language create precise pictures for the reader.	The writer uses similes, metaphors, and descriptive and figurative language most of the time.	Some of the descriptive and figurative language is confusing or vague.
Sentence Fluency	Sentence variety is enhanced with transitions that link ideas.	Most short sentences have been combined with transitions to make the writing flow.	Most sentences show a variety of length, beginnings, and structure. Transitions are helpful.
Conventions	Plural and possessive nouns and articles are correct.	There are a few minor errors with plural and possessive nouns and articles, but they do not distract the reader.	There are a few minor errors in plural and possessive nouns or articles that may confuse the reader.

+Presentation Use neat handwriting or a limited number of clear fonts.

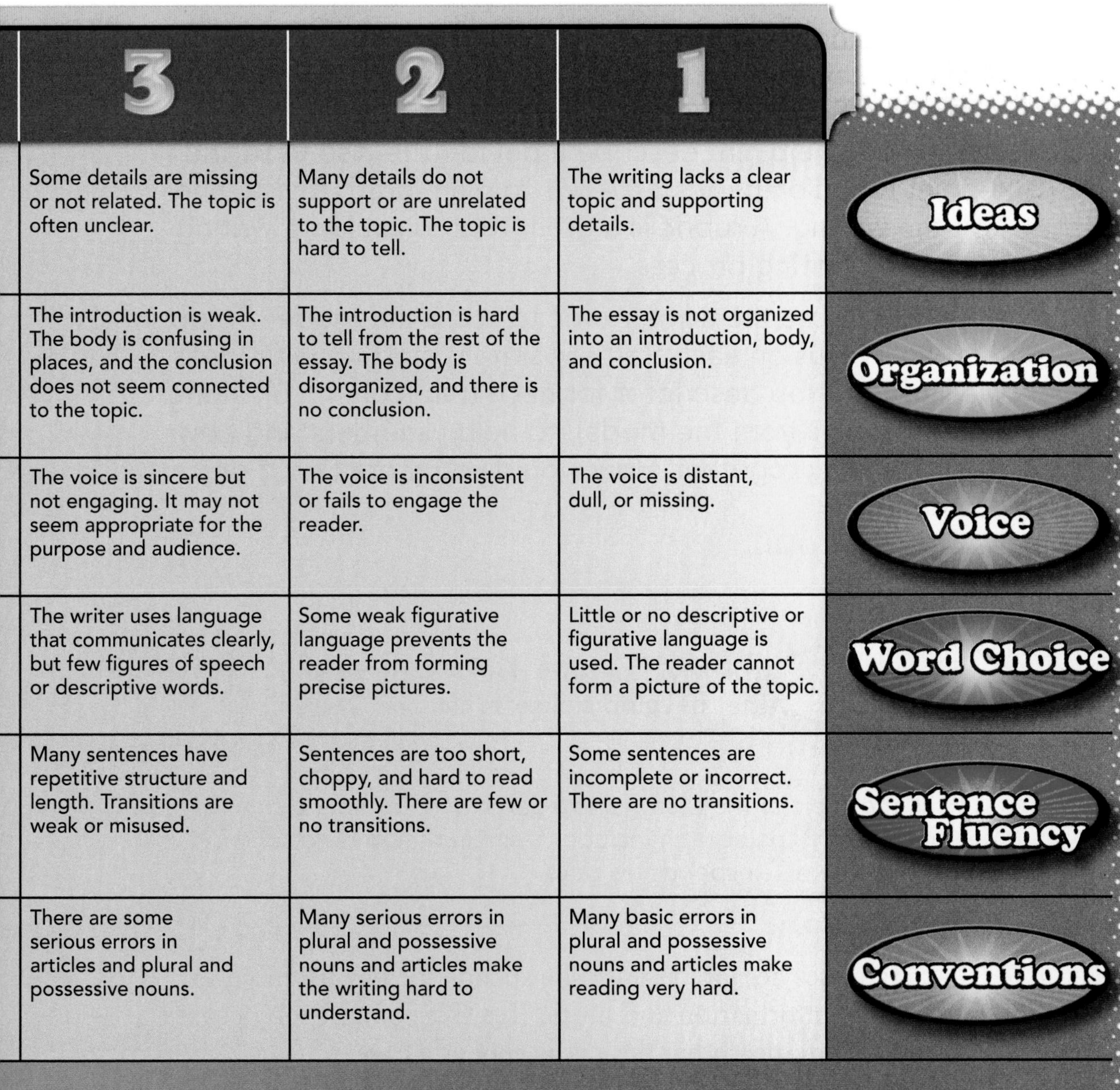

3	2	1	
Some details are missing or not related. The topic is often unclear.	Many details do not support or are unrelated to the topic. The topic is hard to tell.	The writing lacks a clear topic and supporting details.	Ideas
The introduction is weak. The body is confusing in places, and the conclusion does not seem connected to the topic.	The introduction is hard to tell from the rest of the essay. The body is disorganized, and there is no conclusion.	The essay is not organized into an introduction, body, and conclusion.	Organization
The voice is sincere but not engaging. It may not seem appropriate for the purpose and audience.	The voice is inconsistent or fails to engage the reader.	The voice is distant, dull, or missing.	Voice
The writer uses language that communicates clearly, but few figures of speech or descriptive words.	Some weak figurative language prevents the reader from forming precise pictures.	Little or no descriptive or figurative language is used. The reader cannot form a picture of the topic.	Word Choice
Many sentences have repetitive structure and length. Transitions are weak or misused.	Sentences are too short, choppy, and hard to read smoothly. There are few or no transitions.	Some sentences are incomplete or incorrect. There are no transitions.	Sentence Fluency
There are some serious errors in articles and plural and possessive nouns.	Many serious errors in plural and possessive nouns and articles make the writing hard to understand.	Many basic errors in plural and possessive nouns and articles make reading very hard.	Conventions

See Appendix B for 4-, 5-, and 6-point descriptive rubrics.

Using the Descriptive Essay Rubric to Study the Model

Did you notice that the model on pages 367–369 points out some key elements of a descriptive essay? As he wrote "Sarah the Sound Engineer," David Morrow used these elements to help him describe a person. He also used the 6-point rubric on pages 370–371 to plan, draft, revise, and edit the writing. A rubric is a great tool to evaluate writing during the writing process.

Now let's use the same rubric to score the model. To do this, we'll focus on each trait separately, starting with Ideas. We'll use the top descriptor for each trait (column 6), along with examples from the model, to help us understand how the traits work together. How would you score David on each trait?

- **Vivid sensory details support and develop a clear topic.**

I think the topic of the essay is how Sarah and Tex spend their time together. This paragraph includes a simile that gives a sensory detail about where Tex spends his days.

> Sarah likes her job because she spends the day listening to interesting information and music. Tex likes Sarah's job because the floor underneath her desk is as cool as a cave.

- **The introduction presents the topic, the body develops it, and the conclusion wraps it up in a satisfying way.**

David states his topic right away, and then the main part of his essay—the body—gives me all the information I want about Sarah and Tex. I liked the way he ends the essay, too. The conclusion gave me a pleasing mental image to take away after reading.

Sarah's life is a lot like most people's lives, but she is different in one way. She never travels alone. She always has the help of a friend named Tex.

- **The voice conveys the writer's purpose and engages the reader.**

David's writing voice is enthusiastic and knowledgeable. As he describes Tex, it's easy for me to connect with what he feels about the Labrador. I think this is important to remember as I write, too.

Tex seems as smart as most people. Absolutely nothing escapes his attention. When he is working, he always wears a harness that Sarah holds in her left hand. He watches traffic, pauses at steps, and understands Sarah's commands.

Using the Descriptive Essay Rubric to Study the Model

- **Descriptive and figurative language create precise pictures for the reader.**

I was curious how Sarah could be a sound engineer, and David uses specific, descriptive words to explain just how she does her job. His simile *like lightning* told me that her hands moved with amazing speed. This helped me imagine Sarah working expertly at the control desk.

> Sarah has memorized the positions and functions of all the knobs on her panel. Her hands move like lightning across the panel. She quickly adjusts the faders as she listens to the different sounds coming through her headphones.

- **Sentence variety is enhanced with transitions that link ideas.**

Instead of writing a series of short sentences, David combines the different things that Sarah and Tex do around town. The transition words *and sometimes* help connect the activities and make the sentences flow smoothly.

> You can see Sarah and Tex all around town. They get on buses, cross busy streets, ride elevators, and sometimes buy lunch at a vendor's stand. They go to restaurants, ice cream shops, concerts, and friends' homes.

- **Plural and possessive nouns and articles are correct.**

I didn't see any spelling or punctuation errors in David's essay, and he capitalizes words correctly. He also uses articles and plural and possessive nouns correctly.

Absolutely nothing escapes his attention. When he is working, he always wears a harness that Sarah holds in her left hand. He watches traffic, pauses at steps, and understands Sarah's commands.

Presentation Use neat handwriting or a limited number of clear fonts.

My Turn!

Now it's my turn to write a descriptive essay! I'll use the rubric and good writing strategies to help me. Follow along to see how I do it.

Prewrite

Focus on **Ideas**

The Rubric Says Vivid sensory details support and develop a clear topic.

Writing Strategy Choose an interesting subject. Gather information about him or her.

When my teacher asked us to write a descriptive essay, I didn't have to think too long before I came up with my topic. My great-grandfather, Joseph Cloud, is the most interesting person I know. I'm even named after him.

I am Native American, and my great-grandfather has taught me a lot about my family's Ute culture and customs. He's also told me lots of stories about himself. He's had a really fascinating life. I have so much I could write about! I will start by making a list of information about him.

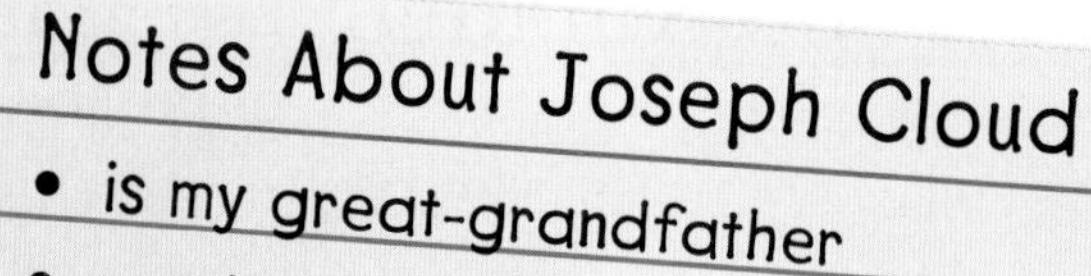

Notes About Joseph Cloud

- is my great-grandfather
- wants to preserve Ute heritage
- tells great stories
- taught me about my forefathers
- became a construction worker
- helped build the Vallecito Dam
- speaks and teaches the Ute language

Apply

Brainstorm a list of people who interest you and then pick one. Gather information about that person and take notes.

Prewrite

Focus on **Organization**

The Rubric Says The introduction presents the topic, the body develops it, and the conclusion wraps it up in a satisfying way.

Writing Strategy Use a Spider Map to organize the notes.

The rubric says the body of my essay should develop the topic. That means I need to include facts and details about my great-grandfather in the body. I'll use a Spider Map to help me organize the information I want to use.

Writer's Term

Spider Map

A **Spider Map** organizes information about a topic. The topic is written in the center. Important details are written on the "legs."

Spider Map

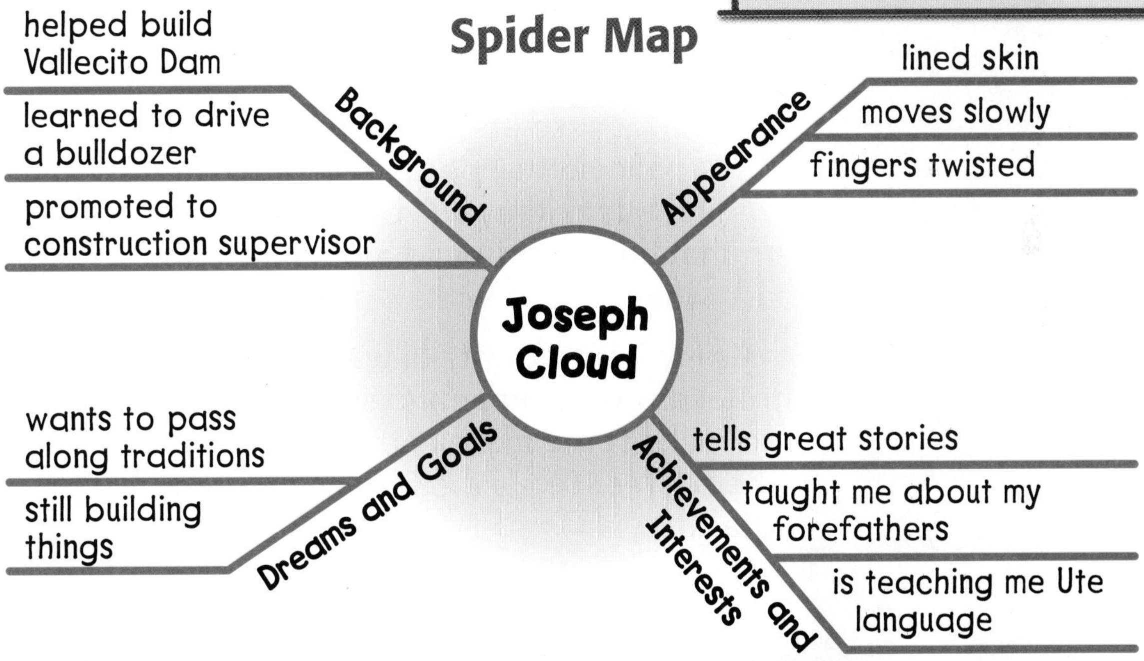

Joseph Cloud

Background
- helped build Vallecito Dam
- learned to drive a bulldozer
- promoted to construction supervisor

Appearance
- lined skin
- moves slowly
- fingers twisted

Dreams and Goals
- wants to pass along traditions
- still building things

Achievements and Interests
- tells great stories
- taught me about my forefathers
- is teaching me Ute language

Reflect

Look at the Spider Map. How is each leg important in describing someone?

Apply

Make your own Spider Map to organize your notes. Be sure to put your information in clear categories.

Draft

Focus on **Ideas**

The Rubric Says Vivid sensory details support and develop a clear topic.

Writing Strategy Choose details that both inform the audience and keep their attention.

I'm ready to start writing now. I've got all my information organized in my Spider Map, and I'll refer to it as I write my draft.

The rubric says that I need details, especially sensory details, to support and develop a clear topic for my descriptive essay. For me the clear topic is my great-grandfather's fascinating life. I want details that let my classmates know what he is like and some special things about his life. I think they will be fascinated to learn that he helped build a gigantic dam. That's what I'll start with.

As I write my draft, I'll watch out for mistakes in grammar and spelling, but if I do make some mistakes, I know I can fix them later. Here's the beginning of my draft.

Proofreading Marks

- ⊐ Indent
- ≡ Make uppercase
- / Make lowercase
- ∧ Add something
- Take out something
- ⊙ Add a period
- ¶ New paragraph
- (sp) Spelling error

[DRAFT]

Still Building

In 1936, my great-grandfather was nineteen years old and living on the Ute reservation in southwestern Colorado. Like many Ute mens, he knew that he could earn better wages working in construction. By the Fall of 1937, he was working on one of Colorados big dam projects, the Vallecito Dam. The dam was being built so people living in the Pine River Valley would have water for crops. To build the large earthen dam, soil had to be dug out of the ground and piled very thick and very high. Joseph Cloud operated a huge bulldozer, sometimes pushing soil up steep embankments. He was not afraid of tipping over, however, because he was very careful. He was so careful that he later became a construction supervisor for other dams being built in Colorado.

sensory details

Reflect

Read the beginning of Joe's draft. What details support his topic?

Apply

Use your Spider Map to write a draft. Include sensory details that support and develop your topic.

Revise

Focus on **Organization**

The Rubric Says The introduction presents the topic, the body develops it, and the conclusion wraps it up in a satisfying way.

Writing Strategy Introduce the topic clearly.

As I reread my draft, I liked the details I included in my introduction. But I don't think I did a great job of introducing my great-grandfather right at the beginning. I want people to know his name and why 1936 was an important year for him. I'll revise the introduction now.

Writer's Term

Introduction

The **introduction** should get the reader's attention and identify the topic.

[DRAFT]

clear topic

Joseph Cloud's journey began in 1936. He ~~In 1936, my great grandfather~~ was nineteen years old and living on the Ute reservation in southwestern Colorado.

Apply

Read your draft. Be sure to present your topic in a clear and interesting way right at the start.

Revise

Focus on **Voice**

The Rubric Says The voice conveys the writer's purpose and engages the reader.

Writing Strategy Share knowledge of and enthusiasm for the topic.

According to the rubric, my voice should let the reader know my purpose for writing. I also want my reader to know that I respect my great-grandfather. My sentences should say that.

Almost everything I know about my Ute heritage, I have learned from him. He teaches me stories of my forefathers.

^ My favorite stories are the ones about Ute

dances. One joyful dance performed every spring was the Bear Dance.

writer's voice

Reflect

How does Joe use his writing voice to connect with the reader?

Apply

Does your voice convey your purpose? Find places to add your knowledge of and respect for your topic.

Revise

The Rubric Says Descriptive and figurative language create precise pictures for the reader.

Writing Strategy Choose words and phrases for effect.

When I reread my draft, I found that some of my descriptions weren't very clear. The rubric says I should use descriptive and figurative language such as similes. I have to be careful not to pick boring similes, such as "his hair is as white as snow." Look at how I used similes to clarify my descriptions. Also notice the adjective *gnarled*. I like that word!

Writer's Term

Simile

A **simile** compares two different things by using the word **like** or **as**.

[DRAFT]

similes

My great-grandfather doesn't move as quickly as he used to. He is an old man now. His hair is long and ^as white as chalk,^ and he pulls it away from his deeply lined face with a piece of leather. His fingers are gnarled ^like the branches of an old tree,^ and they often rest upon a wooden cane.

Apply

Look over your draft again. Find places to add similes and other descriptive language that make your writing stronger.

Edit

Focus on **Conventions**

The Rubric Says Plural and possessive nouns and articles are correct.

Writing Strategy Check to see that plural nouns and possessive nouns are formed correctly and that articles are correct.

I'm ready to check my draft for spelling, punctuation, and capitalization. According to the rubric, I also have to make sure I used articles (*a*, *an*, *the*) and nouns correctly.

Writer's Term

Plural and Possessive Nouns

Plural nouns name more than one noun. **Possessive nouns** show ownership.

[DRAFT]

southwestern Colorado. Like many Ute mens, he knew that he could earn better wages working in construction. By the Fall of 1937, he was working on one of Colorados big dam projects, the Vallecito Dam.

corrected plural noun

corrected possessive noun

Reflect

Look at Joe's edits. How did he fix his mistakes? How do Joe's edits help you, the reader, understand the text?

Apply

Conventions

Edit your draft for spelling, punctuation, and capitalization. Correct any mistakes with plural and possessive nouns.

For more practice fixing articles and nouns, use the exercises on the next two pages.

Plural and Possessive Nouns

Know the Rule

Plural Nouns

- Add *-s* or *-es* to form the plural of most nouns. *(voice/voices; dish/dishes)*
- Change *y* to *i* and add *-es* to form the plural of some nouns ending in *y*. *(sky/skies)*
- Change *f* to *v* and add *-es* to form the plural of some nouns ending in *f*. *(leaf/leaves)*
- Some nouns change their spelling or remain unchanged in their plural form. *(man/men; sheep/sheep)*

Possessive Nouns

- Add an apostrophe and *-s* to form the possessive of singular nouns and plural nouns that do not end in *s*. *(the man's face/the men's faces)*
- Add only an apostrophe to form the possessive of plural nouns that end in *s*. *(the workers' boots)*

Practice the Rule

Number a sheet of paper 1–10. Then find the error in each sentence below and write the correct plural or possessive noun form. Label it **PL** for plural and **POSS** for possessive.

1. Zookeepers care for animals at zoos, especially the babys.
2. Most peoples become zookeepers because they love animals.
3. They take time to answer childrens questions.
4. They help children ride the ponys.
5. Zookeepers have a powerful influence on the animals lives.
6. They must know when an animal needs a veterinarians help.
7. Zookeepers protect animals from many varietys of disease.
8. Healthy animal's are happy animals.
9. Zookeepers know how to care for many animals, even sheeps.
10. A zookeepers life is always busy.

Articles

Know the Rule

An **article** is a special type of adjective. English has two articles: *the* and *a/an*. *The* is called a **definite article** because it describes a particular person, place, thing, or idea.

Example: He chose **the** new Mexican restaurant for his birthday party.

A and *an* are called **indefinite articles** because they describe nouns that are not specific. Use *a* before nouns that begin with a consonant.

Example: She has not sent **a** reply to our invitation.

Use *an* before nouns that begin with a vowel or vowel sound.

Example: We sent **an** invitation to her weeks ago.

Practice the Rule

Each of the sentences below has a missing article. Write the missing article to complete the sentence. Use the definitions above to choose the correct article.

1. (indefinite) My grandmother, Vera Scotti, is _____ sculptor.
2. (indefinite) Before she creates any statue of _____ animal, she always studies the animal closely on videos.
3. (definite) With pencil or pen, she sketches _____ animal.
4. (definite) My grandmother uses modeling clay to make small and large studies of _____ animal.
5. (indefinite) After she decides about size and position, she builds _____ model from wire, pipes, and modeling clay.
6. (indefinite) Then she takes it to _____ foundry to make a rubber mold that closely matches her model.
7. (definite) Workers at _____ same foundry pour hot wax into the mold to make a wax model.
8. (indefinite) Vera works carefully with special tools before the foundry transforms it into _____ impressive bronze statue.

Publish

+Presentation

Publishing Strategy Publish the descriptive essay in a class newsletter.

Presentation Strategy Use a limited selection of clear fonts.

I've finished my descriptive essay! I'm going to submit it to the editorial committee for our class newsletter. I think my classmates will enjoy reading about Joseph Cloud. I will type my essay on a computer, using easy-to-read fonts. Then I'll type a cover letter to the committee that explains why I think my essay should be published. After it's published, I'll give a copy to my great-grandfather. Before I submit my essay to the newsletter, though, I'll read through it to make sure I've done everything on my final checklist.

My Final Checklist

Did I—

- ✓ check my spelling, punctuation, and capitalization carefully?
- ✓ use nouns and articles correctly?
- ✓ use just a couple of clear, readable fonts?
- ✓ put my name on my paper?

Apply

Use this checklist to prepare a final copy of your essay. Then submit it for publication in your class or school newsletter. You can also submit a photograph of your topic.

Send | Reply | Attach | Print

Still Building

by Joe

Joseph Cloud's journey began in 1936. He was nineteen years old and living on the Ute reservation in southwestern Colorado. Like many Ute men, he knew that he could earn better wages working in construction. By the fall of 1937, he was working on one of Colorado's big dam projects, the Vallecito Dam. The dam was being built so people living in the Pine River Valley would have water for crops. To build the large earthen dam, soil had to be dug out of the ground and piled very thick and very high. Joseph Cloud operated a huge bulldozer, sometimes pushing soil up steep embankments. He was not afraid of tipping over, however, because he was very careful. He was so careful that he later became a construction supervisor for other dams being built in Colorado.

Joseph Cloud is my teacher. He is an elder in the Ute community, but he is also my great-grandfather. Almost everything I know about my Ute heritage, I have learned from him. He teaches me stories of my forefathers. My favorite stories are the ones about Ute dances. One joyful dance performed every spring was the Bear Dance. It went on for many days, and afterwards there was a tremendous feast. The dance included an instrument that sounded like a bear roaring after being asleep all winter. Dances celebrated everything from successful battles to buffalo hunts.

My great-grandfather doesn't move as quickly as he used to. He is an old man now. His hair is long and as white as chalk, and he pulls it away from his deeply lined face with a piece of leather. His fingers are gnarled like the branches of an old tree, and they often rest upon a wooden cane. There is one thing about him that still seems young. It is his eyes. They are bright and alert.

Joseph Cloud has seen many things in his long life, and he has lots of stories and wisdom to share. His voice rumbles like thunder whenever he speaks. He urges us to preserve our heritage. He tells us about his hopes for the Ute and our way of life. He says that he is still a construction worker, but now he is helping to build our future. We are all lucky to have Joseph Cloud in our lives, especially me!

Reflect

Use the rubric to score this essay. What are some ways that it shows the traits of a good descriptive essay? Be sure to use the rubric to score your own essay.

What's an Observation Report?

An observation report is an essay that describes in detail an object, person, event, or process.

What's in an Observation Report?

Why write an Observation Report?

People write observation reports for different reasons. Here are two reasons that I thought of.

Information

Observation reports are really important for scientists. Many scientists in history recorded important observations. Their observations have changed how people think and what they do.

Other people make observation reports, too. The police describe the scene of a crime or an accident. Doctors observe their patients and include their observations in medical reports.

Change

Observation reports can give important information to support changes. For example, sometimes a business or a school may not be performing well. Observers may come and report what they see. They may use their observations to recommend ways to improve how things work.

Linking Descriptive Writing Traits to an Observation Report

In this chapter, you will write a report on something you observed firsthand. This type of descriptive writing is called an observation report. Joe will guide you through the stages of the writing process: Prewrite, Draft, Revise, Edit, and Publish. In each stage, Joe will show you important writing strategies that are linked to the Descriptive Writing Traits below.

Descriptive Writing Traits

 Ideas	• a clear, focused, and complete topic • sensory details that are related to and develop the main ideas
 Organization	• well-constructed paragraphs that are organized into an introduction, a body, and a conclusion • paragraphs that each have a topic sentence and supporting details • transitions that connect ideas
 Voice	• a voice and tone that are appropriate for the purpose and audience
 Word Choice	• precise, descriptive language that creates a picture for the reader
 Sentence Fluency	• a variety of sentences that make the writing interesting and easy to read aloud
 Conventions	• no or few errors in grammar, usage, mechanics, and spelling

Before you write, read Evan Burns's observation report on the next page. Then use the observation report rubric on pages 392–393 to decide how well he did. (You might want to look back at What's in an Observation Report? on page 388, too!)

New Mexico Piñon Pines

November 25

by Evan Burns

Today, I visited an area near Chimayó, New Mexico. I wanted to take a closer look at the many piñon trees that grow there and produce such tasty seeds. I was amazed at the different locations in which I found them. They were everywhere. I saw them growing high up on the rims of canyons, on dry mesas and plateaus, on the slopes of rocky foothills, and in forest groves.

topic

Piñon pines are not large. The tallest one I saw was about 35 feet high, about as tall as a three-story building. The trunks are only one to two feet in diameter, and most of the trunks are crooked and irregular. Reddish branches reach up to form a rounded top on many piñon pines. Sprouting from these branches are short pine needles that grow in pairs. They give off a wonderful evergreen scent. Nestled within the needles are small, egg-shaped pinecones. The largest ones I saw were only two inches long. The pinecones are yellowish-brown, and a sticky resin coated my hands after I touched them.

topic sentence

sensory details

Piñon pinecones contain large seeds. These seeds are the sweet, rich piñon nuts, or pine nuts, that I like to eat. When the pinecone opens up, the piñon seeds fall out. Walking among the trees, I talked to some people who were harvesting the seeds. Proudly, they showed me burlap bags stuffed with piñon seeds. In one year, a single piñon pine can produce nine bushels of seeds!

sensory details

People are not the only creatures who enjoy eating piñon nuts. I spotted jays, quails, and wild turkeys eating every seed they could find. I've heard that bears and deer eat piñon seeds, too, but I didn't see any today. I did, however, see porcupines and many wood rats. One wood rat ran into a hole in a tree. After he left, I looked inside and saw that he had put away seeds for the winter.

focus

When I had dinner this evening, there were delicious piñon nuts on my salad. I thought about these trees that can grow out of rock, endure the wind and heat, survive dry conditions, and provide food for both humans and animals. They are truly a wonder!

Observation Report Rubric

Use this 6-point rubric to plan and score an observation report.

	6	5	4
Ideas	Each main idea is supported with accurate and interesting sensory details.	Each main idea is supported with several accurate sensory details.	Most details are clear and concise, but a few may be confusing.
Organization	Each paragraph contains a topic sentence and related supporting details. Transitions link ideas between sentences and between paragraphs.	Most paragraphs contain topic sentences and transitions that link ideas effectively.	Some topic sentences are unclear or missing. Some ideas lack transitions or have unclear transitions.
Voice	A strong voice shows that the writer knows and cares about the topic.	The writer's voice is appropriate and fairly strong, but needs to be consistent throughout the report.	Most of the time, the writer's commitment to the topic is clear. Voice is sincere but ordinary.
Word Choice	Carefully chosen, precise words create a vivid picture for the reader.	More precise words could create better pictures for the reader.	The writing creates some vivid pictures for the reader. In some places, words are vague or dull.
Sentence Fluency	Sentences of different structures and lengths make the report enjoyable to read.	Most sentences have varied structures and lengths.	The writing is easy to read in most places. There is some variety in sentence length and structure.
Conventions	Spelling, punctuation, and capitalization are correct. Subjects and verbs agree.	There are a few minor errors with subjects and verbs, but they do not distract the reader.	There are some errors with subjects and verbs, but they do not confuse the reader.
+Presentation	Indent each new paragraph.		

3	2	1	
Some details do not support or enhance the main ideas.	Some ideas are unsupported, with limited use of sensory details.	The report does not contain clear, focused ideas or related details.	Ideas
In several places it is hard to follow the ideas because paragraphs lack topic sentences or transitions.	Few or no paragraphs have topic sentences. Few transitions are used, making the ideas hard to follow.	The report is a list of sentences with nothing to connect them.	Organization
The voice may not be appropriate for the topic, purpose, and audience. The reader is confused.	The writer's voice is weak or distant; the writer needs to connect with the reader.	The writer's voice fails to communicate purpose or connect with the reader.	Voice
Too few precise words leave the reader confused.	Incorrect or imprecise words do not provide clear pictures.	Words are misleading, confusing, and vague. The writer shows no interest in purpose or meaning.	Word Choice
Many sentences share the same length and structure, making the writing awkward.	Little or no sentence variety causes the reader to lose interest and the writing to be choppy and awkward.	The writing is very difficult to follow. Repetitive sentence beginnings and run-ons and fragments interrupt meaning.	Sentence Fluency
Several errors with subjects and verbs make the writing hard to follow in places.	Major errors with subjects and verbs confuse the reader.	Many errors with subjects and verbs stop the reader. The reader cannot understand the report.	Conventions

See Appendix B for 4-, 5-, and 6-point descriptive rubrics.

Using the Observation Report Rubric to Study the Model

Did you notice that the model on page 391 points out some key elements of a personal narrative? As he wrote "New Mexico Piñon Pines," Evan Burns used these elements to help him describe a special kind of pine tree. He also used the 6-point rubric on pages 392–393 to plan, draft, revise, and edit the writing. A rubric is a great tool to evaluate writing during the writing process.

Now let's use the same rubric to score the model. To do this, we'll focus on each trait separately, starting with Ideas. We'll use the top descriptor for each trait (column 6), along with examples from the model, to help us understand how the traits work together. How would you score Evan on each trait?

- **Each main idea is supported with accurate and interesting sensory details.**

Evan went out to look at piñon pines closely and reported what he saw. In each paragraph of the report, he states a main idea and supports it with interesting sensory details. Notice how he describes the seeds of the pinecones.

> Piñon pinecones contain large seeds. These seeds are the sweet, rich piñon nuts, or pine nuts, that I like to eat. When the pinecone opens up, the piñon seeds fall out.

- **Each paragraph contains a topic sentence and related supporting details.**
- **Transitions link ideas between sentences and between paragraphs.**

Evan begins each paragraph in his report with a topic sentence. The first sentence of the paragraph below tells me the main idea is the size of the trees. Look back at the essay to see that Evan mentions pinecones later on in the paragraph. This works as a transition to the main idea of the next paragraph.

Piñon pines are not large. The tallest one I saw was about 35 feet high, about as tall as a three-story building. The trunks are only one to two feet in diameter, and most of the trunks are crooked and irregular.

- **A strong voice shows that the writer knows and cares about the topic.**

Evan sounds knowledgeable as he describes his topic in detail. His voice conveys enthusiasm and a sense of wonder, too.

When I had dinner this evening, there were delicious piñon nuts on my salad. I thought about these trees that can grow out of rock, endure the wind and heat, survive dry conditions, and provide food for both humans and animals. They are truly a wonder!

Using the Observation Report Rubric to Study the Model

- **Carefully chosen, precise words create a vivid picture for the reader.**

Evan uses precise words to convey the shape, color, and size of the pinecones. The adjectives *small, egg-shaped, yellowish-brown,* and *sticky* help the reader "see" and "feel" what he experienced. The precise verb *coated* really "shows" me what his hands were like.

Nestled within the needles are small, egg-shaped pinecones. The largest ones I saw were only two inches long. The pinecones are yellowish-brown, and a sticky resin coated my hands after I touched them.

- **Sentences of different structures and lengths make the report enjoyable to read.**

Evan uses a variety of sentence lengths and structures. In this example, a short, three-word sentence is followed by a much longer sentence. Variety helps make the report flow.

They were everywhere. I saw them growing high up on the rims of canyons, on dry mesas and plateaus, on the slopes of rocky foothills, and in forest groves.

- **Spelling, punctuation, and capitalization are correct. Subjects and verbs agree.**

Evan makes sure that the subjects he uses agree with the verbs. When subjects and verbs agree, the reader does not have to guess at the writer's meaning.

I've heard that bears and deer eat piñon seeds, too, but I didn't see any today.

+Presentation Indent each new paragraph.

My Turn!

Now I'm going to write my own observation report. Follow along, and you'll see how I use good writing strategies and the rubric to guide my writing.

Prewrite

Focus on **Ideas**

The Rubric Says Each main idea is supported with accurate and interesting sensory details.

Writing Strategy Take detailed notes.

Right before our spring break, my teacher told us we were going to write an observation report. He asked us to take notes on something we observed while we were on break. My family planned to visit my grandmother. She lives near a salt marsh on the Atlantic coast. Salt water flows in and out with the tide, and all kinds of plants and animals live there.

I made notes of sights, sounds, and smells in the salt marsh. I also made sketches of what I saw. Later I used a field guide to help identify some of the things I saw. Here are my notes.

Notes

high and low tides
salt water
herons and egrets in marsh
birds eat–snails
fiddler crabs
fish
insects
sounds–crickets
frogs
birds
spartina grass
cattails
algae
strong smell
shrubs along edge

Apply

Think about interesting natural places, plants, or animals that you could observe. Take notes and make sketches of what you see.

Prewrite

Focus on **Organization**

The Rubric Says Each paragraph contains a topic sentence and related supporting details.

Writing Strategy Use a Network Tree to organize the notes.

The rubric reminds me that organization is important. I used a Network Tree to help me group details around my main points. This will help me organize my information into paragraphs.

Writer's Term

Network Tree

A **Network Tree** organizes information. The topic goes at the top, and main points about the topic go on the next level. Details about each main point go on the bottom.

Network Tree

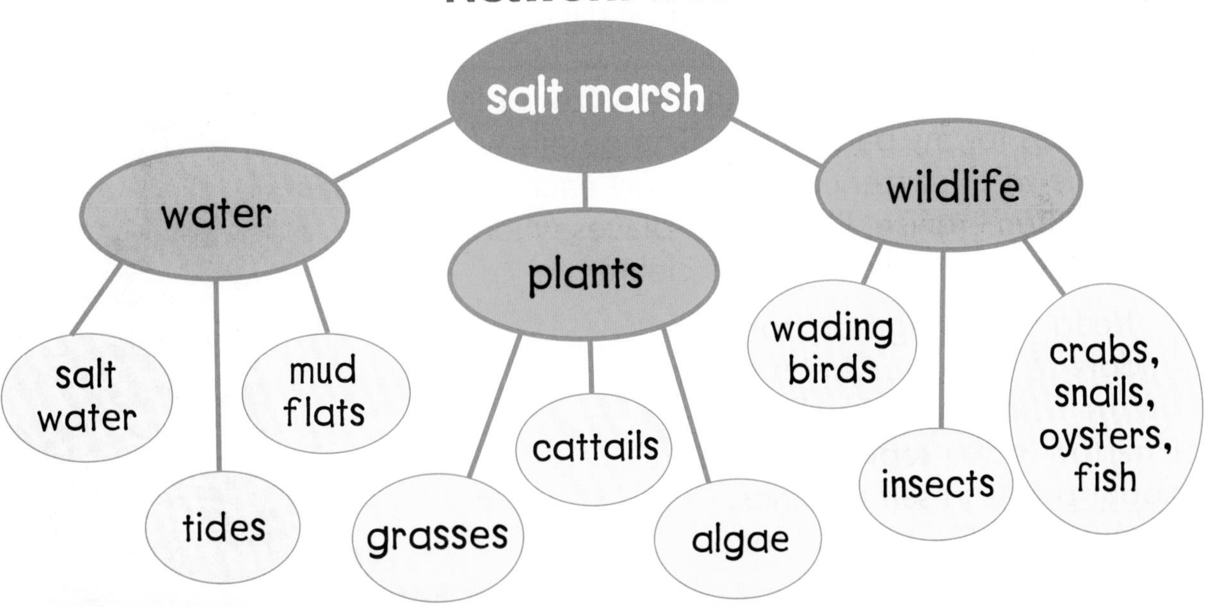

Reflect

What are the main points on Joe's Network Tree?

Apply

Make your own Network Tree. Use it to help you organize your notes and ideas about your topic.

Draft

Focus on **Organization**

The Rubric Says Each paragraph contains a topic sentence and related supporting details. Transitions link ideas between sentences and between paragraphs.

Writing Strategy State the main point, or idea, of the paragraph in a topic sentence.

Now I'm ready to write my draft. The rubric reminds me that my paragraphs should have topic sentences, supporting details, and transitions.

Writer's Term

Topic Sentence, Detail Sentence

A **topic sentence** states the main idea of the paragraph. It is often the first sentence, but it may be placed in the middle or at the end of the paragraph.

A **detail sentence** supports the paragraph's main idea. The detail sentences in each paragraph should tell about the main idea.

The main points on the Network Tree will help me write topic sentences for my paragraphs. The details will help me write sentences to support each main idea. When I revise, I'll look for places where transitions will make my ideas clearer.

Read the paragraph from the middle of my observation report on the next page. You'll see that I started with a topic sentence about plants in salt marshes. Then I added detail sentences to tell about plants that grow in the salt marsh.

Proofreading Marks

⊐	Indent	ℓ	Take out something
≡	Make uppercase	⊙	Add a period
/	Make lowercase	¶	New paragraph
∧	Add something	(sp)	Spelling error

[DRAFT]

topic sentence

The moist salt marsh is a perfect area for plants to grow. Cordgrass gives the marsh its yellowish-green color. It stands five or six feet tall, and its long thin reeds sway in the breeze. Black needle rush reaches my waist, and the shorter spartina grass comes up to my knees. As I examine the standing water and tidal creeks, I can see colorful saltwater plankton and clumps of algae floating on the surface. Both are blooming, and they make the water thick and soupy. Along the edges of the marsh are cattails and shrubs. Salt myrtle and marsh elder are two shrubs I can identify.

repeated word as transition

detail sentences

Reflect

Read the middle of Joe's observation report. Do all of Joe's sentences support the topic sentence?

Apply

Use your Network Tree to draft your observation report. Be sure each paragraph has a topic sentence, supporting detail sentences, and transitions that connect ideas.

Revise

Focus on **Voice**

The Rubric Says A strong voice shows that the writer knows and cares about the topic.

Writing Strategy Use first person (*I, me*) to show a personal connection with the writing.

From the rubric, I understand that my voice should convey that I know and care about the salt marsh. In my draft I found places where my voice could come through more.

Writer's Term

First-Person Pronouns

Use **first-person pronouns—I, me, my, mine, we, us, our,** and **ours**—to connect directly with the reader.

By using first-person pronouns, I show that my knowledge comes from my personal experience. By sharing what I saw, heard, touched, and smelled, my voice really connects with the reader!

[DRAFT]

first-person point of view

The marsh stretches as far as ~~the eye~~ [my eyes] can see. ~~When~~ [As I step into the marsh,] the sun is high, ~~it is a warm, sticky place.~~ [and a warm, humid stickiness surrounds me.] ~~It has a~~ [I take a deep breath and inhale the] strong smell of salt water, plants, and decay.

first-person point of view

Apply

Read your draft again. Use the first-person point of view to share your observations.

Revise

Focus on **Word Choice**

The Rubric Says Carefully chosen, precise words create a vivid picture for the reader.

Writing Strategy Describe the scene with precise adjectives and verbs.

The rubric reminds me to choose precise adjectives and verbs that help create a vivid picture of the salt marsh. In my draft I added some adjectives that I hope will help my readers feel like they are in the marsh themselves. Notice that the adjectives all relate to the senses. They describe sights and sounds.

[DRAFT]

use a specific verb

I take a deep breath and inhale the strong ^, murky smell of salt water, ^lush green plants, and ^muddy decay. The air is filled with the ^blended sounds of ^buzzing insects and ^singing birds. My grandma calls this "marsh music."

added precise adjectives

Reflect

Look at Joe's new words. How do his carefully chosen words paint a vivid picture for the reader?

Apply

Look through your draft. Replace vague adjectives and verbs with precise ones.

Revise

The Rubric Says Sentences of different structures and lengths make the report enjoyable to read.

Writing Strategy Make the sentences different kinds and lengths.

At this point, my observation report included all my main ideas and the important details. But it just didn't flow along. In fact, some of the report was boring to read.

The rubric reminds me to vary my sentences, both in length and structure. I found sections where almost all the sentences began with the subject. That can get boring! I'll try starting some sentences with phrases or adverbs to add variety and connect my ideas, too.

added adverbs

added phrase

[DRAFT]

The salt marsh is a tidal wetland that connects the ocean and the land. ^Twice daily, ~~T~~the tide floods in and out of it. ^Now ~~T~~the tide is low. ^Throughout the morning, ~~W~~water has been draining out of the marsh and back into the ocean.

Apply

Look over your draft again. To improve the flow of your report, revise your sentences so they are different types and lengths.

Edit

Focus on **Conventions**

The Rubric Says Spelling, punctuation, and capitalization are correct. Subjects and verbs agree.

Writing Strategy Make sure the subject always agrees with the verb.

Now I need to proofread my report. I always check my spelling, punctuation, and capitalization. But I'm also going to pay careful attention to my verbs. Here are a few of the corrections I made while editing.

Writer's Term

Subject-Verb Agreement

Subjects and **verbs agree**, or go together correctly, in a sentence when a singular subject is used with a singular verb, or when a plural subject agrees with a plural verb.

[DRAFT]

Soggy mud flats stands where tidal water has been, and a small tidal creek glisten^s as it snakes out of sight.

corrected subject-verb agreement

corrected subject-verb agreement

Reflect

What will you check first when you edit your report? What errors do you make often?

Apply

Conventions

Edit your draft for spelling, punctuation, and capitalization. Make sure all subjects and verbs agree, including the forms of *be*.

For practice making subjects and verbs agree, use the exercises on the next two pages.

Conventions **Grammar, Usage & Mechanics**

Subject-Verb Agreement

Know the Rule

Singular subjects take **singular verbs**.
- Add *-s* or *-es* to a verb when the subject is singular.
  Example: A carnivorous **plant eats** animals.

Plural subjects take **plural verbs**.
- Do not add *-s* or *-es* when the subject is a plural noun or is one of the pronouns *I, you, we,* or *they*.
  Examples: **Venus flytraps** grow in bogs.
  They trap insects.

Using Forms of the Verb "to be"
- Use *am* after *I*.
  Example: **I am** interested in carnivorous plants.
- Use *is* or *was* with singular subjects.
  Example: My Venus flytrap **plant is** very healthy.
- Use *are* or *were* with plural subjects.
  Example: Carnivorous **plants are** rare.

Practice the Rule

If the sentence contains an error in subject-verb agreement, rewrite the sentence correctly. If a sentence is correct, write **Correct**.

1. Venus flytraps grow in the bogs of North and South Carolina.
2. They eats flies and ants.
3. The Venus flytrap leaf lies on the ground.
4. A bright red color on the leaf attract insects.
5. A sweet liquid also lure insects onto the leaf.
6. Then the two sections of the leaf snaps together quickly.
7. Only small insects escapes between the sharp points.
8. After a while, the leaf closes tightly.
9. The Venus flytrap surround the body with liquid.
10. The decomposing insect give the plant its nitrogen.

Forms of *Be*

Know the Rule

Am, is, was, are, and *were* are forms of the verb *be*.
Use the verbs *is* and *was* after a **singular subject** or after the pronouns *he, she,* or *it*.

Example: The pine tree **is** taller than our house. It **was** planted many years ago.

Use the verbs *am* and *was* after the pronoun *I*.

Example: I **am** in a new school now. Last year I **was** in a different school.

Use the verbs *are* and *were* after a **plural subject** or after the pronouns *we*, *you*, or *they*.

Example: We **were** here early, but you **are** just on time.

Practice the Rule

Write the correct form of the verb to correctly complete each sentence.

1. An exhibit about frogs (is/are) at the science museum now.
2. At the exhibit, I (was/were) amazed at how large and how small frogs can be.
3. Some, such as the litter-leaf frog, (are/is) the size of a dime.
4. At the other extreme, the goliath frog (are/is) about a foot long.
5. The habitat of goliath frogs (are/is) rainforests in western Africa.
6. The range of colors for frogs (was/were) also a surprise to me.
7. If you (are/is) someone who thinks that all frogs are green, this exhibit will change your mind.
8. Some frogs I saw (was/were) brilliant blue.
9. When we (was/were) at the museum last summer, the frog exhibit was not open yet.
10. If you want to see the frog exhibit, I (am/is) happy to go again.

Publish

+Presentation

Publishing Strategy Record the report in an observation journal.

Presentation Strategy Indent each new paragraph.

I've finished writing my observation report! I like the idea of keeping it and other observations in an observation journal. I can read what I've written whenever I like. Then I'll remember the things I've seen. I could also use my report for science class, or present it as an oral report with pictures so that my classmates can learn about what I observed.

As I wrote my report, I tried to indent each paragraph. When I indent, I make it easy for the reader to see information about one main idea at a time. Before copying my report into my journal, I read through it one more time. Here's the final checklist I used.

My Final Checklist

Did I—

- ✔ check my spelling, punctuation, and capitalization carefully?
- ✔ make sure my subjects and verbs agree?
- ✔ indent every paragraph?
- ✔ use neat handwriting or word processing?
- ✔ put my name on my paper?

Apply

Use this checklist to prepare a final copy of your observation report for your journal. Include any sketches you made while observing, too.

The Salt Marsh Behind Grandma's House

April 15

by Joe

The salt marsh I am exploring is behind my grandmother's house in Georgia, near the coast of the Atlantic Ocean. The marsh stretches as far as my eyes can see. As I step into the marsh, the sun is high, and a warm, humid stickiness surrounds me. I take a deep breath and inhale the strong, murky smell of salt water, lush green plants, and muddy decay. The air is filled with the blended sounds of buzzing insects and singing birds. My grandma calls this "marsh music." Walking into the salt marsh is like entering a different world.

The salt marsh is a tidal wetland that connects the ocean and the land. Twice daily, the tide floods in and out of this special marsh. Now the tide is low. Throughout the morning, salt water has been draining out of the marsh and back into the ocean. Soggy mud flats stand where tidal water has been, and a small tidal creek glistens as it snakes out of sight. The tidal creek is there only at low tide. At high tide, that whole area is under water. Damp and mushy, the ground sucks at my shoes wherever I step.

The moist salt marsh is a perfect area for plants to grow. Cordgrass gives the marsh its yellowish-green color. It stands five or six feet tall, which is taller than I am. Its long thin reeds sway in the breeze. Black needle rush reaches my waist, and the shorter spartina grass comes up to my knees. As I examine the standing water and tidal creeks, I can see colorful saltwater plankton and clumps of algae floating on the surface. Both are blooming, and they make the water thick and soupy. Along the edges of the marsh are cattails and shrubs. Salt myrtle and marsh elder are two shrubs I can identify.

Although tall grasses make it hard to see what's here, the salt marsh is full of wildlife. The first things I notice are the large wading birds. A great blue heron not far from me is nearly four feet tall and has bent its long neck into an "S" shape. Smaller blue herons and white egrets circle overhead and land in the marsh. Other birds stand quietly as they scan the water and mud flats for food. They search for fiddler crabs, snails, oysters, clams, and small fish. These smaller creatures live in the mud flats, on plants, or in the marsh waters. The wading birds also eat insects. Looking more closely, I see grasshoppers, deer flies, and dragonflies. Although I can't see them, I know the "no-see-ums" are out. They keep biting my arms and legs!

This salt marsh is a good example of the ecosystems I learned about in school. The tidal waters, the mud, the plants, and the wildlife all work together. Each part depends on the other parts. These plants could not live here without the saltwater tide every day, and the wildlife would not be here at all if there were no plants. I am glad that my grandmother lives here and that I get to visit her often. I can't wait to explore this salt marsh again!

Reflect

Use the rubric to check Joe's observation report. Which of the traits would you rate as excellent? Check your observation report against the rubric, too!

What's a Biographic Sketch?

It's a short description of the life of a real person.

What's in a Biographic Sketch?

Facts
The facts about a person are true pieces of information. This includes a person's name, where he or she lives, and important events that happened.

Characteristics
These are the special qualities that the person has, such as determination, honesty, or curiosity. Characteristics could also include special talents a person has.

Achievements
These are what a person has accomplished in life, the ways in which he or she has been successful.

Interesting Details
Details are words or phrases that give more information about a person or event. I will include interesting details, so my person will seem real to my readers.

Why write a Biographic Sketch?

Here are some reasons for writing a biographic sketch.

Entertainment
People are so interesting! People can be quiet or adventuresome, heroes or villains. They change over time. They make good decisions or bad ones. Exploring the world of people is fascinating!

Information
Learning about the lives of others can inspire us. It can help us solve problems, see things from new perspectives, or set new goals for ourselves.

Understanding
Describing other people can help us understand them better. We can recognize what we have in common. We can learn to appreciate our differences.

Linking Descriptive Writing Traits to a Biographic Sketch

In this chapter, you will write about the life of someone you admire. This type of descriptive writing is called a biographic sketch. Joe will guide you through the stages of the writing process: Prewrite, Draft, Revise, Edit, and Publish. In each stage, Joe will show you important writing strategies that are linked to the Descriptive Writing Traits below.

Descriptive Writing Traits

- a clear, focused, and complete topic
- sensory details that are related to and develop the main ideas

- well-constructed paragraphs that are organized into an introduction, a body, and a conclusion
- paragraphs that each have a topic sentence and supporting details
- transitions that connect ideas

- a voice and tone that are appropriate for the purpose and audience

- precise, descriptive language that creates a picture for the reader

- a variety of sentences that make the writing interesting and easy to read aloud

- no or few errors in grammar, usage, mechanics, and spelling

Before you write, read Laurie Duncan's biographic sketch on the next page. Then use the biographic sketch rubric on pages 416–417 to decide how well she did. (You might want to look back at What's in a Biographic Sketch? on page 412, too!)

Benjamin Banneker: A Passion for Learning

by Laurie Duncan

facts

Benjamin Banneker was born on a farm in rural Maryland to a family of freed slaves. He was raised in a log house, set in an area of lush hills and dense forests. His childhood was filled with chores, such as feeding the farm animals, picking fruit, and tending the crops. He could not have imagined that one day he would become a well-known scientist and writer.

Young Benjamin had very little schooling. He learned to read from his grandmother, who used the family's only book, the Bible, as a lesson book. Although he went to school whenever he could, most of what he learned he taught himself from books that he borrowed. He read fiction, history, mathematics, and science.

achievement

fact

When Benjamin Banneker was 58 years old, he became fascinated with the night sky. A neighbor lent him a brass telescope and some books on astronomy. Through his window, he watched the stars. Then he used a ruler and compass to plot their positions and predict their locations throughout the year.

interesting detail

The neighbor found Benjamin a job surveying the land for the nation's new capital at Washington, D.C. Banneker worked through the frigid winter months in the marshy forests of the region. At night, he worked in a special tent with a hole cut in the top. He used the main telescope, which pointed upward to a patch of sky. Through careful observation, Banneker maintained the astronomical clock. The clock made sure that the crew's data were accurate. The crew used this data to plot the map of the new city.

fact

achievement

When Banneker returned to his farm, he began writing almanacs. An almanac is a kind of written calendar that tells the positions of the sun, moon, stars, and planets throughout the year. Banneker became well known for his work. As he aged, his hair grew white, which gave him a distinguished look. He also had an upright stance and always dressed neatly. Although he had lived a simple life, his appearance and knowledge commanded respect. He spoke and wrote on topics of science and also called for an end to slavery. He pointed to his own accomplishments as proof that all people are created equal.

interesting details

Biographic Sketch Rubric

Use this 6-point rubric to plan and score a biographic sketch.

	6	5	4
Ideas	The ideas are clear. Unusual details show in-depth knowledge and make the subject come alive.	Ideas are clear. The writing includes some unusual details that show in-depth topic knowledge.	Some of the ideas are clear and supported by relevant details.
Organization	Well-organized paragraphs have a topic sentence, engaging details, and helpful transitions.	Most paragraphs have a topic sentence, supporting details, and helpful transitions.	Most paragraphs have a topic sentence. Some may lack supporting details. Transition words are used correctly in most places.
Voice	The writer sounds sincere and knowledgeable about the subject from beginning to end.	The voice is sincere and knowledgeable in all but a few places.	The writer's passion is evident most of the time. The voice sounds sincere but not always knowledgeable.
Word Choice	Precise, original words help the reader easily understand the subject of the sketch.	Most of the writing is clear, original, and precise.	A few precise words are used, but the description could be clearer.
Sentence Fluency	A variety of sentence types makes the writing flow smoothly.	A variety of sentence types makes the writing smooth most of the time.	A few paragraphs lack variety in sentence types, making the writing choppy.
Conventions	Spelling, punctuation, and capitalization are correct. Commas and the words *that, which,* and *who* are used correctly.	There are a few minor errors with conventions, commas and *that, which,* and *who*, but they do not interfere with meaning.	Conventions are mostly correct. Some minor errors with commas and *that, which,* and *who* are noticeable but do not distract the reader.

+Presentation The biographic sketch is neatly prepared and legible.

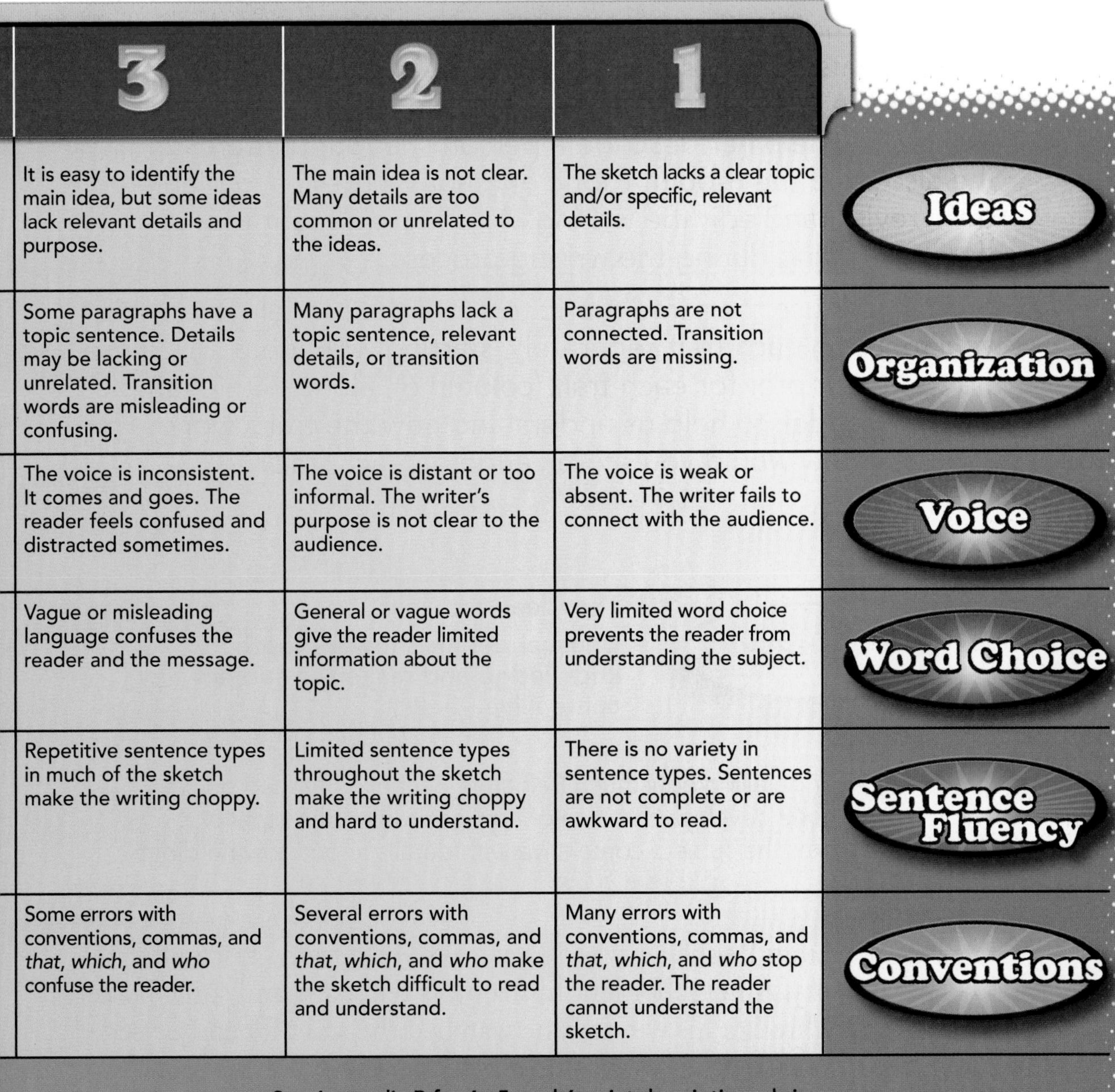

3	2	1	
It is easy to identify the main idea, but some ideas lack relevant details and purpose.	The main idea is not clear. Many details are too common or unrelated to the ideas.	The sketch lacks a clear topic and/or specific, relevant details.	Ideas
Some paragraphs have a topic sentence. Details may be lacking or unrelated. Transition words are misleading or confusing.	Many paragraphs lack a topic sentence, relevant details, or transition words.	Paragraphs are not connected. Transition words are missing.	Organization
The voice is inconsistent. It comes and goes. The reader feels confused and distracted sometimes.	The voice is distant or too informal. The writer's purpose is not clear to the audience.	The voice is weak or absent. The writer fails to connect with the audience.	Voice
Vague or misleading language confuses the reader and the message.	General or vague words give the reader limited information about the topic.	Very limited word choice prevents the reader from understanding the subject.	Word Choice
Repetitive sentence types in much of the sketch make the writing choppy.	Limited sentence types throughout the sketch make the writing choppy and hard to understand.	There is no variety in sentence types. Sentences are not complete or are awkward to read.	Sentence Fluency
Some errors with conventions, commas, and *that*, *which*, and *who* confuse the reader.	Several errors with conventions, commas, and *that*, *which*, and *who* make the sketch difficult to read and understand.	Many errors with conventions, commas, and *that*, *which*, and *who* stop the reader. The reader cannot understand the sketch.	Conventions

See Appendix B for 4-, 5, and 6-point descriptive rubrics.

Using the Biographic Sketch Rubric to Study the Model

Did you notice that the model on page 415 points out some key elements of a personal narrative? As she wrote "Benjamin Banneker: A Passion for Learning," Laurie Duncan used these elements to help her describe a person she found interesting. She also used the 6-point rubric on pages 416–417 to plan, draft, revise, and edit the writing. A rubric is a great tool to evaluate writing during the writing process.

Now let's use the same rubric to score the model. To do this, we'll focus on each trait separately, starting with Ideas. We'll use the top descriptor for each trait (column 6), along with examples from the model, to help us understand how the traits work together. How would you score Laurie on each trait?

- **The ideas are clear.**
- **Unusual details show in-depth knowledge and make the subject come alive.**

After detailing how much Benjamin Banneker learned on his own, Laurie develops the idea of how he studied the night sky. She makes the subject come alive with details about how he did it.

When Benjamin Banneker was 58 years old, he became fascinated with the night sky. A neighbor lent him a brass telescope and some books on astronomy. Through his window, he watched the stars. Then he used a ruler and compass to plot their positions and predict their locations throughout the year.

- **Well-organized paragraphs have a topic sentence, engaging details, and helpful transitions.**

In this paragraph, Laurie uses transition words to add details to explain Benjamin Banneker's work.

Banneker worked through the frigid winter months in the marshy forests of the region. At night, he worked in a special tent with a hole cut in the top.

- **The writer sounds sincere and knowledgeable about the subject from beginning to end.**

In her introduction, Laurie shows her knowledge of Banneker's early life and of how much he would achieve. Her sincere admiration comes through to the reader. In fact, her voice is very consistent all the way through.

His childhood was filled with chores, such as feeding the farm animals, picking fruit, and tending the crops. He could not have imagined that one day he would become a well-known scientist and writer.

Using the Biographic Sketch Rubric to Study the Model

- **Precise, original words help the reader easily understand the subject of the sketch.**

When Laurie describes Benjamin Banneker as an older man, her precise words clearly convey the impression he made on people. *Had an upright stance* is a great phrase!

As he aged, his hair grew white, which gave him a distinguished look. He also had an upright stance and always dressed neatly. Although he had lived a simple life, his appearance and knowledge commanded respect.

- **A variety of sentence types makes the writing flow smoothly.**

Laurie's sketch is fun to read because she uses lots of different kinds of sentences. She uses both short and long sentences to keep the pace moving.

Young Benjamin had very little schooling. He learned to read from his grandmother, who used the family's only book, the Bible, as a lesson book. Although he went to school whenever he could, most of what he learned he taught himself from books that he borrowed. He read fiction, history, mathematics, and science.

- **Spelling, punctuation, and capitalization are correct. Commas and the words *that, which,* and *who* are used correctly.**

I checked Laurie's sketch, and I didn't see any errors in spelling, punctuation, or capitalization. She uses words and commas in a series correctly.

An almanac is a kind of written calendar that tells the positions of the sun, moon, stars, and planets throughout the year.

+Presentation The biographic sketch is neatly prepared and legible.

My Turn!

Now it's my turn to write a biographic sketch! Read along to see how I use the rubric and good writing strategies to help me.

Prewrite

Focus on **Ideas**

The Rubric Says The ideas are clear. Unusual details show in-depth knowledge and make the subject come alive.

Writing Strategy Pick a historic figure. Take notes about him or her.

My teacher says that our biographic sketch should be about a historic person we admire.

I like stories about people who try to make the world a better place. Eleanor Roosevelt did that in her work to defend others' rights. She was the wife of President Franklin D. Roosevelt. In class we studied about him but not much about her.

I'll start by taking some detailed notes on her.

Notes About Eleanor Roosevelt

- ✔ lost both parents when she was little
- ✔ was plain looking
- ✔ went away to school in England as a teenager
- ✔ called "First Lady of the World"
- ✔ became delegate to United Nations
- ✔ helped write Universal Declaration of Human Rights
- ✔ worked for civil rights for African Americans
- ✔ worked for women's rights
- ✔ married Franklin D. Roosevelt when she was 21
- ✔ held press conferences as first lady

Apply

Brainstorm about some historic figures, and then choose one to write about. Make notes about that person.

Prewrite

Focus on **Organization**

The Rubric Says Well-organized paragraphs have a topic sentence, engaging details, and helpful transitions.

Writing Strategy Use a Web to organize notes.

I'll use a Web to make categories for the periods in Eleanor Roosevelt's life and group the details that belong together.

Writer's Term

Web

A **Web** organizes information about a topic. The topic is written in a center circle. Categories are attached to the center, and related information is attached to each category.

Web

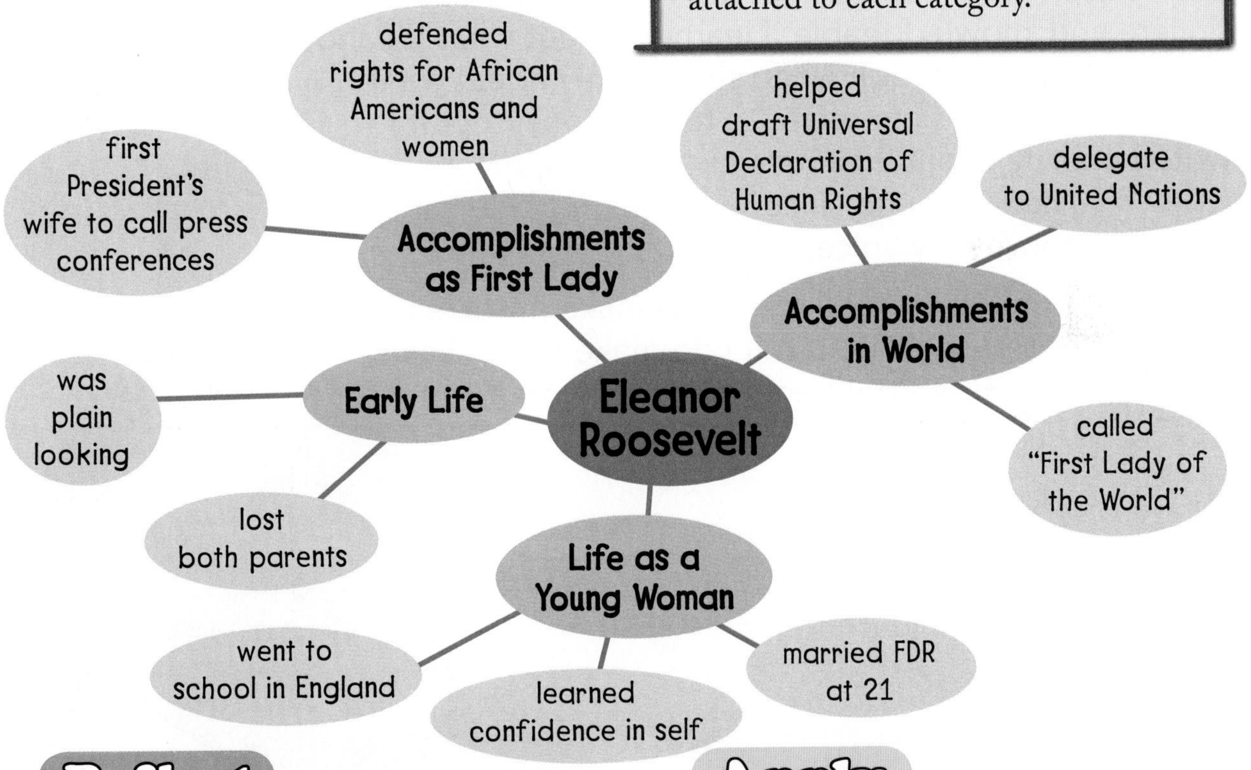

Eleanor Roosevelt

- Accomplishments as First Lady
  - defended rights for African Americans and women
  - first President's wife to call press conferences
- Accomplishments in World
  - helped draft Universal Declaration of Human Rights
  - delegate to United Nations
  - called "First Lady of the World"
- Early Life
  - was plain looking
  - lost both parents
- Life as a Young Woman
  - went to school in England
  - learned confidence in self
  - married FDR at 21

Reflect

How does Joe's Web organize information?

Apply

Make your own Web. Create clear categories and group details that belong together.

Draft

Focus on **Voice**

The Rubric Says The writer sounds sincere and knowledgeable about the subject from beginning to end.

Writing Strategy Think about the reason for writing and the audience.

I'll use my Web to write my draft. I can't wait to share what I've learned about Eleanor Roosevelt's life! I'd like my mom to read it because she told me that Eleanor Roosevelt was her hero.

The rubric reminds me that my voice should sound sincere and knowledgeable. I learned about what Eleanor Roosevelt went through when she was my age. I want the students in my class to relate to her feelings, too. If I write honestly about Eleanor's experiences, my writer's voice will sound sincere. In fact, my title can also help convey my voice.

As I draft my sketch, I'll try not to make mistakes in grammar and spelling, but if I do make some, I can fix them later. Here's the beginning of my draft.

[DRAFT]

Proofreading Marks

]	Indent	ℓ	Take out something
≡	Make uppercase	⊙	Add a period
/	Make lowercase	¶	New paragraph
∧	Add something	(sp)	Spelling error

A Beautiful Person

Eleanor Roosevelt was not what most people would consider pretty, but she had a beauty inside of her. People loved her. They joined her in her fight for the rights of others. She was often called the "First Lady of the World."

voice

Eleanor's early life was painful. Her family was rich, but she was a plain girl. Her mother sometimes made fun of her in front of other people. This made Eleanor even more timid. Then both of her parents died when she was still a child. She became lonly and began to look for ways to be happy.

voice

When Eleanor was a teenager, she went away to school at allenswood in London. At school, many of her fears went away. Learned to think for herself and speak up. Helping others became her focus.

voice

Reflect

Read the beginning of Joe's draft. What are some words or phrases that convey Joe's sincerity?

Apply

Use your Web to draft a biographic sketch. As you write, think of ways to share the knowledge and feelings you have about your person.

Revise

Focus on **Ideas**

The Rubric Says Unusual details show in-depth knowledge and make the subject come alive.

Writing Strategy Choose details that will make the subject come alive.

When I finished my draft, I asked a friend to look it over. After reading it, he asked how the facts about the press conference were important. I looked at the rubric and saw that I forgot to add details to make it clear how the press conference showed Eleanor Roosevelt's confidence as the first lady. Do you think the details I've added make that clearer?

[DRAFT]

She answered reporters' questions calmly. After that, she often held press conferences to talk about important issues, such as equal rights for women.

This were something no other first lady had ever done.

added details

Apply

Read your draft. Check to see that all your details make the person seem real to the reader.

Revise

Focus on **Word Choice**

The Rubric Says Precise, original words help the reader easily understand the subject of the sketch.

Writing Strategy Choose words and phrases to convey ideas precisely.

As I look at the rubric, I see that I need to use exact words to describe Eleanor Roosevelt. There are a few places where I haven't done that. Look how I added precise words to make my description clearer.

[DRAFT]

added precise words

Eleanor's early life was painful. Her family was rich, but she was
with a small chin, oversized
teeth, and baggy eyes , who was very good-looking,
a plain girl^. Her mother^sometimes made fun of her in front of other
people.

added precise words

Reflect

Do Joe's words describe Eleanor and her mother clearly?

Apply

Read your draft. Add precise words to sharpen your description for your readers.

Revise

The Rubric Says A variety of sentence types makes the writing flow smoothly.

Writing Strategy Combine short, choppy sentences.

The rubric reminds me to use a variety of sentence types. After reading my draft aloud, I could hear the choppy sound of too many similar sentences in a row. I'll combine them to see if I can improve the flow.

Writer's Term

Sentence Types

Simple sentences have a subject and a predicate.

Compound sentences have two or more independent clauses that are joined with a comma and a conjunction.

Complex sentences have a subject, a predicate, and a dependent clause.

[DRAFT]

She went to a conference in Alabama, where ~~There~~ there were strict segregation laws. Blacks had to sit on one side of the aisle, and ~~Whites~~ whites had to sit on the other side.

created complex sentence

created compound sentence

Apply

Read your draft aloud and listen for choppy sentences that you could combine.

Edit

Focus on **Conventions**

The Rubric Says Spelling, punctuation, and capitalization are correct. Commas and the words *that, which,* and *who* are used correctly.

Writing Strategy Check that commas are used correctly.

I'll go through my draft now and check for spelling, punctuation, and capitalization. The rubric reminds me also to check that I've used commas correctly. I found where I needed to add commas in a series.

Writer's Term

Commas in a Series

Separate items in a series with a **comma.** Put the last comma before **and** or **or.**

[DRAFT]

added commas in a series

her focus. Throughout her life she would champion the causes of others as a teacher, a lecturer, a newspaper writer, an international traveler, and first lady of the United States.

Reflect

What difference do Joe's corrections make? What happens when you come across errors in someone's writing?

Apply

Conventions

Edit your draft for spelling, punctuation, and capitalization. Correct any mistakes with commas in a series.

For practice in using commas and *that, which,* and *who* correctly, use the exercises on the next two pages.

Conventions **Grammar, Usage & Mechanics**

Commas in a Series

Know the Rule

Use a **comma** to separate items in a series. Put the last comma before *and* or *or*.

Example:
Lyle participated in football, basketball, track, and baseball.

Practice the Rule

Number a sheet of paper 1–10. Rewrite each sentence below by adding commas in the appropriate places in a series.

1. Since 1789, American women have looked up to first ladies as models for fashion hairstyles and speech.
2. Hosting parties attending ceremonies and accompanying the president on trips are some of a first lady's duties.
3. First ladies have championed many social causes, including civil and women's rights literacy and health care.
4. First ladies today may travel by car bus train or plane.
5. Presidents with no wives depend on daughters nieces or daughters-in-law to take on the first lady's role.
6. Presidents Jefferson Jackson and Wilson were widowers.
7. Presidents' wives have been called such names as "Lady Washington" "Mrs. President" and "First Lady of the Land."
8. First ladies who have earned college degrees include Grace Coolidge Lou Hoover, Hillary Rodham Clinton, and Michelle Obama.
9. First ladies who have served two terms include Dolley Madison Julia Grant Eleanor Roosevelt and Laura Bush.
10. Whether she is redecorating the White House raising money for a soup kitchen or visiting a foreign palace, the first lady is always in the news.

That, Which, Who

Know the Rule

Use **that** to refer either to people or to things.

Example: The watch **that** he always wore was a gift from the aunt **that** lived in Argentina.

Use **that** instead of **which** to begin a clause that is necessary to the meaning of the sentence.

Example: Please bring the watch **that** I left at your house.

Use **who** to refer to people. Use **which** to refer to things.

Example: People **who** repair watches and timepieces use special tools. Most buy their own tool collection, **which** can cost a lot.

Practice the Rule

Write **that, which,** or **who** to complete each of the sentences.

1. The art assignment, _____ surprised us, was to write about someone famous.
2. For ideas, some students went straight to the *Book of World Records,* _____ is in our room.
3. Gina chose Jackie Robinson, _____ is in the National Baseball Hall of Fame.
4. Some students chose players _____ are in the Basketball Hall of Fame.
5. The topic _____ I wanted to explore was past presidents.
6. I chose Theodore Roosevelt, _____ was known as Teddy.
7. Like me, President Roosevelt loved outdoor life, _____ had saved his health as a child.
8. In his military service, he joined a group _____ was called the Rough Riders.
9. One cause _____ he was known for was land conservation and the creation of our national park system.
10. Before writing, I did most of my research online, _____ was more fun than I expected.

Publish

+Presentation

Publishing Strategy Share the biographic sketch with a classmate.

Presentation Strategy Write very neatly or use a limited number of clear fonts.

I've finished my biographic sketch of Eleanor Roosevelt. I think I've captured several of her characteristics and showed her overall character. I can see why she's my mom's hero. My teacher wants us to exchange our sketches with a classmate, so I need to be sure I prepare a neat, legible copy. I'm going to include a picture of Eleanor and possibly find an audio clip of her voice. Before I give my classmate my sketch, though, I'll check it over one more time.

My Final Checklist

Did I—

- ✔ check my spelling, punctuation, and capitalization carefully?
- ✔ make sure commas and the words *that*, *which*, and *who* are correct?
- ✔ indent every paragraph?
- ✔ use neat handwriting or word processing?
- ✔ put my name on my paper?

Apply

Use this checklist to prepare a final copy of your biographic sketch. Be sure to write neatly or use a limited number of clear fonts, and include a photograph, if you like.

A Beautiful Person

by Joe

Eleanor Roosevelt was not what most people would consider pretty, but she had a beauty inside of her. People loved her. They joined her in her fight for the rights of others. She was often called the "First Lady of the World."

Eleanor's early life was painful. Her family was rich, but she was a plain girl with a small chin, oversized teeth, and baggy eyes. Her mother, who was very good-looking, sometimes made fun of her in front of other people. This made Eleanor even more timid. Then, both of her parents died when she was still a child. She became lonely and began to look for ways to be happy.

When Eleanor was a teenager, she went away to school at Allenswood in London. At school, many of her fears went away. She learned to think for herself and speak up. Helping others became her focus. Throughout her life she would champion the causes of others as a teacher, a lecturer, a newspaper writer, an international traveler, and first lady of the United States.

In 1905, when Eleanor was 21, she married Franklin Delano Roosevelt. Many years later she began to help him in his political career. When he was elected president of the United States in 1933, Eleanor called a press conference. This was something no other first lady had ever done. She answered reporters' questions calmly. After that, she often held press conferences to talk about important issues, such as equal rights for women.

Eleanor also worked to defend civil rights for African Americans. In 1939, she went to a conference in Alabama, where there were strict segregation laws. At the conference, blacks had to sit on one side of the aisle, and whites had to sit on the other side. Eleanor decided to sit next to a friend on the black side. Police officers ordered her to move, so Eleanor picked up her chair and sat in the middle of the aisle instead. This act made newspaper headlines throughout the country. People began to pay attention to her fight against segregation laws.

After President Roosevelt died in 1945, Eleanor stayed active in politics. She was named as a delegate to the United Nations. She and others wrote the Universal Declaration of Human Rights. This paper was written to protect people throughout the world. When it was approved, all the members of the United Nations stood up and clapped for Eleanor Roosevelt, First Lady of the World!

Reflect

Use the rubric to score Joe's sketch. Which of the traits is strongest? Use the rubric to check your own writing.

What's a Poem?

It's a piece of writing that expresses thoughts or ideas or describes a topic. It is written in lines that may or may not rhyme. A group of lines in a poem is called a verse or stanza.

What's in a Poem?

Lines

Poems are written in lines. These may be sentences or parts of sentences. Some poems have a specific number of lines, only a few lines, or pages of lines. Line length helps give a poem rhythm. You can choose to break the lines in a poem in different ways to give a poem different feelings.

Literary Techniques

A poem uses figurative language, such as metaphors, personification, and alliteration. A metaphor compares one object to another. Personification gives an object the characteristics of a person. Alliteration is the repeating of the same beginning sound in several words in a row. For example, *A dozen donkeys doze* is alliteration.

Imagery

When you listen to a poem, you form images in your head of what the poem describes. This is called imagery. A poet uses imagery to help a reader "see" exactly what he or she means.

Why write a Poem?

There are many reasons to write a poem. Here are a few of the reasons.

Description
Poems can describe just about anything—an object, a person, a place, a feeling. A poem can give its readers a new way of looking at something. For example, a poem might compare the moon to a chocolate chip cookie or a man's face. This comparison helps readers to think of the moon in a new way.

Expression
A poem is a piece of writing in which a writer can express his or her thoughts, observations, ideas, or feelings. The purpose of the poem is to help the reader understand the writer's thoughts and ideas.

Personal Reflection
When you reflect on a topic, you give it careful thought and consideration. In a personal reflection, you think carefully about something in your own life and how it affects you. For example, you might write a poem about the importance of a pet in your life, or a grandparent. A poem that is a personal reflection is an opportunity for you to share something about yourself with readers.

Linking Descriptive Writing Traits to a Poem

In this chapter, you will write a poem about a math topic. This type of descriptive writing is called a poem. Joe will guide you through the stages of the writing process: Prewrite, Draft, Revise, Edit, and Publish. In each stage, Joe will show you important writing strategies that are linked to the Descriptive Writing Traits below.

Descriptive Writing Traits

	• a clear, focused, and complete topic • sensory details that are related to and develop the main ideas
	• well-constructed paragraphs that are organized into an introduction, a body, and a conclusion • paragraphs that each have a topic sentence and supporting details • transitions that connect ideas
	• a voice and tone that are appropriate for the purpose and audience
	• precise, descriptive language that creates a picture for the reader
	• a variety of sentences that make the writing interesting and easy to read aloud
	• no or few errors in grammar, usage, mechanics, and spelling

Before you write, read Delia Mayer's poem on the next page. Then use the poem rubric on pages 438–439 to decide how well she did. (You might want to look back at What's in a Poem? on page 434, too!)

Parallel Lines

by Delia Mayer

Parallel lines are
Railroad tracks leading to the next town,
The lanes of a bowling alley sending the ball to the pins,
The opposite sides of a rectangle or square,
The tines of a fork.

Parallel lines are not
The X that marks the spot on a treasure map,
The curves of a ball flying through the air,
An intersection of streets at a stoplight or stop sign,
Two wiggly worms.

Parallel lines are
Equidistant, equally eternal, everlasting,
Motionless, side by side, without end,
Never touching, never talking, never smiling,
Straight forever.

descriptions that create imagery

metaphor

stanza of short and long lines

alliteration

rhythm

imagery

Poem Rubric

Use this 6-point rubric to plan and score a poem.

	6	5	4
Ideas	The poem focuses on a single subject. Descriptive details create clear images for the reader.	The poem focuses on a single subject. Most of the details create clear mental images.	The poem focuses on a single subject. One or two details are not descriptive.
Organization	The lines and stanzas, if used, are organized logically. The ideas are easy to follow.	The lines and stanzas, if used, are organized. Most of the ideas are easy to follow.	One line may be out of order, making ideas hard to follow.
Voice	The writer's voice is clear and consistent. It connects with the audience.	The writer's voice is consistent. It could reach out to the audience more in one part.	The voice is not consistent enough. It could connect with the audience more.
Word Choice	Carefully chosen words bring the subject to life. Figurative language makes the poem memorable.	Most of the words bring the subject to life. Figurative language is memorable.	Most of the words bring the subject to life. Most of the figurative language is memorable.
Sentence Fluency	The lines flow smoothly. The lines are easy to read aloud.	Most of the lines flow smoothly. Most of the lines are easy to read aloud.	The beginning of the poem flows smoothly. Some lines are not easy to read aloud.
Conventions	The writing has been carefully edited. Verb tense is consistent and correct.	Minor errors are present but do not interfere with meaning. Verb tense is consistent and correct.	Few errors cause confusion. Most verbs are used correctly.

+Presentation The poem is placed attractively on the page. The font is clear.

	3	2	1
Ideas	The poem focuses on a subject. Some of the details stray from the subject.	The poem does not focus on a single subject. The details may not be related.	The subject is not clear. Details do not describe.
Organization	Many lines may be out of order, making ideas hard to follow.	The lines run together. The ideas are hard to follow.	The writing is not organized into lines.
Voice	The voice is clear in the beginning, but then it fades. The connection is weak.	The voice is not clear. It does not connect with the audience in the beginning.	The voice is not consistent or clear. The audience does not know who is speaking.
Word Choice	Many words are overused or ordinary. Figurative language may be overused or cliché.	The meaning of some words may be confused. Figurative language is not used.	Many words are used incorrectly. Figurative language is not used.
Sentence Fluency	Only a few of the lines flow smoothly. The lines may sound choppy or incomplete.	The lines do not flow. The lines may be too long.	The lines do not flow.
Conventions	Many errors are repeated. Shifts in verb tense cause confusion.	Serious errors interfere with meaning. Verb tense is incorrect.	The writing has not been edited.

See Appendix B for 4-, 5-, and 6-point descriptive rubrics.

Using the Poem Rubric to Study the Model

Did you notice that the model on page 437 points out some key elements of a poem? As she wrote "Parallel Lines," Delia Mayer used these elements to help her describe a concept she learned in math class. She also used the 6-point rubric on pages 438–439 to plan, draft, revise, and edit the writing. A rubric is a great tool to evaluate writing during the writing process.

Now let's use the same rubric to score the model. To do this, we'll focus on each trait separately, starting with Ideas. We'll use the top descriptor for each trait (column 6), along with examples from the model, to help us understand how the traits work together. How would you score Delia on each trait?

- **The poem focuses on a single subject.**
- **Descriptive details create clear images for the reader.**

Delia chose a specific topic for her poem. She uses details to create clear images for the reader. Here she describes parallel lines not just by defining them, but by creating pictures of them for the reader.

Parallel lines are
Railroad tracks leading to the next town,
The lanes of a bowling alley sending the ball to the pins,

- The lines and stanzas, if used, are organized logically.
- The ideas are easy to follow.

Delia uses three stanzas in her poem. The first introduces the reader to the topic of parallel lines and describes what parallel lines are. The second stanza describes what parallel lines are not. The third stanza, shown below, concludes the poem.

Parallel lines are
Equidistant, equally eternal, everlasting,
Motionless, side by side, without end,
Never touching, never talking, never smiling,
Straight forever.

- The writer's voice is clear and consistent. It connects with the audience.

The writer uses the same voice throughout the poem. It is clear that the poet is speaking. She connects with her audience through descriptions people can easily imagine.

Parallel lines are not
The X that marks the spot on a treasure map,

Using the Poem Rubric to Study the Model

- Carefully chosen words bring the subject to life.
- Figurative language makes the poem memorable.

Delia uses figurative language, such as metaphors, alliteration, and personification, throughout the poem. The line below personifies parallel lines by giving them the characteristics of a person.

Never touching, never talking, never smiling,

- The lines flow smoothly.
- The lines are easy to read aloud.

No matter how many lines or stanzas, or how short or long each line is, a poem should have a rhythm when you read it. Delia gives her poem a rhythm by writing three stanzas that each have the same number of lines. She starts each stanza with a short line, then writes three longer lines, and ends the stanza with another short line.

Parallel lines are not
The X that marks the spot on a treasure map,
The curves of a ball flying through the air,
An intersection of streets at a stoplight or stop sign,
Two wiggly worms.

- **The writing has been carefully edited.**
- **Verb tense is consistent and correct.**

Delia makes sure that she uses correct verb tenses in her poem. The verb tense tells when the action takes place. She uses the same verb tense, present tense, throughout her poem.

The X that marks the spot on a treasure map,
The curves of a ball flying through the air.

+Presentation The poem is placed attractively on the page. The font is clear.

My Turn!

Now it's my turn to write a poem! I'll use the rubric and good writing strategies to help me. Follow along to see how I do it.

Prewrite

Focus on **Ideas**

The Rubric Says The poem focuses on a single subject. Descriptive details create clear images for the reader.

Writing Strategy Choose a topic. Make a list of the key points.

My teacher told us we are going to write a poem to show what we have learned in math class. She wants us to write a poem about a term from geometry.

I decided to write a poem about cubes. In order to write a poem about cubes, I need to know what makes a cube unique. I also need to think of how I can help the reader to picture a cube. Here are my notes. Have I listed enough ideas?

Notes

cube

6 sides

sides are all squares

8 vertices

12 edges

all right angles

each square
has right angles
and sides the same length

building blocks

a present

stacked up high to
make a skyscraper

cube towers that kids
knock over

ice cubes

cheese cubes on a plate

sugar cubes

Apply

Think about a term from geometry like a shape, a figure, or a kind of angle that you could write about in a poem. Make a list of key points about your topic.

Prewrite

Focus on **Organization**

The Rubric Says The lines and stanzas, if used, are organized logically. The ideas are easy to follow.

Writing Strategy Use a Network Tree to organize notes.

The rubric reminds me that organization is important. I decided to make a Network Tree to organize the notes I wrote about cubes.

Writer's Term

Network Tree

A **Network Tree** organizes information. The topic goes at the top, and main points about the topic go on the next level. Details about each main point go on the bottom.

Network Tree

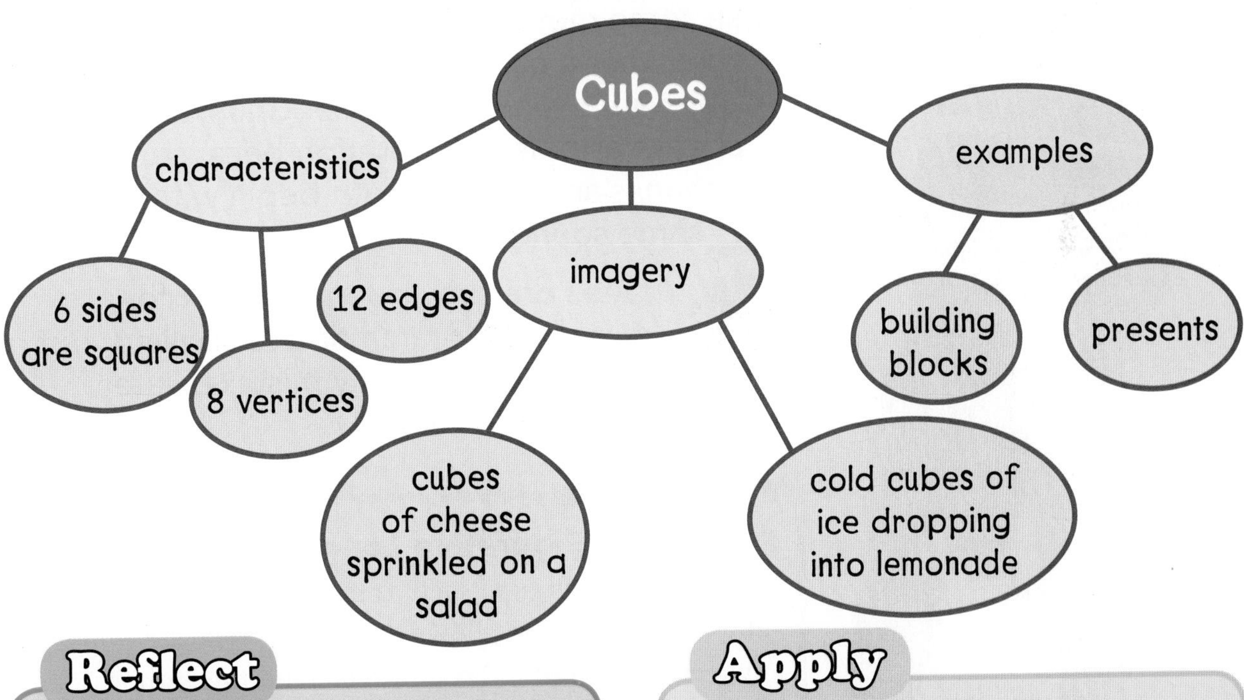

Reflect

How will Joe's Network Tree help him write a poem?

Apply

Make your own Network Tree. Use it to help you organize your notes and ideas about the topic of your poem.

Draft

Focus on **Word Choice**

The Rubric Says Carefully chosen words bring the subject to life. Figurative language makes the poem memorable.

Writing Strategy Choose words carefully.

Now I'm ready to use my Network Tree to write a draft of my poem. Words are always important when I write. But they are especially important when I write a poem because there are so few of them. I will choose my words carefully to say exactly what I mean.

I need to use figurative language in my poem. I'll use some metaphors to help my readers picture what a cube is. I like the metaphor *Cubes are chunks of cheese. Chunks of cheese* also uses alliteration because *chunks* and *cheese* both begin with the same sound.

As I draft my poem, I'll look for mistakes in grammar and spelling, but I know I can fix my mistakes later. Here's my draft.

Writer's Term

Figurative Language

Figurative language, such as metaphors, alliteration, and personification, allows the author to create imagery to help the reader understand the author's meaning.

Proofreading Marks

Indent	Take out something
Make uppercase	Add a period
Make lowercase	New paragraph
Add something	Spelling error

[DRAFT]

alliteration

metaphor

Chunks of cheese on salad,

Unbeatable with lemonade with cubes of ice in it.

Enormous presents complete the party.

metaphor

Square faces six without frowns

sit still and straight.

personification

Reflect

Read the poem. Does the figurative language help you "see" the images Joe is trying to create?

Apply

Use your Network Tree to draft your poem. Be sure your poem focuses on a single topic and uses figurative language to help readers create a picture in their minds.

Revise

Focus on **Ideas**

The Rubric Says The poem focuses on a single subject. Descriptive details create clear images for the reader.

Writing Strategy Use details that make a lively picture of the subject.

The rubric reminds me that all the details in a poem should be useful and create a picture in the reader's mind, so I decided to add more details. For example, I can add details about the chunks of cheese to create a clearer picture.

Writer's Term

Details

Details are words that describe something more specifically to give the reader a better picture.

added interesting details

[DRAFT]

Chunks of cheddar cheese sprinkled on salad,
Unbeatable with lemonade with cubes of ice in it.

Enormous presents complete the party.

Apply

Read your draft again. Add interesting, specific details to create a lively picture for your reader.

Revise

Focus on **Organization**

The Rubric Says The lines and stanzas, if used, are organized logically. The ideas are easy to follow.

Writing Strategy Organize the lines of the poem so that they make sense.

When I read my poem to myself, something was missing. The two parts of my poem didn't feel connected. I decided to put in a question—twice—to tie the two sections together. What do you think?

[DRAFT]

added two lines to organize the poem

What's a cube?

Chunks of cheddar cheese sprinkled on salad,

Unbeatable with lemonade with cubes of ice in it.

Enormous presents complete the party.

What's a cube?

Reflect

Look at Joe's revisions. Are his ideas easier to follow?

Apply

Read your poem. Make sure your ideas are easy to follow. Move or add lines if you need to.

Revise

Focus on **Sentence Fluency**

The Rubric Says The lines flow smoothly. The lines are easy to read aloud.

Writing Strategy Break the lines in logical places.

After I made some revisions, my poem included details and the ideas flowed together smoothly. But when I read it aloud, it didn't sound quite right.

Poems are different from other writing. Where the lines break affects the rhythm, or how the poem sounds, as well as what it means and how it looks on the page.

To figure out where to break the lines, I read the poem aloud to hear where the breaks should be.

[DRAFT]

What's a cube?

Chunks of cheddar cheese

  sprinkled on salad,

Unbeatable with ice cubes

  floating in lemonade.

Big presents in boxes complete the festive party.

added line breaks

added a word to change the rhythm

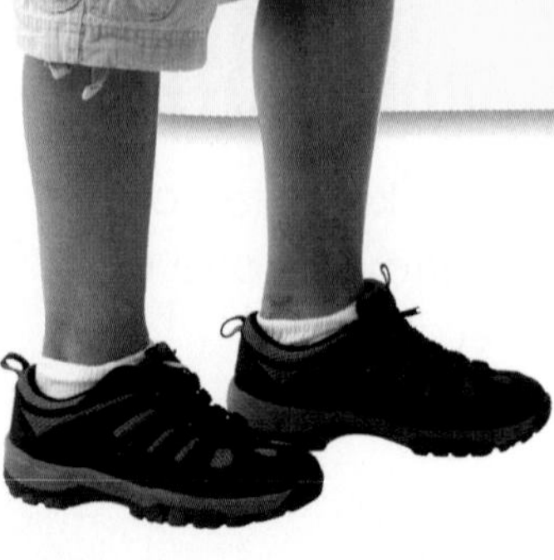

Apply

Read your poem aloud. Your poem should have a rhythm when you read it. Try breaking your lines in different places to see how it changes your poem.

Edit

Focus on Conventions

The Rubric Says The writing has been carefully edited. Verb tense is consistent and correct.

Writing Strategy Recognize and correct inappropriate shifts in verb tense.

Next I will proofread my poem. I will check my spelling, punctuation, and capitalization.

The rubric also reminds me to make sure my verb tenses are correct. A poem might use different verb tenses, but the verb tense should always make sense. Here are some changes I made while editing:

Writer's Term

Verb Tense

Verbs can be past tense, present tense, or future tense. The **tense** of a verb shows when an action happens.

[DRAFT]

Six faces, eight vertices, and twelve edges
make
~~made~~ a cube, you see.

corrected verb tense

Reflect

Look at Joe's poem. Do his lines break where they should? Did Joe proofread and make sure all his verbs are the correct tense?

Apply

Conventions

Edit your poem for spelling, punctuation, and capitalization. Make sure all verbs are in the correct tense.

For more practice with verb tenses, use the exercises on the next two pages.

Past and Present Tense Verbs

Know the Rule

A **verb** tells what the subject of a sentence does. The tense of a verb helps show when an action happens. Make sure each verb tense agrees with the time in which the action takes place.

Present tense verbs show that an action happens regularly or is true now.

Example:
This year, José **likes** math better than science.

Past tense verbs show that an action has already happened. Many past tense verbs end in *-ed*. Irregular verbs change spelling in their past tense form.

Example:
Last year, José **studied** fractions in math class.

Practice the Rule

For each sentence, write the correct verb tense.

1. Alicia draws an equilateral triangle yesterday.
2. To make sure it was equilateral, she measures the angles.
3. All of the angles of an equilateral triangle must had the same measure.
4. Now she wanted to draw another equilateral triangle that is congruent to her first triangle.
5. This time, she used a ruler as she draws the sides.
6. For homework yesterday, Alicia finishes her triangles.
7. In math class now, she practiced drawing line segments and angles.
8. The first angle she makes did not turn out straight.
9. Her teacher tells her to use a ruler, so she tried again.
10. Today it was perfect.

Verb Tenses

Know the Rule

Remember that the tense of a verb tells when an action happens. **Future tense verbs** tell that an action is going to happen. Add the helping verb *will* to the present tense form of a verb to form the future tense.

Examples:
Grace **finished** her homework before dinner.
Grace and her family **eat** at six o'clock.
After dinner, she **will read** a book.

Practice the Rule

For each sentence, write the correct verb tense. The correct verb tense may be past, present, or future.

1. Tyler has always likes math.
2. When he was in kindergarten, he does math problems for fun.
3. Then in first grade, he joins a math club after school.
4. Now that he is in fifth grade, he helped first graders with their math homework.
5. Once he is there, he will play lots of math games with the students.
6. Last week, Tyler will leave his calculator in the first grade classroom.
7. The first grade teacher called his classroom to say that she brings it to him later.
8. When the first graders finish their math problems, Tyler gave them a sticker.
9. When they get ten stickers, they got to play a math game on the computer.
10. Tyler is certain that when he is an adult he is a math teacher.

Publish +Presentation

Publishing Strategy Publish the poem in a class book of math poems.

Presentation Strategy An illustration helps get the message across to the reader.

My poem is finished. I am going to present it by publishing it in a class book of math poems.

I will type my poem on a word processor in a font that is easy to read. I'll use hard returns and tabs to make sure my line breaks and indents stay where they need to be. To make my poem stand out on the page, I will leave white space around it. Another thing I will do is add an illustration of a cube to make it clear to the reader what the poem is about.

Before adding my poem to the class book, I will read through it one more time. I'll make sure I've done everything on my checklist.

My Final Checklist

Did I—

- ✔ check for correct verb tenses?
- ✔ edit my poem carefully?
- ✔ center the title of my poem at the top of the page?
- ✔ type my final copy on a word processor so it is easy to read?
- ✔ set my poem with white space around it to present it?

Apply

Use Joe's list to check your own poem. Be sure to present your poem so that it is easy to read.

Cubes

by Joe

What's a cube?

Chunks of cheddar cheese

sprinkled on salad.

Unbeatable with ice cubes

floating in lemonade.

Big presents in boxes complete the festive party.

What's a cube?

Square faces six without frowns

sit still and straight.

Faces meet at edges twelve.

Edges meet at corners eight,

otherwise known as vertices.

Six faces, eight vertices, and twelve edges

make a cube—yes, that's a cube!

Reflect

Use the rubric to check the poem. Did Joe meet all the criteria of a good poem? Use the rubric to check your poem, too.

Descriptive test writing

Read the Writing Prompt

When you first look at your writing prompt, look for three important parts: the setup, the task, and the scoring guide. Most writing prompts have these three parts.

Setup This part of the writing prompt gives you the background information you need to get ready for writing. It "sets you up" to write a great essay!

Task This part of the writing prompt tells you exactly what you're supposed to write: a descriptive essay about a special day you look forward to each year.

Scoring Guide This part tells how your writing will be scored. To get the best score, do each of the things on this list.

You've used a rubric to help you write each descriptive piece in the book. When you are writing a test essay, you won't always have all the information that a rubric gives you. But the scoring guide is a lot like a rubric. Like the rubric, the scoring guide lists everything you need to think about as you write your test essay. Scoring guides will often include the six important traits of writing that you've already seen in rubrics:

Every year brings around favorite holidays, family outings, and events. What is your favorite special day of the year—the day you look forward to for twelve long months until it comes around again?

Write a descriptive essay about the special day you look forward to.

Be sure your descriptive essay

- provides specific details that support and develop the topic.
- presents the topic, the body develops it, and the conclusion wraps it up in a satisfying way.
- has a voice that fits the audience and purpose.
- uses precise language to explain the topic and create interest.
- includes a variety of lively, energetic sentences.
- has correct grammar, spelling, capitalization, and punctuation.

Writing Traits in the Scoring Guide

The scoring guide in the writing prompt on page 457 has been made into this chart. Take a look: Does the chart remind you of the rubrics you've used? Not all prompts include all of the writing traits, but this one does. Use them to do your best writing. Remember to work neatly and put your name on each page!

- Be sure your writing provides specific details that support and develop the topic.

- Be sure your writing presents the topic, the body develops it, and the conclusion wraps it up in a satisfying way.

- Be sure the voice in your descriptive essay fits the audience and purpose.

- Be sure your writing uses precise language to explain the topic and create interest.

- Be sure your descriptive essay includes a variety of lively, energetic sentences.

- Be sure your descriptive essay has correct grammar, spelling, capitalization, and punctuation.

Take a look at Ruthie Perez's descriptive essay on the next page. Did Ruthie use the scoring guide to write a good essay?

Cinco de Mayo

by Ruthie Perez

If you enjoy Mexican food, music, and dancing, then come to the *Cinco de Mayo* celebration! May 5th is a special day for Mexicans and Mexican Americans. It's the day we celebrate the victory of a small band of Mexican soldiers who defeated a large army of French invaders. All that happened a long time ago—in 1862! But we love to remember the courage of our ancestors with pride and festivities.

Listen! The celebration is beginning—it's a loud, triumphant melody from the high school marching band. Leading the parade, the drum major is twirling his silver baton. He tosses it high above his tall, plumed hat and catches it as he keeps on moving with high, bold strides. The players follow, stepping lively, swaying to the beat of a patriotic song. Trumpets blare, cymbals crash, and the snare drum rolls. Five brass tubas polished to a mirror shine reflect the bright blue uniforms trimmed in gold.

Crowds line the street cheering and clapping to the beat. Little kids squeal, and people tap their feet. A cool breeze carries the music, the laughing, and the wonderful aromas. Food carts are everywhere—*tacos, enchiladas, tamales, pasteles.* Mmmmmmm! A small woman pats a tortilla between her hands and puts it on a hot, flat pan. She takes it out and places it on a board. She fills it with beans, rice, shredded cheese, and chopped tomato. She folds the tortilla over and folds up the edges. I give her a dollar, and she hands me the *burrito.* I add salsa and hot peppers. It's warm, nourishing, spicy, delicious!

Next in the parade, dancers are filling the street! The women turn this way and that, twirling their full, brightly colored skirts. The men stand tall in black pants and white shirts. They hold their hands behind them as they click the heels of their boots and step in time to the music of *mariachis.* The crowd is singing. Many start dancing, too. We can't help it—dancing is something we love to do!

The mariachi violins are wailing a *danzón*! Everyone knows this dance from the town of Vera Cruz. Now the trumpets take up the tune. Then the flutes join in. The big bass guitar, the *guitarón,* holds a steady beat. The mariachis march in black suits embroidered with white flowers. Silver spangles twinkle on their black hats like the stars in tonight's sky. It's getting late, but the fun of our three-day celebration has just begun!

Using the Scoring Guide to Study the Model

Let's use the scoring guide to study Ruthie's writing test, "Cinco de Mayo." We can find examples in her writing that show how well she did on each part of the scoring guide.

- **Specific details support and develop the topic.**

The topic of Ruthie's essay is clear. It's Cinco de Mayo Day! All the details relate directly to the celebration.

If you enjoy Mexican food, music, and dancing, then come to the *Cinco de Mayo* celebration! May 5th is a special day for Mexicans and Mexican Americans.

- **The writing presents the topic, the body develops it, and the conclusion wraps it up in a satisfying way.**

Ruthie's lead sentence gets the attention of her audience with an invitation! The body of the essay is filled with interesting details about the celebration. The details in the conclusion bring the exciting day to a close.

Silver spangles twinkle on their black hats like the stars in tonight's sky. It's getting late, but the fun of our three-day celebration has just begun!

- **The voice in the descriptive essay fits the audience and purpose.**

Ruthie's purpose is to describe her favorite celebration, Cinco de Mayo. It is easy for the audience to pick up on her enthusiasm and enjoyment of the event.

A cool breeze carries the music, the laughing, and the wonderful aromas. Food carts are everywhere—*tacos, enchiladas, tamales, pasteles*. Mmmmmmm!

- **The essay uses precise language to explain the topic and create interest.**

The scoring guide doesn't just say to use interesting descriptive words—it says that the words should be precise. Well-chosen words help readers to picture the descriptions. In this example, Ruthie's words describe the mariachis so well that readers could actually draw them!

The mariachis march in black suits embroidered with white flowers. Silver spangles twinkle on their black hats like the stars in tonight's sky.

Using the Scoring Guide to Study the Model

- **The essay includes a variety of lively, energetic sentences.**

Ruthie's sentences are as lively as the celebration she describes. She uses all kinds of punctuation to "spice up" her essay, and she varies the length of sentences to keep the essay flowing.

Listen! The celebration is beginning—it's a loud, triumphant melody from the high school marching band. Leading the parade, the drum major is twirling his silver baton. He tosses it high above his tall, plumed hat and catches it as he keeps on moving with high, bold strides.

The crowd is singing. Many start dancing, too. We can't help it—dancing is something we love to do!

- **The descriptive essay has correct grammar, spelling, capitalization, and punctuation.**

The scoring guide will usually remind you to check the grammar, spelling, capitalization, and punctuation. Ruthie edited carefully before preparing her final copy. Her page design looks great, and she includes a title and her name.

Planning My Time

Before my teacher hands out the writing prompt, he always tells us how much time we have to complete the writing test. Knowing how much time I have to work helps me plan how much time to spend on each part of the writing process. I also plan for time to study the writing prompt. Take a look at how I divided my writing time into four parts.

Prewrite

Focus on **Ideas**

Writing Strategy Study the writing prompt to find out what to do.

The first thing I do when I get the writing prompt is study it to make sure I know exactly what I'm supposed to do.

Most writing prompts have three parts. When you study the prompt, you should find and label each part: the setup, the task, and the scoring guide. See how I did this below? Then you circle key words in the prompt that tell you what kind of writing to do. I circled *Write a descriptive essay* because it tells what kind of writing I'll be doing. Also, I circled *a place that is special to you* because that is the subject of my essay.

My Writing Test Prompt

Setup — Most people have places that are special to them and that they love to visit. These places may be in the city, out in nature—anywhere!

Task — Write a descriptive essay about a place that is special to you.

Scoring Guide — Be sure your descriptive essay

- provides specific details that support and develop the topic.
- presents the topic, the body develops it, and the conclusion wraps it up in a satisfying way.
- has a voice that fits the audience and purpose.
- uses precise language to explain the topic and create interest.
- includes a variety of lively, energetic sentences.
- has correct grammar, spelling, capitalization, and punctuation.

I've studied the prompt. Like the rubrics, this scoring guide has the six traits of a good essay. If you see a scoring guide that doesn't list all six traits, think back to the rubrics you've used, and remember what's important in a good essay.

Ideas

- **Be sure your writing provides specific details that support and develop the topic.**

I'll choose interesting, specific details about my special place so readers understand why I'm describing it.

Organization

- **Be sure your writing presents the topic, the body develops it, and the conclusion wraps it up in a satisfying way.**

I'll use a graphic organizer to organize my essay. I want to be sure I put my details in the right order.

Voice

- **Be sure the voice in your descriptive essay fits the audience and purpose.**

I want my readers to feel like they're visiting this special place with me right from the beginning.

Word Choice

- **Be sure your writing uses precise language to explain the topic and create interest.**

Whenever I can, I'll use precise words that create a picture for the reader. I won't just write that a place is colorful. Instead, I'll describe the colors I saw there.

Sentence Fluency

- **Be sure your descriptive essay includes a variety of lively, energetic sentences.**

I'll use a variety of sentence lengths and kinds of punctuation.

Conventions

- **Be sure your descriptive essay has correct grammar, spelling, capitalization, and punctuation.**

I'll proofread my essay carefully after I write my first draft.

Prewrite

Focus on **Ideas**

Writing Strategy Respond to the task.

I shouldn't just start writing. First I should get the information to help me write. It's important to do this when you write for a test because you won't have time to start over if your draft gets away from the assigned task.

I'll start by seeing what information I can gather from the writing prompt. Look again at the task in the writing prompt. This section of my writing prompt tells me to write a descriptive essay about a place that's special to me. So first I'll make a list of special places. Then I can decide which place to describe in my essay.

Task — Write a descriptive essay about a place that is special to you.

Places I Could Write About

- the cliff dwellings of Mesa Verde
- the San Juan Skyway near our home
- the science museum in Denver
- the work shed at my grandparents' house

Apply

Before you start writing, think about how you'll respond to the writing prompt task. Collect ideas by jotting down notes or making a short list.

Prewrite

Writing Strategy Choose a graphic organizer.

It's time to start organizing my ideas. I've decided to write about a special stretch of highway near my home, the San Juan Skyway. The last time I wrote a descriptive essay, I used a graphic organizer called a Spider Map. I can use it again to organize the details by the senses.

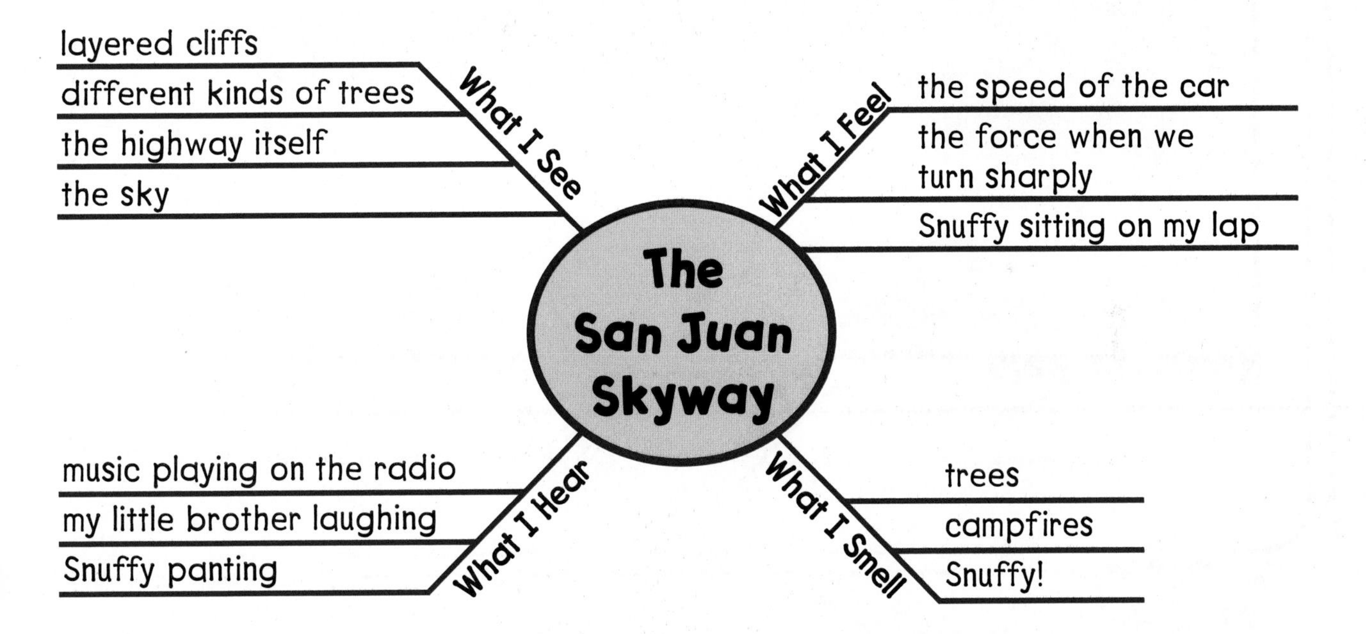

Reflect

Which set of sensory details is strongest? Why?

Apply

Choose the best graphic organizer for the assignment. Include the most important details in the organizer.

Prewrite

Focus on **Organization**

Writing Strategy Check the graphic organizer against the scoring guide.

I can see from my writing plan that I won't have much time to revise my essay. Therefore, it is important that I do a good job of prewriting! Before I start writing my draft, I'd better check my Spider Map against the scoring guide in the writing prompt. I need to be sure that I'm writing about the assigned topic—a place that is special to me.

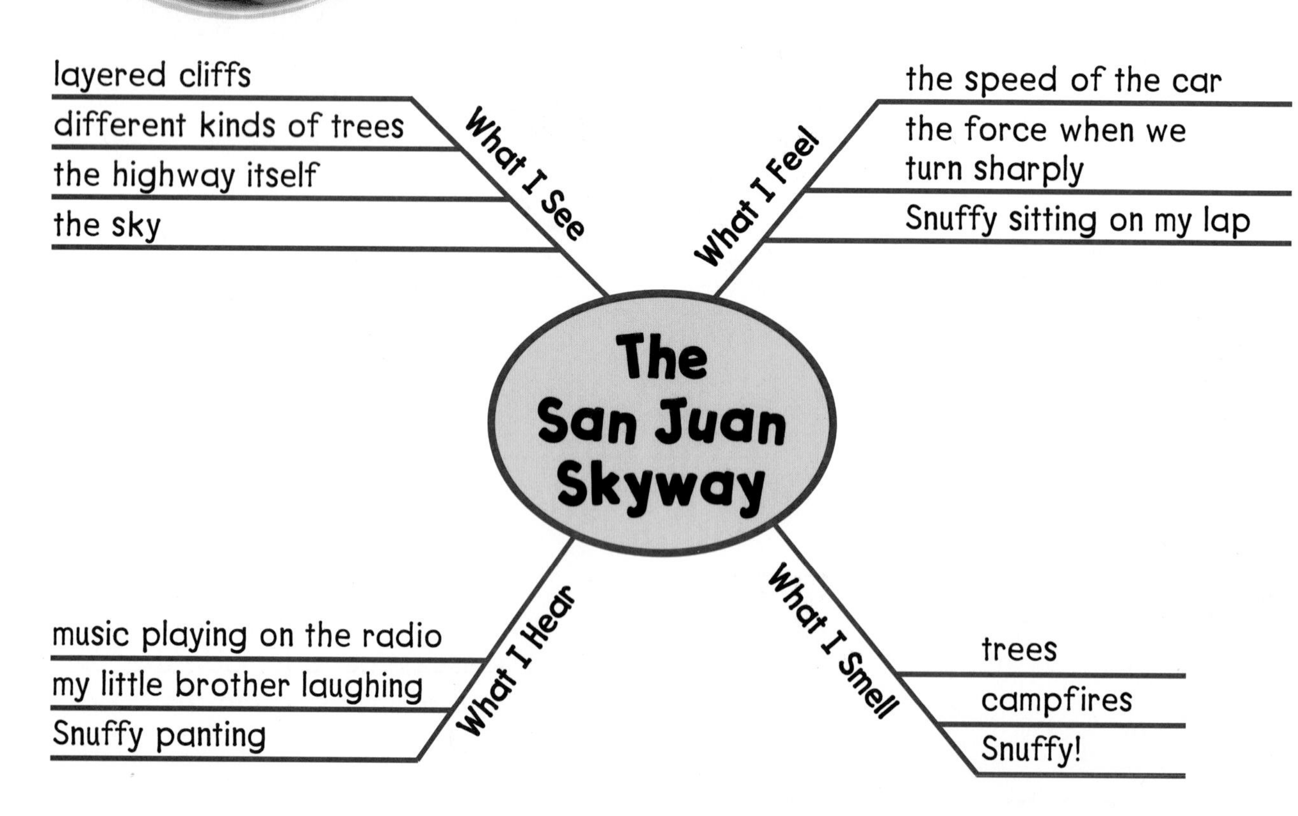

Ideas

- **Be sure your writing provides specific details that support and develop the topic.**

My topic is the San Juan Skyway. I need to make sure all my details add to my readers' knowledge about it.

Organization

- **Be sure your writing presents the topic, the body develops it, and the conclusion wraps it up in a satisfying way.**

I'll need to think about organizing my writing into an introduction, body, and solid conclusion.

Voice

- **Be sure the voice in your descriptive writing fits the audience and purpose.**

I need to connect with my audience from start to finish.

Word Choice

- **Be sure your writing uses precise language to explain the topic and create interest.**

In my Spider Map, I used general words such as *trees*. I'll replace these with exact words as I write.

Sentence Fluency

- **Be sure your descriptive essay includes a variety of lively, energetic sentences.**

My Spider Map doesn't help much with this part of the scoring guide, but I remember how Ruthie energized her writing by varying sentence length and using punctuation to make the writing flow.

Conventions

- **Be sure your descriptive essay has correct grammar, spelling, capitalization, and punctuation.**

I'll check grammar and mechanics when I edit my draft.

Reflect

How does Joe use the scoring guide to plan his essay?

Apply

Before you start writing, ask yourself, "Do I understand everything I need to do?"

Draft

Focus on  Ideas

Writing Strategy Use specific details that support the topic.

The Spider Map helps me focus on my topic. In my draft, I'll add details to describe the location and the best parts of the San Juan Skyway.

[DRAFT]

Mountain Memories

by Joe

On a Saturday in September my mom, my brother, and I pile into our car with our dog, Snuffy. We are going for a drive along one of the prettiest stretches of highway anywhere in the world. It is the San Juan Skyway, one of my favorite places. It runs in a loop in southwestern Colorado. After tuning the radio to our favorite station, we set out. It is a beautiful day in the San Juan Mountains. I see high white clouds against the blue sky. Sunlight flashes on the hood of the minivan. The whole drive is terrific, but the best part is the stretch of Highway 550 from the town of Ouray to the old

supporting detail

topic

Proofreading Marks

⊐ Indent	ℓ Take out something
≡ Make uppercase	⊙ Add a period
/ Make lowercase	¶ New paragraph
∧ Add something	(sp) Spelling error

mining town of Silverton. The road goes around the mountainside in twists and turns. Below us the cliff drops straight down to the canyon floor. It almost makes me dizzy looking down. The slopes are blanketed with pines and other trees. Cliffs rise in colorful rock layers around us. The road disapears under our car as the seenery goes by.

supporting details

supporting details

Mom drives like a pro. Going into a curve, she slows down just right so the force presses them gently against their safety belts. They sway to the side as she rounds a bend. It's as if they're on a roller coaster.

Snuffy leans against my chest as I lean my head toward the window, I smell his doggy smell mixed with the smells pine forests and campfires. The cool air ruffles our hair as we take in the sights. A still mountain lake mirrors the sky. Cattle graze in a field. These seenes flash before my eyes and are gone in a moment. The drive is over before I know it, too.

Reflect

Read Joe's draft. Which details help you picture the drive?

Apply

Add supporting details that will help the reader picture your topic.

Revise

Focus on **Organization**

Writing Strategy Write an introduction, a body, and a conclusion.

My first draft is complete. The scoring guide reminds me to organize the parts of my essay. I will read my draft to find out if my paragraphs are in order.

I found a place in my essay where I should have indented and begun a new paragraph. I think this change will help my reader follow my descriptions better.

[DRAFT]

It is the San Juan Skyway, one of my favorite places. It runs in a loop in southwestern Colorado. After tuning the radio to our favorite station, we set out.

It is a beautiful day in the San Juan Mountains. I see high white clouds against the blue sky. Sunlight flashes on the hood of the minivan. The whole drive is terrific, but the best part is the stretch of Highway 550 from the town of Ouray to the old...

Apply

Focus on the reader to write a strong beginning.

Revise

Focus on 

Writing Strategy **Use first-person point of view to connect with the reader.**

The scoring guide reminds me to keep my purpose and audience in mind as I write. I'm writing about my special place. I'll make sure my pronouns are in the first person, too.

[DRAFT]

first-person point of view

Mom drives like a pro. Going into a curve, she slows down just right so the force presses ~~them~~ us gently against ~~their~~ our safety belts. ~~They~~ We sway to the side as she rounds a bend. It's as if ~~they're~~ we're on a roller coaster.

first-person point of view

Reflect

What do you think about the revised text? What do the revisions tell you?

Apply

How strong is your voice in your draft? Be sure to convey your own feelings about the place that is special to you.

Revise

Focus on **Word Choice**

Writing Strategy Use precise words to create interest.

The scoring guide reminds me to use specific words when I can. I'll check the words I use to name or describe things and actions. I've already used some exact words, such as *minivan* to describe our car.

Now I'll see what other general words I can replace with more precise and interesting words.

[DRAFT]

~~Snuffy leans~~ Snuffy's warm weight presses against my chest as I lean my head toward the window, I smell his doggy smell mixed with the ~~smells~~ scent of pine forests and the bite of smoke from campfires.

used precise words

used precise words

Apply

Look at your draft to find general words that could be replaced with specific, interesting words.

Edit

Writing Strategy Check the grammar, spelling, capitalization, and punctuation.

The scoring guide says to use spelling and grammar correctly. Proofreading takes time, but I set aside the time to do it when I made my writing plan. Now I'll read my draft carefully one more time.

[FINAL DRAFT]

Mountain Memories

by Joe

On a sunny Saturday in September my mom, my brother, and I pile into our ~~car~~ minivan with our dog, Snuffy. We are going for a drive along one of the prettiest stretches of highway anywhere in the world. It is the San Juan Skyway, one of my favorite places. It runs in a loop in southwestern Colorado. After tuning the radio to our favorite station, we set out.

It is a beautiful day for a drive in the San Juan Mountains. ~~I see high white clouds against the blue sky. Sunlight flashes on the hood of the minivan.~~ The whole drive is terrific, but the best part is the stretch of Highway 550 from the town of Ouray to the old mining town of Silverton. The road ~~goes around~~ hugs the mountainside

Apply

When you plan your test writing time, always leave time to proofread your essay.

FINAL DRAFT

in twists and turns. Below us the cliff drops straight down to the canyon floor. It almost makes me dizzy looking down~~.~~—so it's a good thing I'm not driving! The slopes are blanketed with pines and other trees. Cliffs rise in colorful rock layers around us. The road ~~disapears~~ disappears under our car as the ~~seenery~~ scenery goes by.

Mom drives like a pro. Going into a curve, she slows down just right so the force presses ~~them~~ us gently against ~~their~~ our safety belts. ~~They~~ We sway to the side as she rounds a bend. It's as if ~~they're~~ we're on a roller coaster.

~~Snuffy leans~~ Snuffy's warm weight presses against my chest~~.~~ As I lean my head toward the window, I smell his doggy smell mixed with the ~~smells~~ scent of pine forests and the bite of smoke from campfires. The cool air ruffles our hair as we take in the sights. A still mountain lake mirrors the sky. Cattle graze in a field. These ~~seenes~~ scenes flash before my eyes and are gone in a moment. The drive is over before I know it, too.

Reflect

Use the scoring guide to check Joe's writing. How did he use the traits to write his essay?

How about that? We used the writing prompt and scoring guide to write a good descriptive essay! These important tips can help when you're writing for a test.

TEST TIPS

1. **Study the writing prompt before you begin to write.** Look for the three parts that most writing prompts have: the setup, the task, and the scoring guide. Label them so that you can review them often and use the helpful information they give you.
2. **Make sure you understand the task before you start to write.**
   - Find and label the setup, task, and scoring guide.
   - Circle key words in the task. Key words tell you what kind of writing you need to do. They may also tell you who your audience is.
   - Read the scoring guide so that you know how your paper will be graded.
3. **Plan your time, and then keep an eye on the clock.** Make sure you know how much time you have to write. Then decide how much time you'll spend on each part of the writing process. You may get a few minutes behind, but stay as close to your plan as you can so that you'll have time to revise and edit your draft.
4. **Check your draft against the scoring guide.** Like the rubrics you've used on other papers, the scoring guide reminds you of what is important. Read your draft to check that it does what the scoring guide says it should do.
5. **Take time to plan.** You won't have much time to revise, so plan well.
6. **Don't quit now—edit your draft!** Watch out especially for errors you often make and correct them. Also, write neatly so that the people scoring your test can read your interesting essay easily!

Appendix A
Grammar Practice

Compound Subjects

Know the Rule

A **compound subject** consists of two or more simple subjects joined by a connecting word. The connecting word is usually *and* or *or.*

Examples:
A **horse** or a **camel** might be your choice of transportation.
Snakes, birds, and other **animals** live in the wild on Kangaroo Island in Australia.

Practice the Rule

Number a sheet of paper 1–10. Next to each number, write the subjects of the sentence. Then write the connecting word that joins the subjects.

1. Planes and boats carry thousands of visitors to Australia each year.
2. A book or a game helps to pass the time on a long plane flight.
3. Australia and New Zealand share no borders with other countries.
4. Huge waves and many beaches make Australia perfect for surfing.
5. The jellyfish and the crocodile are two dangerous animals that live in Australia's waters.
6. Experienced lifeguards, warning signs, and colored flags help people enjoy the waters safely.
7. Mountains, rain forests, and deserts are all part of the vast Australian landscape.
8. Australia and the United States are about the same size.
9. Beautiful yarns, clothing, and blankets are made from the wool of Australian sheep.
10. A toy koala bear or a toy kangaroo would be a nice gift from Australia.

Compound Predicates

Know the Rule

A **compound predicate** has two or more verbs that share the same subject. The verbs are joined by a connecting word, such as *and*, *or*, or *but*.

Example:

Ana **read** the message and **typed** a response.

Practice the Rule

Number a sheet of paper 1–10. Next to each number, write the verbs that make up the compound predicate. Then write the connecting word that joins the verbs.

1. Last summer Sami traveled to India and met his cousin for the first time.
2. Together, the cousins saw many interesting places and did lots of fun things.
3. Sami liked the museums but preferred the parks.
4. In one park, Sami saw some monkeys and rode an elephant.
5. Other days, Sami and his cousin played games or identified birds.
6. Sami's uncle drove the cousins into town and bought them lunch.
7. Sami saw and tasted many exotic foods.
8. The dishes were very spicy and had unusual names.
9. In the evening, nightingales flew through the sky and made strange sounds.
10. Sami will write a story or paint a picture about his trip.

Object of a Preposition

Know the Rule

A noun or pronoun that follows a preposition is the **object of the preposition**. Prepositions include *at, in, over, of, to, by, about, with, from, down*, and *before*.

Example:

Sloths are animals that live **in South America**.

Practice the Rule

Write each numbered sentence on a separate sheet of paper. Underline each preposition once and the object of the preposition twice.

1. A typical sloth spends most of the day sleeping.
2. The sloth sleeps hanging from the branch of a tree.
3. It supports itself with its strong arms.
4. At the end of each arm are huge claws.
5. The sloth is the slowest mammal in the world.
6. The sloth's diet of leaves doesn't provide the animal with much energy.
7. The sloth's fur resembles the color of the trees in the rain forest.
8. Its coloring helps keep the sloth safe from predators.
9. Humans and jaguars are the main predators of sloths.
10. Sloths also live in the rain forests of Central America.

Complex Sentences

Know the Rule

A **complex sentence** is made up of one **independent clause** (or simple sentence) and at least one **dependent clause**. A dependent clause is a group of words that has a subject and a predicate but cannot stand alone.

Examples:

We used to live in a warm climate. (independent clause)
where there were never any snowstorms (dependent clause)
We used to live in a warm climate where there were never any snowstorms. (complex sentence)

Practice the Rule

Number a sheet of paper 1–10. Identify whether the item is a dependent clause, an independent clause, or a complex sentence.

1. If the storm moves in this direction, we can expect two feet of snow.
2. Since Dad broke his shovel, he will have to buy a new one.
3. Dad will go to the hardware store to buy a new snow shovel.
4. It is not safe to drive when it is snowing hard.
5. Even though there is lots of snow all around.
6. As soon as the storm passes, people will begin to shovel.
7. If there is too much snow, school might be called off!
8. Until all the streets and sidewalks are cleared.
9. Wet snow is good for making a snowman.
10. I hope the snow doesn't melt before I have a chance to play in it!

Comma Splices

Know the Rule

A **comma splice** occurs when two complete sentences are separated by a comma without a joining word such as *and, or, so,* or *but*. This results in a run-on sentence. You can correct a comma splice by adding a joining word after the comma or by replacing the comma with a period to form two complete sentences.

Examples:

Amsterdam has narrow streets, riding a bicycle makes good sense. (comma splice)

Amsterdam has narrow streets, **so** riding a bicycle makes good sense. (corrected sentence)

Practice the Rule

Correct the comma splice by adding a joining word after the comma or by replacing the comma with a period to form two sentences.

1. There are all types of bicycles in Holland, most people prefer sturdy bikes.
2. It is not unusual to see a bicycle with a box used for carrying groceries, the box might also be used for carrying a pet.
3. Some bicycles have extra seats, young children can ride on the back of the bicycle.
4. Bicycle riders may be both young and old, they may be on their way to work or simply out for pleasure.
5. Bicycles come in normal sizes and colors, they might be highly decorated by the owners.
6. It is a good idea to have a bike stand out, the owner can find it easily among the crowds of bikes parked on the same corner.
7. You wouldn't think that bike theft would be a problem in Holland, actually many bikes are stolen.
8. People use strong locks to secure their bikes to bike racks, they also take their bikes inside at night.

Articles

Know the Rule

A, *an*, and *the* are special adjectives called **articles**. They are used before nouns. Use *a* before a noun that begins with a consonant sound. Use *an* before a noun that begins with a vowel sound. Use *the* when talking about a specific person, place, or thing.

Example:

The book *Zeely* by Virginia Hamilton won **an** award.

Practice the Rule

On a separate sheet of paper, write each sentence using the correct article, **a** or **an**. Then underline the article **the** wherever it appears.

1. Virginia Hamilton grew up on (a/an) farm in Ohio.
2. Her grandfather had been brought into that state as (a/an) infant by way of the Underground Railroad.
3. Her grandfather had been born in the state of Virginia and had been the son of (a/an) slave.
4. As (a/an) adult, Virginia became (a/an) writer of stories for young people.
5. She was the first African American to win (a/an) award called the Newbery Medal.
6. Hamilton's books often focus on (a/an) African American character.
7. In her novels, the characters are almost sure to have (a/an) encounter with something unusual or mysterious.
8. Hamilton wrote nonfiction books, too, including (a/an) biography of Paul Robeson.
9. Paul Robeson was (a/an) African American who was famous as (a/an) athlete and as (a/an) singer.
10. (A/An) collection of her folktales, called *The People Could Fly*, is (a/an) favorite of many readers.

Comparative Adverbs

Know the Rule

The **comparative form** of an adverb compares two actions. Most adverbs that end in *-ly* form their comparative by adding *more* before the adverb (*more boldly*). The comparative form of an adverb is often followed by the word *than.*

Examples:
Kelly ran **swiftly** past her competitors.
Kelly ran **more swiftly than** Emily.

Practice the Rule

Number a sheet of paper 1–10. Next to each number, write the correct form of the adverb in parentheses.

1. Abigail jogs (smoothly/more smoothly) along the dirt trail.
2. She watches the path ahead (closely/more closely) to avoid tripping over a twig or stone.
3. Her new running shoes fit (comfortably/more comfortably) than her old ones.
4. Abigail stretches (faithfully/more faithfully) before every run.
5. She plans to run (frequently/more frequently) than she has in the past.
6. Every so often, she stops running and walks (quickly/more quickly) for a short while.
7. She has learned to save energy by running up hills (slowly/more slowly) than she used to.
8. Soon she is able to run a longer distance while still breathing (evenly/more evenly).
9. Abigail's goal is to enter a 5-kilometer race and run it (quickly/more quickly) than her brother.
10. Abigail imagines people cheering (loudly/more loudly) as she crosses the finish line.

Concrete and Abstract Nouns

Know the Rule

A **concrete noun** names something that you can recognize through your senses—sight, hearing, smell, touch, and taste (*tomato, cat, thunder*). An **abstract noun** names something that cannot be recognized by your senses, such as an idea, a quality, or an emotion (*safety, beauty, jealousy*).

Examples:
The **spider** wove an intricate **web**. (concrete nouns)
I can't get over my **fear** of spiders. (abstract noun)

Practice the Rule

Number a sheet of paper 1–5. List the concrete noun or nouns in each sentence. A sentence might contain an abstract noun or nouns. Do not include the abstract nouns in your list.

1. A female mosquito is biting my arm.
2. A scorpion has a sharp stinger on its tail.
3. Beetles feed on plants and live in many different regions of the world.
4. My fear of your pet tarantula is not reasonable.
5. I would get the creeps if I let that snake crawl on me.

On the same paper, write the numbers 6–10. Next to each number, list the abstract noun or nouns in that sentence. A sentence might contain a concrete noun or nouns. Do not include concrete nouns in your list.

6. I feel great comfort when my cat is curled up next to me.
7. It takes a lot of patience to give my dog a bath.
8. It was a shock to find out that he owned a boa constrictor.
9. Communication between people and dolphins is amazing.
10. A turtle is not known for its speed.

Demonstrative Adjectives

Know the Rule

Adjectives describe nouns and pronouns. The adjectives that tell which one are called **demonstrative adjectives**. The demonstrative adjectives are *this, that, these,* and *those.*

Example:
Those wild horses in the photograph live on an island off the coast of Maryland.

Practice the Rule

Number a sheet of paper 1–10. Next to each number, write the demonstrative adjective in that sentence.

1. This beach is part of the Cape Cod National Seashore.
2. I want to climb that dune and look at the ocean.
3. Those historic forts are on the Gulf Islands National Seashore.
4. May we climb out on these rocks?
5. That lighthouse is very old.
6. I have visited those national seashores.
7. This photograph shows sea turtles on Padre Island.
8. Look at these photos of surfers on Cape Hatteras.
9. This picture of a fort was taken at Gulf Islands National Seashore.
10. Do you see those birds wading in the water?

Helping Verbs

Know the Rule

A **helping verb** appears with the main verb in a sentence. A helping verb usually comes before the main verb. Common helping verbs include *are, can, have, must, should,* and *will.*

Examples:
Raccoons **have** knocked the covers off our trash cans again.
Those pesky raccoons **are** adapting well to city life.

Practice the Rule

Write the numbers 1–10 on a sheet of paper. Next to each number, write the helping verb in that sentence.

1. Loss of their natural habitats has forced some wild animals into urban areas.
2. Raccoons have become a familiar sight.
3. Now coyotes are appearing in many areas.
4. In Alaska, people have spotted the occasional moose wandering around town.
5. People must learn the best ways of sharing space with them.
6. People can take precautions against unwanted wild animals.
7. Pet owners should keep their pets inside at night.
8. Homeowners can keep trash in a garage or shed.
9. Coyotes can be helpful by eating rodents, insects, and other pests.
10. In books and on the Internet, you can find many good suggestions for dealing with urban wild animals.

Interjections

Know the Rule

An **interjection** is a word or group of words used to express strong feeling. A strong interjection stands alone and is followed by an exclamation point. A mild interjection that begins a sentence is followed by a comma. When you write, use the punctuation that gives the effect you are looking for.

Examples:
Wait! I need to talk to you.
Sorry, now is not a good time.

Practice the Rule

Number a sheet of paper 1–10. Next to each number, write the interjection that is in that sentence. Tell whether each is strong or mild.

1. Wow! The graphics in this game are outstanding.
2. Hmm, I'm not sure what kind of character to make.
3. Hey! I'm glad you came over, Darnell.
4. Yes, I do need help with the game.
5. No! I do not want to play a troll.
6. Shh, I'm thinking.
7. Hurray! I know what I want to be—an elf.
8. Great! The character looks really cool.
9. Help! Some critter just attacked me.
10. Oh, so that's how you do it.

Grammar, Usage & Mechanics

Linking Verbs

Know the Rule

A **linking verb** connects the subject of a sentence to a word or words in the predicate that tell about the subject. The following verbs are common linking verbs: any form of the verb *be* (*am, is, are, was, were, has been, are being, might have been,* etc.), *become,* and *seem.*

Examples:

Bread **is** an important food for people around the world.

Pizza **has been** popular in the United States for many years.

Practice the Rule

Number a sheet of paper 1–10. Next to each number, write the subject, the linking verb, and the word to which the subject is linked. Then circle the subject. For example, next to number 1 you would write **bread was medicine**. Then you would circle the word **bread**.

1. Moldy bread was a useful medicine for people of ancient Egypt.
2. Penicillin in the mold was effective in killing bacteria.
3. Penicillin became a wonder drug in the twentieth century.
4. In many countries, a meal is incomplete without bread.
5. Rice is more popular than bread in Japan, China, and other Asian countries.
6. Toast is a common breakfast for many people.
7. The French are fond of long loaves of bread.
8. A soft pretzel is another form of bread.
9. People were excited about the invention of a bread-slicing machine.
10. I am curious about making my own bread.

Grammar, Usage & Mechanics

More Linking Verbs

Know the Rule

A **linking verb** connects the subject of a sentence to a word or words in the predicate that tell about the subject. Not all linking verbs are forms of the verb *be*. Other words may also be linking verbs if they show a state of being, not an action. Some of these linking verbs are *look, taste, appear, grow,* and *smell.*

Examples:

The cat **looked** hungry. (linking verb: state of being hungry)

The cat **looked** for a mouse. (action verb: act of looking for a mouse)

Practice the Rule

Number a sheet of paper 1–10. Next to each number, write the verb in the sentence and tell whether it is a linking verb or an action verb.

1. Elena tasted the spicy chili.
2. The cat smells our salmon dinner.
3. I grew tired of leftovers.
4. This bread looks moldy.
5. Jamal appeared suddenly at our table.
6. The corn grows quickly.
7. The toast appears burnt.
8. That milk smells sour.
9. I looked for the tomato sauce.
10. The vegetable pizza tastes delicious.

Past-Perfect Verb Tense

Know the Rule

The **past-perfect tense** shows action that was completed by a certain time in the past. It is formed by using *had* with the past participle of the verb.

Example:

For many years, the Irish people **had depended** on potatoes as their most important food.

Practice the Rule

Number a sheet of paper 1–10. Next to each number, write the past-perfect verb in the sentence.

1. For hundreds of years, poor people in Ireland had grown potatoes as their main crop.
2. Potatoes had supplied most of the people's nutritional needs.
3. In 1845, a potato farmer discovered that all his potatoes had rotted.
4. It wasn't long before thousands of farmers had made the same discovery.
5. The potato blight had become a crisis for the country.
6. Before the blight ended, millions of people had died from starvation and disease.
7. Landlords had responded by evicting farmers who couldn't pay their rent.
8. At first, people had refused to abandon the country they loved.
9. But finally, staying in Ireland had become too difficult.
10. In the end, about two million Irish had left their homeland for other countries, including the United States.

Present-Perfect Verb Tense

Know the Rule

The **present-perfect verb tense** shows action that started in the past and was recently completed or action that is still happening. It is formed by using *has* or *have* before the past participle of the verb.

Examples:
My little sister **has** just **learned** to ride her pony. (The action was recently completed.)
We **have started** to ride together. (The action is still happening.)

Practice the Rule

Number a sheet of paper 1–10. Next to each number, write the present-perfect verb in the sentence.

1. This is the first time my cousin JD has ridden a horse.
2. He has visited us on our ranch often but was afraid to try riding.
3. I have chosen the perfect horse for him.
4. Her name is Maisie, and she has carried many beginners.
5. JD has dressed in jeans, boots, and a flannel shirt.
6. I gave him a helmet and explained that we have always worn helmets for protection from head injuries.
7. Soon JD and I have settled into our saddles.
8. I have suggested that we go at a slow pace until he feels secure.
9. After we have been on the trail for about an hour, we will go faster.
10. My cousin has become a real rider!

Reflexive Pronouns

Know the Rule

A **reflexive pronoun** ends in *-self* or *-selves* and refers to a preceding noun or pronoun. Singular reflexive pronouns are *myself, yourself, himself, herself,* and *itself.* Plural reflexive pronouns are *ourselves, yourselves,* and *themselves.*

Example:
We went to a fundraiser for the Furry Friends Shelter, since **we** volunteer there **ourselves**.

Practice the Rule

Number a sheet of paper 1–10. Next to each number, write the reflexive pronoun that completes the sentence.

1. My sister gave the first speech, which she had written _____.
2. She spoke passionately about opportunities to help those who can't help _____.
3. I can't imagine _____ speaking before a crowd of people.
4. My brother agrees with me and shudders at the thought of seeing _____ on stage.
5. Just the microphone _____ is scary.
6. My sister says we won't be afraid once we have tried it _____.
7. She said that we shouldn't think about _____, but about the points we are trying to get across.
8. The more you concentrate on the subject of the speech, the more you will forget about _____.
9. After listening to my sister, my friends decided that they would say a few words _____.
10. My brother and I reluctantly agreed that we would eventually force _____ to give a speech.

Homophones

Know the Rule

Homophones are words that sound alike but have different meanings and, often, different spellings. *Their, there,* and *they're* are homophones that are often confused. *Their* is a possessive pronoun that means "belonging to them." *There* is an adverb that usually means "in that place." *There* can also be an introductory word. *They're* is a contraction of the words *they are.*

Examples:

Gabriella and Josh got **their** two cats from a shelter.

Many potential pet owners visit the shelter to see the animals **there**.

They're very happy with the cats.

Practice the Rule

Number a sheet of paper 1–10. After each number, write the correct homophone in parentheses for each sentence.

1. Mom and Dad have said that (their/there/they're) willing to get my brother and me each a pet.
2. They have heard so much about the animal shelter that they want us to go (their/there/they're) for our pets.
3. That dog in the cage over (their/there/they're) looks sad and lonely.
4. (Their/There/They're) are so many great animals in the shelter.
5. The owners took some animals out of (their/there/they're) cages so that we could hold and pat them.
6. They gave us (their/there/they're) instructions for pet care.
7. Those two kittens have lost their mother, and (their/there/they're) very attached to each other.
8. (Their/There/They're) are two dogs my brother really likes.
9. (Their/There/They're) were three adoptions that day.
10. My brother took home the dog, and I took home the two kittens that had lost (their/there/they're) mother.

More Homophones

Know the Rule

Homophones are words that sound alike but have different meanings and, often, different spellings. There are many homophones in the English language. A few are *blue/blew, fir/fur, pole/poll, toe/tow, role/roll, see/sea,* and *sale/sail.*

Example:
From the top of the cliff, she could **see** far out to **sea**.

Practice the Rule

On a separate sheet of paper, write each sentence using the correct word(s) in parentheses. Check in a dictionary if you are uncertain which word to use.

1. The (tide/tied) was (hi/high) as the old sailor pushed his small boat into the water.
2. He unfurled the (sale/sail) from the (mast/massed).
3. The sailor and his dog headed out to (sea/see).
4. As he rowed, the sailor (herd/heard) the cries of the seagulls overhead.
5. Soon they (passed/past) the first (boy/buoy) and turned toward the small island.
6. The old man hauled the boat onto the (beech/beach).
7. He rested a bit until his dog thought the (wait/weight) was long enough and began to bark.
8. The man took his fishing (poll/pole) and other gear out of the boat.
9. Then the man and the dog walked to a freshwater pond that very few people (new/knew) about.
10. As he fished, the man felt the warmth of the sun's (rays/raise).

Irregular Verbs

Know the Rule

The past tense and past participle of most verbs are formed the same way: by adding *-ed* to the present tense of the verb (*walk, walked, walked*). The past tense and past participle of **irregular verbs** are not formed by adding *-ed*. These verbs have different forms (*feel, felt, felt; go, went, gone*). Remember, use *has* or *have* with the past participle to form the present perfect tense. Use *had* with the past participle to form the past perfect tense.

Examples:

My dog **hid** under the bed during the thunderstorm. (past tense)

I **have hidden** there myself during storms. (present perfect tense)

Practice the Rule

Number a sheet of paper 1–10. After each number, write the correct form of the irregular verb in parentheses.

1. The storm (hit/hitted) our area in the middle of the night.
2. Wind (tore/teared) through the trees.
3. I (felt/feeled) the house shake.
4. I have (feeled/felt) the house shake only once before.
5. I looked out the window and (seen/saw) leaves and some roof shingles fly by.
6. Then I (heared/heard) a loud clap of thunder.
7. The house (shaked/shook) again.
8. I (creeped/crept) back under the covers.
9. In the morning, I discovered that lightning had (striked/struck) our neighbor's tree.
10. I had never (saw/seen) anything quite like it.

Multiple-Meaning Words

Know the Rule

Multiple-meaning words are words that are spelled the same but have different meanings depending on how they are used in a sentence. Many multiple-meaning words are used as both a noun and a verb.

Examples:

Last week we had an inch of **rain**. (noun)

It will **rain** again tomorrow. (verb)

Practice the Rule

Number a sheet of paper 1–5. Next to each number, write the letter of the sentence that uses the underlined word in the same way as the numbered sentence.

1. It was hard not to slip on the ice.
   - **A.** I gave the teacher my permission slip.
   - **B.** I saw a man slip on a banana peel.
2. That's the place that has great pizza.
   - **A.** Please place your pencils on your desks.
   - **B.** Which place sells the best skateboards?
3. My dog likes to roll in the mud.
   - **A.** I ate a roll with my soup.
   - **B.** I get dizzy when I roll down hills.
4. The alarm clock rings too early.
   - **A.** Saturn has more rings around it than any other planet.
   - **B.** The telephone rings, but no one answers.
5. I notice your family has a new car.
   - **A.** I waved, but you didn't seem to notice.
   - **B.** Post the notice on the door.

More Multiple-Meaning Words

Know the Rule

Multiple-meaning words are words that are spelled the same but have different meanings depending on how they are used in a sentence. Many multiple-meaning words are used as both a noun and a verb.

Examples:
That painting has a beautiful **frame**. (noun)
I will **frame** my poster tomorrow. (verb)

Practice the Rule

Number a sheet of paper 1–12. Write **verb** or **noun**, depending on how the underlined word is used in the sentence.

1. Many young children like to color.
2. Ethan's favorite color is blue.
3. My sister and I have the same eye color.
4. Many artists use oil paint on canvas.
5. My parents worked hard to paint our house.
6. What is the plan for tonight?
7. Plan your time carefully so that your report will be done on time.
8. Before you paint a piece of wood, you need to sand it.
9. Please don't track sand into the house!
10. The kite rose gracefully into the sky.
11. Yesterday the sun rose at 7:03 A.M.
12. A honeybee landed on the rose.

Connotation and Denotation

Know the Rule

The **connotation** of a word refers to the feelings that the word brings to mind. Connotations can be positive or negative. **Denotation** is the dictionary definition of the word, or the word's literal meaning.

Example:
These words have the same denotation ("thin") but different connotations.
scrawny (negative)
slender (positive)

Practice the Rule

Number a sheet of paper 1–10. Read each sentence and think about the connotation of the underlined word. After each number, write the underlined word. Then write **positive** or **negative** to describe the connotation of the underlined word.

1. The dress in the store window looks really cheap.
2. Mrs. Benson made a generous donation to the school fundraiser.
3. The audience snickered at the bad acting in the movie.
4. My father thought that my behavior was childish.
5. Thomas thought the concert was boring.
6. The class liked Dwayne's inspiring speech.
7. The cherry pie you made was delicious.
8. I loved the exciting ending of the novel.
9. My little brother's bedroom is a total mess.
10. Clara giggled at Chris's joke.

Grammar, Usage & Mechanics

Compound Words

Know the Rule

A **compound word** is made when two words are joined to form a new word. A compound word may be spelled as one word, as a hyphenated word, or as two words.

Examples:
bedroom (*bed* and *room*)
ready-made (*ready* and *made*)
pen pal (*pen* and *pal*)

Practice the Rule

Number a sheet of paper 1–10. Next to each number, write the compound word found in that sentence and the two words that make up the compound.

1. Iceland is an island country completely surrounded by water.
2. The country has many natural wonders, such as glaciers, volcanoes, and waterfalls.
3. Most of the people live along the seacoast because the interior of the country consists of mountains and fields of sand.
4. Horseback riding and hiking are two popular activities.
5. The horses are small and sturdy and can safely cross the rough countryside.
6. Soccer is the most popular sport, but handball is also very popular.
7. I wonder if cross-country skiing is popular.
8. The ocean around the country contains many kinds of shellfish.
9. In summer, there is sunlight all day and all night.
10. If you flew to this country, you might suffer jet lag.

Appositives

Know the Rule

An **appositive** is a word, phrase, or clause that identifies, or means the same thing as, a noun. Appositives follow the nouns they identify and are usually separated from the rest of the sentence by commas.

Example:

The owl**, a creature of the night,** swoops towards its prey.

Practice the Rule

Number a sheet of paper 1–10. After each number, write the appositive phrase in the sentence and the noun it identifies.

1. The little field mouse, a seed-eating animal, creeps out of its nest at night.
2. Owls, animals that see and hear extremely well at night, can locate tiny animals in the dark.
3. Bushbabies, animals that live in Africa, have very large eyes that help them see well at night.
4. The serval, an African wildcat, has big ears that help it find small prey at night.
5. Bats, nocturnal animals, hunt for food at night.
6. Skunks, critters known for their smell, hunt at night for bugs, frogs, and other small animals.
7. The flying squirrel, a rarely seen nocturnal animal, does not have real wings.
8. Leopards, ferocious hunters, rest in trees during the day and hunt at night.
9. The opossum, a strange-looking animal, carries its young in a pouch.
10. The aye-aye, an animal of the rain forest, is now an endangered species.

Correlative Conjunctions

Know the Rule

Conjunctions connect parts of a sentence. **Correlative conjunctions** connect similar, balanced parts of a sentence. They always appear in pairs.

Example:
You should wear **either** your blue sweater **or** your green one.

Correlative Conjunctions

either, or	not only, but also
neither, nor	both, and
not, but	whether, or

Practice the Rule

Number a sheet of paper 1–10. Write the correlative conjunction from each sentence and its missing partner.

1. Ben likes to read either mysteries _____ adventure stories.
2. I have read _____ Stephen King's books nor any other books that will scare me.
3. In school, we read _____ *Charlotte's Web* and *Stuart Little.*
4. I love not only the words _____ the illustrations in both books.
5. The animated movie of *Charlotte's Web* was neither well drawn _____ well adapted.
6. Natalie has read both *Stone Fox* _____ *Hatchet.*
7. In fact, she has read _____ *Hatchet* but also *Dogsong* and *The Winter Room.*
8. Do you know whether you will read an electronic book _____ you will read a printed book?
9. I like to read both after dinner _____ before going to bed.
10. It doesn't matter _____ you like biographies or you enjoy folktales; reading is a great activity!

Conventions **Grammar, Usage & Mechanics**

Verb Tenses

Know the Rule

The **present tense** of a verb tells that something is happening now or that something happens regularly. To make the third-person singular form of the present tense, add *-s* or *-es* (*he throws, she catches*).

Example:

Cats **are** very interesting animals.

The **past tense** of a verb tells that something has already happened. Regular verbs form the past tense by adding *-ed* or *-d.*

Example:

Cats **lived** in Egypt as long ago as 1400 B.C.

The **future tense** of a verb tells that something is going to happen. Use *will* before the present tense to form the future tense.

Example:

We **will visit** the cat show next Monday.

Practice the Rule

Number a sheet of paper 1–10. Next to each number, write the verb in the sentence and tell whether it is in the present, past, or future tense.

1. "Natural" breeds of cats developed on their own with no human input.
2. A Siamese is an example of a natural breed.
3. Humans created other breeds by mixing two breeds together.
4. A Bengal cat is a mix of a domestic cat and an Asian leopard.
5. As a result, the Bengal has leopard markings.
6. Every breed displays some unique characteristics.
7. I will ask the school librarian for some interesting books on cats.
8. My friend Felipe once owned two cats.
9. I will read my report on unusual cats to my class this afternoon.
10. I already printed out some photographs of cats for my presentation.

Grammar, Usage & Mechanics

Capitalization

Know the Rule

A **common noun** names any person, place, thing, or idea.

Example:

Two popular **dishes** are **bratwurst** and **sauerbraten**.

A **proper noun** names a particular person, place, thing, or idea. Proper nouns are capitalized. If a proper noun is two words, both words are capitalized (*South Africa, Civil War*).

Example:

Germany, a country in **Europe,** is known for certain foods.

Practice the Rule

Write the sentences on a separate sheet of paper, capitalizing the proper nouns.

1. During world war II, the united states, great britain, france, and the soviet union fought against germany and its allies.
2. When germany lost the war in 1945, the country was divided into two parts.
3. West germany was under the power of the united states, great britain, and france.
4. East germany was under the control of the soviet union.
5. The former capital of germany, berlin, was divided into two parts: west berlin and east berlin.
6. In 1961, the government of east germany built a concrete wall to keep the people of east berlin and west berlin apart.
7. The wall, officially known as the berlin wall, divided families and friends.
8. The united states president at the time was john f. kennedy.
9. It wasn't until 1989 that the berlin wall finally came down.
10. The leader of the Soviet Union was mikhail gorbachev.

Conventions **Grammar, Usage & Mechanics**

Colons

Know the Rule

A **colon** is used after an independent clause that introduces an explanation, an example, or a series. Do not use a colon unless the words that come before it make a complete sentence.

Practice the Rule

Write the sentences on a separate sheet of paper. If the sentence needs a colon, write the sentence correctly. If the sentence does not need a colon, write **Correct**.

1. My favorite pizza toppings include mushrooms, green peppers, and onions.
2. Our pizzas come in the following sizes small, medium, and large.
3. These are the pizza toppings Jermain always orders pepperoni, onion, and extra cheese.
4. Instead of pizza, we would like to order a tuna rollup, a Caesar salad with chicken, and a chicken salad.
5. Ella and I prefer the following pasta dishes tortellini, spaghetti and meatballs, and ravioli.
6. I now know what is on a pizza bianca garlic, Romano cheese, mozzarella cheese, olive oil, and no tomato sauce.
7. The pizza places I like are Sarpino's, Giordano's, and Tony's.
8. My pizza crust is made with the following ingredients yeast, flour, salt, olive oil, sugar, and water.
9. These are my three favorite vegetarian foods pizza with veggies, bean and cheese burritos, and stir-fried vegetables.
10. Please don't order anchovies, spinach, or sausage.

Contractions

Know the Rule

A **contraction** is a word formed by combining two words. One of the words is shortened. An apostrophe is used in place of the missing letters of the shortened word. Commonly used contractions include *I've* (*I have*), *you'll* (*you will*), and *don't* (*do not*).

Examples:

It is fun to live in an apartment building.

It's fun to live in an apartment building.

Practice the Rule

Write the numbers 1–10 on a separate sheet of paper. Next to each number, write the contraction for the words in parentheses.

1. (We have) always lived in an apartment in the city.
2. I (would not) want to live anywhere else.
3. One thing I like about this building is that (it is) full of different kinds of people.
4. (I am) lucky to live near families from Mexico, Kenya, Italy, and Hungary.
5. My best friend Ty says (it is) like the United Nations of apartment buildings.
6. Ty lives four floors up from me, but we can ride an elevator if we (do not) feel like walking.
7. Another nice thing about living here is (what is) outside.
8. In back of the building (there is) a playground.
9. (You will) find that most of the people who live here are friendly.
10. All the residents think that (it is) a great place to live.

Parentheses

Know the Rule

Parentheses are used to set off explanatory matter within a sentence. The words within the parentheses can be omitted without changing the meaning of the sentence.

Example:
China (a large country in East Asia) was the first country to use paper money.

Practice the Rule

Write the numbers 1–10 on a separate sheet of paper. Write each sentence, using parentheses to set off information that could be omitted without changing the meaning of the sentence.

1. He withdrew six hundred dollars $600 from his checking account.
2. United States paper money is designed to make it more secure harder for criminals to make counterfeit bills.
3. The penny has President Lincoln's profile side view of his head on one side and the Lincoln Memorial on the other.
4. Hundred-dollar bills last much longer about nine years than one-dollar bills.
5. A nickel is the only coin named for a metal nickel.
6. The British pound also called a quid is Britain's version of our dollar.
7. In February 2010, the English pound was worth about $1.55 these rates change often.
8. Most European countries exceptions include Britain and Denmark now use a single currency called the Euro.
9. When the United States first issued paper bills, each note was signed by hand the signature of the U.S. Treasurer.
10. A dollar coin honoring Susan B. Anthony a women's suffrage crusader is easily confused with a quarter.

Semicolons

Know the Rule

A **semicolon** can be used instead of a comma and conjunction to separate the independent clauses in a compound sentence. The ideas in the independent clauses should be very closely related if you use a semicolon to separate them.

Example:
A giraffe can grow as tall as nineteen feet; eight feet of its height is its neck.

Practice the Rule

Number a separate sheet of paper 1–10. Write each sentence, using a semicolon to separate the independent clauses.

1. A giraffe's height allows it to eat leaves other animals can't reach a giraffe commonly eats hundreds of pounds of leaves in a week.
2. The giraffe eats all the time it has to travel miles each day to find enough food.
3. The giraffe's height enables it to see predators that are far away in this way, the giraffe acts as a lookout for smaller animals.
4. Fortunately, giraffes only need to drink every few days this is a lucky thing because drinking from a water hole is very awkward for them.
5. A giraffe's legs are about six feet tall its legs are taller than many humans.
6. Adult giraffes have very few enemies predators tend to go after baby giraffes.
7. A mother giraffe is very protective she hides her baby under her body.
8. A giraffe will kick an attacking predator the kick can knock out or even kill the other animal.
9. Giraffes travel in small herds a herd may have only six giraffes.
10. Giraffes are known for the beautiful patterns on their coats no two giraffes have exactly the same pattern.

More Practice

Compound Subjects

Number your paper 1–5. Beside each number, write the subjects of the sentence. Then write the connecting word that joins the subjects.

1. Can a cat or a dog see colors?
2. Humans and many animals have good color vision.
3. Cats, dogs, and mice have limited color vision.
4. Apparently, these animals and rabbits see only shades of grays, blues, and yellows.
5. Books or online resources provide lots of information about how people see color.

Compound Predicates

Number your paper 1–5. Beside each number, write the verbs of the sentence. Then write the connecting word that joins the verbs.

1. This morning, Nina cleaned her room and alphabetized her books.
2. Her younger brother stayed home but played a computer game.
3. Nina taped a poster to her wall and placed a plant on the table.
4. Her brother wanted a plant and asked Nina for hers.
5. Their mother thanked them and made them popcorn for an afternoon snack.

Object of a Preposition

Number a sheet of paper 1–5. Copy each sentence. Circle the preposition. Underline the object.

1. During a fire drill, we line up at the door.
2. We walk down the hall.
3. Everyone goes through the front doors.
4. The fire truck pulls along the curb and stops.
5. Finally, we return to the classroom.

More Practice

Complex Sentences

Number your paper 1–5. Write each complex sentence. Underline the independent clause once and the dependent clause twice.

1. I was almost late for class because I was talking to some friends in the hallway.
2. Tanya will finish her report as soon as she can use the computer.
3. I'm not sure how I did on the spelling test.
4. When the bell rang, we ran out the door to the playground.
5. When lunch period ended, we went back to the classroom.

Comma Splices

Number your paper 1–5. Rewrite each sentence that has a comma splice by adding a joining word after the comma or by changing the comma to a period to form two sentences. If the sentence does not have a comma splice, write **Correct** after the number.

1. I wanted to go swimming, it seemed too cold.
2. If the sun were shining, I would feel more like getting wet.
3. My friends jumped in the pool, they yelled at me to join them.
4. I touched the water with my toe, the water didn't seem too cold.
5. I finally jumped in, my friends and I had a great time.

More Practice

Articles

Number your paper 1–5. Choose the correct article in parentheses and write it next to the number.

1. My older sister took me to (an/the) Carolina Zoo.
2. I was very excited to see (a/the) elephants.
3. I had seen (a/an) elephant only in picture books.
4. We also saw (a/an) monkey.
5. My sister and I were both scared by (a/an) anaconda, a very large snake.

Comparative Adverbs

Number your paper 1–5. Write each sentence, using the correct form of the adverb in parentheses. Some of the sentences require the comparative form of the adverb. Others do not.

1. Damon practices his instrument (frequently) than I do.
2. Lea played her violin solo (carefully).
3. The teacher (patiently) explained the piece of music.
4. Sarina can learn music (quickly) than other students.
5. Todd takes his music class (seriously) than most of us.

Concrete and Abstract Nouns

Number your paper 1–5. Write **abstract** or **concrete** to describe the underlined noun in each sentence.

1. We had fun in the <u>gym</u> this afternoon.
2. I barely had the <u>strength</u> to finish my five chin-ups.
3. Elliot dribbled the <u>basketball</u> across the gym.
4. Troy is always talking about his <u>love</u> of baseball.
5. Tiffany threw the football almost twenty <u>yards.</u>

More Practice

Demonstrative Adjectives

Number your paper 1–5. Choose the correct demonstrative adjective in parentheses.

1. (This/That) trail over there is the one we will hike today.
2. Does (this/that) map here show the scenic spots along the trail?
3. Just look at (that/these) field of wildflowers!
4. (That/Those) hiking boots look really comfortable.
5. (That/This) hill we are hiking up is pretty steep.

Helping Verbs

Number your paper 1–5. Rewrite each sentence using one of the helping verbs **is, are, has, have, must, can,** or **should** with the verb in parentheses.

1. Honey bees (buzzing) around their hive.
2. People (eaten) honey for thousands of years.
3. You (wear) protective clothes when handling bees.
4. The gardener (looking) for ladybugs among her plants.
5. Ladybugs (be) very helpful to gardeners.

Interjections

Number your paper 1–5. Write each sentence. Add the punctuation that is missing after each interjection.

1. Wow I am really looking forward to watching this movie.
2. Oh this seat has gum on it.
3. Ouch I pinched my finger in the seat.
4. Oh, no she spilled her soft drink.
5. Well she didn't really want it anyway.

More Practice

Linking Verbs

Number your paper 1–5. Copy each sentence. Circle the linking verb. Underline the subject and the word that is linked to it.

1. Cats are very quiet.
2. Your dog looks friendly.
3. This fat cat is my family's pet.
4. Your old hound smells bad.
5. Ellen's snake looks harmless.

More Linking Verbs

Number your paper 1–5. Beside each number, write the verb in the sentence. Then identify the kind of verb each is by writing **linking verb** or **action verb**.

1. Conrad smells the chili on the stove.
2. We are all really hungry.
3. The cornbread tastes pretty good to me!
4. My sister is a great cook.
5. Ivan appears suddenly at the table.

Present-Perfect Tense and Past-Perfect Tense

Number your paper 1–5. Write the verb from each sentence and tell whether it is present-perfect tense or past-perfect tense.

1. I have chosen a book for my book report.
2. I had thought about doing a report on *Hoot*.
3. Jared had already decided to do his report on *Hoot*.
4. In fact, Jared has already written his whole report!
5. Therefore, I have made a decision to read *Holes*.

More Practice

Reflexive Pronouns

Number your paper 1–5. Write the reflexive pronoun that correctly completes each sentence.

1. Kaito taught _____ to speak English.
2. Kaito's mother was teaching _____ to speak English, too.
3. Kaito and his mother were pleased with _____ for learning a new language.
4. Kaito's friend Karen said, "I wish I knew another language that well _____."
5. She said, "You will be able to find _____ a good job someday."

Homophones

Number your paper 1–5. Write a homophone pair that can complete each sentence.

1. Nana and Papa said that _____ on _____ way to the restaurant.
2. Meshawn and Masani _____ up the red and _____ balloons.
3. When the guests arrive, they can put _____ coats over _____.
4. From the window in the dining room, you can _____ the boats on the _____.
5. I am glad I got _____ celebrate Mom and Dad's anniversary by eating _____ pieces of cake!

More Practice

Irregular Verbs

Number your paper 1–5. Beside each number, write the correct past-tense, present-perfect tense, or past-perfect tense form of the verb in parentheses.

1. Constanza quietly (creep) downstairs.
2. She (know) that her parents had been up late packing.
3. She hoped that she had not (overdo) her own packing.
4. Her family had (send) the most important things in boxes a few weeks ago.
5. Constanza (think) that leaving her friends was going to be difficult.

Multiple-Meaning Words

Number your paper 1–5. Write whether the underlined multiple-meaning word is a noun or a verb.

1. I feel a <u>paw</u> on my leg.
2. I reach down and <u>pet</u> my dog Sniffles.
3. It's time to start him on his new <u>diet</u>.
4. I wonder if the new food has a different <u>taste</u>.
5. I watch Sniffles <u>wolf</u> the new food.

Connotation and Denotation

Number your paper 1–5. The following words have negative connotations. For each word, write another word that has a similar meaning but a positive connotation. If you are unsure what a word means, look it up in a dictionary to find its denotation.

1. smirk
2. nosy
3. rowdy
4. cheap
5. weird

More Practice

Compound Words

Number your paper 1–5. Combine each word from row 1 with a word from row 2 to write a compound word. Some of the words in row 2 can be combined with more than one word in row 1.

Row 1:	skate	moon	book	key	rain
Row 2:	pad	coat	board	worm	light

Appositives

Number your paper 1–5. Write the words that make up each appositive.

1. Wilma Rudolph, a famous track star, was the first American woman to win three gold medals in the Olympics.
2. Elliot, my best friend, wants to write a biography about Wilma Rudolph.
3. Fortunately, Ms. Langston, our English teacher, thinks it's a great idea.
4. I'm going to write my report on Hank Aaron, a famous professional baseball player.
5. Uncle Ray, my mother's brother, has some old baseball cards of Hank Aaron.

Correlative Conjunctions

Number a sheet of paper 1–5. Write the correlative conjunction in each sentence and its missing partner.

1. Ana plays both soccer _____ ice hockey.
2. Nick likes neither football _____ baseball.
3. We can either go to the pool _____ stay home.
4. Manny can speak not only Spanish _____ Portuguese.
5. Sonya plays both violin _____ piano.

More Practice

Verb Tenses

Number your paper 1–5. Write the verb in each sentence in the present tense, past tense, or future tense as indicated.

1. Josh (go, future tense) to a special camp this summer.
2. It (be, present) a computer camp.
3. He and I (attend, past) the camp last year.
4. Josh (enroll, past) in an advanced programming course.
5. I (ask, future) about an athletic camp for later in the summer.

Capitalization

Number your paper 1–10. The paragraph below contains ten proper nouns that should be capitalized. Write each proper noun with the correct capitalization.

Our teacher wants us to write about a country. I have chosen cuba. My grandparents were born there. My friend eduardo is going to write about china. I don't know why he chose that country. Elissa said that she was going to write about moscow. I explained to her that it was a city and not a country. I pointed out to her that she could write about russia, which is a country. Another student wanted to write about africa. I explained to him that it was a continent, not a country. Other classmates are going to write about mexico, canada, italy, and belize.

More Practice

Colons and Semicolons

Number your paper 1–5. Write each sentence, using a colon or semicolon where needed. If the sentence does not need a colon or semicolon, write **Correct**.

1. I went to the store with my uncle he needed to buy some tools.

2. He put the following tools in his cart a hammer, a saw, and two boxes of nails.

3. The store was pretty crowded my uncle told me that the store was having a big sale.

4. In one aisle, my uncle picked out some paint, paintbrushes, and rollers.

5. Next week I am going to help my uncle do these things paint the kitchen, fix the bathroom sink, and clean the basement.

Contractions

Number your paper 1–5. Write the two words that have been combined to form each contraction.

1. didn't **2.** couldn't **3.** we'll **4.** I've **5.** she's

Parentheses

The following paragraph contains four examples of incidental matter that should be enclosed within parentheses. Copy the paragraph, adding parentheses where appropriate.

I was amazed to see a tree filled with beautiful butterflies monarchs. The butterflies travel a great distance up to 2,500 miles every year to escape the cold weather in the North. They begin their migration about the same time October each year. They fly until they reach the warm climates of California or Mexico. Each year, the butterflies fly to the same place literally the exact same tree as they did the year before.

Transitions

Transitional words and phrases help to make the meaning of a paragraph clearer.

Words and phrases that can be used to show time order:

about	after	at	before
during	first	second	to begin
yesterday	meanwhile	today	tomorrow
until	next	soon	later
finally	then	as soon as	in the end

Words and phrases that can be used to show cause and effect:

and so	as a result	because	consequently
once	since	so	therefore

Words and phrases that can be used to compare and contrast:

Compare:	also	as	both
	in the same way	like	likewise
	one way	similarly	
Contrast:	although	but	even though
	however	yet	otherwise
	still	on the other hand	

Appendix B
Rubrics

4-Point Rubrics

5-Point Rubrics

6-Point Rubrics

Narrative Writing Rubric

	4	3	2	1
Ideas	The topic is just the right size—not too big or too small. Descriptive details introduce and develop the setting, narrator, characters, and plot. Carefully selected ideas completely satisfy the needs of the reader.	The topic is the right size. Details introduce and develop the setting, narrator, characters, and plot. The ideas selected by the author frequently meet the needs of the reader.	The topic is too big or too small. Some details develop the setting, narrator, characters, and plot. The ideas selected by the author sometimes meet the needs of the reader.	The writing is not a narrative. Details are unrelated or not included.
Organization	The narrative unfolds logically and naturally. Transition words and phrases help sequence the events. A strong beginning leads to a satisfying conclusion.	Some events are not connected or are out of order. Transition words and phrases are needed to help sequence the events. The beginning and the conclusion work, but may not be strong.	The narrative does not unfold logically and naturally. Events are out of order. Transition words and phrases are confusing or missing. The beginning or the conclusion is weak.	The writing is disorganized and very difficult to follow. Transition words and phrases are not used. No beginning or conclusion is evident.
Voice	The voice, mood, and tone are just right for the purpose. Dialogue, if used, reveals each character's voice clearly.	The voice, mood, and tone are just right in places, but inconsistent. Dialogue, if used, somewhat reveals the characters' voices.	The voice sounds disinterested. Mood and tone are weak. Dialogue, if used, does not uniquely distinguish the characters' voices.	Voice is flat. Mood and tone are absent. Dialogue, if used, does not sound right for some of the characters.
Word Choice	Words and phrases consistently help the reader "see" the characters and "experience" the events. Nouns and verbs are clear and precise, supported by a few carefully selected modifiers.	Some words and phrases help the reader picture characters and events, but some are too general. Certain nouns and verbs are weak, requiring too much help from modifiers. Modifiers are satisfactory.	Many words and phrases are too general. They keep the reader from picturing the characters and events clearly. Nouns and verbs lack clarity or precision. Too many or too few modifiers are used, and many of them are weak.	Many words are not used correctly. They distract the reader.
Sentence Fluency	Varied sentence beginnings, lengths, and patterns make the writing flow smoothly. Several particularly well-crafted sentences add style and interest. The paper is effortlessly read aloud with inflection or feeling.	There is some variation in sentence beginnings, lengths, and patterns. The sentences are correct, and one or two sentences add style. The paper can be read aloud with inflection or feeling.	Many sentences have the same beginnings, lengths, and patterns. This interrupts the flow of the writing. The sentences are mostly correct but ordinary. It is difficult to read the paper with inflection.	Sentences are poorly written or incorrect. The writing does not flow.
Conventions	Spelling, grammar, punctuation, and capitalization are correct. The narrative contains no errors.	There are a few grammatical errors that may cause the reader to pause momentarily, but meaning is clear.	Many errors are present, and some confuse the reader.	The writing has not been edited. Serious errors make the narrative hard to understand.

Informative/Explanatory Writing Rubric

	4	3	2	1
Ideas	The topic is introduced clearly. Information and examples develop the main idea(s). Carefully selected ideas completely answer the reader's main questions.	A topic is introduced. Most of the information and examples develop the main idea(s). The ideas chosen by the author frequently answer the reader's main questions.	A topic is introduced, but little of the information or examples develops the main idea(s). Some of the reader's questions are answered.	A topic is not introduced. Information and examples are incomplete or unrelated to the topic.
Organization	Information is organized into a strong and thoughtful introduction, a body, and a satisfying conclusion. Varied and appropriate transitions connect the ideas.	Information is organized into an introduction, a body, and a conclusion. More or better transitions are needed.	Information is not well organized. The introduction, body, and conclusion may be poorly developed. Transitions are confusing or not helpful.	The writing is not organized. Introduction and conclusion may both be missing. Transitions are not used.
Voice	The voice sounds interested and informative. It fully connects with the audience and conveys the writer's purpose well.	The voice sounds informative and mostly connects with the audience. It conveys the purpose some of the time.	The voice sounds informative in places. It conveys the purpose, but often fades out.	Voice is weak or absent. It does not connect with the audience or convey the writer's purpose.
Word Choice	Precise language and domain-specific vocabulary are used. Definitions are complete and helpful. Nouns and verbs are clear and precise, supported by a few carefully selected modifiers.	Some precise language, domain-specific vocabulary, and definitions are used. Some nouns and verbs are weak, requiring help from modifiers. Modifiers are satisfactory.	Little precise language and domain-specific vocabulary is used. Definitions are missing or incorrect. Nouns and verbs lack clarity or precision. Too many or too few modifiers are used, and many of them are weak.	Precise language and domain-specific vocabulary are not used.
Sentence Fluency	Clear, concise sentences make the text flow smoothly. Sentence beginnings, lengths, and patterns are varied for effect. The paper is effortlessly read aloud with inflection.	One or two sections of the writing do not flow smoothly. In these sections, several sentences may have the same beginnings, lengths, or patterns. The paper can be read with inflection.	In many places, the writing does not flow smoothly due to repetitive sentence beginnings, lengths, and patterns. It is difficult to read the paper with inflection.	Sentences are incomplete or incorrect.
Conventions	The text contains no errors. Spelling, grammar, punctuation, and capitalization are correct.	The text contains some errors in spelling, grammar, punctuation, and capitalization. One or two errors may cause the reader to pause momentarily, but meaning remains clear.	Many errors are present. Some errors are basic or repeated. The errors interfere with meaning in places.	The writing has not been edited. Serious errors make the writing hard to understand.

Opinion Writing Rubric

	4	3	2	1
Ideas	The writer states a clear opinion. The perfect details and facts are chosen to support the writer's reasons.	The writer states an opinion. Some details and facts are well chosen to support the writer's reasons.	The writer states an opinion, but few details are well chosen to support the writer's reasons.	The writer does not state an opinion. Reasons are not provided.
Organization	The text is organized logically and creatively. Helpful, appropriate, even unique transitions link the writer's opinion and reasons. A compelling conclusion clearly supports the opinion statement.	The text is organized logically. More or better transitions are needed to link the opinion and reasons. The beginning and the conclusion are functional. The conclusion relates to the opinion statement.	The text is not organized logically. Transitions may not show how the writer's ideas are related. Either the beginning or the conclusion is weak. The conclusion may not relate to the opinion statement.	The text is not organized as an opinion. Transitions are not used. Ideas are hard to follow. No beginning or conclusion is evident.
Voice	The voice is clearly convincing and totally fits the writer's purpose. The mood and tone are appropriate and engage the audience.	The voice is convincing and fits the writer's purpose. The mood and tone are engaging some of the time.	The voice is convincing in some places. The mood and tone are incorrect or inconsistent. They lose the audience.	The voice is weak or absent. The tone is not appropriate.
Word Choice	Precise words and fair language convey the writer's opinion. No biased words or phrases are used. Nouns and verbs are clear and precise, supported by a few carefully selected modifiers.	Some words are too general. One biased word or phrase may be used. Some nouns and verbs are weak, requiring help from modifiers. Modifiers are satisfactory.	Most words are weak. A few biased words or phrases may be used. Nouns and verbs lack clarity or precision. Too many or too few modifiers are used, and many of them are weak.	Words are weak, biased, or used incorrectly.
Sentence Fluency	A variety of sentence patterns adds interest and style. Great variation in sentence beginnings and lengths makes the writing flow very smoothly. The paper is effortlessly read aloud with inflection.	Some sentence patterns are varied and add interest. Some variation in sentence lengths and beginnings is evident. The writing flows smoothly in some places, but not in others. The paper can be read with inflection.	Too many sentences share the same pattern. The writing does not flow smoothly due to a lack of variation in sentence lengths and/or beginnings. It is difficult to read the paper with inflection.	Sentences are poorly written or incomplete. The writing is hard to follow.
Conventions	The text contains no errors. Spelling, grammar, punctuation, and capitalization are correct.	There are some errors in spelling, grammar, punctuation, and capitalization. One or two of these errors may cause the reader to pause momentarily, but meaning remains clear.	Many errors are present. Some errors are basic or repeated. The errors interfere with meaning in places.	The writing has not been edited. Serious errors make the writing hard to understand.

Descriptive Writing Rubric

	4	3	2	1
Ideas	The topic is clear, focused, and complete. Sensory details and examples are related to and develop the main ideas. The description helps the reader experience what is being described very clearly.	The topic is clear but may not be focused or complete. Sensory details and examples develop most of the main ideas. The description sometimes helps the reader experience what is being described.	The topic is not clear or focused. Details and examples develop some of the main ideas. The reader cannot always experience what is being described.	The topic is not clear. Details and examples are unrelated or missing. The reader cannot experience what is being described.
Organization	The description is well organized into a strong introduction, body, and conclusion. Details support the topic. Appropriate transitions connect the ideas and guide the reader.	Most of the description is organized. The introduction, body, and conclusion are functional. Most of the details support the topic. More or better transitions are needed to connect the ideas and guide the reader.	Some of the description is organized. The introduction, body, or conclusion may be weak. Few of the details support the topic. More and better transitions are needed to connect the ideas and guide the reader.	The description is not organized and does not have an introduction or conclusion. Details are missing. Transitions are not used.
Voice	The writer's voice connects strongly with the audience. The mood and tone match the purpose perfectly.	The writer's voice connects with the audience in places. The mood and tone match the purpose, but are inconsistent.	The writer's voice does not fit the purpose or the audience well. The mood and tone are inappropriate or inconsistent.	The writer's voice is weak or absent. It does not connect with the audience.
Word Choice	Precise, descriptive language and creative comparisons create a clear picture of the subject. Nouns and verbs carry the descriptive load with help from a few carefully chosen modifiers.	Some of the language is precise, but some is vague. Some of the comparisons create a clear picture of the subject. Many nouns and verbs depend upon modifiers for specificity. Modifiers are satisfactory.	Most of the language is not descriptive. Comparisons are ineffective. Nouns and verbs lack clarity or precision. Too many or too few modifiers are used, and many of them are weak.	The language is very basic and limited. Comparisons are not used.
Sentence Fluency	A variety of sentence beginnings, lengths, and patterns keeps the description interesting. It is effortless to read aloud with inflection or feeling. The writing flows very smoothly.	Some sentences share the same beginnings, lengths, or patterns. Some of the writing flows smoothly. The paper can be read aloud with inflection or feeling.	Several sentences in a row have the same beginnings, lengths, or patterns. The flow of the writing may slow or stall in parts. The paper is difficult to read aloud with inflection or feeling.	Sentences are not varied or interesting. The writing does not flow. The description is very difficult to read.
Conventions	The description contains no errors. Spelling, grammar, punctuation, and capitalization are correct.	The description contains some errors in spelling, grammar, punctuation, and capitalization. One or two of these errors may cause the reader to pause momentarily, but meaning remains clear.	Many errors are present. Some errors are basic or repeated. The errors interfere with meaning in places.	The writing has not been edited. Serious errors make the writing hard to understand.

Narrative Writing Rubric

	5	4	3	2	1
Ideas	The topic is just the right size—not too big or too small. Descriptive details introduce and develop the setting, narrator, characters, and plot. Carefully selected ideas completely satisfy the needs of the reader.	The topic is the right size. Most details introduce and develop the setting, narrator, characters, and plot. Carefully selected ideas satisfy most of the reader's needs.	The topic is the right size. Some details introduce and develop the setting, narrator, characters, and plot. The ideas selected by the author frequently meet the needs of the reader.	The topic is too big or too small. Some details develop the setting, narrator, characters, and plot. The ideas selected by the author sometimes meet the needs of the reader.	The writing is not a narrative. Details are unrelated or not included.
Organization	The narrative unfolds logically and naturally. Transition words and phrases help sequence the events. A strong beginning leads to a satisfying conclusion.	One or two events in the middle are not connected or are out of order. Transition words and phrases help sequence most of the events. The beginning or the conclusion is strong.	Some events are not connected or are out of order. Transition words and phrases are needed to help sequence the events. The beginning and the conclusion work, but may not be strong.	The narrative does not unfold logically and naturally. Events are out of order. Transition words and phrases are confusing or missing. The beginning or the conclusion is weak.	The writing is disorganized and very difficult to follow. Transition words and phrases are not used. No beginning or conclusion is evident.
Voice	The voice, mood, and tone are just right for the purpose. Dialogue, if used, reveals each character's voice clearly.	The voice, mood, and tone are just right most of the time. Dialogue, if used, reveals the characters' voices.	The voice, mood, and tone are just right in places, but inconsistent. Dialogue, if used, somewhat reveals the characters' voices.	The voice sounds disinterested. Mood and tone are weak. Dialogue, if used, does not uniquely distinguish the characters' voices.	Voice is flat. Mood and tone are absent. Dialogue, if used, does not sound right for some of the characters.
Word Choice	Words and phrases consistently help the reader "see" the characters and "experience" the events. Nouns and verbs are clear and precise, supported by a few carefully selected modifiers.	Words and phrases frequently help the reader "see" most of the characters and "experience" most of the events. Nouns and verbs are mostly clear and precise. Most modifiers are carefully selected.	Some words and phrases help the reader picture characters and events, but some are too general. Certain nouns and verbs are weak, requiring too much help from modifiers. Modifiers are satisfactory.	Many words and phrases are too general. They keep the reader from picturing the characters and events clearly. Nouns and verbs lack clarity or precision. Too many or too few modifiers are used, and many of them are weak.	Many words are not used correctly. They distract the reader.
Sentence Fluency	Varied sentence beginnings, lengths, and patterns make the writing flow smoothly. Several particularly well-crafted sentences add style and interest. The paper is effortlessly read aloud with inflection or feeling.	Most sentence beginnings, lengths, and patterns are varied. One or two sentences add style. The paper is easily read aloud with inflection or feeling.	There is some variation in sentence beginnings, lengths, and patterns. The sentences are correct but ordinary. The paper can be read aloud with inflection or feeling.	Many sentences have the same beginnings, lengths, and patterns. This interrupts the flow of the writing. The sentences are mostly correct but ordinary. It is difficult to read the paper with inflection.	Sentences are poorly written or incorrect. The writing does not flow.
Conventions	Spelling, grammar, punctuation, and capitalization are correct. The narrative contains no errors.	There are a few minor errors, but they do not make the narrative difficult to read.	There are a few grammatical errors that may cause the reader to pause momentarily, but meaning is clear.	Many errors are present, and some confuse the reader.	The writing has not been edited. Serious errors make the narrative hard to understand.

Informative/Explanatory Writing Rubric

	5	4	3	2	1
Ideas	The topic is introduced clearly. Information and examples develop the main idea(s). Carefully selected ideas completely answer the reader's main questions.	The topic is introduced clearly. Most of the information and examples develop the main idea(s). Almost all of the reader's main questions are answered.	A topic is introduced. Some of the information and examples develop the main idea(s). The ideas chosen by the author frequently answer the reader's main questions.	A topic is introduced, but little of the information or examples develops the main idea(s). Some of the reader's questions are answered.	A topic is not introduced. Information and examples are incomplete or unrelated to the topic.
Organization	Information is organized into a strong and thoughtful introduction, a body, and a satisfying conclusion. Varied and appropriate transitions connect the ideas.	Information is organized into an introduction, a body, and a conclusion. Most transitions are varied and appropriate.	Information is organized into an introduction, a body, and a conclusion. More or better transitions are needed.	Information is not well organized. The introduction, body, and conclusion may be poorly developed. Transitions are confusing or not helpful.	The writing is not organized. Introduction and conclusion may both be missing. Transitions are not used.
Voice	The voice sounds interested and informative. It fully connects with the audience and conveys the writer's purpose well.	The voice sounds informative and mostly connects with the audience. It conveys the purpose fairly well.	The voice sounds informative and connects with the audience somewhat. It conveys the purpose some of the time.	The voice sounds informative in places. It conveys the purpose, but often fades out.	Voice is weak or absent. It does not connect with the audience or convey the writer's purpose.
Word Choice	Precise language and domain-specific vocabulary are used. Definitions are complete and helpful. Nouns and verbs are clear and precise, supported by a few carefully selected modifiers.	Precise language and domain-specific vocabulary are used. Most definitions are complete and helpful. Nouns and verbs are mostly clear and precise. Most modifiers are carefully selected.	Some precise language, domain-specific vocabulary, and definitions are used. Some nouns and verbs are weak, requiring help from modifiers. Modifiers are satisfactory.	Little precise language and domain-specific vocabulary is used. Definitions are missing or incorrect. Nouns and verbs lack clarity or precision. Too many or too few modifiers are used, and many of them are weak.	Precise language and domain-specific vocabulary are not used.
Sentence Fluency	Clear, concise sentences make the text flow smoothly. Sentence beginnings, lengths, and patterns are varied for effect. The paper is effortlessly read aloud with inflection.	Most of the sentences flow smoothly. The sentence beginnings, lengths, and patterns are varied. The paper is easily read aloud with inflection.	One or two sections of the writing do not flow smoothly. In these sections, several sentences may have the same beginnings, lengths, or patterns. The paper can be read with inflection.	In many places, the writing does not flow smoothly due to repetitive sentence beginnings, lengths, and patterns. It is difficult to read the paper with inflection.	Sentences are incomplete or incorrect.
Conventions	The text contains no errors. Spelling, grammar, punctuation, and capitalization are correct.	The text contains very few errors in spelling, grammar, punctuation, or capitalization. The meaning remains clear.	The text contains some errors in spelling, grammar, punctuation, and capitalization. One or two errors may cause the reader to pause momentarily, but meaning remains clear.	Many errors are present. Some errors are basic or repeated. The errors interfere with meaning in places.	The writing has not been edited. Serious errors make the writing hard to understand.

Opinion Writing Rubric

	5	4	3	2	1
Ideas	The writer states a clear opinion. The perfect details and facts are chosen to support the writer's reasons.	The writer states a clear opinion. Most details and facts are well chosen to support the writer's reasons.	The writer states an opinion. Some details and facts are well chosen to support the writer's reasons.	The writer states an opinion, but few details are well chosen to support the writer's reasons.	The writer does not state an opinion. Reasons are not provided.
Organization	The text is organized logically and creatively. Helpful, appropriate, even unique transitions link the writer's opinion and reasons. A compelling conclusion clearly supports the opinion statement.	The text is organized logically. One or two more transitions are needed to link the opinion and reasons. The beginning is strong, and the conclusion supports the opinion statement.	The text is organized logically. More or better transitions are needed to link the opinion and reasons. The beginning and the conclusion are functional. The conclusion relates to the opinion statement.	The text is not organized logically. Transitions may not show how the writer's ideas are related. Either the beginning or the conclusion is weak. The conclusion may not relate to the opinion statement.	The text is not organized as an opinion. Transitions are not used. Ideas are hard to follow. No beginning or conclusion is evident.
Voice	The voice is clearly convincing and totally fits the writer's purpose. The mood and tone are appropriate and engage the audience.	The voice is convincing and fits the writer's purpose. The mood and tone are appropriate and engaging most of the time.	The voice is somewhat convincing and fits the writer's purpose. The mood and tone are engaging some of the time.	The voice is convincing in some places. The mood and tone are incorrect or inconsistent. They lose the audience.	The voice is weak or absent. The tone is not appropriate.
Word Choice	Precise words and fair language convey the writer's opinion. No biased words or phrases are used. Nouns and verbs are clear and precise, supported by a few carefully selected modifiers.	Most words are precise and fair. No biased words or phrases are used. Nouns and verbs are mostly clear and precise. Most modifiers are carefully selected.	Some words are too general. One biased word or phrase may be used. Some nouns and verbs are weak, requiring help from modifiers. Modifiers are satisfactory.	Most words are weak. A few biased words or phrases may be used. Nouns and verbs lack clarity or precision. Too many or too few modifiers are used, and many of them are weak.	Words are weak, biased, or used incorrectly.
Sentence Fluency	A variety of sentence patterns adds interest and style. Great variation in sentence beginnings and lengths makes the writing flow very smoothly. The paper is effortlessly read aloud with inflection.	Most sentence patterns are varied and add interest. Variation in sentence beginnings and lengths makes the writing flow smoothly. The paper is easily read aloud with inflection.	Some sentence patterns are varied and add interest. Some variation in sentence lengths and beginnings is evident. The writing flows smoothly in some places, but not in others. The paper can be read with inflection.	Too many sentences share the same pattern. The writing does not flow smoothly due to a lack of variation in sentence lengths and/or beginnings. It is difficult to read the paper with inflection.	Sentences are poorly written or incomplete. The writing is hard to follow.
Conventions	The text contains no errors. Spelling, grammar, punctuation, and capitalization are correct.	The text contains very few errors in spelling, grammar, punctuation, or capitalization. The meaning remains clear.	There are some errors in spelling, grammar, punctuation, and capitalization. One or two of these errors may cause the reader to pause momentarily, but meaning remains clear.	Many errors are present. Some errors are basic or repeated. The errors interfere with meaning in places.	The writing has not been edited. Serious errors make the writing hard to understand.

Descriptive Writing Rubric

	5	4	3	2	1
Ideas	The topic is clear, focused, and complete. Sensory details and examples are related to and develop the main ideas. The description helps the reader experience what is being described very clearly.	The topic is clear and focused. Most sensory details and examples are related to and develop the main ideas. The description helps the reader experience what is being described most of the time.	The topic is clear but may not be focused or complete. Sensory details and examples develop most of the main ideas. The description sometimes helps the reader experience what is being described.	The topic is not clear or focused. Details and examples develop some of the main ideas. The reader cannot always experience what is being described.	The topic is not clear. Details and examples are unrelated or missing. The reader cannot experience what is being described.
Organization	The description is well organized into a strong introduction, body, and conclusion. Details support the topic. Appropriate transitions connect the ideas and guide the reader.	Most of the description is organized, featuring an introduction, body, and conclusion. Most details support the topic. One or two more transitions are needed to connect the ideas and guide the reader.	Most of the description is organized. The introduction, body, and conclusion are functional. Some of the details support the topic. More or better transitions are needed to connect the ideas and guide the reader.	Some of the description is organized. The introduction, body, or conclusion may be weak. Few of the details support the topic. More and better transitions are needed to connect the ideas and guide the reader.	The description is not organized and does not have an introduction or conclusion. Details are missing. Transitions are not used.
Voice	The writer's voice connects strongly with the audience. The mood and tone match the purpose perfectly.	The writer's voice connects with the audience most of the time. The mood and tone match the purpose.	The writer's voice connects with the audience in places. The mood and tone match the purpose, but are inconsistent.	The writer's voice does not fit the purpose or the audience well. The mood and tone are inappropriate or inconsistent.	The writer's voice is weak or absent. It does not connect with the audience.
Word Choice	Precise, descriptive language and creative comparisons create a clear picture of the subject. Nouns and verbs carry the descriptive load with help from a few carefully chosen modifiers.	Most of the language is precise. Most comparisons create a clear picture of the subject. Nouns, verbs, and modifiers are mostly strong.	Some of the language is precise, but some is vague. Some of the comparisons create a clear picture of the subject. Many nouns and verbs depend upon modifiers for specificity. Modifiers are satisfactory.	Most of the language is not descriptive. Comparisons are ineffective. Nouns and verbs lack clarity or precision. Too many or too few modifiers are used, and many of them are weak.	The language is very basic and limited. Comparisons are not used.
Sentence Fluency	A variety of sentence beginnings, lengths, and patterns keeps the description interesting. It is effortless to read aloud with inflection or feeling. The writing flows very smoothly.	Most of the sentences feature varied beginnings, lengths, and patterns, making the writing interesting. Most of the writing flows smoothly. The paper is easy to read aloud with inflection or feeling.	Some sentences share the same beginnings, lengths, or patterns. Some of the writing flows smoothly. The paper can be read aloud with inflection or feeling.	Several sentences in a row have the same beginnings, lengths, or patterns. The flow of the writing may slow or stall in parts. The paper is difficult to read aloud with inflection or feeling.	Sentences are not varied or interesting. The writing does not flow. The description is very difficult to read.
Conventions	The description contains no errors. Spelling, grammar, punctuation, and capitalization are correct.	The description contains very few errors in spelling, punctuation, or capitalization. Grammar is correct, and meaning is clear.	The description contains some errors in spelling, grammar, punc–tuation, and capitalization. One or two of these errors may cause the reader to pause momentarily, but meaning remains clear.	Many errors are present. Some errors are basic or repeated. The errors interfere with meaning in places.	The writing has not been edited. Serious errors make the writing hard to understand.

Narrative Writing Rubric

	6	5	4	3	2	1
Ideas	The topic is just the right size—not too big or too small. Descriptive details introduce and develop the setting, narrator, characters, and plot. Carefully selected ideas completely satisfy the needs of the reader.	The topic is the right size. Most details introduce and develop the setting, narrator, characters, and plot. Carefully selected ideas satisfy most of the reader's needs.	The topic is the right size. Some details introduce and develop the setting, narrator, characters, and plot. The ideas selected by the author frequently meet the needs of the reader.	The topic is too big or too small. Some details develop the setting, narrator, characters, and plot. The ideas selected by the author sometimes meet the needs of the reader.	The topic is undeveloped. Too few details develop the narrative. Some details are unrelated. The author did not consider the needs of the reader.	The writing is not a narrative. Details are not included.
Organization	The narrative unfolds logically and naturally. Transition words and phrases help sequence the events. A strong beginning leads to a satisfying conclusion.	One or two events in the middle are not connected or are out of order. Transition words and phrases help sequence most of the events. The beginning or the conclusion is strong.	Some events are not connected or are out of order. Transition words and phrases are needed to help sequence the events. The beginning and the conclusion work, but may not be strong.	The narrative does not unfold logically and naturally. Events are out of order. Transition words and phrases are confusing or missing. The beginning or the conclusion is weak.	The narrative does not unfold logically. Events are out of order. Transition words and phrases are not used. The beginning or the conclusion is missing or problematic.	The writing is disorganized and very difficult to follow. No beginning or conclusion is evident.
Voice	The voice, mood, and tone are just right for the purpose. Dialogue, if used, reveals each character's voice clearly.	The voice, mood, and tone are just right most of the time. Dialogue, if used, reveals the characters' voices.	The voice, mood, and tone are just right in places, but inconsistent. Dialogue, if used, somewhat reveals the characters' voices.	The voice sounds disinterested. Mood and tone are weak. Dialogue, if used, does not uniquely distinguish the characters' voices.	The voice, mood, and tone are not consistent. Dialogue, if used, does not sound right for some of the characters.	Voice is flat. Mood and tone are absent. Dialogue is not used.
Word Choice	Words and phrases consistently help the reader "see" the characters and "experience" the events. Nouns and verbs are clear and precise, supported by a few carefully selected modifiers.	Words and phrases frequently help the reader "see" most of the characters and "experience" most of the events. Nouns and verbs are mostly clear and precise. Most modifiers are carefully selected.	Some words and phrases help the reader picture characters and events, but some are too general. Certain nouns and verbs are weak, requiring too much help from modifiers. Modifiers are satisfactory.	Many words and phrases are too general. They keep the reader from picturing the characters and events clearly. Nouns and verbs lack clarity or precision. Too many or too few modifiers are used, and many of them are weak.	Most words do not help the characters and events come alive for the reader. Nouns and verbs are vague, unclear, or confusing. Modifiers may be missing entirely.	Many words are not used correctly. They distract the reader.
Sentence Fluency	Varied sentence beginnings, lengths, and patterns make the writing flow smoothly. Several particularly well-crafted sentences add style and interest. The paper is effortlessly read aloud with inflection or feeling.	Most sentence beginnings, lengths, and patterns are varied. One or two sentences add style. The paper is easily read aloud with inflection or feeling.	There is some variation in sentence beginnings, lengths, and patterns. The sentences are correct but ordinary. The paper can be read aloud with inflection or feeling.	Many sentences have the same beginnings, lengths, and patterns. This interrupts the flow of the writing. The sentences are mostly correct but ordinary. It is difficult to read the paper with inflection.	All or almost all the sentences follow the same pattern. Lengths and beginnings do not vary, making the writing robotic or rambling.	Sentences are poorly written or incorrect. The writing does not flow.
Conventions	Spelling, grammar, punctuation, and capitalization are correct. The narrative contains no errors.	There are a few minor errors, but they do not make the narrative difficult to read.	There are a few grammatical errors that may cause the reader to pause momentarily, but meaning is clear.	Many errors are present, and some confuse the reader.	Several serious errors make the narrative hard to understand.	The writing has not been edited.

Informative/Explanatory Writing Rubric

	6	5	4	3	2	1
Ideas	The topic is introduced clearly. Information and examples develop the main idea(s). Carefully selected ideas completely answer the reader's main questions.	The topic is introduced clearly. Most of the information and examples develop the main idea(s). Almost all of the reader's main questions are answered.	A topic is introduced. Some of the information and examples develop the main idea(s). The ideas chosen by the author frequently answer the reader's main questions.	A topic is introduced, but little of the information or examples develops the main idea(s). Some of the reader's questions are answered.	A topic is introduced, but information and examples do not develop the main idea(s). The author did not think about what questions the reader might have.	A topic is not introduced. Information and examples are incomplete or unrelated to the topic.
Organization	Information is organized into a strong and thoughtful introduction, a body, and a satisfying conclusion. Varied and appropriate transitions connect the ideas.	Information is organized into an introduction, a body, and a conclusion. Most transitions are varied and appropriate.	Information is organized into an introduction, a body, and a conclusion. More or better transitions are needed.	Information is not well organized. The introduction, body, and conclusion may be poorly developed. Transitions are confusing or not helpful.	Information is only partly organized. The introduction or the conclusion is missing. Transitions are not used.	The writing is not organized. Introduction and conclusion may both be missing. Transitions are not used.
Voice	The voice sounds interested and informative. It fully connects with the audience and conveys the writer's purpose well.	The voice sounds informative and mostly connects with the audience. It conveys the purpose fairly well.	The voice sounds informative and connects with the audience somewhat. It conveys the purpose some of the time.	The voice sounds informative in places. It conveys the purpose, but often fades out.	The voice consistently sounds flat. It may sound uninformed or uninterested. It does not convey the purpose.	Voice is weak or absent. It does not connect with the audience or convey the writer's purpose.
Word Choice	Precise language and domain-specific vocabulary are used. Definitions are complete and helpful. Nouns and verbs are clear and precise, supported by a few carefully selected modifiers.	Precise language and domain-specific vocabulary are used. Most definitions are complete and helpful. Nouns and verbs are mostly clear and precise. Most modifiers are carefully selected.	Some precise language, domain-specific vocabulary, and definitions are used. Some nouns and verbs are weak, requiring help from modifiers. Modifiers are satisfactory.	Little precise language and domain-specific vocabulary is used. Definitions are missing or incorrect. Nouns and verbs lack clarity or precision. Too many or too few modifiers are used, and many of them are weak.	Some domain-specific vocabulary is used incorrectly. Clarification and definition are not provided for the reader. Nouns and verbs are vague, unclear, or confusing. Modifiers may be missing.	Precise language and domain-specific vocabulary are not used.
Sentence Fluency	Clear, concise sentences make the text flow smoothly. Sentence beginnings, lengths, and patterns are varied for effect. The paper is effortlessly read aloud with inflection.	Most of the sentences flow smoothly. The sentence beginnings, lengths, and patterns are varied. The paper is easily read aloud with inflection.	One or two sections of the writing do not flow smoothly. In these sections, several sentences may have the same beginnings, lengths, or patterns. The paper can be read with inflection.	In many places, the writing does not flow smoothly due to repetitive sentence beginnings, lengths, and patterns. It is difficult to read the paper with inflection.	All or almost all the sentences have similar beginnings, lengths, or patterns. The writing sounds robotic or rambling.	Sentences are incomplete or incorrect.
Conventions	The text contains no errors. Spelling, grammar, punctuation, and capitalization are correct.	The text contains very few errors in spelling, grammar, punctuation, or capitalization. The meaning remains clear.	The text contains some errors in spelling, grammar, punctuation, and capitalization. One or two errors may cause the reader to pause momentarily, but meaning remains clear.	Many errors are present. Some errors are basic or repeated. The errors interfere with meaning in places.	Serious errors stop the reader frequently and make the writing hard to understand.	The writing has not been edited.

Opinion Writing Rubric

	6	5	4	3	2	1
Ideas	The writer states a clear opinion. The perfect details and facts are chosen to support the writer's reasons.	The writer states a clear opinion. Most details and facts are well chosen to support the writer's reasons.	The writer states an opinion. Some details and facts are well chosen to support the writer's reasons.	The writer states an opinion, but few details are well chosen to support the writer's reasons.	The writer's opinion is not clear. Facts are inaccurate or unrelated to the writer's reasons.	The writer does not state an opinion. Reasons are not provided.
Organization	The text is organized logically and creatively. Helpful, appropriate, even unique transitions link the writer's opinion and reasons. A compelling conclusion clearly supports the opinion statement.	The text is organized logically. One or two more transitions are needed to link the opinion and reasons. The beginning is strong, and the conclusion supports the opinion statement.	The text is organized logically. More or better transitions are needed to link the opinion and reasons. The beginning and the conclusion are functional. The conclusion relates to the opinion statement.	The text is not organized logically. Transitions may not show how the writer's ideas are related. Either the beginning or the conclusion is weak. The conclusion may not relate to the opinion statement.	The text is not organized logically. Transitions are not used. Ideas are hard to follow. The beginning or the conclusion is missing.	The text is not organized as an opinion. No beginning or conclusion is evident.
Voice	The voice is clearly convincing and totally fits the writer's purpose. The mood and tone are appropriate and engage the audience.	The voice is convincing and fits the writer's purpose. The mood and tone are appropriate and engaging most of the time.	The voice is somewhat convincing and fits the writer's purpose. The mood and tone are engaging some of the time.	The voice is convincing in some places. The mood and tone are incorrect or inconsistent. They lose the audience.	The voice is flat and does not fit the writer's purpose. The mood and tone do not engage the audience.	The voice is weak or absent. The tone is not appropriate.
Word Choice	Precise words and fair language convey the writer's opinion. No biased words or phrases are used. Nouns and verbs are clear and precise, supported by a few carefully selected modifiers.	Most words are precise and fair. No biased words or phrases are used. Nouns and verbs are mostly clear and precise. Most modifiers are carefully selected.	Some words are too general. One biased word or phrase may be used. Some nouns and verbs are weak, requiring help from modifiers. Modifiers are satisfactory.	Most words are weak. A few biased words or phrases may be used. Nouns and verbs lack clarity or precision. Too many or too few modifiers are used, and many of them are weak.	Many words are overused and ineffective. Several biased words and phrases are used. Nouns and verbs are vague, unclear, or confusing. Modifiers may be missing.	Words are weak, biased, or used incorrectly.
Sentence Fluency	A variety of sentence patterns adds interest and style. Great variation in sentence beginnings and lengths makes the writing flow very smoothly. The paper is effortlessly read aloud with inflection.	Most sentence patterns are varied and add interest. Variation in sentence beginnings and lengths makes the writing flow smoothly. The paper is easily read aloud with inflection.	Some sentence patterns are varied and add interest. Some variation in sentence lengths and beginnings is evident. The writing flows smoothly in some places, but not in others. The paper can be read with inflection.	Too many sentences share the same pattern. The writing does not flow smoothly due to a lack of variation in sentence lengths and/or beginnings. It is difficult to read the paper with inflection.	Almost all sentences are alike. The writing is boring and does not flow smoothly.	Sentences are poorly written or incomplete. The writing is hard to follow.
Conventions	The text contains no errors. Spelling, grammar, punctuation, and capitalization are correct.	The text contains very few errors in spelling, grammar, punctuation, or capitalization. The meaning remains clear.	There are some errors in spelling, grammar, punctuation, and capitalization. One or two of these errors may cause the reader to pause momentarily, but meaning remains clear.	Many errors are present. Some errors are basic or repeated. The errors interfere with meaning in places.	Serious errors stop the reader frequently and make the writing hard to understand.	The writing has not been edited.

Descriptive Writing Rubric

	6	5	4	3	2	1
Ideas	The topic is clear, focused, and complete. Sensory details and examples are related to and develop the main ideas. The description helps the reader experience what is being described very clearly.	The topic is clear and focused. Most sensory details and examples are related to and develop the main ideas. The description helps the reader experience what is being described most of the time.	The topic is clear but may not be focused or complete. Sensory details and examples develop most of the main ideas. The description sometimes helps the reader experience what is being described.	The topic is not clear or focused. Details and examples develop some of the main ideas. The reader cannot always experience what is being described.	The topic and main ideas are not clear. Few sensory details and examples are included. The reader has to work to experience what is being described.	The topic is not clear. Details and examples are unrelated or missing. The reader cannot experience what is being described.
Organization	The description is well organized into a strong introduction, body, and conclusion. Details support the topic. Appropriate transitions connect the ideas and guide the reader.	Most of the description is organized, featuring an introduction, body, and conclusion. Most details support the topic. One or two more transitions are needed to connect the ideas and guide the reader.	Most of the description is organized. The introduction, body, and conclusion are functional. Some of the details support the topic. More or better transitions are needed to connect the ideas and guide the reader.	Some of the description is organized. The introduction, body, or conclusion may be weak. Few of the details support the topic. More and better transitions are needed to connect the ideas and guide the reader.	The description is not well organized. The introduction or conclusion is missing or problematic. Details are missing. Transitions are misused or missing.	The description is not organized and does not have an introduction or conclusion. Details are missing. Transitions are not used.
Voice	The writer's voice connects strongly with the audience. The mood and tone match the purpose perfectly.	The writer's voice connects with the audience most of the time. The mood and tone match the purpose.	The writer's voice connects with the audience in places. The mood and tone match the purpose, but are inconsistent.	The writer's voice does not fit the purpose or the audience well. The mood and tone are inappropriate or inconsistent.	The writer's voice does not fit the purpose or the audience. The mood and tone are inappropriate.	The writer's voice is weak or absent. It does not connect with the audience.
Word Choice	Precise, descriptive language and creative comparisons create a clear picture of the subject. Nouns and verbs carry the descriptive load with help from a few carefully chosen modifiers.	Most of the language is precise. Most comparisons create a clear picture of the subject. Nouns, verbs, and modifiers are mostly strong.	Some of the language is precise, but some is vague. Some of the comparisons create a clear picture of the subject. Many nouns and verbs depend upon modifiers for specificity. Modifiers are satisfactory.	Most of the language is not descriptive. Comparisons are ineffective. Nouns and verbs lack clarity or precision. Too many or too few modifiers are used, and many of them are weak.	The language is not descriptive. Comparisons are confusing. Nouns and verbs are vague, unclear, or confusing. Modifiers may be missing.	The language is very basic and limited. Comparisons are not used.
Sentence Fluency	A variety of sentence beginnings, lengths, and patterns keeps the description interesting. It is effortless to read aloud with inflection or feeling. The writing flows very smoothly.	Most of the sentences feature varied beginnings, lengths, and patterns, making the writing interesting. Most of the writing flows smoothly. The paper is easy to read aloud with inflection or feeling.	Some sentences share the same beginnings, lengths, or patterns. Some of the writing flows smoothly. The paper can be read aloud with inflection or feeling.	Several sentences in a row have the same beginnings, lengths, or patterns. The flow of the writing may slow or stall in parts. The paper is difficult to read aloud with inflection or feeling.	Many sentences have the same beginnings, lengths, or patterns. The writing does not flow smoothly.	Sentences are not varied or interesting. The writing does not flow. The description is very difficult to read.
Conventions	The description contains no errors. Spelling, grammar, punctuation, and capitalization are correct.	The description contains very few errors in spelling, punctuation, or capitalization. Grammar is correct, and meaning is clear.	The description contains some errors in spelling, grammar, punctuation, and capitalization. One or two of these errors may cause the reader to pause momentarily, but meaning remains clear.	Many errors are present. Some errors are basic or repeated. The errors interfere with meaning in places.	Serious errors stop the reader frequently and make the writing hard to understand.	The writing has not been edited.

Index